Design of Building Frames

by

JOHN S. GERO

Associate Professor of Architectural Science
University of Sydney

and

HENRY J. COWAN

Professor of Architectural Science
University of Sydney

APPLIED SCIENCE PUBLISHERS LTD
LONDON

APPLIED SCIENCE PUBLISHERS LTD
RIPPLE ROAD, BARKING, ESSEX, ENGLAND

ISBN: 0 85334 644 5

WITH 7 TABLES AND 251 ILLUSTRATIONS

Printed in Great Britain by Galliard (Printers) Ltd Great Yarmouth

To our wives

ANNETTE AND RENATE

Preface

The majority of all the building structures designed nowadays have some type of frame. Although both architects and engineers have always been fascinated by other structural types such as shells, suspension structures and similar three-dimensional forms, the predominant structural form still remains the frame. Undoubtedly, part of the reason for its popularity resides in the continual urbanisation throughout the world with the resultant need to produce increased densities of population, both for work and for residential purposes. Multi-storey construction with its vertical walls and horizontal floors has made the building frame an economic structural solution. Some books on structural design devote space specifically to frames but there are very few books devoted entirely to the subject.

The aim of this book is to provide the reader with sufficient background not only to be able to predict the behaviour of a building frame under the action of loads and hence to understand its behaviour but also to provide guidance for the design of these structures, particularly at the preliminary stages. For this reason extensive use has been made of design charts, tables and graphs.

The first three chapters provide an introduction to the basic forms of building frames, some of the problems associated with their design, the loads they are likely to experience, a discussion of load factors and some pertinent concepts associated with the materials of construction. Chapters 4 and 5 present classical methods for the elastic analysis of isostatic (statically determinate) and hyperstatic (statically indeterminate) frames including the moment-distribution method, which still remains the most popular hand method of analysis for vertical loadings. Chapter 6 is devoted to the virtual-displacement method as this not only provides a simple introduction to matrix methods presented in Chapter 7, but also because it is a most powerful technique for the analysis of deformation in a variety of situations. An introduction to matrix methods of analysis is presented within the context of computer-based methods of analysis and design in Chapter 7. Both the flexibility and stiffness methods are discussed.

Buckling of columns, beams and frames is discussed in Chapter 8. Whilst many readers may wish to avoid some of the derivations presented here, this chapter concludes with a series of charts which make the determination of the buckling load of a frame relatively simple. Chapter 9 covers the plastic theory of steel structures and concludes with a set of charts which facilitates the design of single storey frames. The elastic and ultimate strength approaches to the design of reinforced and prestressed concrete structures are presented in Chapter 10. This includes the design of beams, columns, slabs and frames. Also presented, is the design of masonry structures.

The behaviour of tall building frames is presented and discussed in Chapter 11. Rigid frames, shear walls, interacting frames and shear walls, 'top-hat' structures, braced-facade (tube) structures, staggered wall structures and panelised construction are all discussed and where appropriate design charts are presented to assist in their preliminary design. The last two chapters deal briefly with the use of physical models in structural design and introduce some optimum design concepts applied to structures. The examples are all worked in metric (SI) units with imperial units provided in parentheses.

The material presented in this book has been presented in lectures in both undergraduate and postgraduate courses. The former to architecture students and the latter to classes including both engineers and architects.

We would like to acknowledge the assistance of the following persons in the preparation of this book: Dr Valerie Havyatt, Dr J. G. Pohl, Mr T. Buchner and Mr P. Reed, who prepared the drawings; Mrs Rita Arthurson and Mrs Brenda Forwood who typed the entire manuscript; Mr J. Deaker, for discussions related to Chapter 7 and Mr T. Buchner who produced a number of the examples.

J. S. G.
H. J. C.

Contents

Chapter 1

Structural Morphology

In this chapter we examine the inter-relation between the structural and the architectural concept of the building frame, and the main considerations which enter into the location and size of the columns and service cores to resist both the vertical and the horizontal loads. We then consider the effect of floor and wall construction on the design of the frame, and the extent to which environmental aspects can influence structural decisions.

1.1. The Effect of Structural Decisions on Architectural Design

A structure must be capable of carrying the loads imposed on it by the weight of the building, the activities carried out inside the building and external forces such as the wind; for this reason structures are usually designed by engineers in accordance with mechanical principles.

This is not the only function of the structure, since in modern architecture the dimensions of the structure have a significant effect on the appearance of the elevation of the building, and the basic structural decisions are therefore also aesthetic decisions. The arrangement of the columns or load-bearing walls has a decisive effect on the layout of the rooms, and structural decisions are therefore also planning decisions. Because of the architectural implications, many architects prefer to make structural decisions personally before handing the detailed structural design over to a consultant. For the same reason, engineers who base their structural decisions purely on mechanical principles are unlikely to produce good buildings.

A structure cannot be designed without knowing something about the building which it is required to support, nor can the building be designed without an appreciation of the mechanical

1

limitations of its structure. It does not follow, however, that a correctly designed structure, honestly exhibited on the facade of a building, will automatically produce good architecture. This fallacy is older than the recent theory of functionalism:

> *The Rationalists were simply that vast body of architects who believed that architectural form was essentially structural form; however ultimately refined and adorned those basic structural forms might be, and they found their most eloquent apologists in France, where architects had held this doctrine consistently throughout the Classical period as a result of its having been bequeathed to them by the master masons of the Middle Ages, from whom many of them could trace a lineal descent. French Classical Doctrine, whether literary or architectural, had always equated truth with beauty, for as Boileau wrote in* Art Poetique: *"Nothing is beautiful but what is true". This idea had expressed itself architecturally by a particular regard for the tectonic integrity of buildings; and the same attitude continued even when the decline in the authority of Antique prototypes caused seventeenth century doctrines also to decline.*
>
> *Peter Collins* [1.1, p. 198].

Apart from this positive aspect of expressing the structure, there is another reason for the interest in structure shown by Neo-Gothic and Modern Movement architects. Composition is easier within a system of rules. Thus musicians like Schoenberg, who abandoned the diatonic scale, chose some other rule, like the twelve-tone scale. Similarly architects who abandoned the classical orders, frequently imposed a structural discipline on their aesthetics.

The 'Orders' have dominated architectural design for most of its history. In Europe the only significant exceptions are the Gothic and Neo-Gothic eras, and the Modern Movement. It is not always appreciated by architects that the direct proportional rule of the Orders does not apply to engineered structures. The proportional rules of structures depend on their use.

Example 1.1. Determine the increase in the thickness of a floor slab resulting from an increase in span for a maximum stress criterion.

Let us consider a floor slab carrying a load w per unit length over a span L. The maximum bending moment in continuous construction is approximately

$$M = wL^2/10$$

and the maximum stress in the slab due to this moment

$$f = kM/bd^2$$

where k is a constant depending on the construction, b is the unit width and d the thickness of the slab.

Assuming that the material is to be stressed to the maximum f, a doubling in the span would require a doubling in the depth.

$$d_1/d_2 = L_1/L_2 \tag{1.1}$$

This direct proportional rule is, however, upset if the weight of the slab is a significant part of the total load. In practice this is often the case. For example, in a flat-plate floor (see Section 5.6) the weight of the concrete slab is usually much greater than the superimposed load. Taking the extreme case of a slab which carries only its own weight

$$w = \gamma bd$$

(where γ is the unit weight of the floor slab), the rule becomes

$$d_1/d_2 = (L_1/L_2)^2 \tag{1.2}$$

In practice the increase in depth will vary between the proportional rules eqns (1.1) and (1.2).

Example 1.2. Determine the increase in the thickness of a floor slab resulting from a maximum-deflection criterion.

Let us consider a timber plank, simply supported, and let us assume that the deflection is limited to $\frac{1}{250}$ of the span.

$$\delta = L/250$$

For a simply supported plank

$$\delta = \frac{5}{384} \frac{wL^4}{EI}$$

where E is the modulus of elasticity, and $I = bd^3/12$ is the second moment of area.

If the load carried by the plank is independent of its own weight and its width is kept constant

$$d_1/d_2 = (L_1/L_2)^{4/3} \qquad (1.3)$$

However, if the width is varied proportional to the depth of the plank

$$d_1/d_2 = L_1/L_2 \qquad (1.4)$$

If the plank carries only its own weight, $w = \gamma bd$ and

$$d_1/d_2 = (L_1/L_2)^{3/2} \qquad (1.5)$$

Example 1.3. Determine the increase in column size due to an increase in span.

Let us consider a square column grid, with square columns measuring d by d. If w is the load per unit area of floor, the load carried by each column

$$P = wL^2$$

If buckling does not occur, the stress in the column

$$f = P/d^2$$

so that doubling the span doubles the column site, if the load per unit area remains the same

$$d_1/d_2 = L_1/L_2 \qquad (1.6)$$

In practice, however, an increase in the span is likely to increase the depth of the slab, and therefore w, so that the direct proportional rule is modified.

Another modification results in a column sufficiently slender to produce buckling, which introduces a term for P which is proportional to d^4, instead of d^2.

While ratios of structural depth to span are frequently used, these can apply only within certain limits, and they do not have the same basis as the direct proportions of the classical orders.

The theory of proportions based on structural principles has been most clearly expressed by Curt Siegel [1.2], although his introductory statement (p. 7) implies too narrow a term of reference:

All attempts to reconcile architecture with art will fail, so long as technology remains unrelated to the process of artistic design. In this context, of course, technology is not to be understood as the provision of technical facilities. Environmental control and sanitary installations have nothing to do with the ultimate quality and expressiveness of even modern architecture. Today, however, the structural framing, which though it has no bearing on comfort, is an essential part of all construction, is emerging as a design factor of critical importance. When we refer to technology, it is these structural aspects that we have in mind.

Sound insulation and fire resistance have a direct bearing on structural dimensions, and few architects would today deny the significant contribution which artificial lighting can make to design of both interiors and exteriors [1.3]. In a more subtle way, thermal comfort is undoubtedly a major design factor, particularly in warm climates where it is more difficult to achieve at a reasonable cost.

Structure, however, has a more immediate effect on the initial decisions of architectural design, and for this reason it is generally introduced both into architectural education and subsequently into the design process at an early stage.

The theory of structures is traditionally taught as a logical development from experimental data, without regard to their historical sequence or authorship. By contrast, architecture is largely taught by studying the work of great masters, even though the masters studied are today contemporary rather than classical. This difference reflects the distinction in the outlook of the scientists, for whom each new theory represents progress over previous knowledge, and the creative artist to whom each work of art is a unique expression, so that there is a progression of masterpieces, rather than progress to greater art.

Modern architecture does not quite fall into either category, because it endeavours to create works of art, but of choice and of necessity does so by means of technology. It must take advantage of the latest technological advances, if building costs are to remain competitive while the standard of living, and therefore the cost of labour is rising. This poses a dilemma:

> An understanding of technological form presupposes technical knowledge; mere intuition is not enough. Even architectural forms, if influenced by technology, are not entirely intelligible without some technical initiation. The fact that technical knowledge is required in order to understand the world of architectural forms indicates an intrusion of cold reason into the sphere of aesthetics ... When technical considerations are made part of the scale of aesthetic values, questions of economy acquire enhanced importance. The word economy is used here not in the sense of saving money, but to denote an intellectual principle, a kind of comprehensive moral law that demands a maximum return.
>
> Curt Siegel [1.2, p. 7].

Some architects have valued this principle more than others, but none more than Mies van der Rohe and his disciples. Mies is credited with the dicta 'More is less' and 'Make it economical however much it costs'. When there is a conflict between structural and cost optimisation on the one hand, and the architect's, possibly ephemeral, conception of structural lightness, then it is necessary to make a choice.

1.2. THE COLUMN GRID

In a single-storey building the column spacing can be varied within fairly wide limits, because only the load transmitted by the roof has to be carried, and this is generally little more than its dead weight.

In a multi-storey building, however, the column grid must be the same for all floors, and the ground floor columns carry the load of all higher floors. Once fixed it is difficult to alter without changing the entire design.

Unless there are special reasons to the contrary, columns are arranged at regular intervals on a square or rectangular grid. This allows standardisation of wall, floor and ceiling components, and the symmetry greatly facilitates structural calculations. If dimensional co-ordination is used, either the distance between centres of columns or the space between columns becomes the co-ordinating dimension [1.4, 1.5].

It is not, however, necessary that every position on the column grid must be occupied by a column. On the higher floors particularly, interior columns can easily be deleted to give a clear floor space. On the ground floor also, where large open spaces, because of their accessibility from the street, are particularly valuable, some columns are often deleted from the grid, although this is bound to increase the cost and require special structural measures (see Section 1.8).

Although it is an advantage to reduce the number of interior columns to a minimum, too much importance can be attached to the concept of complete interior flexibility. In actual fact, movable partitions, once installed, are frequently left in position for many

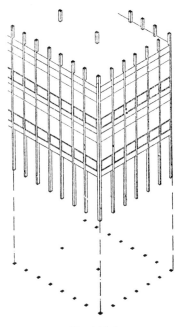

Fig. 1.1(a).

years, and block partitions can be demolished and erected elsewhere without much trouble if their weight is allowed for. It is, moreover, difficult to obtain good sound insulation with movable partitions.

The spacing of columns on the exterior wall may, with advantage, be kept much closer. We have therefore a basic choice (Fig. 1.1)

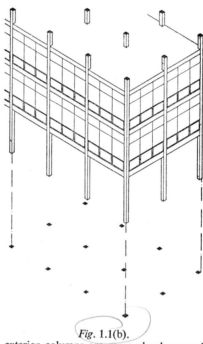

Fig. 1.1(b).

(a) When the exterior columns are more closely spaced than the interior columns, they are generally fairly close, and therefore appear smaller on the facade of the building (*Narrow Grid*).

(b) When the exterior and interior columns have the same spacing, the columns on the facade are larger and more prominent (*Wide Grid*).

between a column grid in which the interior and exterior columns have the same spacing (*wide grid*), and a column grid in which the exterior columns are more closely spaced than the interior columns (*narrow grid*).

Since the facade of a curtain-walled multi-storey building is essentially an assembly of rectangular panels, it makes a significant difference whether the vertical lines are more closely spaced, or more prominent and widely apart. The curtain wall can, of course, be supported on cantilever overhangs clear of the structure. However, it then loses the accent provided by the structural frame, and the designer frequently reintroduces it by making the frame visible through a transparent glass wall (Fig. 1.2). This is a device of dubious validity since a transparent glass wall has environmental limitations, particularly in a warm climate.

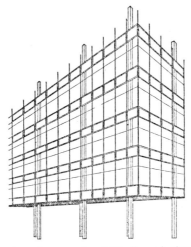

Fig. 1.2.   Interior columns only, visible through glass curtain wall.

In a low-rise multi-storey building the columns carry mainly vertical loads, and it is then economical to keep the spans at about $7\frac{1}{2}$ m (25 ft). Shorter spans are customary for flat plates (reinforced concrete slabs without beams or enlarged column heads) because of the deflection caused by creep. This is more troublesome than the instantaneous elastic deflection because it continues for many months after the completion of the building, and therefore leads to cracking of brick walls and brittle finishes, and even to the jamming of doors.

In high-rise buildings the lateral loads acting on the frame due to wind (and in some regions due to earthquake), become a dominant factor. Interior columns are not well-placed to contribute to the lateral bending resistance of the frame. The omission of interior columns naturally produces a heavier floor structure (see Sections 1.5 and 1.6).

1.3. COLUMN SIZE

The size of the walls or columns has always been a factor in deciding the height of buildings. There are stories of collapses from Ancient Rome and from medieval cities where residential buildings sometimes reached a height of seven storeys. However, the objection to walking too many stairs normally sets the limit at five floors.

Following the development of the passenger lift (elevator) in New York in the 1860s buildings rose to ten storeys and more. The limit was reached in 1889 when the Monadnock Building in Chicago was built to a height of sixteen storeys with load-bearing walls 1·83 m (72 in) thick. The limitations of load-bearing walls had become apparent some years earlier, and in 1883 the first steel-framed building, the Home Insurance Building, was erected in Chicago.

Thereafter it is debatable whether column size or wall thickness was ever a factor limiting the height of buildings. In the early years the space required for vertical transportation was considerable because lift speeds were low, and this restricted the economic height because it left too little for useful occupancy. In 1931 when lift speeds had improved, 380 m (1250 ft) was reached with the erection of the Empire State Building. It held the record until 1971 when the World Trade Center (110 floors, 413 m or 1350 ft) in New York was completed; this utilised sky lobbies (Fig. 1.3) to reduce the space required for vertical transportation.

While perhaps not a decisive factor, column size is a matter of great importance, and it may dictate the mode of construction. The higher the building the greater is the load carried by the ground floor columns, although the cross-sectional area of columns is not directly proportional to height. Since it is unlikely that every floor will simultaneously carry the maximum load (see Section 2.2) a reduction in column loading is permissible for multi-storey buildings. The tendency towards buckling is reduced with increase in column size over a standard storey height, so that unit stresses are higher in large

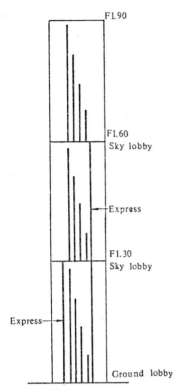

Fig. 1.3.   The space occupied by lifts can be reduced by subdividing the vertical transportation system into units utilising the same shafts. The lifts of each unit start from sky lobbies, which in turn are served by express lifts. A further space-saving is possible with double-deck lifts which load at two ground lobbies and unload at two sky lobbies; however, extra space is needed for lobbies, hoistways, engines and controls; and operating speeds are reduced.

columns (see Section 8.1). Concrete encasement or other fire protection adds proportionately less to the size of a larger column, *e.g.* 50 mm (2 in) cover is relatively less over a 600 mm (24 in) column than over a 300 mm (12 in) column. High strength steel and high strength concrete can be used in the larger columns, whereas it is often not economical to use them for the smaller sizes (see Section 10.1).

Although space is often rented or sold per unit area, inclusive of columns, the price must make allowance for lost space. The obstruction of free-standing columns to a flexible layout, and the unsightliness of columns projecting from a corner into a room, are other objections.

The size of the columns is therefore an important element in the design of high-rise buildings. The size of floor slabs and beams does not increase significantly with the height of the building (although

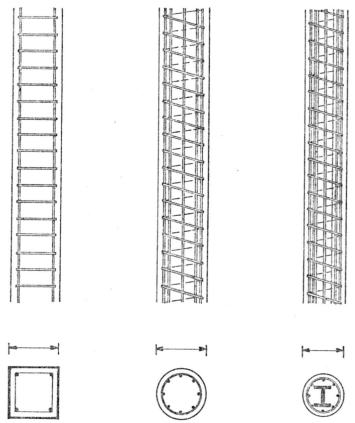

Fig. 1.4.   A concrete column with spiral reinforcement requires a smaller cross-sectional area than a column with tied reinforcement; the area can be still further reduced by employing a composite column with a structural steel core. If all columns are placed on the outside wall, however, their size is less important if they are allowed to project beyond the facade.

wind loads affect the depth of floor members), whereas column sizes increase rapidly with height.

The choice between steel and concrete is determined by several, at times conflicting, requirements. The erection of steel frames tends to be faster because so much of the work is done off-site prior to erection; but this advantage may be cancelled out by delay in floor construction and in the finishing trades.

Fire regulations vary considerably from country to country and even from city to city. Steel frames may be acceptable bare, may need only sprayed vermiculite or similar superficial fireproofing, or may need to be encased in solid concrete to the extent of 50 mm (2 in) or more. When concrete encasement is required, steel is not economical for frames of small and medium height, because reinforced concrete columns require only a little more concrete and far less steel.

Steel columns are generally used for the tallest buildings. However, the economic margin between concrete and steel can be reduced by the use of lightweight aggregate. Structural lightweight concrete has about the same strength as normal concrete, but only about ¾ of its weight, and the vertical column loads are thus greatly reduced. The concrete may be a little dearer, but the columns are smaller and the available floor space is increased [1.6]. The relative economics of steel and concrete frames alter with changing conditions, and buildings already designed in one material have from time to time been redesigned in the other to reduce cost [1.7].

The size of reinforced concrete columns can be reduced by spiral reinforcement and by steel cores (Fig. 1.4). The service core, which is usually constructed in concrete, can be designed to provide the interior support in place of columns (Fig. 1.5). Even normal reinforced concrete columns can be made less obstructive by employing elongated or L-shaped sections which fit into a wall (Fig. 1.6).

1.4. SERVICE CORES

All multi-storey buildings, except for walk-up apartments, require lifts.

All require plumbing, and while the water pipes, being under pressure, can be sharply bent, the drains require downward runs

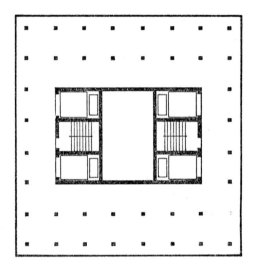

Fig. 1.5.   Using the service core as a main structural support.

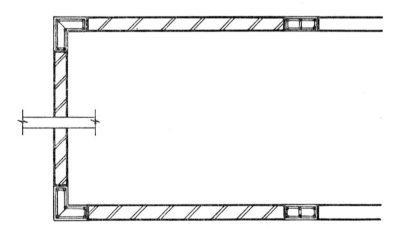

Fig. 1.6.   Reinforced concrete columns can be made to fit into walls by using elongated rectangles of L-shapes.

with gentle bends. For this reason drain pipes have frequently been put on the outside of buildings, but this is unsightly and exposes the pipes to freezing in cold weather.

The larger the building, the greater is the economy of a central heating plant. Heat can be conveyed by hot water or steam pipes, but there is an increasing tendency to use forced air which can also serve to ventilate the building and air condition it in summer. Sealing the building greatly reduces pollution from dust, etc., and in libraries and various industrial buildings, even if not strictly required, it saves more money on cleaning than it costs to install. Air conditioning, *i.e.* cooling and drying the air in warm and humid weather, is coming to be expected for office buildings and to a lesser extent for residential buildings, particularly in tropical and sub-tropical regions. Forced ventilation requires vertical plenum ducts of substantial size to connect the floor ducts. If the building is sealed, return ducts are also needed.

Plenum ducts, drains and lifts require much space, and in addition there are electrical conduits and water pipes to be accommodated. It thus becomes economical to group the services together in one or more vertical shafts.

Fire control is discussed in detail in another book in this series, [1.8], and it depends on a number of factors, such as the type of occupancy and the amount of combustible material in the building. We would like to draw attention to only one factor, *viz.* the effect of height. Fire regulations are minimal in single-storey buildings, because the occupants can leave the building without stairs or lifts. A multi-storey building is low in this sense, so long as the fire can be fought from the outside, *i.e.* the height of the building is no greater than that of longest extension ladder owned by the fire brigade; this is commonly 45 m (150 ft). In a tall building the fire must be fought from the inside, and it is thus necessary to ensure that there is water and fresh air available, and that some of the lifts continue to function; it would clearly not be practicable for fire-fighters to walk up emergency stairs to the hundredth floor. In addition to the fire-proofing of the structural frame, the lifts, the water pipes and the air ducts must be protected from fire. By far the best material for the purpose is reinforced concrete, and its use in the service cores of tall buildings is common, except for very tall buildings in North America.

Reinforced concrete, apart from its value in protecting the services, can also provide some, or indeed all, the structure needed to carry the vertical and the horizontal loads, and the taller the building, the more important becomes the design of this core which calls for close co-operation between the architect, the structural engineer and the mechanical/electrical engineer.

In low-rise buildings the services are frequently separated into two cores (Fig. 1.7). Persons and goods entering by one door need

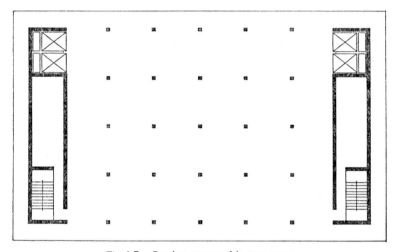

Fig. 1.7.   Services arranged in two cores.

not go to the centre of the building; in department stores, for example, the service lifts can be kept separate from those for customers. From a structural viewpoint, this arrangement has the advantage that the separation of the service units provides a lever arm to resist the horizontal forces in one direction (Fig. 1.8).

The higher the building, the greater the tendency to provide a single core (Fig. 1.5). Tall buildings are invariably on valuable land, and for constructional reasons alone, the central location on a restricted building site has advantages. The core is built first and temporary lifts operating in the regular shafts are then used for vertical transportation for the construction of the rest of the building.

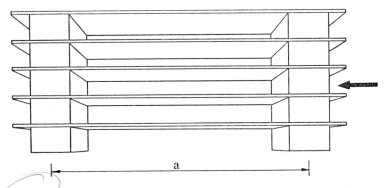

Fig. 1.8. Wind bracing with twin service cores. The floors provide the web, and each service core provides one flange of a beam, separated by a lever arm *a*. If necessary, the depth of the core walls provides the horizontal resistance at right angles.

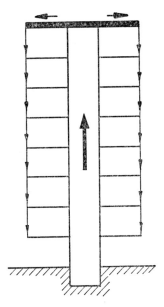

Fig. 1.9. Floors supported by hangers suspended from cantilevers.

For buildings of low or medium height, the core can be made strong enough to carry the entire vertical and horizontal loads, and the outer walls are then supported on tension members hung from the roof (Fig. 1.9). From a purely structural point of view it is not sensible to hang the floors from the roof, whence they have to be sent back to the ground, since it is possible to carry them directly on columns to the foundation. However, both constructional and aesthetic advantages are claimed for suspended curtain walls [1.9], and a number of such buildings have been erected.

The scaffolding used for the construction of the central core can be designed to form subsequently the reinforcement for an outer ring of concrete columns [1.10] in an otherwise conventional construction.

1.5. Wind Bracing

Inevitably a premium must be paid for building high. Since the columns or load-bearing walls of the lower floors of a tall building must carry the load of all the floors above, more material is needed than for the same space built single-storey on the ground. The economic justification of tall buildings is based on high land values in the city centre, on the convenience of having an entire operation in a single building, or on the prestige value attached to a building generally known as a landmark.

It is usually necessary to pay a further premium for the resistance to lateral loads (Fig. 1.10). The taller the building, the greater the surface exposed to wind, the greater the wind loads per unit area (see Section 2.5), and the longer the span of the cantilever. However, with good design it may be possible to utilise the vertical-load structure so effectively that no additional material is needed for resisting lateral loads.

In the first place it is necessary to anchor the building into the ground with a sufficiently deep foundation, or to provide a basement or podium sufficiently wide to prevent overturning (Fig. 1.11). Few authorities today allow an entire building site to be covered by a tall building, but there is generally no objection to a basement or podium over the whole of the property; indeed access from major buildings to underground railways and to pedestrian subways is encouraged.

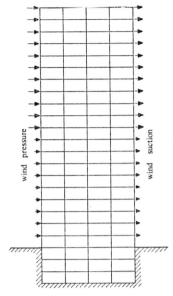

Fig. 1.10. Wind pressure on the windward side, and wind suction on the leeward side produce a bending moment which increases rapidly with height, since the magnitude of the wind pressure, the surface exposed, and the span of the cantilever all increase with height.

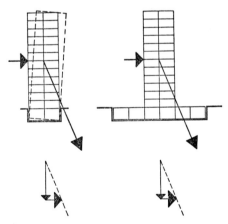

Fig. 1.11. The foundation of a building must be sufficiently deep or sufficiently wide to prevent overturning.

In the circumstances it is improbable that the configuration would have to be altered to meet this stability requirement.

On the other hand, buildings have overturned due to settlement of the foundations. The most spectacular recent failure was that of the Sao Luis Rei Building, an 11-storey reinforced concrete building under construction in Rio de Janeiro in 1957 [1.11]. This was inadequately founded on soft clay, toppled over during construction because of slow, uneven settlement, and was a total loss. Many old buildings had inadequate foundations, and settled unevenly. The best-known example is the Leaning Tower of Pisa, founded on volcanic ash; it, too, started to settle unevenly during construction, but it has survived for more than eight centuries. Foundation design

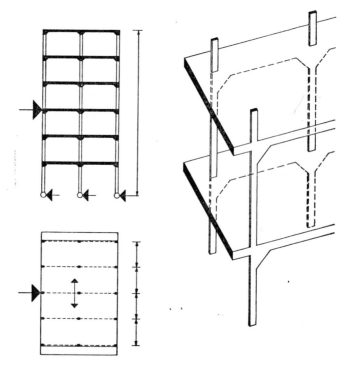

Fig. 1.12. Horizontal forces due to wind taken by rigid frame action. If the building is exposed to wind also at right angles, rigid connections are needed to beams in both directions.

is covered in another book in this series [1.12] and will not be further considered.

Our main concern is therefore with the strength of the building as a vertical cantilever. Evidently the columns individually have very little bending strength over cantilevered spans of 45 m (150 ft) or more. The first step in resisting wind and earthquake loads is therefore to connect the beams and columns into rigid frames (Fig. 1.12). It is sufficient to do this in one direction, if the building is protected by adjacent structures from wind at right angles; otherwise the rigid connections between columns and beams must be made in both directions.

An alternative approach is to utilise existing walls (Fig. 1.13). Each building is likely to have either solid walls in one direction, or else solid walls within the service core, and these can be used even if they are perforated by windows or doors in lift shafts.

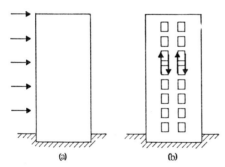

Fig. 1.13. (a) Solid shear wall; (b) shear wall with window or door openings; there must be sufficient solid material to resist the vertical shear.

Either rigid connections between beams and columns, or shear walls, will often be able to resist the horizontal forces for buildings up to about twenty storeys without a substantial premium of additional material. A further increase in lateral strength can be obtained by interconnecting a rigid frame with shear walls. The interconnection forces the two structural systems to deflect together, and the combined system has a much smaller deflection than either acting separately (Fig. 1.14). Dr. Khan has produced tables and

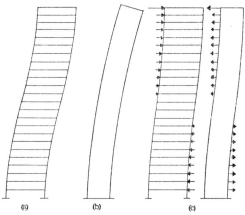

(a)   (b)   (c)

Fig. 1.14.   Deflection of: (a) free rigid frame; (b) free shear wall; (c) combined frame and shear wall. (From Khan and Sbarounis [1.13, p. 288].)

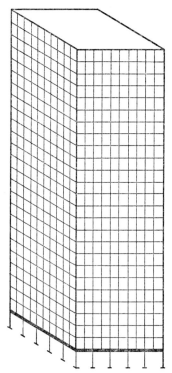

Fig. 1.15.   Framed tube type structure. (From Khan [1.14, p. 9].)

charts [1.13] which enable an estimate of the distribution of loads between shear walls and frames to be made for various ratios of relative stiffness, in terms of the total shear force existing at ground level. He has since applied these principles to the design of a number of tall buildings.

Another possibility is to treat the facade of the building as a perforated tube (Fig. 1.15), using very closely spaced exterior columns and connecting them at each floor with deep perimeter spandrel beams [1.14].

The effectiveness of the framed-tube concept is reduced by the shear lag occurring in a thin tube subjected to bending [1.15] which increases the stresses near the corners of the facade on the leeward side (Fig. 1.16).

The problems of large shear lag and excessive number of joints in the framed tube can be largely overcome by using diagonal braces. This was used on the grand scale for the first time by Dr. Khan in

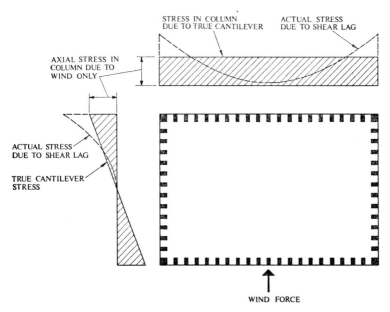

Fig. 1.16.   Stress distribution in a true cantilever, and actual stress distribution due to shear lag. (From Khan [1.14, p. 9].)

1967 in the 100-storey John Hancock Centre in Chicago (Fig. 1.17).
In this system the exterior columns can have normal spacing of 6 to
18 m (20 to 60 ft), instead of the close spacing required for the framed
tube.

Service floors can also be used to increase the lateral strength of
tall buildings. Generally there is a service floor at the top of the

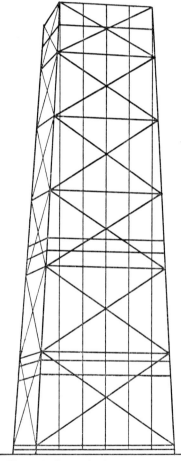

Fig. 1.17.   The John Hancock Centre in Chicago uses structural windbracing.
It is both an important factor in the structural design of the building, and the
most significant visual feature.

building which can be given a blank wall without serious inconvenience. When this is connected to the shear walls of the service core, the 'top hat' greatly reduces the deflection and increases the stiffness (Fig. 1.18).
Tall buildings generally have several service floors, at intervals of 15 to 30 storeys. These are commonly higher than ordinary floors,

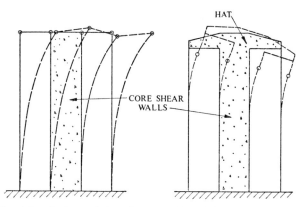

Fig. 1.18. A 'top hat', consisting of an extension of the service-core shear walls into the topmost service floor, greatly increases the stiffness of a tall building.

so that a substantial stiffener can be fitted into the space, and it is thus possible to extend the 'top hat' concept to the lower service floors. The stiffener may be visually more acceptable on the facade if a truss, rather than a solid shear wall, is used (Fig. 1.19).

1.6. FLOOR CONSTRUCTION

Concrete is an excellent material for floor construction, because it is stiff, fireproof and a good sound insulator. Thus some concrete is almost invariably used as a topping even in steel-framed buildings with metal deck floors, and conventional concrete floor construction may be used in conjunction with a conventional steel frame. On the other hand, a concrete frame always has a concrete floor.
In a tall building the floor structure is subordinate, both in

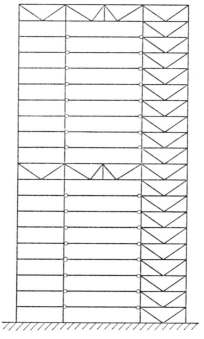

Fig. 1.19.   Horizontal stiffening trusses used in conjunction with a vertical shear truss. (From Khan [1.14, p. 6].) This is the system employed in the 43-storey B.H.P. Building, Melbourne.

structural decision-making and in cost, to the vertical structure; however, the reverse is true for buildings of only a few storeys.

In tall steel-framed buildings cellular metal decking is frequently used because of its lightness and because of the ease with which the electrical services can be accommodated in the cells. The minimum depth is determined by the electrical requirements, and this depth permits quite large spans between joists. For further lightness, triangulated open-web joists are used, unless the floor joists are needed to stiffen the vertical structure. Mechanical services can be accommodated between the joists so that the overall depth of this floor need not be great. This method has particular attraction when site labour costs are high, because the concrete-topped metal deck requires no formwork or temporary support.

The material cost, however, is usually lower for reinforced concrete floors, described below, supported on rolled steel joists. The two can be made to act together by welding shear connectors to the top of the joists, so that the steel and the concrete act as composite construction, and this is particularly appropriate when the floor structure plays a significant part in resisting the lateral forces due to wind or earthquake.

A reinforced concrete slab may either span in both directions between major beams (Fig. 1.20) or in one direction over secondary

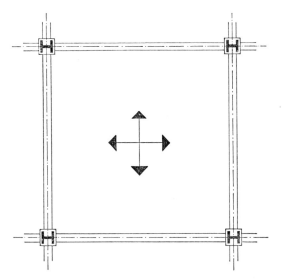

Fig. 1.20. Two-way reinforced concrete span; this can be used either for steel or for concrete frames.

beams which in turn are supported on primary beams (Fig. 1.21). It can be used either in conjunction with a steel or a reinforced concrete frame. The concrete slab may be either cast in place, or precast. The first avoids the transport problems associated with heavy prefabricated units, the second avoids the need for site formwork for the wet concrete. The relative economics of site-cast versus precast concrete vary appreciably from place to place.

When the concrete is cast in place, the slab contributes to the

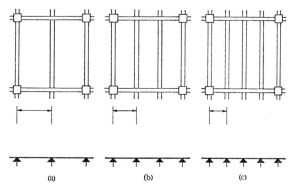

Fig. 1.21. One-way reinforced concrete slab supported on secondary beams, which span between primary beams. The panel can be divided into two, three or four secondary spans; the sub-division into three is usually advantageous, because it produces low bending moments in the primary beams, and a reasonable ratio of slab span to primary beam span.

strength of reinforced concrete beams by forming the flange of a T-beam (see Chapter 10). A similar result can be achieved with steel beams if shear connectors are used for composite construction.

Ribbed floors (Fig. 1.22) are particularly advantageous for floors carrying heavy loads, such as parking, storage and mechanical service areas, and also for buildings with long spans because there are few or no interior columns. The ribs can be formed by wooden, steel, plastic or carboard pans placed on flat formwork, or permanent filler blocks may be used for additional insulation. Column heads (shown in Fig. 1.22) may be needed because of the high shear stresses surrounding columns without beams; but these can be avoided by using a greater thickness of concrete, or else by using shear reinforcement in the concrete slab surrounding the column. The ribbed floor provides an attractive ceiling in parking areas, and it offers complete freedom for running the services when a false ceiling is used.

As has been mentioned in Section 1.2, the simplest of all floors is the flat plate, a beamless concrete floor without column heads; however, it requires close spacing of the columns or load-bearing walls or else very thick slabs to limit the creep deflection (see Section 3.5). It is therefore particularly suitable for buildings in which closely spaced interior columns are acceptable, *e.g.* apartment houses, and where false ceilings are not required, since its economy is largely based on the clean appearance of the soffit of the slab which can be used to form the ceiling of the room below with only minimal treatment.

Concrete beams, ribbed slabs and flat plates can all be prestressed if it is desired either to use greater spans or smaller floor depths.

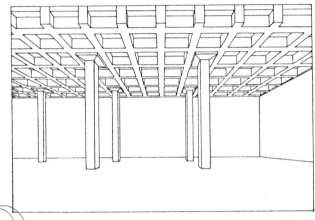

Fig. 1.22. Ribbed slab spanning in two directions. It can be considered as a flat slab from which some of the concrete in the tension zone (which serves no useful purpose) has been cut away, and the steel concentrated in the ribs; or else as a series of interacting concrete beams carrying short-span slabs.

Higher strength concrete and steel can be used economically in prestressed concrete so that less weight is required, and the prestressing operation sets up bending moments opposite to those caused by the load, which may be utilised to cancel out the dead-load moments. The economics of prestressing vary from place to place, but nowhere is it at present a common alternative to reinforced concrete in multi-storey buildings.

The floors must meet the fire-resisting requirements [1.8], and it is desirable that they should offer an adequate barrier to noise. Sound insulation is covered in another book in this series [1.16]; however, we would like to draw here attention to the excellent noise-attenuating properties of concrete. A small increase in thickness may alter an unpleasant to a satisfactory environment, and excessive structural lightness may thus be a shortsighted policy. Some building authorities lay down minimum soundproofing requirements, and others permit a bonus in site utilisation if minimal standards are met. The frequent complaints about inadequate soundproofing of floors, particularly in low-cost multi-storey residential buildings, suggests that such restrictions should be more widely imposed.

1.7. WALL CONSTRUCTION

The concept of the structural frame was gradually developed in the closing years of the last century, and it took some time before it was accepted. In the early years of the 20th century the realisation that the walls were structurally superfluous ('Buildings consisting of skin and bones' [1.17]) found expression in a number of completely glass-walled buildings. Fascination with the lightness of the structural frame and the transparency of glass ('Architecture is a crystal') has since waned. Some people are worried by a completely transparent wall at great height, while others do not wish to conduct their affairs too much in the public view. Glass breaks in a fire, and in a tall building it is necessary to have either a horizontal or a vertical projection of fireproof material between floors. The cost of air-conditioning is greatly increased without the thermal barrier offered by an insulating wall. In some cities glass is still an important material for curtain walls, generally backed in part by insulation, while in others it has in recent years been restricted to comparatively small windows.

Some conventional materials have returned to be used in curtain walls in a new manner: stone cut into thin slabs, backed with insulating material, and bricks often prefabricated into panels. Steel and aluminium sheets have been used in various forms.

The most important material in recent years has been concrete. This has led to great improvements in its surface finish which had previously imposed severe limitations. However, there are still many tall buildings where exposed aggregate is not used to the best advantage. Concrete panels which look excellent at close quarters may blur to an undistinguished grey at a distance of several hundred feet, *i.e.* when seen from the ground at the top of a tall building [1.18].

The use of concrete panels which have considerable strength led to a re-examination of the building consisting of 'skin and bones'. Concrete wall panels have been designed in some buildings to carry the lateral loads, and in others also the vertical loads. For residential buildings in particular, prefabricated concrete panels have been used without beams and columns, notably in Russia. These panels form, in fact, a structural frame; but unlike the traditional load-bearing walls of the 19th century, the new engineered version uses much thinner walls and therefore far less material. Apartment buildings 30 storeys high have been built with wall panels 20 cm (8 in) thick without a conventional frame [1.19].

1.8. THE TOP FLOOR AND THE GROUND FLOOR OF THE TALL BUILDING

The roofs of low buildings are commonly designed with a view to their appearance from above. In many cities the height of buildings was absolutely restricted, and the taller buildings were all of the same height. Since their roofs could only be seen occasionally by somebody who took the trouble to go up a cathedral or town hall tower, their appearance was given little attention. The effect of this neglect can easily be seen from the new buildings erected since the height limitations were removed.

The early tall buildings also tended to clutter their roofs with lift shafts, cooling towers for the air conditioning plant, and other functional but unattractive parts of the mechanical services. It seems very likely that the roof of every building now erected will some day be seen from an even taller building, and for aesthetic reasons alone the services at the top of a building should therefore be enclosed.

There is, however, also a structural reason for doing so. A stiff wall or truss can easily be incorporated into the top floor, and this greatly stiffens the frame (Figs. 1.18 and 1.19), and thus saves material in the spandrels and/or columns at lower levels.

The ground floor has particular importance because of its accessibility to the general public. Columns create obstructions, and in this commercially valuable space it may be worthwhile to remove them, in spite of the structural premium which must be paid for taking away vertical supports at the level where they are most needed.

In a low multi-storey building the removal of interior columns at ground level can be accomplished by inserting a rigid frame, a full floor in depth, at first-floor level (second-floor level in American terminology) (Fig. 1.23); more complex rigid frames are needed for higher buildings. If it is not too tall, the entire building can be

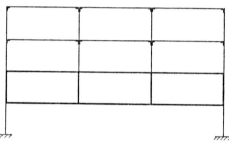

Fig. 1.23. Non-rigid multi-storey frame without interior ground floor columns. The lowest two floors are joined into a rigid Vierendeel girder, a full floor in height.

propped up on stilts, and this may lead to interesting designs clearly expressing the structure; *e.g.* the UNESCO Building in Paris, designed by Professor P. L. Nervi, which is supported off the ground by a series of frames with inclined legs [1.2, pp. 100–2 and 168–9].

1.9. ENVIRONMENTAL ASPECTS

The effect of tall buildings on the environment, and vice versa, pose problems far more complex and important than their structural design [1.20]. At worst, tall buildings may be said to 'pollute the environment' by their very presence; at best they provide a civic focus, as the cathedrals and town halls did in previous centuries. Buildings are growing taller both in cities where planning is centrally controlled and in cities where developers are given much freedom, and it seems likely that this trend will continue. Clearly much more research is needed to ensure that tall buildings make the city a better place to live or work in, rather than the reverse.

We can mention here only a few aspects which affect the structure. Tall buildings, whether they are residential or commercial, create huge traffic problems because they house so many people. This could be avoided if people lived and shopped in the building in which they work, but this seems unlikely even in mixed-occupancy buildings. The problem is aggravated by the fact that some of the tallest buildings are in narrow streets, such as Wall Street, New York, or Pitt Street, Sydney, which were laid out for a small town, and whose alignments are now, for economic reasons, very difficult to alter. Even when buildings are located favourably, as on Michigan Avenue, Chicago, the question of car access remains controversial. Car parking requires special structural provision, as do the access ramps for the cars. The debate on vehicular access is therefore of great importance to the structural engineer.

Provision must be made for pedestrian passages to other buildings, particularly if car access is restricted, and, if at all possible, to underground railway stations. Indeed, there is much to be said for locating a very tall building so that a station can be built in its basement. This clearly affects the design of the foundations, and possibly also the superstructure.

The location of tall buildings relative to one another also has structural implications. There is justifiable opposition to lining an entire street with tall buildings, and thus turning it into an artificial canyon. It is equally undesirable to place the buildings too far apart if the city is to have a proper centre. Buildings placed at a distance comparable to their own height create wind effects, which affect existing buildings, whose structural design can no longer be altered, just as they affect the new building.

It is possible that some of the present discussions on urban planning have structural implications which are not yet appreciated, and the subject is one which the structural designer should keep under constant review.

Chapter 2

Loads, Load Factors and Safety

In this chapter we examine the various loads to which a building is subject, and the probability of their occurrence. We next consider safety and load factors, and progressively more accurate methods of determining their magnitude. Stresses caused by temperature and moisture movement are discussed in Chapter 10.

2.1. LOADS ON BUILDINGS

The principal forces acting on a building are:

(i) the dead weight of the structural member, which acts vertically;
(ii) the dead load superimposed by other structural members, non-structural finishes, etc., which also act vertically;
(iii) the live load resulting from the occupancy of the building, which usually acts vertically, although there may be horizontal forces due to moving machinery;
(iv) snow load, which is vertical irrespective of the slope of the roof; snow will not, however, be retained on a steeply sloping roof;
(v) wind load, which acts perpendicularly to the wall or roof, and may be either positive (pressure) or negative (suction);
(vi) forces due to earthquakes or explosions, which are commonly treated as dynamic horizontal forces.

The exact magnitude of most of these loads depends on the definition of the load factor or the factor of safety. The dead weight of the structural member is the only load which can be accurately predicted. Even the superimposed dead loads could be different from those intended in the initial design. For example, if a very small factor of safety were to be used, as is customary in aircraft design, then it would be necessary to re-design and possibly strengthen the building if a cork floor over a structural concrete slab was replaced by marble paving.

The live loads due to the occupancy of the building could either be estimated at their highest possible value, or a moderately high load could be used, allowing exceptional overloads to be covered by the factor of safety (see Section 2.3).

Snow loads can be estimated with some accuracy, but wind loads are less predictable. Whilst major buildings should not collapse in a high wind, it is uneconomical to ensure that the roof of every building remains undamaged during a wind of hurricane force. If this were done, the cost of building would become unduly high. Just as people use motor cars although they run the risk of being killed, so people must accept the very much smaller risk of damage to a building, or even loss of life from the collapse of a building (see Section 2.8).

Neither can complete security from earthquakes be achieved, although in regular earthquake zones the horizontal forces assumed in the calculations should be sufficiently high to prevent collapse absolutely. In the case of resistance to explosions, however, this is no longer possible, and it is a matter of opinion whether protection of buildings against blasts from bombs of megaton size is even worth considering (see Section 2.6).

There are some uncertaintres in the assesments of the dead loads ?

2.2. DEAD LOADS

At first sight it may seem that the weight of the structure can be determined precisely, and indeed it is the load acting on the structure which is known with the greatest accuracy.

There are only some minor uncertainties:

1. The field strength of gravity varies; however, the maximum variation between pole and equator, the effect of height, of time and of local anomalies amount to less than a 1 per cent variation.
2. In the design of most structures it is necessary to assume the dimensions of the structural members before the strength of the structure can be determined. Designers tend to assume dimensions slightly larger than they anticipate for the purpose of computing the weight of the structure. If the final volume of the structure is

more than 10 per cent larger than that assumed, the design calculations are generally repeated.

3. The volume of structural and non-structural elements may be higher than that specified by the designer, due to tolerances allowed for construction. However, if the structure is oversized, it will also be stronger, and this error is insignificant.

4. The weight of the structure is computed by multiplying the volume by the unit weight of the structural material, specified in the relevant building code [2.1–3]. S. M. Johnson [2.4] considers that the actual weight may vary from that specified by up to 20%.

5. In the design of the supporting structure it is commonly assumed that the proportion of the total load carried by each supporting member is the same as for simple supports. In continuous construction this can be seriously in error, particularly if the spans are of unequal length (see Section 5.3). This error could be greater than the combined effect of the four previously considered, and an accurate assessment of the support reactions may be needed if the spans are unequal.

2.3. LIVE LOADS DUE TO OCCUPANCY

Although there are some uncertainties in the assessments of the dead loads, there is a far larger range of variation in the live loads. Let us examine first of all office buildings, since these have received the greatest attention. Two early detailed investigations were undertaken by C. M. White for the British Steel Structures Research Committee in 1931 [2.5] and by the U.S. Department of Commerce Building Code Committee in 1924 [2.6]. More recently office loads have been surveyed in England by G. R. Mitchell and R. W. Woodgate [2.7, 2.8] and in America by J. W. Dunham, G. N. Brekke and G. N. Thomson [2.9], and by J. O. Bryson and D. Gross [2.10].

Weighing all the items in an office and recording the data is tedious and time-consuming, and the recent surveys are more thorough due to the introduction of automatic weighing equipment and data recording systems. Thus G. R. Mitchell's survey [2.8] consisted of a sample of 32 buildings (chosen from a total of 473), involving over 100 occupying organisations and having a total area of 160 000 m² (1 750 000 ft²).

Retail stores have also received careful attention [2.9, 2.12]. Thus G. R. Mitchell [2.12] surveyed 26 premises covering a wide range of activities, from butchery to bookselling, and comprising 48 500 m² (523 000 ft²).

Other investigations have dealt with storage occupancies [2.9], industrial occupancies [2.9], churches and theatres [2.10] and residential buildings [2.13].

Weighing the furniture, movable equipment, filing cabinets, books, etc., is an objective activity, and provided that the sample is sufficiently large, the result should be entirely reliable. Some problems may arise in warehouses and retail stores where the quantity of goods stored can vary considerably, but even this can be overcome with reasonable accuracy by sampling.

Investigators differ, however, in their assessment of the weight of the people. J. W. Dunham [2.9] filled the spaces open to the public with people:

Two department stores were included in the survey. The surveying was done when few people were present, in order to cause a minimum of inconvenience to the stores. The human load was therefore small. It must be appreciated that, in general, the areas over which live loads were averaged were larger than a single floor bay and that consequently some portions had loads of greater intensity than the average.

Within each area the aisle space, which might be crowded at special times, such as around Christmas, was noted as a percentage of the total area. The data contained under 'unit live load as surveyed' include the weight of people actually present at the time the observations were made. Under the heading 'unit live load, with aisles crowded' in the table, are given additional data that include the weight of persons in aisles calculated on the basis of 60 lb/ft² (2·9 kPa) of aisle space. This is believed to represent a fairly crowded condition.

J. W. Dunham then gives layout drawings and detailed loads on all public floors of the two stores. The following may serve as an example:

*Live loads in department store, New York, N.Y.—Second Floor
(first floor in European and Australian usage)*

Department	Area			Unit live load	
	Part surveyed ft^2	Whole department ft^2	Aisle space %	As surveyed lb/ft^2	With aisles crowded lb/ft^2
Women's hats	3 040	18 378	54	16·5	48·9
Negligees and lingerie	3 570	20 673	37	10·7	32·9
Corsets and girdles	1 020	5 932	18	15·0	25·8
Men's suits	2 140	17 733	50	11·4	41·4
Storage (men's suits)	260	1 668	0	39·1	—
Men's shoes	1 470	3 777	55	10·6	43·6
Storage (men's shoes)	990	1 856	0	57·0	—
Men's shirts, etc.	1 230	9 213	39	22·2	45·6
Women's dresses	4 590	14 056	43	8·6	34·4

Evidently, the weight of the people is a very important part of the total load.

G. R. Mitchell [2.12] relied on observations:

Observations of numbers of persons present in sales areas were made on days indicated by the manager of the establishment to be peak periods—these could be at lunchtimes, at the weekend, at 'sales' times or just before Christmas or Easter, depending on the nature and situation of the establishment . . . .

An allowance of 50 lb/ft^2 (2·4 kPa) was made for crowding at stairheads and at shop exits, the area involved depending on the numbers of persons present and the disposition of the exits. Toilets were assumed loaded to 40 lb/ft^2 (1·92 kPa).

However, the report does not give the difference between the loads in 'empty' and 'full' premises.

In addition, G. R. Mitchell made an allowance for change of occupancy:

The figures quoted are, of course, for the sample as surveyed, i.e. they are for one arrangement of the items and for a single arrangement of different kinds of business in the available premises. As changes are made in the disposition and nature of the loads, a given *floor zone will experience different loadings and the probability of a particular loading level being experienced will be changed. It is reasonable to assume that, in the absence of any major change in the nature and method of storage of items, the new loadings that such a floor zone experiences will already exist and have been surveyed elsewhere in the retail trade occupancy. In these circumstances a loading that occurs with cumulative probability P for a single arrangement will occur with cumulative probability P^n after n arrangements.*

Assuming an average life of 100 years for the buildings and an average occupancy of 7 years, G. R. Mitchell made $n = 14$, and then computed the load intensity levels after 14 occupancies, which showed a substantial increase over the one-occupancy figures.

The magnitude of the unit load is also affected by the length of the span. Some building codes require that an area of less than 10 ft² (0·94 m²) be considered to carry the load corresponding to a loaded area of 10 ft². In addition a *single* large load, such as an office safe, computer or storage shelf, is more significant over a short span than over a long span, compared to the uniformly distributed load. J. W. Dunham [2.9] thus suggested that high concentrations of load in offices should be provided for by a requirement that the floor must be capable of supporting a load of 2000 lb (8900 N) on a specified limited area in any location.

On the other hand, over large areas a reduction is possible, since it is improbable that the maximum loads will be realised simultaneously over the entire area. This is particularly important for assessing the loads carried by columns. G. R. Mitchell [2.8] has considered 'the reduction in column loads made possible by considering the joint probabilities of different levels of loadings on the column-tributary zones on the several floors, to derive the appropriate loadings from those present on an identical area of floor on one level only'. On this basis he obtained reductions in column loading of up to 57% (*i.e.* more than half) for a ten-storey building. He then modified these reductions to allow:

(1) *That some buildings are more heavily loaded as a whole than others;*

(2) *That in many buildings some columns tend to be consistently loaded on all floors* (e.g. *those supporting toilet areas and areas where fire practice crowding may occur;*

(3) *that, although all floors above ground floor have been aggregated to obtain appropriate loading intensities, there is nevertheless a tendency for the lower floors to carry somewhat heavier loadings.*

The percentage reductions resulting from these considerations of Mitchell are shown in the following table:

Size group Mean area ft^2	151	336	624
m^2	14	31	58
Number of floors supported	Percentage reduction in loading intensity of 99% probable load		
1	0	0	0
2	22·2	25·0	20·1
3	21·2	26·8	22·4
4	23·1	26·8	23·1
5	26·2	27·5	26·5
6	24·9	27·8	25·4
7	22·5	27·5	23·5
8	19·4	26·8	18·6
9	25·7	21·1	—
10	20·7	—	—

These are still considerable reductions, although not as great as those permitted by some building codes.

Finally, some allowance must be made for significance of a particular part of a building in case of an emergency. The taller a building, the more stringent are the regulations to protect it from collapse in case of fire. However, fires cannot at present be entirely prevented, and the occurrence of a fire may result in crowding of escape stairs and passages. It is therefore necessary to assign sufficiently high loads to them, even though one hopes that they will never be realised.

2.4. Loads Due to Snow

Snow loads on the ground stipulated by building codes vary from nil in Sydney, Australia, to 120 lb/ft² (5·7 kPa) on the coast of Labrador [2.13]. Most cities or geographical areas which contain large buildings have records of snow falls from which the weight of the snow can be derived.

The heaviest snow loads often occur when an early spring rain falls into, and is retained by, the snow cover, and this is generally allowed for in the specified snow loads.

Snow loads can be greatly increased by the effect of wind. Monitors, high roofs adjacent to low roofs, and other configurations which offer shelter can produce substantial accumulations of snow. W. R. Schriever reports a 14 ft (4·3 m) snowdrift near Montreal which produced a load of 189 lb/ft² (8·6 kPa) causing the collapse of the roof [2.14].

Solar radiation can reduce snow loads by melting even when the air temperature does not rise above 0°C, if suitable drainage is provided.

On the other hand, melting of the snow followed by subsequent freezing can produce an ice barrier at the edge of a sloping roof which increases the depth of snow which is retained. This is accentuated by unsuitable heating of the roof space.

2.5. Loads Due to Wind

Very high wind velocities occur over very short periods (less than a second), and a distinction must be made between these and the *average* wind velocity measured over longer periods. Short-term gusts can be more than double the average wind speed. They are important in the design of roof coverings and curtain walls, particularly if suction is likely to result. Once a fastening has been loosened by the suction of a gust of wind, the roof or wall covering may roll up, thus presenting a front to the wind, which leads to rapid failure.

The structure has too much inertia to be able to fail under the action of a gust, at least if we exclude light domestic buildings, and average wind speeds are therefore used in the static design of structures. It is, of course, essential that multi-storey buildings should not collapse due to wind loading; but this has never occurred. Very few cases of serious structural wind damage to multi-storey buildings have been reported, and in only one instance (the Meyer–Kiser Building, damaged by a hurricane in Miami in 1926) has yielding of the steel been claimed. On the other hand, collapse of domestic buildings and damage to multi-storey buildings by cyclones (hurricanes, tornadoes, typhoons) is frequently reported. More could be done to minimise such damage [2.24], but the complete elimination of cyclone damage is probably not economically feasible.

While average wind-speeds are used for static design, short-term gusts seem to determine the dynamic behaviour of the building [2.26]. The very tall (above 400 m) steel-framed buildings with lightweight fireproofing erected in the U.S.A. in the late 1960s have appreciable deformation, with frequencies of the order of 0·1 Hz (0·1 c/s), and visco-elastic dampers may need to be incorporated in the structural frame. The aerodynamic behaviour of buildings is a specialised field, and the reader is referred to the papers in References [2.17, 2.19, 2.21–23, 2.25, 2.30].

The aerodynamic design criterion for building frames is the perceptibility of motion to the occupants, which must not happen more frequently than, say, once in ten years. Prevention of aerodynamic failure, such as occurred in the collapse of the Tacoma Narrows Suspension Bridge near Seattle, U.S.A., is not sufficient.

Because of the complexity of aerodynamic analysis many problems are solved by model investigations, using a boundary-layer wind-tunnel in which the roughness or smoothness of the ground, and particularly the effect of surrounding buildings, are imitated with considerable accuracy. In addition, the building under investigation must be modelled aerodynamically to produce movements and forces in the wind tunnel from which the behaviour of the building can be predicted by dimensional analysis [2.25].

The static design of buildings is based on the average wind speed which is determined from anemometer measurements over a period of years, usually at airfields or on the roof of meteorological offices. However, in recent years a number of measurements have also been made on actual buildings in the U.S.A., Canada, England, France,

Germany and Holland [2.25], which allow comparison with the wind velocities recorded by the meteorological bureaux. The most recently revised national code for wind loads [2.27] gives design speeds ranging from 59 mph (26 m/s) in the built-up areas of Brisbane to 130 mph (58 m/s) on the north-west coast of Australia. Wind speeds are specified both by a table (listing the major towns) and by a contour map of the continent.

At ground level wind speeds are about 30% lower in built-up areas than in exposed positions. Tall buildings are, however, protected by low buildings for only part of their height, and the wind velocity can therefore increase sharply at the higher levels. In addition to the lack of protection there is also an increase of wind velocity with height, because the wind velocity near the ground is reduced by the friction, or drag, of the ground.

The wind velocity V_1 at a height H_1 above the ground is obtained from the velocity V_0 at the standard height H_0 (usually 10 m or 30 ft) by the power law

$$\frac{V_0}{V_1} = \left(\frac{H_0}{H_1}\right)^{\alpha} \tag{2.1}$$

where α varies from 0·07 to 0·4 depending on the nature of the terrain. A commonly accepted value for $\alpha = 1/7$, a ratio first derived by R. H. Blasius in the early 20th century from experiments on pipes. A. G. Davenport has discussed the effect of the earth's boundary layer [2.17, 2.29] and N. C. Helliwell [2.25] the effect of the average gust duration on the value of α.

From the wind velocity we can determine the pressure exerted by the wind, which is proportional to its kinetic energy

$$P = \tfrac{1}{2}\rho V^2 \tag{2.2}$$

where ρ is the density of the air. In S.I. units

$$P = 0·60V^2 \tag{2.3}$$

where P is measured in pascals and V in m/s. In British units

$$P = V^2/400 \tag{2.3}$$

where P is measured in lb/ft^2 and V in mph.

From the overall wind pressure corresponding to a certain height above ground level we can now calculate the distribution of wind pressure or wind suction on the building. Taking the simple case of a rectangular building (Fig. 2.1), the wind pressure produces positive pressure on the windward side, but suction on all other faces and on the roof. For the strength and stability of the frame as a whole, the pressure on the windward face and the suction on the leeward face are additive (Fig. 1.10).

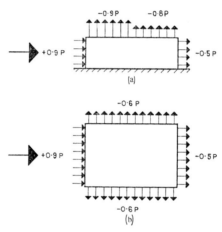

Fig. 2.1.   Allowance for wind pressure and suction required by the Australian Loading Code [2.27] for a rectangular building not exceeding 100 ft (30 m) in height. (a) Elevation; (b) Plan.

Roofs are generally subject to uplift, and pressure occurs only if the angle of the roof slope exceeds 30°. Since the weight of the roof is commonly greater than the wind suction, the stresses in the roof structure tend to be highest in calm weather for flat-roofed buildings (see also eqns 2.7 and 2.8). The wind suction may, however, cause failure of the much lighter roof covering, even to the extent of stripping the roof, without damaging the structural frame. Special problems arise in the case of suspension structures which are very light and flexible.

Wind pressure and suction coefficients for standard shapes are specified in the various loading codes [2.1, 2.2, 2.27] and they are revised from time to time in the light of additional data derived from observations on actual buildings and from wind-tunnel tests. Special problems arise when a building is shielded [2.16], and this may subject the structural frame to torsion [2.28]. (See also Fig. 3.5c.)

The resistance of the structure to wind forces has been outlined briefly in Section 1.5 and Figs. 1.7 to 1.9, and it is considered in more detail in Chapter 11.

2.6. LOADS DUE TO EARTHQUAKES AND EXPLOSIVES

Major earthquakes occur only in some parts of the earth's surface, including the west coast of North and South America, New Zealand, Japan and several Mediterranean countries. Some areas of high seismicity, such as northern New Guinea, are fortunately only sparsely inhabited. Only minor disturbances have been reported during the last century in the United Kingdom, in Australia and in eastern North America.

G. W. Housner [2.32] describes the causes:

The shaking of the ground during an earthquake is caused by the passage of seismic waves generated by the release of stored-up stresses in the earth's crust when sudden slips take place along a geological fault. Three main types of fault have generated significant destructive ground shaking: strike-slip faults, normal thrust faults, and shallow-angle thrust faults. It is thought that the characteristics of surface ground shaking very close to the fault differ somewhat for the three types of fault.

A strike-slip fault, such as the famous San Andreas Fault in California, lies in an essentially vertical plane, and the slip is mainly a relative horizontal displacement across the fault plane.

The normal thrust fault, which generated the 9 February, 1971, San Fernando, California, earthquake [2.35], had a fault plane making an angle of approximately 45 degrees with the ground surface and the slip reflected a horizontal compression in the earth's crust so that during the earthquake the upper rock mass moved uphill over the lower rock mass. A relative horizontal component of displacement across the fault plane also occurred.

A normal thrust fault can be thought of as a plane of shear failure resulting from horizontal compression in the rock forming the earth's crust. The 1964 Alaska earthquake was generated on a shallow-angle thrust fault making an angle of approximately 15 to 20 degrees with respect to the ground surface and the slip was one which predominantly represented movement of the lower rock mass into and beneath the upper rock mass. The fault displacement is attributed to the relative motion of two large crustal plates moving into each other with the result that the oceanic plate is thrust under the continental plate, deep into the earth's mantle.

At the present time the precise nature of these waves is not well understood, and all earthquake-resistant design is therefore based on simplifications.

The ground moves and takes the foundation of the building with it, while leaving the upper part of the building temporarily behind because of its high speed and the inertia of the building. The movement of the building relative to the ground has horizontal and vertical components. The building is generally strong enough to resist the vertical movement, and the simplest form of analysis is thus based on the premise that the building is subject to a horizontal force. Building codes in earthquake zones stipulate the minimum values of the horizontal forces which must be allowed for in the design; examples of such codes are the Uniform Building Code of the International Conference of Building Officials (which covers the American West Coast), the New Zealand Standard Model Building Bylaw, and the Building Standard Law of Japan.

The concept of a static analysis has led to progressively stiffer buildings, incorporating massive concrete frames and shear walls. Some of the damage observed during recent earthquakes [2.33–35] has indicated that great stiffness is not necessarily a protection against earthquake damage, particularly to ground floor columns. Capacity to absorb the energy transmitted by the earthquake to the structure, and to dissipate it dynamically, may be more important. Recent earthquake studies have therefore concentrated on dynamic analysis [2.36] and this is emphasised in current textbooks on the design of earthquake-resistant buildings [2.37, 2.38].

The danger of serious structural damage from *internal blast* was considered remote until the spectacular partial collapse of Ronan

Point, a block of flats in London, system-built from load-bearing precast concrete panels without a structural frame [2.39]. Serious loss of life was prevented only by the fact that the part of the building which collapsed as a result of the gas explosion was almost unoccupied at the time.

The most effective cure is to have a window or light brick wall which is blown out by the explosion and thus prevents the maximum pressure from building up and then being sustained for some centiseconds. Rasbash [2.40] has suggested the formula

$$P_{max} = aP_{vent} + bK$$

where P_{vent} is the pressure at which the venting panel breaks or is blown out, K is the ratio of the cross-sectional area of the room in which the explosion occurs to the area of the vent and a and b are constants.

An additional precaution is to design the structure against progressive collapse, which could spread upwards through the removal of a support, or downwards by the impact loads of falling debris (which happened in the Ronan Point collapse). This can be done either by designing for a specified additional load due to an internal explosion, or by providing additional paths through the structure in the event of the removal of one of its members. Design against progressive collapse seems entirely possible for structural steel or reinforced concrete frames, and also for buildings with load-bearing walls which are rigidly connected to form box frames. Buildings with load-bearing precast concrete or masonry walls (which rely on gravitational stability) are more prone to progressive collapse, as are flat-plate structures (beam-less concrete plates supported directly on the columns) because of the danger of punching shear (see also Section 2.10).

During the 1939–45 War the superiority of buildings with steel or reinforced concrete frames for resisting *bomb explosions*, as compared with those constructed with load-bearing brick walls, was amply demonstrated, and many structural engineers during the 1940s considered the desirability of designing structural frames in future to resist both the air blasts and the earth shocks likely to be produced by the largest bombs in a future war [2.41]. The development of atomic bombs with megatons of explosives has made this unrealistic [2.42].

The problem of protecting the population from nuclear fallout is, of course, an entirely separate problem.

The possibility of damage by *sonic booms* generated by aeroplanes is also disregarded, since no supersonic plane is likely to be permitted to pass through the sound barrier near a populated area in peacetime. *Collision between an aeroplane and a tall building* must, however, be considered. Indeed, the Empire State Building in New York has suffered the impact of an aeroplane. If the weight of the plane is W_{plane}, and its speed is V_{plane}, then its kinetic energy is $\frac{1}{2}W_{plane}V^2_{plane}$. If the mass of the portion of the building which is struck by the plane is W_{bld}, then the amount of energy conveyed to the structural frame is

$$\frac{1}{2}W_{plane}V^2_{plane}\ \frac{W_{plane}}{W_{plane} + W_{bld}}$$

2.7. FIRE LOADS

This section is included merely to point out that fire loads are not loads in the sense in which the term is defined in this chapter. Fire loads are frequently assessed at the same time as dead loads [2.10], because the same observations can be partly used for both. The fire load of a building is the thermal energy generated if all its combustible contents are burned. Thus, if the building contains x kg of books, and each kilogram of books produces y J (BTu, cal) of thermal energy, then the fire load is xy J, etc. The design of structures to resist fire is a special field which is discussed elsewhere [1.8, 2.43, 2.44]. (See also Section 1.4.)

2.8. SAFETY FACTORS AND LOAD FACTORS

Building codes go back to the earliest days of history. The oldest known is by Hummurabi, a king of Babylon about 3800 years ago (Fig. 2.2). One of its clauses states:

If a builder has built a house for a man and his work is not strong, and if the house he has built falls and kills the householder, that builder shall be slain.

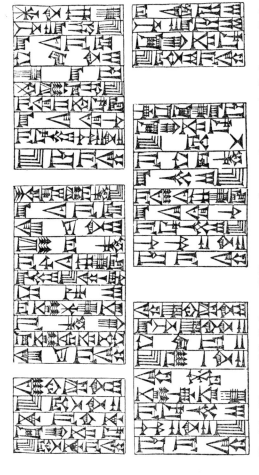

Fig. 2.2. Hammurabi's Code, *ca.* 1950 B.C., engraved on a column now in the Louvre, Paris:

If a builder has built a house for a man and his work is not strong, and if the house he has built falls in and kills the house-holder, that builder shall be slain. If goods have been destroyed, he shall replace all that has been destroyed; and because the house he built was not made strong, and it has fallen in, he shall restore the fallen house out of his own material.

(Quoted by Lyman W. Wood (1954). *Structural performance requirements for housing codes,* Symposium on Methods of Testing Building Constructions, *Special Technical Publication No. 166, American Society for Testing and Materials, Philadelphia, p.* 12.)

This type of code is designed to ensure structural safety, but it is also likely to result in excessively heavy and unadventurous structures since the builder makes certain there will be no collapse. The late medieval attitude, exemplified by the late Gothic cathedrals, is typical of the opposite approach. Collapse of the masonry appears to have occurred frequently, judging from the evidence of structural repairs and from mentions in monastic chronicles. Blame was not necessarily attributed to the builder's incompetence; it may have been that he, or even the whole community, had failed to find favour in the eye of God.

A more pragmatic approach existed in Ancient Rome, where some masonry structures (such as arches) were designed by geometric rules limiting the ratio of depth to span. However, the concept of a *factor of safety* was never introduced into the design of traditional masonry structures, partly because their mechanics were not properly understood until after they became obsolescent, and partly because the loads could not be properly estimated at the time [2.45].

The building of the railways, which included numerous bridges, required a new approach. The iron bridges were expensive and material was used sparingly. The loads imposed by the trains could be controlled, and the strength of the iron could be measured. The concept of a working stress developed, and it was later defined as the strength of the material, divided by a factor of safety.

The factor was at first a round number determined by experience, and it could be quite high. In 1866 J. Rankine, suggested a factor of safety of 4 to 6 for his column formula (see Section 8.2), but as recently as 1921 E. H. Salmon considered that, in the design of cast iron columns, a factor of safety of 10 for dead loads and of 20 for live loads would be prudent 'when applying formulae . . . the constants for which were determined from carefully prepared laboratory specimens [2.46]'.

The factor of safety has been progressively reduced by better controls, in some instances to well below 2.

An alternative approach, developed in the 20th century for ultimate strength design, is to factor the loads.

$$\text{Factor of safety} = \frac{\text{Failing stress (yield stress, crushing strength)}}{\text{Working stress used in design}} \qquad (2.4)$$

$$\text{Load factor} = \frac{\text{Ultimate load}}{\text{Working load}} \qquad (2.5)$$

The distinction between a factor of safety and a load factor is thus essentially that one applies the safety margin to the stresses and the other to the loads. Either could be used for elastic design (see Chapters 4 and 5) or for ultimate strength design (see Chapters 9 and 10). In practice, however, factors of safety are traditionally used for elastic design, for which the maximum permissible (or working) stresses are obtained from eqn (2.4), while load factors are normally associated with ultimate strength design.

A constant load factor numerically equal to the traditional factor of safety evidently is of little benefit if one wants to design a more economical structure. A committee of the *Institution of Structural Engineers* [2.47] has proposed a series of load factors which take account of the principal variables. It bases the choice of the load factor on two groups.

Group X : *Probability of Collapse*, includes the following factors:

    A—Material, workmanship, inspection, maintenance.

    B—Accuracy of loading assumption, control of use.

    C—Accuracy of analysis, type of structure.

Group Y : *Seriousness of Collapse*, includes the following factors:

    D—Danger to human life.

    E—Economic losses.

In each factor of Group X there are four ratings: very good (vg), good (g), fair (f) and poor (p). In each factor in Group Y there are three ratings: not serious (ns), serious (s), very serious (vs).

The Committee assigned the following values to the factors, based on its collective judgement and experience:

Values of X factors

Characteristic		B = Very good	Good	Fair	Poor
A = very good	C = very good	1·1	1·3	1·5	1·7
	good	1·2	1·45	1·7	1·95
	fair	1·3	1·6	1·9	2·2
	poor	1·4	1·75	2·1	2·45
A = good	C = very good	1·3	1·55	1·8	2·05
	good	1·45	1·75	2·05	2·35
	fair	1·6	1·95	2·3	**2·65**
	poor	1·75	2·15	**2·55**	**2·95**
A = fair	C = very good	1·5	1·8	2·1	2·4
	good	1·7	2·05	2·4	**2·75**
	fair	1·9	2·3	**2·7**	**3·1**
	poor	2·1	**2·55**	**3·0**	**3·45**
A = poor	C = very good	1·7	2·15	2·4	**2·75**
	good	1·95	2·35	**2·75**	**3·15**
	fair	2·2	**2·65**	**3·1**	**3·55**
	poor	2·45	**2·95**	**3·45**	**3·95**

Factors above 2·5 are given in the above table in bold type, and the Committee recommends that it would be better, if the design passes into that range, either to alter the practical conditions envisaged, or to adopt statistical methods of load and strength assessment, or to use superior methods of calculation.

Values of Y factors

Characteristic		D = Not serious	Serious	Very serious
E = Not serious		1·0	1·2	1·4
	Serious	1·1	1·3	1·5
	Very serious	1·2	1·4	1·6

The ultimate load factor is then obtained multiplying X by Y. The following examples are taken from the Report:

Example 2.1. Consider a reinforced concrete tank designed for erection on a tower for use as a source of water supply in a country district.

The factors are assessed as follows:

$$A = g; \quad B = vg; \quad C = g; \quad D = ns; \quad E = s$$

Consequently from the two tables $X = 1\cdot45$ and $Y = 1\cdot1$. The ultimate load factor $= 1\cdot45 \times 1\cdot1 = 1\cdot60$.

Example 2.2. Consider the steel structure of the gallery of a metropolitan theatre.

$$A = g; \quad B = vg; \quad C = g; \quad D = vs; \quad E = s$$

The ultimate load factor $= 1\cdot45 \times 1\cdot5 = 2\cdot18$.

Example 2.3. Consider the load bearing walls of a large block of flats, to be built of brick under ordinary municipal conditions.

$$A = p; \quad B = g; \quad C = p; \quad D = s; \quad E = vs$$

The ultimate load factor $= 2\cdot95 \times 1\cdot4 = 4\cdot13$.

It will be noted that load factors determined by this method can be quite high, much more than the factors traditionally stipulated in building codes. The nominal factors of codes, however, do not provide the only safety margin. When unreliable materials are used, lower stresses may be assumed. Higher loads may be stipulated in uncertain loading conditions. Finally engineers and architects often increase arbitrarily the calculated structural dimensions in an unfamiliar situation. When a more rational method of assessing the load factor is employed, these additional safeguards can be discarded.

2.9. QUALITY CONTROL CRITERIA

Our first measure towards a more accurately determined, and therefore lower, safety margin is to treat our data statistically (Fig. 2.3). The superimposed loads carried by the structure could have different values under different conditions. Instead of taking the average load W_0, we choose W_1 which includes, say, 95% of all possible loading conditions. There is then a 5% chance of a higher load. Similarly we do not choose the strength of the material, or load

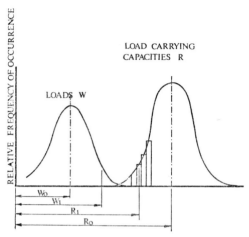

Fig. 2.3. Frequency distribution curves of the actual loads and the actual load carrying capacities of structural materials. (After W. R. Schriever (1960). Loads and load factors, *Trans. Engineering Institute of Canada*, **4**, 72–81.)

carrying capacity of the structural member, which represents the average of all material tests R_0, but a lower value R_1 which covers, say, 95% of all likely tests [2.48].

We next define our problem as providing a reasonable margin of safety against failure of the structure under load, and we therefore multiply the loads individually, depending on the uncertainty, by a load factor.

The individual load factor method has two advantages. In hyperstatic structures at high loads, the stress is not proportional to the load (see Chapters 9 and 10), so that factoring the loads is more realistic. A more important advantage is the flexibility gained by factoring the loads separately, since each load can be given an appropriate factor, instead of employing a single factor for all.

Complete certainty is statistically impossible, and we must first of all stipulate a probability of failure which is low enough to be acceptable. O. G. Julian in a report published by a Committee of the *American Society of Civil Engineers* [2.49] assumes a probability of 10^{-4}, *i.e.* a chance of 1 in 10 000, that the structure will collapse. Although some designers prefer to think in terms of a chance of 1 in a million, the ratio compares favourably with safety standards on the roads. In 1960, for example, in the State of New South Wales, 998 persons were killed in road accidents, which means that 260 per million of population were killed, or a probability of 2·6 × 10^{-4} per year. If the rate remained constant for 50 years (and it has not changed significantly in 12 years), the probability would be 130 × 10^{-4} in fifty years. If we take the useful life of a building also as fifty years, the probability of its prior collapse is only 1/130 of the designer being killed on the road during the same period.

If we use a lower probability of collapse, we must use a higher load factor, and therefore more material. On the other hand, we can obtain more favourable rates for insuring the building against damage or collapse and subsequent replacement, if we wish to transfer the risk from the building owner to an insurance company. There is a load factor at which the two just balance (Fig. 2.4), and it could be argued that this is the optimum factor.

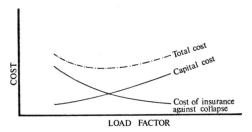

Fig. 2.4. Cost of a structure as a function of the load factor. (After W. R. Schriever, *loc. cit.*)

We have already examined the variation in the loads carried by the structure (see Sections 2.2 and 2.3). For the load of the structure itself, the coefficient of variation* is less than 0·05; for wind loads it might be more than 0·25. The coefficient of variation for the strength of structural steel with a guaranteed yield or proof stress is less than 0·1; for the cheaper reinforcing steels it might be as high as 0·15. For concrete the coefficient of variation ranges from 0·1 with good control to 0·3 with poor control.

* The definition and significance of the coefficient of variation may be found in any elementary book on statistics.

O. G. Julian [2.49] determined the load factor which corresponds to these coefficients of variation:

Load factor required for various coefficients of variation of loads and materials, for a probability of failure of 10^{-4}

Coefficient of variation of loads	Coefficient of variation of materials				
	0	0·05	0·10	0·25	0·40
0	—	1·21	1·46	2·58	4·51
0·05	1·20	1·30	1·52	2·62	4·56
0·10	1·44	1·51	1·69	2·76	4·71
0·25	2·42	2·47	2·62	3·65	5·72
0·40	3·89	3·94	4·10	5·24	7·58

O. G. Julian then investigated the increase in the load factor which would be needed to lower the probability of failure from 10^{-4} to 10^{-6} (*i.e.* a condition 10 000 times more favourable than the present road casualty figures). For coefficients of variation of 0·10 the load factor increases from 1·69 to 1·96 (an increase of 16%), and for coefficients of variation of 0·40 from 7·58 to 13·3 (138%).

Probably the two most advanced formulations embodied in actual building codes at the time of writing are those of the CEB-FIP Recommendations [2.50] and the ACI Code [2.51, 2.52].*

These are similar in character. The latter gives three equations for the load factor U, and the one which gives the most severe condition must be chosen:

$$U = 1\cdot4D + 1\cdot7L \tag{2.6}$$

$$U = 0\cdot75(1\cdot4D + 1\cdot7L + 1\cdot7W) = 1\cdot15D + 1\cdot28L + 1\cdot28W \tag{2.7}$$

$$U = 0\cdot9D + 1\cdot3W \tag{2.8}$$

where D is the dead load, L is the live load and W is the wind load (see also Section 2.5).

In addition, however, the method specified for testing the concrete gives its *minimum* strength (R_1 in Fig. 2.3). This means that

---

* The more sophisticated method of factoring used in the Code of Practice for the Structural Use of Concrete, CP 110:1972, is discussed in Chapter 10.

the *average* strength for a 3500 psi concrete and a coefficient of variation of 1·10 is 14% higher than the design strength, giving a load factor of about 1·85.

These concepts could, in principle, be taken further to develop a comprehensive *limit states* philosophy, which would permit reliability optimisation procedures producing minimal, but consistent load factors [2.13, 2.53]. One obvious possibility is to vary the load factor for columns with the height of the building, since the failure of the ground-floor columns of a 100-storey building would be far more serious than the failure of the penthouse columns in the same building, or the failure of the columns in a single-storey building. Another desirable innovation is to make an accurate allowance for dimensional errors (*e.g.* undersized concrete beams or slabs, reinforcement too close to the neutral axis [2.54]), lack of fit (*e.g.* of steel sections, of precast concrete elements to be joined), and inadequate connections (*e.g.* in welded structures).

While the probability theory has reached a suitable state of development, data cannot be assigned to many of the factors. For example, we mentioned in Section 2.6, a collision between an aeroplane and a building. This has happened only once and it is clearly not possible from this one occurrence in New York to make a reliable prediction of it happening elsewhere in the future. However, the question of assessing and reporting uncertainties, both for aircraft structures and for architectural structures, is receiving much attention [2.54–59].

2.10. THE FAIL-SAFE CONCEPT

Fail-safe structures originated in the 1920s in aircraft research. Sir Alfred Pugsley [2.46] gives the following example:

Consider the statically determinate plane frame (see Section 4.6) in Fig. 2.5(a), in which two members are of equal area and of the same material. The load W is shared equally between the two members AC and BC, and so long as these respond elastically, the vertical deflection d will increase linearly with W. At some load W_0, when $d = d_0$, the two members will start simultaneously to *yield, and if this occurs in idealised fashion at constant load (see Fig. 3.12), the W–d relationship will be as shown in Fig. 2.5b. Finally, at some total deflection $d = d_1$, when the ductility of the bars is exhausted (see Section 3.4), fracture will occur and the structure will fail.*

Suppose now that a vertical bar be added to the structure of Fig. 2.5a to produce the structure of Fig. 2.5c. This is now redundant (see Section 4.6), and, in the elastic range, the loads on the members due to the force W will be dependent on their relative extensibilities.

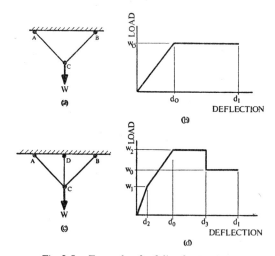

Fig. 2.5. Example of a fail-safe structure.
(a) Statically determinate structure.
(b) Load-deformation diagram of (a).
(c) Structure (a) modified by the fail-safe concept.
(d) Load-deformation diagram for (c).
(After Sir A. Pugsley [2.46].)

For convenience of illustration let us assume that the central bar has the same modulus of elasticity as the others, but is of less area in the ratio of 1 to $(2)^{\frac{1}{2}}$. In this case, in the elastic range, the load in the central bar DC will be $\frac{1}{2}W$ and the remainder of W will be supported by the inclined bars.

Let us assume that the central bar starts to yield at some load P before the inclined bars do likewise. This will happen when

$W = W_1 = 2P$ and $d = d_2$, where d_2 is less than d_0. Up to this stage the frame will have been wholly elastic, but stiffer than the frame of Fig. 2.5a, and its behaviour is illustrated by the first part of the full line of Fig. 2.5d. Thereafter, as W is increased beyond W_1, DC will continue to yield whilst the inclined bars remain elastic until, when $d = d_0$, they too start to yield. The total load carried by the structure at this stage will be $W = W_2 = W_0 + P$. Thereafter, all the members will yield until $d = d_3$, if less than d_1, at which the central bar snaps. This behaviour is illustrated by the full line in Fig. 2.5d.

The structure remaining—consisting of the inclined bars AC and BC—is still capable of carrying a load $W = W_0$, and this residual strength will remain until $d = d_1$, when the inclined bars themselves fracture and the whole structure fails.

It is evident that by the simple addition of a member a frame which suddenly reaches the ultimate load is changed into one which gives clear warning of collapse at a lower load, whose level can be controlled at will. In addition, the extra member increases the strength of the frame so that the material is not wasted.

While the fail-safe approach was specifically developed for aircraft structures whose load factors must be kept low if the planes are to fly economically, it has evident advantages for the optimisation of architectural structures. One specific example is the rule in the ACI Code [2.50] which limits the amount of tensile steel in a concrete beam to ensure a primary tension failure. Because steel yields with considerable plastic deformation, such failure is preceded by extensive cracking of the concrete over a period of time which gives warning of collapse (see Chapter 10), while a primary concrete failure, because of the brittle nature of concrete (see Section 3.4), occurs suddenly without warning.

Chapter 3

The Elastic and Inelastic Deformation of Materials, and the Criteria for Structural Design

In this chapter we look at the various criteria for structural design and pin-point those which determine the sizes of the structural members; we note that these are not the same in modern engineered structures and in traditional construction.

We next distinguish between ductile and brittle materials, and examine their deformation and strength, and the effect of crystal structure and moisture content on deformation. Finally we note that simple standard tests are not always simple, and discuss the interpretation of the test data.

3.1. CRITERIA FOR STRUCTURAL DESIGN

Design based on the strength and stability of the structure is a comparatively recent concept [2.45], and the theory is still perhaps not fully developed.

The most basic cause of failure is the loss of gravitational stability of the structure (Fig. 3.1). In architectural structures this is now rare, although it could result from grossly deficient foundations, from mining subsidence, or from an earthquake. It was, however, the basis of the design of traditional masonry structures, and it is still a dominant factor in determining the dimensions of many dams and retaining walls. Failure through overturning does not depend on the strength or deformation of the structural materials, and we need not consider it further in this chapter.

Most of our present design calculations determine the relation between the loads acting on the structure and the stresses caused in it. We can then either determine structural dimensions which are sufficient to carry the maximum permissible loads when the stresses in the structural materials reach the maximum permissible stresses (*elastic design*), or the ultimate loads when the structural materials just reach their ultimate strength (*ultimate strength design*) (see Chapters 9 and 10). Since materials deform under stress, we may reach our conclusions through determining the deformations and then translating them into stresses (see Section 4.5); but this is merely a means to an end.

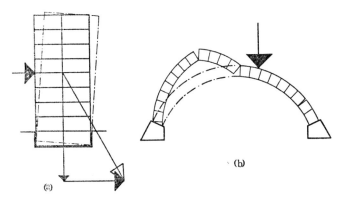

Fig. 3.1. Failure by loss of gravitational stability.
(a) Overturning of the entire building.
(b) Failure of traditional masonry arch. The joints between the blocks of stone (*voussoirs*) open to form hinges, and when the fourth hinge forms, the arch becomes a mechanism and collapses. Unless the stone is exceptionally weak (say, chalk), it is unlikely to be overstressed. If the voussoirs fall on soft ground after the collapse and are undamaged, the entire arch can be re-erected with new mortar joints and re-used at its safe load.

Excessive deformation may, in itself, be a criterion of failure. Elastic deformation is not usually serious in buildings. The elastic deformation under the dead loads can be allowed for, if necessary, by giving the structural member a slight camber; *i.e.* it is built to curve slightly upwards, and becomes horizontal when the permanent load begins to act, usually when the formwork is removed. Generally architectural structures are fairly stiff, and the ratio of live load to dead load is low, so that movement due to elastic deformation of the structure is unlikely to be noticeable. However, it might damage brittle finishes, such as plaster, and the remedy is then to use more flexible finishes or a less flexible structure. Inelastic deformation is more serious because the action of the dead load cannot be compensated (see Section 3.3).

Finally, a structure could fail by buckling. This is a loss of stability, but unlike stability failure through overturning (Fig. 3.1a), the structure recovers its shape if the material is not damaged in the process. If a very long and slender column is loaded in compression, it will at a certain load suddenly deflect sideways (Fig. 3.2a), and

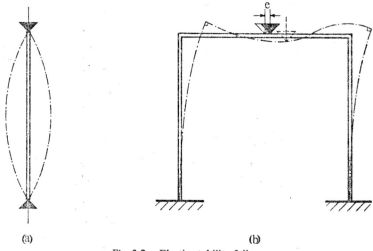

(a)   (b)

Fig. 3.2.   Elastic stability failure.

(a) Buckling of a slender column. The column deflects sideways due to loss of elastic stability; it may buckle either to the right or the left. Buckling implies a slight, but unavoidable imperfection in straightness or concentricity of loading. Theoretically one should be able to balance a pin on its point, and theoretically a perfect column should not buckle.

(b) Buckling of slender frame. The buckling load is greatly reduced by a small eccentricity of loading *e*, or by a slight departure from straightness of the compression members.

(See also Fig. 3.7.)

cease to be a useful load bearing member. However, when the load is removed, the original shape is recovered, and the material is undamaged. On the other hand, the deflection due to buckling may overstress the material, or the deformation caused by overstressing the material may cause a member to buckle. Buckling, like deflection, can be either an elastic or an inelastic phenomenon (see Chapter 8).

3.2. PRIORITIES IN STRUCTURAL DESIGN

Up to the 18th century structural design was based on craft tradition or on geometry [2.45]. Even if one considers classical structures in the light of modern knowledge, the strength of the materials is still not a decisive criterion. Traditional masonry structures depend on the stability of the blocks which compose them (Fig. 3.1b), and only in the case of very weak materials, *e.g.* soft chalk, could failure through overstressing result. Classical timber structures generally used more material than modern methods would require, and the connections were their weakest feature.

In the 19th century design based on strength became so generally accepted for engineering structures, that it is sometimes overlooked that it need not necessarily be the basic criterion. Strength calculations have greatly reduced the quantity of material required, sometimes by more than 100 to 1. In this process some structures have become so light that deflection or buckling have been turned into critical design factors.

The strongest aluminium alloys have today a greater strength than structural steel had at the beginning of the century. Steel, in turn, has been produced in high-strength alloys far better than those previously available. Unfortunately the methods used to increase strength do not raise the value of the modulus of elasticity (see Section 3.4); indeed, the modulus of elasticity of steel and aluminium cannot be improved by any known means. In this respect concrete has an advantage, because its modulus of elasticity increases with strength.

Since deflection and buckling depend primarily on the modulus of elasticity, the use of high strength materials is liable to cause buckling and excessive deflection before the critical stresses are reached.

These are still exceptions, however, and in most structures the primary design calculations are concerned with the relation between the loads and the consequential stresses.

In this respect we must make a further sub-classification. Members of architectural structures may be divided into those under direct compression (Fig. 3.3a and b), direct tension (Fig. 3.3c), bending (Fig. 3.3d) and a combination of these. Apart from the fact that compression members (columns) are liable to buckling, their design

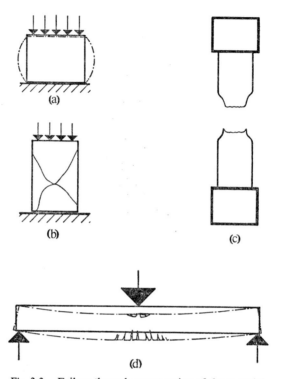

Fig. 3.3.   Failure through overstressing of the material.
(a) Compression failure of a ductile material through plastic flow.
(b) Compression failure of brittle material through rupture.
(c) Tension failure, always by rupture.
(d) Bending failure of a brittle material; crushing on top, cracking on the bottom.
(See also Figs. 3.14 and 3.15.)

and that of tension members is straightforward. Most calculations are concerned with the solution of bending problems.

Let us consider a horizontal gap to be spanned by a structure to carry vertical loads (Fig. 3.4a) and let us consider some section B-B. The forces acting to the left of B are the vertical loads between A and B and the vertical reaction at A. These form a moment M about B, and this is called the *bending moment* (Fig. 3.4c). The structure must have sufficient structural material at the section B to resist it. This can be done in several different ways. A beam provides a resultant tension and compression within its own depth to form a resistance moment M (Fig. 3.4d). A truss does so with separate tension and compression flanges with bracing members between (Fig. 3.4e). An arch provides the resistance moment by the product of the compression within the arch and its rise (Fig. 3.4f). Similarly a suspension cable relies on the tension and the sag of the cable (Fig. 3.4g). The bending moment is therefore basically a function of the loads, and not of the structure.

The bending moment is usually the factor which determines the dimensions of the structure, and the calculations are primarily concerned with it and its effect on the structure. There are, however, secondary effects. The compression flanges of a truss, or even of an I-shaped beam, may buckle under the influence of the direct compressive force due to bending, unless their effective length is reduced by bracing. Arches may buckle if they are long and slender, but not suspension cables; this is one reason why they are so suitable for large spans.

The most important secondary effect of the vertical loads is the shear force. Let us consider the vertical forces to the left of B in Fig. 3.4a. These consist of the vertical reaction at A and the vertical loads between A and B. Except at one point where they cancel out, there is a residual force which tends to cut, or shear, through the

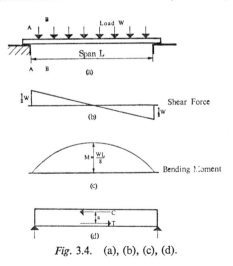

Fig. 3.4. (a), (b), (c), (d).

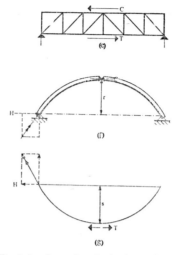

Fig. 3.4. Spanning the horizontal gap.

(a) Load on simply supported span.

(b) Shear force.

(c) Bending moment.

(d) *Beam action.* The bending moment M is resisted by a couple formed by the resultant compressive force C, the resultant tensile force T, and the lever arm a.

(e) *Truss action.* The bending moment M is resisted by the force in the compression flange C, the force in the tension flange T, and the lever arm formed by the depth of the truss. The shear force is resisted by the vertical and the diagonal members.

(f) *Arch action.* The bending moment M is resisted by the compressive force at the crown C, the horizontal component of the reaction H, and the lever arm formed by the rise of the arch r.

(g) *Cable action.* The bending M is resisted by the cable tension at the lowest point T, the horizontal component of the reaction H, and the lever arm formed by the sag of the cable s.

member (Fig. 3.4b). Beams must be designed to resist it; but in architectural structures it is usually a secondary effect which may modify the details of the structural member, but does not drastically alter basic dimensions such as depth. It should be noted, however, that this is not universally true; for example, the shear force is more important than the bending moment in many engine parts.

In trusses the shear force is resisted by the bracing members (Fig. 3.4e). In cables shear is eliminated by the shape (Fig. 3.4g). The same

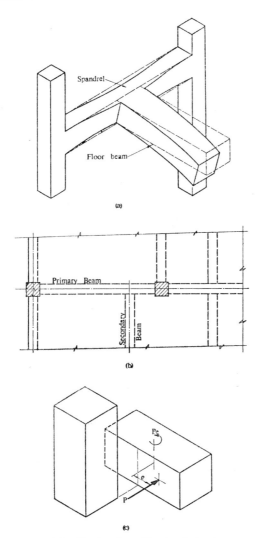

Fig. 3.5.   Torsion in architectural structures.

(a) Torsion in spandrel beam on the facade of a building, due to absence of a balancing load on the other side of the beam.

(b) Torsion in primary beam, due to displacement of the secondary beam. This can produce very large twisting moments.

(c) Torsion due to eccentric wind load *P*, caused by shelter from a taller building.

is possible in arches, either completely or partially, depending on shape.

Torsion which is, for example, the primary design factor for engine shafts, is only a secondary factor in architectural structures. It occurs mainly through an eccentricity of the loading (Fig. 3.5). It should, however, be noted that the rectangular structural shape most efficient for bending is not efficient for resisting torsion, and if the torsion is a significant, even though a secondary factor, this must be allowed for (Fig. 3.6).

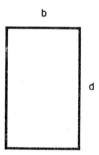

Fig. 3.6. Effect of secondary torsion on the choice of structural sections. The bending strength is proportional to $bd^2/12$, whereas the torsional strength is proportional to b^2d/k (where k varies from 5 for squares to 3 for narrow rectangles). The most efficient rectangle to resist bending is a deep section which has negligible torsional strength; the most efficient rectangle for resisting torsion is the square, which has quite acceptable bending strength.

In emphasising the primary importance of direct and bending stresses in the design of structural frames for buildings we must, however, make one reservation. Light rectangular steel frames (*i.e.* frames of low to medium height) are liable to buckle before they fail in bending and compression, if they have no encasement, or only lightweight fireproofing (Fig. 3.7). This is normally prevented by concrete encasement, which is still the most common method of fireproofing, because the stiffness is then increased to an extent where bending failure occurs before buckling. For the same reason buckling is not usually a primary cause of failure in reinforced concrete frames.

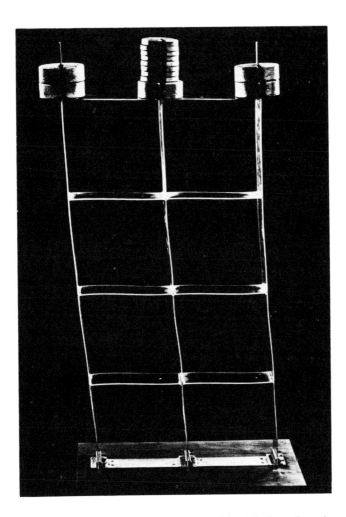

Fig. 3.7.   Stability failure of building frame. At this load the frame is on the point of elastic stability failure, followed by collapse. Stability is instantly recovered, without material damage, if the load is removed. The load-carrying capacity of the frame is greatly increased (in this instance about three-fold) if sidesway is prevented by bracing, by shear walls, etc.

3.3. ELASTIC AND INELASTIC DEFORMATION

The relation between the loads acting on the structure and the stresses in it have for more than a century been determined almost exclusively by assuming that structures consist of perfect materials which are:

homogeneous   *i.e.* of consistently uniform composition;

isotropic   *i.e.* behaving the same way in all directions and without a fibrous structure;

elastic   *i.e.* deforming instantly on loading and fully recovering that deformation instantly on unloading; and obeying *Hooke's Law*, so that loads are proportional to deformations.

Without these assumptions the design of structures would become extremely difficult. The assumptions of isotropy and homogeneity permit us to treat each small piece like any other piece of the same material. The assumption of elasticity implies that there is a unique relation between load and deformation, so that it is not necessary to know how often the load has been applied, or how long it has been acting. Hooke's Law implies a linear relationship, so that double the load produces double the deformation.

The high degree of perfection which the mathematical theory of elasticity achieved in the late 19th and early 20th centuries owes a great deal to its temporary significance in cosmology, through the supposition of the existence of the ether as an elastic fluid permeating space as a medium for the transmission of electromagnetic waves. Many of the precise solutions have been so complex that they have served as a hindrance rather than a help to structural design. The remedy is to make approximations, not to abandon the assumptions, as any theory based on a non-linear relation between load and deformation can only be more complex.

We must bear in mind, however, that the above assumptions are idealisations to which actual materials may conform only in part. Timber has different properties along and across the grain, and is therefore not isotropic. The deformation of concrete is not purely elastic, and if the inelastic deformation is included in the calculations, as it must be, it no longer obeys Hooke's Law. We must also remember that keeping stresses below the maximum permissible values is no protection against cracking and creep, because these occur well within the working range.

These are not defects, but simply normal characteristics of materials, which are not inferior because they do not conform to the assumptions of a classical theory. If we normally modify the constants to make them conform to this theory, it is only to produce a simple design method.

The departure of structural materials from the ideal properties enumerated above can be either helpful or unhelpful. Thus, the creep of concrete and the plastic deformation of steel at high stresses can produce troublesome deflections, but they can also increase the load-bearing capacity of structures by redistributing stresses and thus lowering the critical maximum stresses.

We will examine the physical properties of structural materials, before considering their effect on structural behaviour.

3.4. Deformation and Crystal Structure

In considering deformation and failure under load, we may classify engineering materials into three main types; *metals, plastics* and *ceramics*.* Wood does not fit into this simple classification since the fibres, which are its chief structural characteristic, are produced by biological growth.

We do not so far employ plastics as principal structural materials in architecture, although they are frequently used for bonding timber, and occasionally concrete and aluminium. Our chief distinction is therefore between the metals, notably the alloys of iron and aluminium, and the ceramics, notably Portland cement, in association with stone and sand, and burnt clay and other silicates, in the form of bricks.

---

* These terms are defined in most modern textbooks on physics or on materials science [3.1]. Basically metals are composed of elements which readily give up electrons to provide a metallic bond and electrical conductivity. The plastics consist of non-metallic elements, which share electrons. Ceramic materials contain compounds of metallic and non-metallic elements, and have both ionic and covalent bonds.

The obvious characteristics of metals are their lustrous appearance and their high electrical conductivity; since they have comparatively few electrons in the outer shell of the atom, metals part relatively easily with them, and this gives them their characteristic 'metallic' behaviour.

It was noted more than a century ago that structural metals, such as wrought iron and steel, were capable of considerable plastic deformation, and that the structure tended to fail through excessive deformation, rather than actual fracture. Structural ceramics, like natural stone, brick and concrete, on the other hand tended to fracture with little deformation. Indeed, Galileo's supposition that the brittle fracture of stone was not preceded by any deformation at all, was widely believed up to the end of the 19th century. There is one important exception. Cast iron fails with a brittle fracture; but in grey cast iron at least, the particles of graphite can be seen in the fracture with the naked eye, and the failure might therefore be attributed to the presence of non-metallic impurities in the metal.

Recent research in materials science has proved this theory to be incorrect. If the force required to produce plastic deformation is higher than that required to produce a cleavage fracture, a brittle

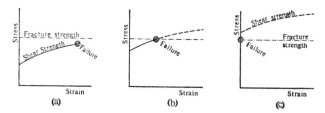

Fig. 3.8.   Ductile and brittle failure.
(a) Ductile shear failure after plastic deformation.
(b) Brittle fracture after some plastic deformation.
(c) Brittle fracture with negligible deformation.

failure results. If the reverse is true, the structural failure is due to plastic deformation (Fig. 3.8). In pure metals plastic deformation occurs relatively early, so that brittle fracture is unlikely. When impurities are introduced, as for example carbon into iron to produce steel, the deformation process is impeded, and the *ductile* force required to produce plastic deformation is raised, even to the extent where brittle fracture may occur before plastic deformation. A drop in temperature, which slows down atomic movement, has the same effect, so that steel which is ductile at normal temperature may produce a brittle failure in cold weather. During the 1939–45 War a number of welded ships broke in half in very cold weather, and low temperature is believed to have been a contributory cause to the failure of the King's Bridge in Melbourne in 1962. In ceramic materials the complexity of the microstructure is such that brittle failure is usually preceded by little plastic deformation. This can be altered by high temperature and pressure, and rocks in the interior

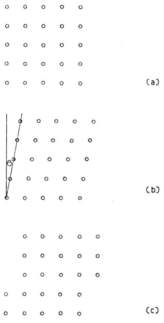

Fig. 3.9.   Deformation of crystalline solid.

(a) The unstrained crystal.

(b) The crystal deformed elastically. The angle θ is a measure of the stiffness, usually given in the form of the elastic modulus E (this is the hypothetical stress which would produce unit deformation). When the load is removed, the atoms spring back to their original positions.

(c) The crystal deformed plastically. When the elastic limit is reached, the atoms jump one position, producing permanent, or 'plastic' deformation.

of the earth do in fact show plastic deformation, as the geological record on numerous exposed cliffs proves. It can even be produced in the laboratory on concrete by triaxial compression [3.2].

Sir Lawrence Bragg [3.3] has devised an analogy to the structure of a simple crystalline material, such as a pure metal or simple alloy, which provides a good visual image of the grouping of atoms, and even of crystal structure. Soap bubbles are blown through a tube on a dish of water. If we apply tension, compression or distortion (shear) to this bubble structure we obtain a picture of elastic deformation.

We can determine the elastic deformation of simple materials (Fig. 3.9b) from solid state physics, and derive the modulus of elasticity from the electrostatic attractions within the crystals. The agreement between theory and experiment is quite good. We can also derive Hooke's Law by this process [3.5]. The electrostatic forces are not influenced significantly by impurities and imperfections, and alloying has therefore no great influence on the value of the modulus of elasticity of metals.

It is also possible to determine theoretically the elastic limit (Fig. 3.9c) at which plastic deformation first occurs. This is, however, 100 to 1000 times higher than the experimental value [3.6]. The reason for the difference between theory and practice lies in the imperfections, or *dislocations* (Fig. 3.10) which crystals inevitably have, unless they are very carefully grown in the laboratory. If a dislocation in one position is removed through filling the vacant space, another one forms adjacent, and the dislocation thus moves across the crystal. This has the same effect as a sliding motion in a perfect crystal (Fig. 3.9c), and can be achieved with much less energy. The hypothesis that plastic deformation of crystals takes place by movement of dislocations was proposed independently by G. I. Taylor, M. Polanyi and E. Orowan in 1934.

The strength of a plastic material therefore depends on the ease with which the dislocations can be moved. If they move readily, the material is soft; *e.g.* a pure iron wire can be twisted around one's finger. If we now introduce an atom of appreciably different size, *e.g.* a carbon atom into iron, we make it more difficult to move the dislocations, and the material becomes harder. Steel is therefore much stronger than pure iron. If there are a great many carbon atoms, as in high-carbon steel, the ductile strength may be raised above the

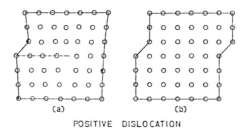

POSITIVE   DISLOCATION

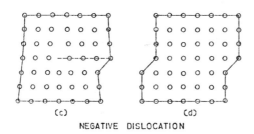

NEGATIVE   DISLOCATION

Fig. 3.10.   Plastic deformation at a dislocation.
(a) Positive dislocation, produced by a gap in the crystal structure.
(b) Plastic deformation at a positive dislocation.
(c) Negative dislocation, produced by an incomplete row of additional atoms in the crystal.
(d) Plastic deformation at a negative dislocation.

brittle strength so that the material fails with little plastic deformation. An increase in ductile strength lowers the ultimate plastic deformation (Fig. 3.8b), because the brittle strength is reached at a smaller deformation.

There is also a very great difference between the theoretical and practical energies required to produce fracture. Fracture consists of the rupture of atomic bonds, as complete as when a solid material is turned into vapour. The energy required to fracture a metal or ceramic is, however, only a small fraction of that required to evaporate it through boiling. This is again due to imperfections, or *cracks*. Most of the current theory of brittle fracture is based on the work of A. A. Griffith [3.7]. When a fine glass filament is freshly drawn in an inert atmosphere, it has a strength approaching the theoretical value.

The slightest touch, however, or exposure to the corrosive effect of air, produces sufficient flaws to lower the strength to about one per cent of the original value. The larger the specimen, the greater the probability of a serious flaw, or Griffith crack, so that large test specimens of brittle material have, on an average, a lower strength than small test pieces.

Cracks exist in all materials; however, ductile materials can relieve the stress concentrations at the end of the Griffith cracks by plastic deformation. In high-carbon steels the carbon atoms block plastic deformation, and brittle fracture results. The complex microstructure of most ceramics produces the same effect.

When a brittle material is tested in compression, the flaws at right angles to the compressive stress cannot open, and therefore do not propagate. Failure is due to the secondary stresses acting on cracks at other angles. Consequently the compressive strength of brittle materials is about ten times their tensile strength. The ratio increases with the brittleness (*i.e.* deficiency of deformation prior to fracture) of the material.

For this reason the tensile strength of concrete with a high compressive strength is not much better than that of ordinary concrete.

Prestressing can be used with great advantage on brittle materials, as for example in prestressed concrete or in safety glass. Prestressing is of limited value in materials whose tensile and compressive strength is similar.

Tensile failure resulting in the production of cracks is not necessarily synonymous with collapse of the structure, or even failure of the structural member concerned. In reinforced concrete, tension cracks bridged by reinforcing steel are stable, and if they are not so large as to allow penetration of moisture to corrode the steel, they could probably remain for centuries without danger.

Even when no reinforcement is present, however, cracks do not necessarily cause collapse. Provided that the crack relieves a local stress concentration, and the remaining structural material is sufficient to carry the loads, then the structure is entirely sound. It follows, of course, that the cracked material need never have been there in the first place; but it may be required for non-structural reasons, such as appearance or fire proofing.

Very strong composite materials can be produced by bonding

high strength fibres of glass or silica in a ductile matrix [3.10], but these are still too expensive for architectural use.

3.5. DEFORMATION AND WATER CONTENT

Wood and concrete contain substantial quantities of water, and the moisture movement gives rise to *shrinkage* and *creep*.* These deformations can be several times as great as the elastic deformations, and seriously alter the stress distribution of the concrete.

Timber should be dried (or *seasoned*) before it is used in a building, but for economic reasons structural timber is rarely fully seasoned, so that some shrinkage usually occurs.

The amount of water required for the chemical reaction of the cement is insufficient to produce a fluid concrete, so that there is always an excess of water when the material is placed in the mould. Consequently concrete shrinks during curing. The shrinkage strain of concrete is approximately 3×10^{-4} (or one part in 3000), and this is also approximately the ultimate tensile strain of concrete. Consequently concrete generally forms some cracks due to shrinkage. These could, in unsuitable designs, propagate and cause serious structural damage.

The phenomenon of creep in concrete is also believed to result from moisture movement although opinions still differ [3.8]. Portland cement is produced by burning together finely divided limestone, which consists mainly of calcium carbonate, and clay, which consists mainly of aluminium silicate. The resulting blend of calcium silicates and calcium aluminates forms partly a microcrystalline structure, and partly a colloidal 'glue' (Fig. 3.11), from which water can be expelled by pressure. This is the reason why concrete 'creeps' under sustained stress. Thus a concrete slab carrying its own weight continues to deflect for many months after the formwork has been removed, and the ultimate creep deflection is much greater than the

---

* The term *creep* is also used for the inelastic deformation of metals. This is caused by the freer movement of electrons at high temperatures, and is entirely different from the creep of concrete and timber, which occur at room temperature, and are due to squeezing of moisture from the pores. Creep of metals is not important in architectural structures.

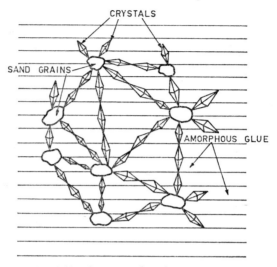

Fig. 3.11.   Structure of sand–cement mortar.

elastic deformation. Since this inelastic deformation occurs gradually over a period of time, it is difficult to compensate for it, as we can compensate the elastic deflection by an upward camber. Furthermore the gradual movement of the concrete is liable to damage brittle finishes, such as plaster, and brick walls with which it is in contact.

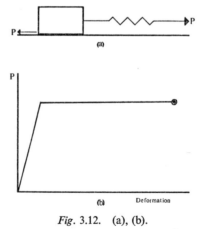

Fig. 3.12.   (a), (b).

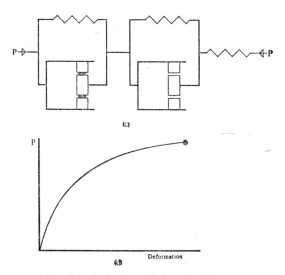

Fig. 3.12. Rheological models for plasticity and creep.

(a) Rheological model for plastic deformation in tension. It consists of a heavy block resting on a rough surface, and a spring. Until the load P exceeds the frictional resistance, the deformation is entirely due to elastic extension of the spring. When the load P reaches the magnitude of the frictional resistance, deformation continues indefinitely without further increases in the load P.

(b) Ideal plastic load–deformation diagram.

(c) Rheological model for creep in compression. It consists of a spring and a dashpot in parallel, and another spring in series. It is not unlike the damping mechanism used in motor cars and motor cycles. As the load P increases, there is an instant elastic response due to the compression of the left-hand spring. The dashpots delay the compression of the other two springs, but the greater the lapse of time, the greater the deformation. The delayed deformation is the creep. In concrete only part of the creep is recoverable. The right-hand dashpot is fitted with non-return valves to model the non-recoverable creep.

(d) Load–deformation diagram of creep model.

The creep of concrete and the plastic flow of steel are both inelastic deformations, but of a very different kind. This is best illustrated by a comparison of their rheological* models (Fig. 3.12).

In spite of their different physical origin, however, the plastic deformation of metals and the creep of concrete have certain

* Rheology is the science of the flow of materials.

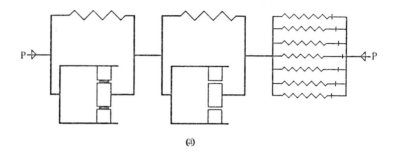

(a)

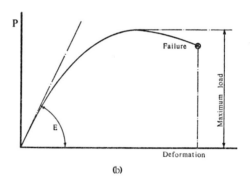

(b)

Fig. 3.13. Rheological model for ultimate strength of concrete.

(a) The pseudo-plastic deformation of concrete at high loads can be represented by a series of brittle springs which replace the single elastic spring in Fig. 3.12c. The springs are elastic up to a certain deformation (which is graded over a range from the beginning of the pseudo-plastic deformation to ultimate brittle failure of the concrete), and then fracture abruptly. As each spring fractures, its share of the load is distributed among the remaining springs, and the deformation therefore increases more rapidly. After the maximum load is reached further deformation of the springs remaining unbroken is possible by reducing the load P, until the last brittle spring fractures.

(b) Load–deformation diagram of concrete up to failure.

similarities. Both serve to redistribute high stresses, particularly those at the end of a crack, where due to the sharp corner stress-concentrations occur over a very small area. This stress redistribution increases the load-bearing capacity of the structure.

When concrete is subjected to very high stresses, the stress–strain diagram shows a much sharper curvature than can be explained by creep. This 'pseudo-plasticity' is now explained by the formation of very fine cracks (Fig. 3.13). In the plastic deformation of metals, however, the atomic bonds reform after slip, while the microcracks of concrete at high loads constitute physical damage which can only be repaired by the chemical action of the cement over very long periods [3.9]. If a structure is loaded to destruction, the concrete consequently breaks, while the structural steel merely deforms to the extent where the structure falls down.

Nevertheless, in concrete, as in steel, deformations occur at high stresses which are very much larger than the elastic deformations, and this fact constitutes the basis of the design theories based on ultimate strength (see Section 10.5).

3.6. INTERPRETATION OF STANDARD TESTS

If we take a brittle material, such as concrete or chalk, and test it in tension, it fails by a crack across the specimen, i.e. in tension (Fig. 3.15a). If we test a ductile material in tension, however, the failure is initiated by plastic deformation, because the brittle fracture strength is not reached (Fig. 3.8a). After the cross-section has been reduced sufficiently by plastic sliding at 45° to the direction of load to reach the brittle-fracture strength, failure occurs with a typical cup-and-cone fracture (Fig. 3.3c).

Materials cannot fail in compression as such. If we lower a piece of steel to the bottom of the ocean, where there are very large hydrostatic pressures, its volume is reduced by elastic compression, but it suffers no permanent damage. If we test a piece of structural steel (or soft iron or copper) in compression, it fails by sliding at 45° to the direction of the load (Fig. 3.14a). The metallic bonds reform after plastic deformation; if the specimen is cut and etched, it shows characteristic diagonal lines, known as Lueder's lines. If we test a

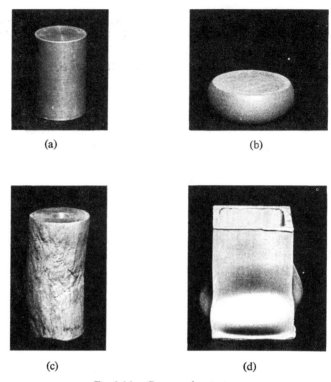

(a)   (b)

(c)   (d)

Fig. 3.14.   Compression tests.
(a) Compression specimen of pure copper.
(b) Plastic compression failure of speciman (a). The piece is squeezed out,
    but not cracked.
(c) Incipient brittle failure of hardened aluminium alloy; note the diagonal
    cracks.
(d) Local buckling of soft aluminium tube.

piece of concrete in compression, it also fails in diagonal shear, but
the material is disintegrated by the sliding action as the atomic bonds
cannot reform in a brittle material.

Direct shear tests are difficult to perform, and it is customary to
test in torsion. Ductile materials again fail in shear, and brittle
materials by diagonal tension failure (Fig. 3.15b).

Ductile materials therefore fail initially in shear, however tested,
and this results in extensive plastic deformation prior to fracture.

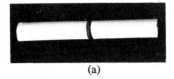 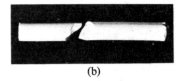

(a)   (b)

Fig. 3.15.   Tension failures.
(a) Brittle failure of chalk in direct tension.
(b) Brittle failure of chalk in diagonal tension, produced by twisting (torsion).

Architectural structures rarely deform sufficiently before collapse to produce actual fracture of ductile materials.

Brittle materials produce a clean cleavage fracture due to tension or shear, and they fail at a much higher stress by diagonal shear when tested in compression; this type of failure produces an appreciable amount of debris, and is easily distinguished from a cleavage fracture.

The phenomena of failure are therefore by no means simple, and they must be taken into account when considering ultimate strength design (see Section 10.5).

Chapter 4

Isostatic Structures

This chapter deals with the structural design methods developed in the late 19th and early 20th centuries. These are still in use for small isostatic plane and space frames. Steel frames are now designed with the aid of computers (see Chapter 7 *et seq.*), but the isostatic approach retains its usefulness because it helps to visualise the structural behaviour of rectangular frames.

4.1. ISOSTATIC AND HYPERSTATIC STRUCTURES

Isostatic or *statically determinate* structures can be solved by statics alone. Most architectural structures have more internal restraints than that, and these cannot be solved by statics alone. Hence they are called *statically indeterminate* or *hyperstatic*. A hyperstatic structure is thus indeterminate unless some equations can be found which are additional to the equations of statical equilibrium, and this is generally possible. The additional equations are either statements about the elastic deformation of the structures, which follow from its geometry (see Chapter 5) or else statements about its mode of collapse (see Chapter 9).

The distinction between isostatic and hyperstatic structures was at one time of the greatest practical importance because design calculations for isostatic structures are simple and direct. Prior to the advent of computers, the solution of hyperstatic structures presented many practical problems. Complete solutions are not available for all hyperstatic structures, and calculations without the aid of computers can be so time-consuming that the precise design of the structure may not be warranted, and empirical approximations are used instead. Furthermore, most hyperstatic structures cannot be calculated unless the cross-sectional properties of the members are known; *i.e.* the structure cannot be directly designed but only

84

analysed to check its safety. If the initial assumptions were seriously in error, the analysis has to be repeated.

Because of the ease with which the computer handles arithmetic, it is now simpler for all but the smaller structures to treat isostatic and hyperstatic structures alike. However the computer-based design methods are not well-suited to visualising structural behaviour, and the isostatic approach remains, therefore, important to an understanding of architectural structures. This applies particularly to complex structures for which computer programs, of necessity, introduce simplifications (which may sometimes be over-simplifications).

The distinction between isostatic and hyperstatic structures also emphasises an important difference in physical behaviour. Since the isostatic structure has just sufficient internal restraints to satisfy the conditions of equilibrium, it follows that the structure collapses (or becomes a *mechanism*) if one of these restraints is removed, *e.g.* by failure of one member. A hyperstatic structure has, by definition, more internal restraints. If the structure has one internal restraint more than is needed for an isostatic structure, then it has *one redundancy*, or it is hyperstatic by one degree. One member could then fail without necessarily causing collapse of the entire structure; the structure becomes a mechanism only after the failure of a second member. Most hyperstatic structures are hyperstatic by many degrees, *i.e.* they have many redundancies.

Hyperstatic structures therefore take longer to collapse, provided the failure of the redundant members takes time. Structures are designed with this end in view (see Chapters 9 and 10), and this is particularly important in structures subject to unexpectedly high, but temporary loads, such as occur during earthquakes and cyclones (hurricanes, typhoons). On the other hand, because of their greater rigidity they are more affected by deformations due to temperature, creep, shrinkage and the subsidence of foundations.

4.2. STATIC EQUILIBRIUM

A structure is in equilibrium if it does not move under the action of the forces acting on it. Consequently we can resolve the forces in various ways, and they must always balance. A force has no components at right angles, so that the conditions of statics are fully satisfied if we resolve vertically (which is the direction in which most loads act), horizontally, and take moments about some convenient point.

$$\left.\begin{array}{l} \Sigma\,V = 0 \\ \Sigma\,H = 0 \\ \Sigma\,M = 0 \end{array}\right\} \qquad (4.1)$$

If the first condition is not satisfied, the structure turns into a rocket without fuel; if the second condition is not satisfied, it becomes a moving vehicle without an engine; and if the third condition is not satisfied, we have a *perpetuum mobile*. All three propositions are manifestly absurd in a building.

Eqn 4.1 is sufficient for the solution of plane isostatic structures. A three-dimensional object can rotate about any of three axes, and the equations of equilibrium therefore become

$$\left.\begin{array}{l} \Sigma\,X = 0 \\ \Sigma\,Y = 0 \\ \Sigma\,Z = 0 \\ \Sigma\,M_x = 0 \\ \Sigma\,M_y = 0 \\ \Sigma\,M_z = 0 \end{array}\right\} \qquad (4.2)$$

4.3. TIES AND STRUTS

If a structural member is subjected to direct tension (Fig. 4.1), the force

$$P = fA \qquad (4.3)$$

where f is the uniform tensile stress, and A the cross-sectional area of the tie. We can use this equation in three different ways. If we have assumed a cross section of area A, the stress

$$f = P/A \qquad (4.4)$$

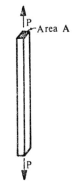

Fig. 4.1. Direct tension member.

If we wish to determine the area required for a given maximum permissible stress p, it is

$$A = P/p \tag{4.5}$$

If we wish to determine the area for a limiting bearing capacity (P_y), for a limiting stress f_y, it is

$$A = P_y/f_y \tag{4.6}$$

None of these equations necessarily requires a knowledge of the material, provided the designer knows the values of p or f_y. If it is suddenly decided to change the tie from mild steel to a high-strength aluminium alloy, with the same value of p, the dimensions are not affected. Furthermore it is unnecessary to assume a value of A and then check its validity; the result is obtained directly.

Provided that buckling does not occur, the same equations apply to a simple strut. When buckling occurs, it is necessary to reduce the stresses p or f_y accordingly (see Chapter 8).

Example 4.1. Design a strut subject to a compressive force of 225 kN (a) if buckling does not occur and the maximum permissible stress is 150 MPa, and (b) if the permissible stress is reduced by buckling to 100 MPa.

(a) Area required $= \dfrac{\text{Force}}{\text{Stress}} = \dfrac{225 \times 10^3}{150 \times 10^6}$

$$= 1 \cdot 5 \times 10^{-3} \text{ m}^2 = 1500 \text{ mm}^2$$

Use 102 × 102 × 8 angle

(b) Area required $= \dfrac{225 \times 10^3}{100 \times 10^6}$

$$= 2 \cdot 25 \times 10^{-3} \ \text{m}^2 = 2250 \ \text{mm}^2$$

Use 102 × 102 × 13 angle

4.4. Plane Frames

From an architectural point of view, plane frames may be of two kinds; those which support a sloping roof (Fig. 4.2), and those which have parallel top and bottom cords. The latter may be used to support either a flat roof or a floor. In the first type the slope of the roof is the determining factor for the geometry. In the second type the structure may be regarded either as a frame, or as a deep girder into which some rather large holes have been made to reduce the weight and the amount of material.

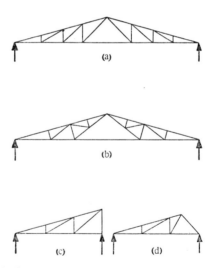

Fig. 4.2. Isostatic frames (trusses) for sloping roofs: (a) Pratt roof truss; (b) Trussed rafter; (c) North-light or south-light roof truss (sub-tropical zone); (d) North-light roof truss (temperate zone).

From a structural viewpoint, trusses may also be divided into two groups; those which are isostatic and those which are hyperstatic (Fig. 4.3). Two members cannot form a truss, and the simplest frame therefore consists of three members connected by three joints.

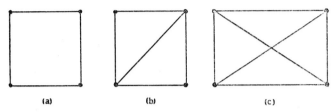

(a)   (b)   (c)

Fig. 4.3. Distinction between a mechanism, an isostatic truss and a hyperstatic truss: (a) Mechanism; (b) Isostatic truss; (c) Hyperstatic truss.

If we wish to add a joint to an isostatic frame, we require two additional members (Fig. 4.4), so that the correct number of members for an isostatic frame

$$n = 2j - 3 \qquad (4.7)$$

where j is the number of joints. The frame is formed by a series of triangles; isostatic frames are, therefore, frequently called triangulated. Triangulated frames are isostatic only if the members are in direct tension or compression. Consequently the joints must not transmit moments, *i.e.* they are pin-jointed. This means that they must either be connected by large pins (which was frequently done in the 19th century) or, as is commonly the case now, consist of

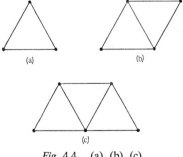

(a)   (b)

(c)

Fig. 4.4. (a), (b), (c).

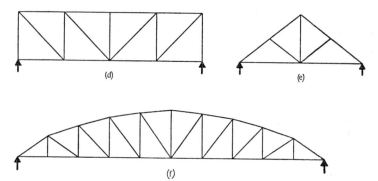

Fig. 4.4. Isostatic trusses with j pin joints require $n = 2j - 3$ members. If there are more, the truss is hyperstatic. If there are fewer, the truss becomes a mechanism.
(a) The simplest truss has 3 members and 3 joints.
(b) Each additional pin requires two additional members.
(c) Warren girder: $j = 5$, $n = 7$.
(d) Pratt truss: $j = 10$, $n = 17$.
(e) King post truss: $j = 6$, $n = 9$.
(f) Hawkesbury River Railway Bridge, Sydney: $j = 20$, $n = 37$.

relatively flexible members joined by relatively small gussets or welds which do not transmit significant bending moment to the far end of the members.

If we remove a member from an isostatic frame, we turn it into a mechanism. This can easily be tried with, say, a Meccano toy set. If we take a member out of a triangulated frame, it can be freely distorted, and it is no longer a load carrying structure. It is possible to add members to an isostatic frame (Fig. 4.5a), and indeed we can

Fig. 4.5. Adding a hyperstatic member to an originally isostatic frame.
(a) Hyperstatic member fits, no initial stresses.
(b) Hyperstatic member too short; new member placed in tension, bottom cord bent before any load is applied.
(c) Hyperstatic member too long; new member placed in compression, bottom bent before any load is applied.

add as many members as we wish. The forces in the frame can then no longer be determined by the laws of statics alone, and the frame becomes *hyperstatic* (see Chapter 5).

The isostatic frame has another important property. If we make any of the members a little too long or too short, they can still be fitted into the frame (Figs. 4.5b and c). We are not, of course, considering serious alterations in length, but only differences of the order of a millimetre. In a hyperstatic frame, a member which is only slightly too long would evidently have to be fitted by force, and this could produce quite high stresses (which may be desirable or undesirable). For example, if a structural steel section in a truss is 1 m long, and there is an error of 1 mm in its length, this produces a strain of 0·001 which, for a modulus of elasticity of 200 GPa, corresponds to a stress of 200 MPa. In materials such as precast concrete, where perfect dimensional control is difficult, there are evident advantages in the use of isostatic trusses.

There are basically three methods of solving isostatic pin-jointed trusses. In the *method of resolution at the joints*, devised by B. J. Jourawski in 1850, we consider the equilibrium at each joint in turn. At each joint we can resolve horizontally and vertically, so that we obtain $2j$ simultaneous equations. Since there are only $2j - 3$ members, we obtain three more equations than there are unknowns, and these provide a useful check. If the last three resolutions, which contain only known quantities, do not equate, something has gone wrong with the arithmetic; the error is not in the statical problem, because every isostatic frame, however unsatisfactory from an architectural or engineering point of view, can be solved by statical means.

Example 4.2. Using resolution of forces at the joints, determine the magnitude of the member forces in the truss shown in Fig. 4.6.

The joints are numbered individually as shown. In writing out the equations it is assumed that all unknown internal forces are tensile, a negative result indicates that the force is compressive. With a simple truss such as used in this example it is possible to assign the direction of the force by inspection but for consistency the method used will be as indicated above.

The symmetry of the truss and loading indicates that the two

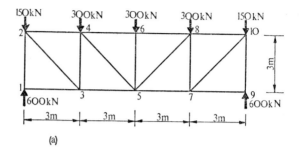

(a)

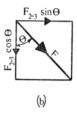

(b)

Fig. 4.6.
(a) Truss and loading detail.
(b) Horizontal and vertical components of force F_{2-3}.

reactions are equal and of magnitude 600 kN each and that the member forces are symmetrical about the centre line of the truss.

Consider Joint 1:
Resolve horizontally:

$$F_{1-3} = 0 \tag{i}$$

Resolve vertically:

$$600 \text{ kN} + F_{1-2} = 0 \tag{ii}$$

or $F_{1-2} = -600$ kN, *i.e.* compressive.
This result could have been determined by inspection.

Consider Joint 2:
Resolve horizontally:

$$F_{2-3} \cos 45° + F_{2-4} = 0 \tag{iii}$$

Resolve vertically:

$$600 \text{ kN} - 150 \text{ kN} - F_{2-3} \sin 45° = 0 \qquad \text{(iv)}$$

i.e.

$$F_{2-3} = (450/0·7071) \text{ kN} = 636·4 \text{ kN (tension)}$$

Substitute in equation (iii):

$$(636·4 \times 0·7071) \text{ kN} = -F_{2-4}$$

or

$$F_{2-4} = -450 \text{ kN (compressive)}$$

Consider Joint 3:
Resolve horizontally:

$$F_{2-3} \cos 45° - F_{3-5} = 0 \qquad \text{(v)}$$

$$636·4 \times 0·7071 = +F_{3-5}$$

or

$$F_{3-5} = 450 \text{ kN (tension)}$$

Resolve vertically:

$$F_{2-3} \sin 45° + F_{3-4} = 0 \qquad \text{(vi)}$$

$$636·4 \times 0·7071 = -F_{3-4}$$

or

$$F_{3-4} = -450 \text{ kN (compressive)}$$

Consider Joint 4:
Resolve horizontally:

$$F_{4-2} + F_{4-6} + F_{4-5} \cos 45° = 0 \qquad \text{(vii)}$$

$$450 \text{ kN} + F_{4-6} + F_{4-5}0·7071 = 0$$

Resolve vertically:

$$F_{3-4} - 300 \text{ kN} - F_{4-5} \sin 45° = 0 \qquad \text{(viii)}$$

$$450 \text{ kN} - 300 \text{ kN} - F_{4-5}0·7071 = 0$$

or

$$F_{4-5} = 212·1 \text{ kN (tension)}$$

Substitute in eqn (vii):

$$-F_{4-6} = 450 \text{ kN} + 212 \cdot 1 \times 0 \cdot 7071 \text{ kN}$$

or

$$F_{4-6} = -600 \text{ kN (compressive)}$$

Consider Joint 5:
Resolve horizontally and we obtain the check equation:

$$F_{5-3} + F_{5-4} \cos 45° = F_{5-7} + F_{5-8} \cos 45°$$

Resolve vertically and we obtain a more meaningful check equation:

$$F_{5-4} \sin 45° + F_{5-8} \sin 45° - 300 \text{ kN} = 0$$

$$(212 \cdot 1 \times 0 \cdot 7071) + (212 \cdot 1 \times 0 \cdot 7071) - 300 \text{ kN} = 0$$

$$150 \text{ kN} + 150 \text{ kN} - 300 \text{ kN} = 0$$

Consider Joint 6:
Resolve horizontally and we obtain the check equation:

$$F_{4-6} = F_{6-8} \tag{ix}$$

Resolve vertically:

$$-F_{6-5} - 300 \text{ kN} = 0 \tag{x}$$

or

$$F_{6-5} = -300 \text{ kN (compressive)}$$

Consider design of tension member 3–5:
A tension member is not subject to stress reduction as a result of buckling effects (necessary with compression members). Area reduction due to holes for fasteners at the joint must therefore be considered in the initial selection of the member. A bolted connection reduces the effective area available to resist tearing across the section, whereas a welded joint does not present this problem. Site welding is, however, expensive and it is usual to use shop welded joints where possible and allow the splice joint to be bolted.
Consider the joints are shop welded for members 3–5:

Allowable stress in tension $= 155$ MPa

Axial tensile force $\qquad = 636 \cdot 4$ kN

Area required $\qquad = \dfrac{636 \cdot 4 \times 10^3}{155 \times 10^6}$ m^2

$\qquad\qquad\qquad = 4100$ mm^2

Use two No. 152 $\times$ 102 $\times$ 9 angles back to back connected along their length in accordance with BS449 clause 51(c) or 54(g)

area provided $= 2 \times 23 \cdot 31 = 4662$ mm^2

Consider design of compression member 4–6:

Allowing for continuity and the restraint provided at node points the effective length of the strut will be taken as $0 \cdot 7$ times the panel length across the X–X axis of the member. Across the Y–Y axis restraint is provided by the connection between the purlin and the truss via the cleat. Partial restraint only is considered in this direction and an effective length at $0 \cdot 85$ times panel length is allowed (see BS449 clause 30(c)).

Axial compressive force $\quad = 600$ kN

Effective length across XX $= 0 \cdot 7 \times 3 = 2 \cdot 1$ m

Effective length across YY $= 0 \cdot 85 \times 3 = 2 \cdot 55$ m

Try two No. 127 $\times$ 127 $\times$ 10 angles back to back connected through a gusset plate 12·7 mm ($\frac{1}{2}$ in thick):

From tables

$$r_{XX} = 39 \cdot 4 \text{ mm}$$

$$r_{YY} = 56 \cdot 9 \text{ mm}$$

Slenderness ratio $= \lambda$

Therefore,

$$\lambda_{XX} = \frac{2 \cdot 1 \times 10^2}{3 \cdot 94} = 53$$

$$\lambda_{YY} = \frac{2 \cdot 55 \times 10^2}{5 \cdot 69} = 44$$

From Table 17(a)(BS499),

$$p_c = 131 \text{ MPa}$$

Therefore

$$\text{area required} = \frac{600 \times 10^3}{131 \times 10^6} \text{ m}^2$$

$$= 4 \cdot 58 \times 10^{-3} \text{ m}^2$$

$$= 4580 \text{ mm}^2$$

Area provided $2 \times 2331 \text{ mm}^2 = 4662 \text{ mm}^2$

Note angles to be connected together along their length in accordance with clause 37 BS499.

The principal disadvantage of Jourawski's method lies in the trigonometric nature of the equations. The dimensions of frames are normally given by horizontal and vertical dimensions, so that it is first necessary to compute the angles, and then look up their sines and cosines. This becomes a particular disadvantage when we come to consider space frames (see Section 4.5) for which we would have to determine solid angles. Sir Richard Southwell introduced the *method of tension coefficients* in 1920 primarily for space frames. The sines and cosines can be expressed as ratios of the vertical and horizontal projection respectively and the length of the members (Fig. 4.7). The tension coefficient is then defined as the force in the member divided by its length, so that the equations at joint A reduce to

$$t_{ab}x_{ab} + t_{ac}x_{ac} + t_{ad}x_{ad} = X_a$$

and

$$t_{ab}y_{ab} + t_{ac}y_{ac} + t_{ad}y_{ad} = Y_a$$

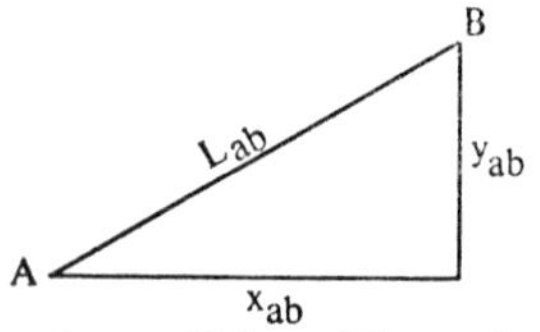

Fig. 4.7. The method of tension coefficients. The tension coefficient $t_{ab} = T_{ab}/L_{ab}$ so that the horizontal component of the force $T_{ab} \cos \theta = t_{ab}x_{ab}$ and the vertical component $T_{ab} \sin \theta = t_{ab}y_{ab}$.

In this equation some x and y terms may be negative or nil, and furthermore X_a is quite likely to be nil, since loads are normally vertical; however, we include all terms so as not to disturb the symmetry of the equations. If we consider 'i' as a typical joint and 'k' as a typical far end of a member, we can write all the equations for a complicated frame briefly in matrix notation:

$$t_{ik}x_{ik} = X_i \qquad (4.8)$$

$$t_{ik}y_{ik} = Y_i$$

This can be readily solved by means of a digital computer, and is therefore the most convenient method for frames so large that the use of a computer is warranted.

Example 4.3. Determine the member forces in the truss shown in Fig. 4.8 using tension coefficients.

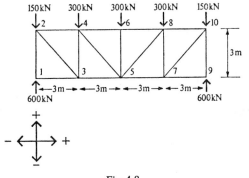

Fig. 4.8.
(a) Truss and loading detail.
(b) Sign convention positive for loads and distances to the right and upwards; negative for loads and distances to the left and downwards.

Consider Joint 4:

Load has negative sign
X distance has negative sign towards 2.
X distance has positive sign towards 6 and 5
Y distance has negative sign towards 3 and 5

The frame being symmetrical, the member forces repeat about the centre line,

hence $t_{3-5} = t_{7-5}$; $t_{4-5} = t_{8-5}$; $t_{4-6} = t_{8-6}$ etc.

Writing out the equations at each joint, considering horizontal and vertical equilibrium we obtain the following tabulation:

Joint	Direction	Equation	Equation number
1	x	$3t_{1-3} = 0$	(i)
	y	$3t_{1-2} + 600 = 0$	(ii)
2	x	$0 \times t_{1-2} + 3t_{2-4} + 3t_{2-3} = 0$	(iii)
	y	$-3t_{2-1} + 0 \times t_{2-4} - 3 \times t_{2-3} - 150 = 0$	(iv)
3	x	$-3t_{1-3} - 3t_{2-3} + 3t_{3-5} = 0$	(v)
	y	$3t_{2-3} + 3t_{4-3} = 0$	(vi)
4	x	$-3t_{2-4} + 3t_{4-6} + 3t_{4-5} = 0$	(vii)
	y	$-3t_{4-3} - 3t_{4-5} - 300 = 0$	(viii)
5	x	$-3t_{3-5} + 3t_{3-5} - 3t_{4-5} + 3t_{4-5} = 0$	(ix)
	y	$3t_{4-5} + 3t_{4-5} + 3t_{6-5} = 0$	(x)
6	x	$-3t_{4-6} + 3t_{4-6} = 0$	(xi)
	y	$-3t_{6-5} - 300 = 0$	(xii)

Solving these equations we obtain the tension coefficients which, when multiplied by the member lengths, give the following values. Negative answers denote compression and positive values denote tension.

Member	Tension coefficient (kN/m)	Length (m)	Force (kN) Tension	Force (kN) Compression
1–2	−200	3	—	600
2–4	−150	3	—	450
2–3	+150	4·242	636·4	—
1–3	0	3	—	—
4–3	−150	3	—	450
4–6	−200	3	—	600
4–5	+50	4·242	212·1	—
3–5	+150	3	450	—
6–5	−100	3	—	300

The *method of sections*, devised by A. Ritter in 1862, utilises the third part of eqn 4.1. We cut the truss along an imaginary line, and replace the internal forces in the members by equivalent external forces. About some convenient point we then take moments of all the external forces holding one of the cut portions of the truss in equilibrium. If the point is so chosen that all but one of the unknown forces have no moment about it, we obtain a direct answer; otherwise the process may have to be repeated until we have sufficient simultaneous equations to solve the problem. The method is particularly suitable for making a preliminary design, in which it is only necessary to work out a few critical sizes.

Example **4.4**. For the Pratt truss shown in Fig. 4.9 determine the maximum tensile and compressive forces in the horizontal chord using the method of sections.

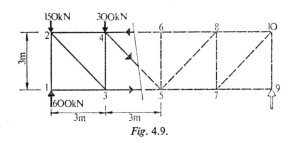

Fig. 4.9.

Since the chords of the truss are parallel, the moment resistance arm is constant throughout and the maximum tensile and compressive forces occur in the central panels.

Cutting the truss as shown and considering forces acting on the left hand side of the cut.

As in Example 4.2 assume force positive if cut member is tensile.

Taking moments about Point 5 eliminates forces F_{4-5} and F_{3-5} and we have

$$(600 - 150) \times 6 - 300 \times 3 + F_{4-6} \times 3 = 0$$

or

$$F_{4-6} = -1800/3 = -600 \text{ kN}$$

i.e. negative result and force is compressive.

Taking moments about Point 4 eliminates forces F_{4-6} and F_{4-5} and we have

$$(600 - 150) \times 3 - F_{3-5} \times 3 = 0$$

or

$$F_{3-5} = 450 \text{ kN (tension)}$$

These values may be compared with those obtained in Example 4.2.

The *reciprocal stress diagram*, published by Clerk Maxwell in 1864, is perhaps the best-known method; but since slide rules and

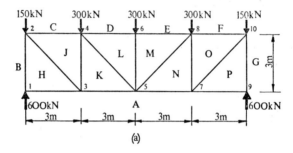

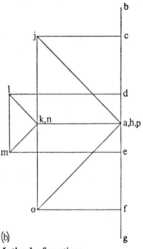

(b)

Fig. 4.10. Method of section.
(a) Truss and loading detail.
(b) Force diagram.

calculating machines have been improved, its use has declined in common with other graphical methods. We consider each joint in turn, and draw the triangle or polygon of the forces converging at it. Provided we start at a point where no more than two unknown members meet, we can complete the diagram, and then utilise our knowledge of the newly determined internal forces as we proceed to the next point. Thus all the diagrams for individual joints merge into a single diagram.

Example 4.5. Determine the forces in the Pratt truss shown in Fig. 4.10a using the method of graphic statics.

The stress diagram is shown in Fig. 4.10b. The magnitude of the various forces are scaled and tabulated below.

Commencing at Joint 1 it can be seen that the force in member 1–3 is zero. In practice this member is normally included and in some designs acts as a horizontal knee brace, which of course results in a stiffer frame and alters the magnitude and signs of various members through the truss.

The vertical reaction is transferred straight through the member 1–2 and hence the column is often carried straight through to Node Point 2 where the truss proper starts.

The force diagram is therefore commenced at Point 2.

The solution proceeds moving from one joint with not more than two unknown forces to the next such joint, any misclosure in the diagram when plotting the final force indicates an error. The forces are tabulated as shown.

Member	Force (kN)	
	Tension	Compression
1–2, 10–9 (bh, pq)		600
2–3, 7–10 (hj, op)	636·4	
2–4, 10–8 (cj, fo)		450
4–6, 8–6 (dl, em)		600
4–3, 8–7 (jk, an)		450
3–5, 5–7 (ak, an)	450	
4–5, 8–5 (kl, mn)	212·1	
6–5 (lm)		300
1–3, 7–9 (ah, ap)	—	—

4.5. SPACE FRAMES

The simplest isostatic space frame, the equilateral tetrahedron, has six members joining four points in space. Each additional point requires three additional members, so that the number of members

$$n = 3j - 6 \tag{4.9}$$

for an isostatic space frame with j joints (see Fig. 4.11).

It is difficult to produce a reciprocal stress diagram in space, although it could be done with a balsa-wood model. It is also difficult to use the method of sections three-dimensionally. The most convenient form is therefore the method of resolution at the joints, particularly when it is expressed in tension coefficients. If eqn 4.8 is extended into three dimensions we obtain:

$$t_{ik}x_{ik} = X_i$$

$$t_{ik}y_{ik} = Y_i \tag{4.10}$$

$$t_{ik}z_{ik} = Z_i$$

Example 4.6. Determine the forces in each of the members of the crane shown in Fig. 4.11 with the boom in the position indicated.

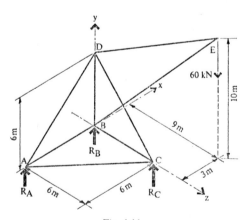

Fig. 4.11.

The reactions may be determined from the equations of statics as:

$$R_A = 30 \text{ kN downwards}$$

$$R_B = 0$$

$$R_C = 90 \text{ kN upwards}$$

Writing down the equations for each joint in turn paying due attention to sign we have:

Joint	Direction	Equation	Equation number
A	x	$+6t_{AB} + 6t_{AD} + 6t_{AC} = 0$	1
	y	$-30 + 6t_{AD} = 0$	2
	z	$6t_{AC} = 0$	3
B	x	$-6t_{AB} + 3t_{BE} = 0$	4
	y	$0 + 6t_{BD} + 10t_{BE} = 0$	5
	z	$6t_{BC} + 9t_{BE} = 0$	6
C	x	$-6t_{AC} = 0$	7
	y	$90 + 6t_{CD} = 0$	8
	z	$-6t_{BC} - 6t_{CD} - 6t_{AC} = 0$	9
D	x	$-6t_{AD} + 3t_{DE} = 0$	10
	y	$-6t_{BD} - 6t_{AD} - 6t_{CD} + 4t_{DE} = 0$	11
	z	$6t_{CD} + 9t_{DE} = 0$	12
E	x	$-3t_{DE} - 3t_{BE} = 0$	13
	y	$-60 - 4t_{DE} - 10t_{BE} = 0$	14
	z	$-9t_{DE} - 9t_{BE} = 0$	15

Solving these equations, we have:

$$t_{AB} = -5$$

$$t_{AD} = +5$$

$$t_{AC} = 0$$

$$t_{BE} = -10$$

$$t_{BC} = +15$$

$$t_{BD} = +100/6$$

$$t_{CD} = -15$$

$$t_{DE} = 10$$

We now tabulate the tension coefficients and lengths of members and obtain the forces:

Member	Tension coefficient (kN/m)	Length (m)	Force (kN)	
AD	+5	8·48	42·4	(T)
AB	−5	6	30	(C)
BD	+100/6	6	100	(T)
BE	−10	13·78	1 378	(C)
BC	+15	6	90	(T)
AC	0	8·48	0	
DE	+10	10·3	10·3	(T)
CD	−15	8·48	127·2	(C)

4.6. BENDING MOMENTS AND SHEAR FORCES

Strictly speaking there are no isostatic beams, since it is only possible to determine the internal moments and forces in a beam. To determine the stress distribution we must make an assumption about the behaviour of the material; however, this is not fundamental to the solution of the problems, and three types of beams are normally classed as isostatic:

(i) the cantilever
(ii) the simply supported beam
(iii) the simply supported beam with cantilever overhangs.

Any of these can be solved for any kind of load distribution. Here it may suffice if we consider a single concentrated load, and a uniformly distributed load. Other solutions are given in many textbooks on the theory of structures [4.1], and in Table 5.1.

A horizontal cantilever carrying a vertical load, built into a rigid support, has two reactions: a vertical force V and a moment M. The beam is firmly restrained at the support, and a load carried by it tends to shear through it (shear force V) and also to bend it downwards (bending moment M). By cutting the beam at any section we can trace the variation of shear force and bending moment along its span. The shear force is the force required to balance the load to the right-hand side of Figs. 4.12a and b. The bending moment is the moment of the loads about that section.

In a simply supported beam there are again two reactions, the two vertical supports. If there are any more restraints the beam is no longer isostatic. This follows from eqn 4.1. Since there are no horizontal forces $\Sigma H = 0$ yields only $0 = 0$. $\Sigma V = 0$ requires that both vertical reactions equal the total load. The third equation $\Sigma M = 0$ enables us to determine how much of the load is taken by

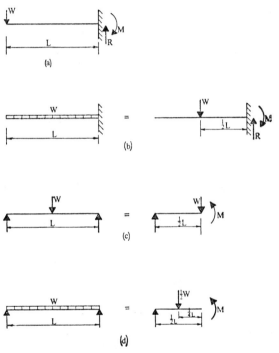

Fig. 4.12.   Maximum shear force and bending moment for cantilevers and simply supported beams: W = total load; L = span; R = reaction; Q = maximum shear force; M = maximum bending moment.

(a) Cantilever carrying a concentrated load: $Q = W$; $M = W.L$.

(b) Cantilever carrying a uniformly distributed load: $Q = W$; $M = W.\frac{1}{2}L$.

(c) Simply supported beam carrying a uniformly distributed load: $Q = \frac{1}{2}W$; $M = \frac{1}{2}W.\frac{1}{2}L = \frac{1}{4}WL$.

(d) Simply supported beam carrying a uniformly distributed load: $Q = \frac{1}{2}W$; $M = \frac{1}{2}W.\frac{1}{2}L - \frac{1}{2}W.\frac{1}{4}L = 1/8\,WL$.

each reaction. In many beams the load is arranged symmetrically, so that as a matter of common sense the reactions must be equal; however, this does not enable us to impose further restraints on the ends of the beam without rendering the problem hyperstatic (Fig. 4.13).

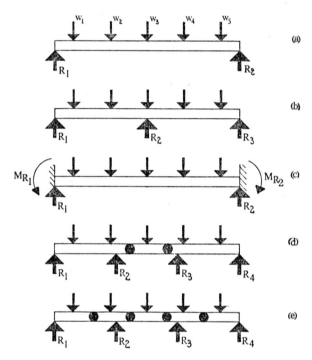

Fig. 4.13.   Isostatic beams, hyperstatic beams and mechanisms.
(a) A beam with two supports is isostatic, or statically determinate.
(b) The third reaction cannot be determined by statics, and the beam is hyperstatic.
(c) A beam built in at the two ends is hyperstatic, because the restraining moments due to the building-in cannot be determined by statics alone.
(d) A beam with two additional supports can be rendered isostatic by inserting two pin joints at which the bending moment is, by definition, nil. These give two additional equations of static equilibrium, which allow the magnitude of the two extra reactions to be determined. This is the *Gerber beam.*
(e) If the number of pin joints exceeds the number of additional reactions, the beams cease to be a structure and become a mechanism.

Having determined the reactions, the shear force is then deter-mined by taking any section at a distance x from the left-hand support, say, and equating vertical forces to the left of the section. The bending moment is determined by taking the moments of all the forces to the left about that section (Fig. 4.12b and c). The beam with cantilever overhangs is essentially a variation of the simply supported beam. The bending moment is, however, nil at the end of the cantilever, and not at the supports (Fig. 4.12d and e). It is evidently not possible to concentrate the entire load on one cantilever, without overturning the beam.

The Gerber beam is an extension of the beam with cantilever overhangs. We can take two beams with cantilever overhangs, and suspend a short span from the ends of the cantilever. By this means we can produce isostatic beams which are continuous over many supports; it is only necessary to have two pin-joints in alternate spans (Fig. 4.13d). If we consider a pin as removing a restraint, the con-ditions of static equilibrium are still satisfied. Since the pin joint allows free rotation, there is no bending moment at that point. We can therefore take moments about each pin in turn, and obtain one reaction in each case. The last reaction is obtained from $\Sigma V = 0$.

Example 4.7. The maximum length available and suitability of transportation limits the length of a standard precast section to 12·8 m. Spans of a multiple bay floor system are set at 10 m. The full length member is to be used in conjunction with an inset span forming a Gerber beam as shown in Fig. 4.14. Determine the bending moments for the beams used and compare with the value of the simply supported condition.

Design Load: equivalent uniformly distributed load to 60 kN/m.

Consider inset Beam FE:

BM $= 60 \times 7·2^2/8 = 388·8$ kNm
Reaction $= 60 \times 7·2/2 = 216$ kN

Consider Beam EG (cantilever moment):
Moment due to point load: $216 \times 1·4 = 302·4$ kNm
Moment due to uniformly distributed load:
$$60 \times 1·4^2/2 = 58·8 \text{ kNm}$$
$$\text{Total} = 361·2 \text{ kNm}$$

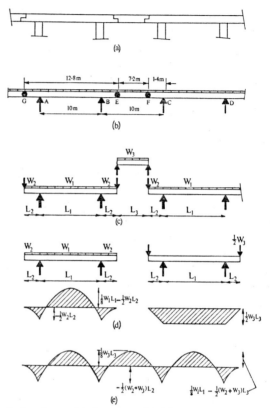

Fig. 4.14. Gerber beam. (a) Structure. (b) Dimensions. (c) System of loads. (d) Components of bending moment diagram. (e) Total bending moment diagram.

Simply supported BM = $60 \times 10^2/8 = 750$ kNm,

i.e. Midspan moment = $750 - 361 \cdot 2$ kNm

= $388 \cdot 8$ kNm

From the above example it can be seen that where the overhang to span is in the ratio of 1·4 to 10 or approximately 1 to 7, equal positive moments result in both spans but the negative moment capacity is not fully realised. Reducing the length of the inset span and hence increasing the cantilever moment results in equal negative and positive moments when the span to overhang ratio is approximately 1 to 6.

It can be seen that a Gerber beam reduces the bending moment to slightly more than 50 % of the freely supported value; however, where it is necessary to consider variation in live load over the various spans the reduction does not have the magnitude indicated above. The pin-jointed cantilever beam was frequently used in long-span bridges in the early days of structural engineering, when it was highly regarded because of its isostatic character. Thus the Firth of Forth Bridge, built in 1883 over two long spans of 523 m each, with a total length of 2500 m (8200 ft), was of the cantilever type. In large span bridges the use of hinges involves elaborate devices. However, in prefabricated steel and precast concrete building frames, which are being used to an increasing extent as part of the move towards industrialised building, the 'hinge' can be achieved by a simple connection, provided that the floor finish permits the necessary rotation (Fig. 4.15).

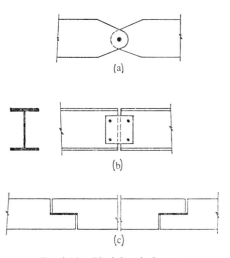

Fig. 4.15.   Pin joints in beams.
(a) The original pin joint was formed by a pin passing through holes in the members to be fitted.
(b) Pin joint in a steel structure, formed by a web connection which offers little resistance to bending, but is strong enough to transmit shear.
(c) Pin joint in precast concrete beam. The halved joints are made strong enough (by additional reinforcement, if need be) to transmit shear, and the joint faces right or left according to the sign of the shear force.

4.7. THE SIMPLE THEORY OF BENDING

Although the shear force and the bending moment can be ascertained, for certain beams, by the laws of statics alone, the distribution of stress resulting from the shear force and the bending moment are not determinable in this way. However, the difference between elastic and ultimate strength solutions for the internal resistance moment of isostatic beams is so small, that this objection may be ignored without creating any serious problem.

Let us consider a simply supported beam, made of an elastic material. If we take very short length x of a simply supported beam which is deflected downwards by a bending moment M (Fig. 4.16) then the upper face is compressed, and the lower face extended. Somewhere there must be a neutral axis, at which the material of the

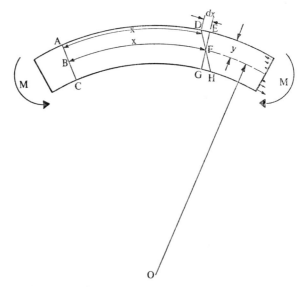

Fig. 4.16. The theory of bending. The beam, under the action of a uniform bending moment M, bends into a circular arc, whose radius of curvature is $R = OF$. Originally plane and parallel sections ABC and EFG thus converge into a centre of curvature O. This causes tensile strains on top, and compressive strains on the bottom. The neutral axis BF is the line of no strain. The maximum tensile strain, at a distance y above the neutral axis, is $DE/AD = dx/x$. The corresponding stresses are shown on the right-hand side of the diagram.

beam is neither tensioned nor compressed. It was assumed by the French mathematician, Jacob Bernoulli, in the early 18th century that in bending, sections which were originally plane and parallel remain plane and converge on a centre of curvature (Fig. 4.17). This has been tested in the late 19th and early 20th centuries with modern instruments on all engineering materials, and it has been found surprisingly close to the truth even beyond the elastic range.

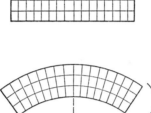

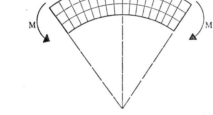

Fig. 4.17.   Bernoulli's assumption. Originally plane and parallel sections remain plane after bending, but converge into a common centre of curvature.

We therefore assume that the original length between plane sections, x, is changed by an amount dx, which is proportional to the distance y from the neutral axis. Depending on whether we are in the tension or compression zone, x is positive or negative.

The *strain*, or change in length per unit

$$e = \frac{dx}{x} = \frac{y}{R} \quad \text{by similar triangles} \qquad (4.11)$$

where R is the radius of curvature at the section. As we shall see presently, the radius of curvature varies with the bending moment, but any infinitesimally short length of beam is bent to some specific radius of curvature.

If the material in the beam is elastic and obeys Hooke's Law (see Section 3.3), *the stress*, or force per unit area, is directly proportional to the strain (Fig. 3.13), so that the stress

$$f = eE = \frac{E}{R} y \qquad (4.12)$$

where E is the modulus of elasticity which is a constant for the material.

If we now consider an element of width b and depth dy, the force acting on it is

$$dP = fb\,dy = eEb\,dy = \frac{E}{R} b\, y\, dy$$

The moment of that force about the neutral axis is

$$dPy = \frac{E}{R} y^2\, dy$$

The total resistance moment of the section is the sum of all these individual moments over the entire section, and this must for equilibrium equal the bending moment at the section.

$$M = \sum dPy = \frac{E}{R} \int y^2\, dy = \frac{E}{R} I \qquad (4.13)$$

where I is the *second moment of area*, sometimes called, rather inappropriately, the *moment of inertia*; it is a geometric property of the section, like its area.

This solution was first derived by C. A. Coulomb in 1773, but in its present form (eqns 4.12 and 4.14) it was published by L. M. H. Navier in 1826, and it is usually quoted as *Navier's Theorem*:

$$\frac{M}{I} = \frac{f}{y} = \frac{E}{R} \qquad (4.14)$$

Thus the relation between the maximum stress (p) and the bending moment

$$M = p\frac{I}{y} = pZ \qquad (4.15)$$

where Z is another geometric property of the section, known as the section modulus. The geometric properties of the section can therefore be directly determined. Section moduli for standard sections are listed on the section catalogues published by steel and aluminium fabricators, etc.

Navier's theorem is not an isostatic equation, because it depends on Bernoulli's assumption that plane sections remain plane during bending, which requires to be substantiated by experiment, and on Hooke's Law which holds only for elastic materials.

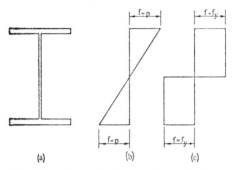

(a) (b) (c)

Fig. 4.18. Stress distribution due to bending.
(a) Shape of cross section.
(b) Elastic stress distribution; p = maximum permissible stress.
(c) Fully plastic stress distribution; f_y = yield stress.

The theorem is, however, still substantially true for a plastic material. In the early stages of inelastic deformation, at least, plane sections remain reasonably plane. In the extreme case of fully plastic stress distribution (Fig. 4.18)

$$f = f_y = \text{constant}$$

and eqn 4.15 becomes

$$M = f_y Z_p \qquad (4.16)$$

where Z is the plastic section modulus. For a rectangle $Z_p/Z = 1.5$, while for an I-section, where most of the material is concentrated in the flanges, Z_p/Z is of the order of 1.1.

For partially inelastic materials the answer lies somewhere

between the elastic and the fully plastic solution. In the case of the isostatic beam, the relation between the bending moment and the limiting stress is therefore not greatly affected by the elasticity or inelasticity of the material. This is not true for hyperstatic beams.

The relation between the limiting shear stress and the shear force also requires an assumption about the nature of the material, but as in the case of the bending moment the answer is not greatly affected by it. If we consider again an element of the beam of length dx, with a shear force Q on the left and $Q + dQ$ on the right, a bending moment M on the left and a bending moment $M + dM$ on the right, and a load w per unit length. Taking moments about the right section A-A in Fig. 4.19a

$$M + Q\,dx + w\,dx \cdot \tfrac{1}{2}\,dx = M + dM$$

If the element is infinitely short, dx^2 is negligible and

$$Q\,dx = dM \qquad (4.17)$$

The shear stress must be nil at the top and bottom of the section, and build up to a maximum somewhere between. In a symmetrical section it is at half-depth, and in an unsymmetrical section at the neutral axis.* The horizontal shear force is $qb\,dx$, where b is the width of the section (not shown in the figure) and this must balance the difference between the compressive force on the left, M/a, and on the right, $(M + dM)/a$, where a is the lever arm between the resultant tensile and compressive forces in the section. For horizontal equilibrium

$$\frac{M}{a} + qb\,dx = \frac{M + dM}{a}$$

Substituting from eqn 4.17

$$qb\,dx = \frac{Q\,dx}{a}$$

so that the limiting shear stress

$$q = Q/ab \qquad (4.18)$$

---

* This is evident by inspection of Fig. 4.19c. A rigorous proof is given in most text-books on the strengths of materials, e.g. [4.2].

This equation is still true for a fully plastic material, except that the length of the lever arm is less. Thus for an elastic rectangular section (which has triangular stress distribution) a is $\frac{2}{3}$ of the depth, while for a fully plastic section (with uniform compression above the neutral axis, and uniform tension below) a is $\frac{1}{2}$ of the depth.

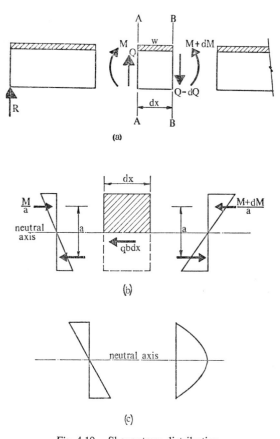

(a)

(b)

(c)

Fig. 4.19.   Shear stress distribution.
(a) Shear forces and bending moment acting on a short element of length dx in a simply supported beam.
(b) Equilibrium at the neutral axis under the action of the compressive forces $(M + dM)/a$, and M/a and the shear force qb dx.
(c) Distribution of direct and shear stress for a rectangular cross section.

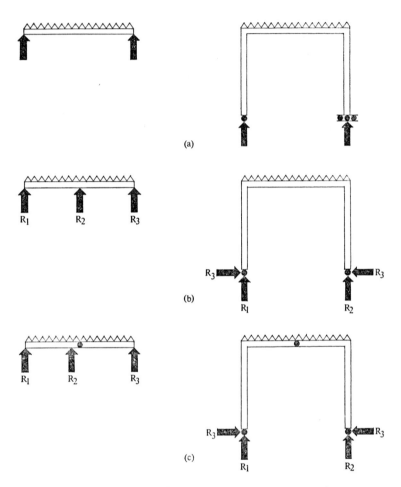

Fig. 4.20. Comparison of beams and corresponding portal frames.
(a) A simply supported beam corresponds to a portal with one sliding joint
(*isostatic*).
(b) A two-pin portal corresponds to a two-span continuous beam (*hyperstatic*).
(c) A three-pin portal corresponds to a Gerber beam (*isostatic*).

4.8. THREE-PIN PORTALS AND ARCHES

If we join several members with rigid connections, we introduce hyperstatic conditions; but we can re-establish the isostatic character of the structure by inserting a sufficient number of hinges. We could turn a portal frame into an isostatic structure by allowing free movement of one end (Fig. 4.20a). This is, however, impractical in a building, and if we restrain horizontal movement at both ends, we introduce horizontal reactions (Fig. 4.20b). These cannot be determined by the conditions of equilibrium of eqn 4.1. The condition $\Sigma H = 0$, gives us $R_3 = R_3$, and the other two conditions give us the vertical reactions. If we now introduce a pin halfway along the beam (Fig. 4.20c) where by definition the bending moment now becomes nil, we can take moments about that point and obtain (Fig. 4.21):

$$R_H \cdot H = R_v \cdot \tfrac{1}{2}L - \tfrac{1}{2}W \cdot \tfrac{1}{4}L$$

which gives the horizontal reactions from the specified load and the previously determined vertical reactions. The horizontal reactions introduce bending moments into the columns, but may reduce the bending moment in the horizontal member of the portal appreciably (see Fig. 3.4). Generally the structural economy is even greater if the three pins are removed, and the portal made in one piece and built in at the supports (see Section 5.4). However, in large-span precast concrete portals it may be quite difficult to achieve the dimensional precision required for a rigid frame, unless it is assembled on the ground and erected by hoisting sideways; this creates serious handling stresses. There are also problems on marshy ground, near a waterway, or on imperfectly compacted fill. Industrial buildings are quite commonly erected in such situations, and as the column loads are low, no problems arise if the structure is isostatic, and can therefore absorb small settlement of the foundations without creating stresses in the structure.

Example 4.8. A rectangular three-pinned portal frame (Fig. 4.22) carries a vertical uniformly distributed load of 15 kN/m. The frame has a span of 12 m and a height of 3 m. Determine bending moments and shear forces.

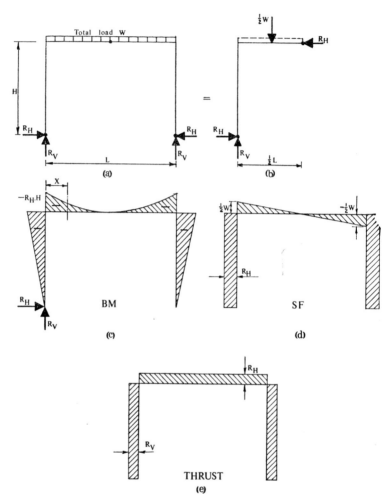

Fig. 4.21.   Solution of rectangular three-pin portal carrying a vertical uniformly
distributed load.
(a) Load diagram.
(b) Forces on left-hand half of portal.
(c) Bending moment diagram.
(d) Shear force diagram.
(e) Thrust diagram.

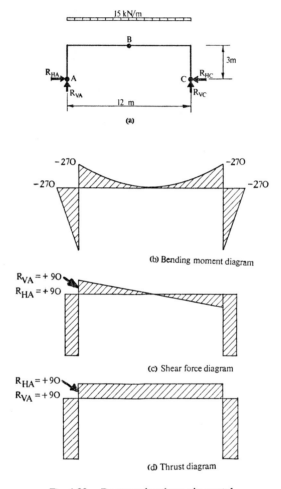

(b) Bending moment diagram

(c) Shear force diagram

(d) Thrust diagram

Fig. 4.22.   Rectangular three pin portal.
(a) Dimensions.
(b) Bending-moment diagram.
(c) Shear-force diagram.
(d) Thrust diagram.

By symmetry $R_{VA} = R_{VC} = \frac{1}{2} \times 15 \times 12 \text{ kN} = 90 \text{ kN}$

Taking moments about B, considering only forces to the left of joint B,

$$90 \times 6 - 15 \times 6 \times 3 - R_{HA} \times 3$$

or

$$R_{HA} = 90 \text{ kN}$$

Maximum negative bending moment at knee of portal =

$$90 \times 3 \text{ kNm} = 270 \text{ kNm}$$

This bending moment reduces parabolically from the knee to zero at point B.

The horizontal thrust constitutes a shear force in the vertical column legs of the frame and the vertical forces constitute shear in the horizontal members.

Example 4.9. A gabled three-pinned portal frame (Fig. 4.23) carries a

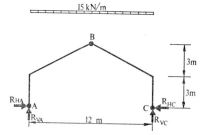

Fig. 4.23.   Gable frame with three pins.

uniformly distributed load of 15 kN/m over a span of 12 m. The overall height of the gable is 6 m and the height to eaves is 3 m. Sketch the bending moments, shear forces and thrust diagrams.

By symmetry $R_{Va} = R_{Vc} = 15 \times 12/2 = 90 \text{ kN}$.

Take moments about B, and considering only forces to the left of joint B

$$90 \times 6 - R_{HA} \times 6 - 15 \times 6 \times 3 = 0$$

or

$$R_{HA} = R_{HC} = 45 \text{ kN}$$

Maximum negative moment at knee $= 45 \times 3 = 135$ kNm. The equation for the bending moment in the gable member is given by

$$R_{VA} \times X - R_{HA}(3 + Y) - 15 \times X^2/2$$

where X is horizontal distance measured from knee
Y is vertical distance measured from knee

For the frame shown $Y = \frac{1}{2}X$ we therefore have

$$BM = 90X - 45(3 + \tfrac{1}{2}X) - 15X^2/2$$

This equation is used to plot the variation of bending moment along the gable member. The shear force in the column is constant and equals the horizontal reaction of 45 kN. In the gable frame the shear force $V = R_V \cos 30° - R_H \sin 30° - 15X \cos 30°$. The thrust in the gable $= R_H \cos 30° + R_V \sin 30 - 15X \sin 30°$.

Example 4.10. A semi-circular three-pin arch (Fig. 4.24) carries a uniformly distributed (in plan) load of 15 kN/m. Sketch the bending moment diagram. The arch has a span of 20 m.

By symmetry $R_{VA} = R_{VC} = 15 \times 20/2 = 150$ kN.

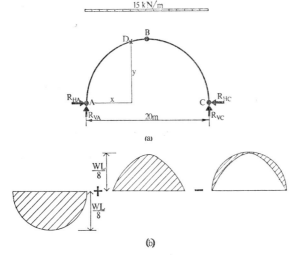

(a)

(b)

Fig. 4.24. Circular three-pin arch.

Taking moments about pin B, and considering only forces to the left of pin B,

$$R_{VA} \times 10 - R_{HA} \times 10 - 15 \times 10 \times 5 = 0$$

$$1500 - 750 = R_{HA}10$$

or

$$R_{HA} = 75 \text{ kN}$$

Taking moments at any point we obtain the bending moment equation for the arch

$$R_{VA}X - R_{HA}Y - 15X^2/2 = M_D$$

or

$$150X - 75Y - 7.5X^2 = M_D$$

This may be expressed as

$$(150X - 7.5X^2) - 75Y = M_D$$

It can be seen that the first part of the expression is the bending moment for a simply supported beam and the second part is a bending moment that follows the function of the arch profile.

If we express the value of Y in terms of the radius R, we have:

$$R^2 = (R - X)^2 + Y^2$$

or

$$Y = (2RX - X^2)^{\frac{1}{2}}$$

and since $R = 10$ m, we have $Y = (20X - X^2)^{\frac{1}{2}}$ and bending moment at any point along arch

$$M_D = 150X - 7.5X^2 - 75(20X - X^2)^{\frac{1}{2}}$$

This equation may be solved at various values of X to give the bending moment diagram the maximum bending moment occurring at the value of X where

$$\frac{dM}{dX} = 0$$

i.e. where $X = 1.35$ m, $Y = 5.01$ m.

Substituting these values in the bending moment equation, we obtain

$$M_{max} = 150 \times 1\cdot35 - 7\cdot5 \times 1\cdot35^2 - 75(20 \times 1\cdot35 - 1\cdot35^2)^{\frac{1}{4}}$$

$$= 187\cdot5 \text{ kNm}$$

4.9. THE ISOSTATIC DESIGN OF STEEL-FRAME BUILDINGS

When the first steel-framed buildings were being designed in the 1880s the theory of hyperstatic structures had not reached the stage of perfection where it could be applied to multi-bay multi-storey buildings. The isostatic method, which was still widely employed in the 1950s, retains its usefulness for illustrating the physical behaviour of simple frames.

Generally the columns are erected first, frequently in lifts of three storeys, and the beams are then set on column cleats. They may therefore be considered as simply supported on the columns (Fig. 4.25). The structural problem is therefore very simple. We must determine the loads carried by the beams, and then select suitable

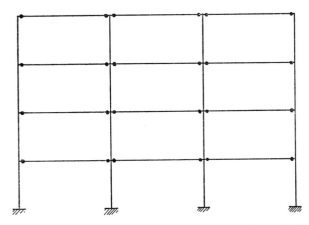

Fig. 4.25. The pinned-frame concept for simple frames with vertical loading. The columns are regarded as cantilevers, supporting the beams. Since a small steel frame has flexible connections between the columns and the beams, this is close to reality.

sections to carry these loads over the chosen spans (see Sections 2.2, 4.6 and 4.7). The steel fabricators publish tables which give this information directly. Generally these contain a limiting line which indicates that some sections would produce excessive deflections, while others require web stiffeners to prevent buckling (see Chapter 8); however, these are secondary effects.

The columns are selected from standard tables with equal ease, again with a limiting line to indicate sections which require stiffeners to avoid buckling.

A pseudo-isostatic method is used, for the horizontal loads. It is assumed that the column cleats are sufficiently strong to withstand the wind loads as rigid connections. The frame then deflects under a horizontal load somewhat as shown in Fig. 4.26. At the points of contraflexure (*i.e.* where the curvature changes from convex to concave) the bending moment is nil and therefore we could insert a hinge without altering the stress distribution.

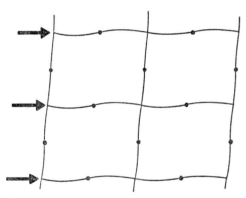

Fig. 4.26.   Deformation of rectangular frame under horizontal loading. Points of contraflexure are formed near the mid-span of each beam and column.

We therefore introduce imaginary hinges at these points of contraflexure (Fig. 4.27), and thus render the structure isostatic; each rigid joint is exactly balanced by a pin-joint. Determination of the exact location of these hinges can be quite complicated, and they are taken as half-way along the beams, and half-way up the columns. We can now take moments about the hinges, and determine the bending

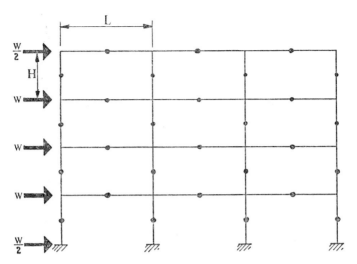

Fig. 4.27. The pinned-frame concept for horizontal loading. Since the bending moment is nil at a point of contraflexure, we can insert a hypothetical pin joint at each.

moments due to horizontal wind loads (Fig. 4.28). The design is now modified to allow for these additional bending stresses. In the case of the columns this means that they become subject to combined bending and compression, *i.e.* the bending and compressive stresses are worked out separately, and then added together.

Example 4.11. Fig. 4.28 shows an interior bay of a steel frame 12 m high, 5 m wide and 60 m long. The frame is subject to wind pressure above the ground. The beams span 5 m in both directions the wind velocity used produces a pressure of 1000 Pa.

The wind force on the building produces both suction and positive pressure. In this example it is assumed that the entire force acts on the windward side as positive pressure.

We have therefore

$$W = 1000 \times 5 \times 3 \text{ N}$$

$$= 15 \text{ kN}$$

The shear force resulting from wind increases from 7·5 kN on the

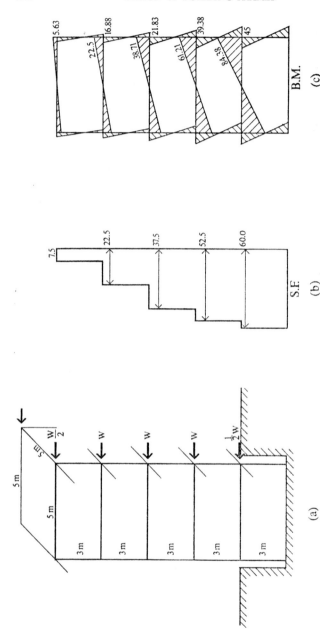

Fig. 4.28.　Distribution of shear force and bending moments due to wind loads in a steel structure designed by the pinned frame concept.

(a) Dimension of frame.
(b) Shear force distribution.
(c) Bending moment distribution.

top floor column by 15 kN through each floor, as shown, to give a maximum force of 60 kN which equals total wind load of 12 × 5 × 1000 N, *i.e.* 60 kN.

If we assume a pin-joint at the mid point of each column and beam when designing against wind forces, the bending moment takes the form shown and has the value of shear force × $\frac{1}{2}$ storey height at each level; *i.e.*

top floor varies from 0 to 0·75 × 1·5 kNm = 1·125 kNm

2nd floor from roof 0 to 2·25 × 1·5 kNm = 3·375 kNm

This moment and the moment from the column above are transmitted into the adjoining floor beam which therefore carry a moment of 4·5 kNm.

The completed bending moment diagram is shown in Fig. 4.28c.

By symmetry, half the bending moment at any particular level is carried by each column.

Chapter 5

The Elastic Theory of Hyperstatic Structures

In this chapter we take a brief look at the classical methods for hyperstatic structures. Although partly superseded by computer programs, they are still mandatory in some building codes, and they remain important because they were used for the design of the majority of the engineered structures in existence today. They retain their value not merely for small structures but also as a basis of understanding more complex design procedures.

5.1. The Elastic Slope and Deflection of Beams

Structures which have more members or restraint than can be solved by statics alone are *statically indeterminate*, or *hyperstatic*. We can solve them by studying the mechanism of their collapse, and this is done in Chapter 9. The older, and still the more common method, is based on the elastic deformation of the hyperstatic structure. The computer programs discussed in Chapter 7 are based on the same principles. Before we can derive the theory, we must therefore examine the elastic deformation of structural members.

Let us consider the same beam as in Section 4.7, *viz.* a short length of a simply supported beam carrying a uniformly distributed load. (The following equations are, however, true for any type of loading.)

Equating all vertical forces in Fig. 4.19a

$$Q + w\,dx = Q - dQ$$

which gives the shear force at the section

$$Q = \int w\,dx \tag{5.1}$$

This means that the shear force is the integral of the loads and support reactions to one side of the section, which is geometrically equivalent to the area of the load diagram.

Taking moments about the section B-B

$$M + Q\,dx + w\,dx \cdot \tfrac{1}{2}\,dx = M + dM$$

If the length dx is infinitely short, $(dx)^2$ is negligible, and the bending moment at the section

$$M = \int Q \, dx \qquad (5.2)$$

which means the area of the shear force diagram to one side of the section.

To obtain the slope of the beam, we consider its deflected shape (Fig. 5.1). The length of the beam from A to B is $R \, d\theta$. Beams in

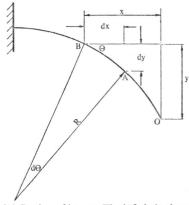

Fig. 5.1. Slope and deflection of beams. The infinitely short length of beam, AB, subtends an angle $d\theta$ at the centre of curvature, the radius of curvature being R. The horizontal and vertical components of AB are dx and dy, and the horizontal and vertical distances from the origin O are x and y.

architectural structures may have only a small elastic deflection, generally less than 1/250, if they are to be effective components of the building. Consequently for a very short length of the beam we may take the length AB as equal to the horizontal projection dx. It follows that

$$R \, d\theta = dx$$

Substituting for the radius of curvature from *Navier's Theorem* (eqn 4.14)

$$d\theta = \frac{M}{EI} \, dx$$

and the slope at the section

$$\theta = \int \frac{1}{EI} M \, dx \qquad (5.3)$$

which means the area of the bending moment diagram to one side of the section, divided by EI (the *stiffness* of the section). The slope of the section $\theta = dy/dx$ and the deflection is therefore

$$y = \int \theta \, dx = \int \int \frac{1}{EI} M \, dx \, dx = \int \int \int \frac{1}{EI} Q \, dx \, dx \, dx$$

$$= \int \int \int \int \frac{1}{EI} w \, dx \, dx \, dx \, dx \tag{5.4}$$

It follows that we can obtain the shear force by integrating, or measuring the area of the load diagram; that we can obtain the bending moment in the same way from the shear force diagram; the slope from the bending moment diagram; and the deflection from the slope diagram. For a uniformly distributed load, the shear force diagram is a straight line, the bending moment diagram is a parabola, the slope diagram is a cubic parabola, and the deflection diagram is a fourth-degree parabola (Fig. 5.2). In practice, however, the quadruple integration is complicated by the fact that each operation produces a constant of integration which must be determined.

A method devised by Otto Mohr in 1893, based on the similarity of eqns 5.1 and 5.3, is therefore generally preferred. The stiffness EI is sensibly constant in architectural structures,* so that the relation between shear force and load (eqn 5.1), and slope and bending moment (eqn 5.3) is the same. Consequently we can derive the slope from the bending moment diagram, as we derive the shear force from the slope diagram.

$$\theta = \frac{1}{EI} \int M \, dx = \int u \, dx \tag{5.5}$$

where $u = M/EI$ is the equivalent load carried by the beam; its shear force diagram is the same as the slope diagram of the original beam, and its bending moment diagram is the same as the deflection of diagram of the original beam.

We can then redraw Fig. 5.2 in two parts (Fig. 5.3). This has one important advantage for the solution of hyperstatic structures which

* The modulus of elasticity, E, is a constant of the material, and the section of beams does not normally vary significantly in buildings, so that the second moment of area, I, is sensibly constant.

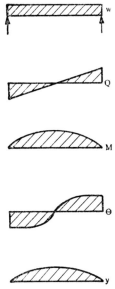

Fig. 5.2. Shear force Q, bending moment M, slope θ and deflection y, obtained by successive integration of the load diagram w.

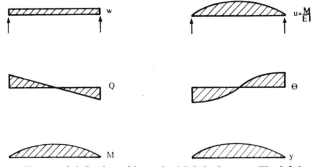

Fig. 5.3. Slope and deflection of beam by Mohr's theorem. The left-hand part of the diagram shows the load diagram for a simply supported beam carrying a uniformly distributed load W. Underneath are the shear force and bending moment diagrams of the same beam. The right-hand part of the diagram shows the load diagram of the equivalent beam, which is the original bending moment diagram, divided by EI. Underneath are the shear force diagram of the equivalent beam (which equals the slope diagram of the original beam) and the bending moment diagram of the equivalent beam (which equals the deflection diagram of the equivalent beam).

Table 5.1

Coefficients for the maximum values of the shear force, the bending moment, the slope and the deflection of isostatic beams

Line No.	Loading Total load $= W$ span $= L$	Maximum shear force (W)	Maximum bending moment (WL)	Maximum slope $\left(\dfrac{WL^2}{EI}\right)$	Maximum deflection $\left(\dfrac{WL^3}{EI}\right)$
1		-1	-1	$+1/2$	$-1/3$
2		-1	$-1/2$	$+1/6$	$-1/8$
3		-1	$-1/3$	$+1/12$	$-1/15$
4		-1	$-2/3$	$+1/4$	$-11/60$
5	Central Load	$\pm1/2$	$+1/4$	$\pm1/16$	$-1/48$
6		$\pm1/2$	$+1/8$	$\pm1/24$	$-5/384$

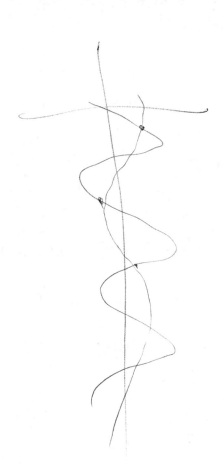

IF YOU CANNOT KEEP YOUR APPOINT
TEL (794) 5411.

YOUR COOPERATION IS APPRECIATED

* Please delete as appropriate

HAROLD COHE

CD-ROM APPO

Yours appointment for * MEDLINE/I

IF YOU ARE MORE THAN 10 MINUTES LA
PERSON WILL BE ALLOWED TO USE THE

IF YOU ARE MORE THAN 30 MINUTES L
THE APPOINTMENT

IF YOU CANNOT KEEP YOUR APPOINTME
TEL (794) 5411.

YOUR COOPERATION IS APPRECIATED.

* Please delete as appropriate

Line No.	Loading span = L	Maximum shear force l^a	Maximum shear force r^a	Maximum bending moment l^a	Maximum bending moment r^a	Maximum slope l^a	Maximum slope r^a	Maximum deflection
7		$l^a + 1/3$	$r - 2/3$		$+0.128$	$1 - 7/180$	$r + 8/180$	$-0.013\ 04$
8	Symmetrical		$\pm 1/2$		$+1/6$		$\pm 5/96$	$-1/160$
9	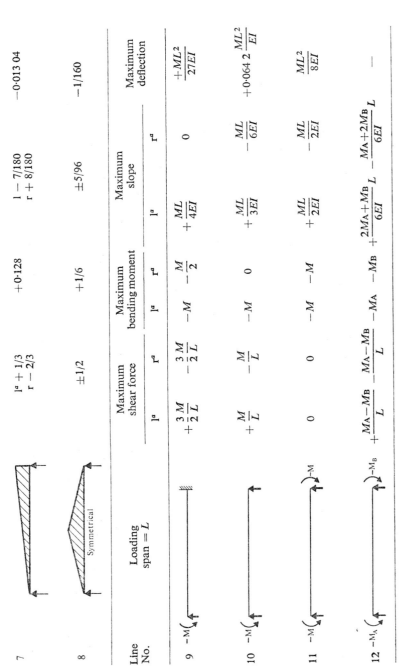	$+\dfrac{3}{2}\dfrac{M}{L}$	$-\dfrac{3}{2}\dfrac{M}{L}$	$-M$	$-\dfrac{M}{2}$	$+\dfrac{ML}{4EI}$	0	$+\dfrac{ML^2}{27EI}$
10		$+\dfrac{M}{L}$	$-\dfrac{M}{L}$	$-M$	0	$+\dfrac{ML}{3EI}$	$-\dfrac{ML}{6EI}$	$+0.064\ 2\ \dfrac{ML^2}{EI}$
11		0	0	$-M$	$-M$	$+\dfrac{ML}{2EI}$	$-\dfrac{ML}{2EI}$	$\dfrac{ML^2}{8EI}$
12		$+\dfrac{M_A-M_B}{L}$	$-\dfrac{M_A-M_B}{L}$	$-M_A$	$-M_B$	$+\dfrac{2M_A+M_B}{6EI}L$	$-\dfrac{M_A+2M_B}{6EI}L$	—

^{a} l = left end; r = right end.

have more members or unknown restraints than static equations; we can determine the unknown quantities by means of the known slopes at the end of the members and thus obtain the additional equations for solving the problem.

From eqn 5.5, the end-slope is the same as the end shear due to the equivalent load u. Furthermore, the shear force at the end of a simply supported beam must always be the same as the support reaction.* Consequently the slope at the end of a beam carrying a load w, is the same as the reaction of a beam carrying a load u over the same span.

Taking the specific case of a simply supported beam carrying a uniformly distributed load w, the bending moment varies parabolically from 0 at the supports to a maximum $\frac{1}{8}wL^2$ (see Fig. 4.12), and the area of the bending moment diagram is $\frac{2}{3} . \frac{1}{8}wL^2 . L = \frac{1}{12}wL^3$. The end-slope is half this area divided by EI.

$$\theta = wL^3/24EI \qquad (5.6)$$

We can obtain the maximum slopes and deflections for other types of loading by the same means, and these, together with the maximum bending moment s and shear forces are shown in Table 5.1.

5.2. Beams Built-in at the Supports

The simplest of all hyperstatic beams is one rigidly restrained at the supports, so that it has, in addition to the usual vertical reactions, restraining moments which are just sufficient, no more and no less, to keep the ends precisely horizontal (Fig. 5.4).

We may therefore resolve the problem into that of a simply supported beam carrying a uniformly distributed load (which is isostatic), and an unloaded beam subjected to a uniform fixing moment M (which is hyperstatic). The end-slope due to the uniformly distributed load, which points downwards (eqn 5.6) is

$$\theta_w = wL^3/24EI$$

* If we cut the beam an infinitesimal distance to the right of the left-hand support in Fig. 5.3, the only force to the left of the cut is the support reaction, which is thus the end-shear.

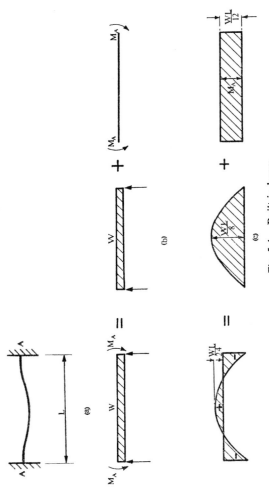

Fig. 5.4. Built-in beam.

(a) Deformation.
(b) The combined system is composed of the sum of the isostatic and the hyperstatic loads.
(c) The total bending moment diagram is the sum of the isostatic and the hyperstatic bending moments.

and the end slope due to the fixing moments M_A, must be exactly equal and opposite (*i.e.* pointing upwards) to cancel it out.

$$\theta_w = -\theta_A$$

The equivalent uniformly distributed load for the purpose of determining the slope θ_A is

$$u = M_A/EI$$

the end slope

$$\theta_A = \tfrac{1}{2}uL = \tfrac{1}{2}M_A L/EI$$

We thus obtain the fixing moment

$$M_A = -\tfrac{1}{12}wL^2 \tag{5.7}$$

From Fig. 5.4c, this is also the maximum negative moment. The maximum positive moment, which occurs at midspan

$$M_+ = \tfrac{1}{8}wL^2 - \tfrac{1}{12}wL^2 = +\tfrac{1}{24}wL^2$$

We can obtain the bending moments for built-in beams with different types of loading by precisely the same means, using the appropriate value of θ_w. With one restraining moment, we can also derive the bending moments for beams built-in at one end only. The results are shown in Table 5.2.

In actual fact, beams are rarely firmly built in. However, in reinforced concrete structures, which are normally cast in one piece, and in steel structures, where substantial end restraints are imposed by heavy welded cleats or similarly stiff high-strength bolted connections, a condition close to the fixed ended support may occur. The true bending moments lie between the simply supported and the fully built-in values. Bending-moment coefficients quoted in some of the earlier building codes for the design of reinforced concrete beams and slabs were based on this principle. However, because of the interaction of adjacent spans it is more accurate to use the theory of continuous beams.

5.3. Continuous Beams

If we take a number of individual spans on simple supports, each span carries its own load, and is unaffected by the loads on adjacent

Table 5.2
End moments in built-in beams (both ends fixed).

Type of Loading	Coefficient of WL
	$-\dfrac{1}{8}$
	$-\dfrac{1}{9}$
	$-\dfrac{5}{48}$
	at A: $-\,a\,(1-a^2)$ at B: $-\,a^2(1-a)$
	$-\dfrac{1}{12}$
	$-\dfrac{5}{48}$
	at A: $-\dfrac{1}{10}$ at B: $-\dfrac{1}{15}$

spans. If we now join the individual beams together, the deflected shape of the beams forms a continuous curve, and the load on each span affects all other spans (Fig. 5.5).

Concrete beams and slabs cast in one piece are continuous, and it would be quite expensive to break the continuity of each span; it would also greatly weaken the structure. In the ordinary steel frame, the beams are connected to the columns with relatively light cleats, which are designed mainly to carry the vertical load, and it is assumed

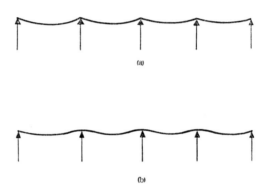

(a)

(b)

Fig. 5.5. Simply supported and continuous beam.
(a) Four simply supported beams.
(b) Beam continuous over the same four spans.

that the beams are simply supported. The same is true in precast concrete, if the beams are simply rested on column cleats. It is possible to establish continuity in steel and precast concrete frames by making the connections sufficiently stiff to transmit moments. Historically, however, the problem of continuity in structural design is associated with the development of reinforced concrete as a major building material.

The establishment of continuity in the beams of Fig. 5.5 creates hyperstatic moments at the supports, and these moments are just sufficient to produce a continuous curve. Let us consider any two adjacent spans L_1 and L_2 in a continuous beam of several spans (Fig. 5.6). The bending-moment diagram consists of the sum of the positive isostatic moments due to the loads acting on the simply supported beam, and the hyperstatic negative restraining moments at the supports A, B and C.

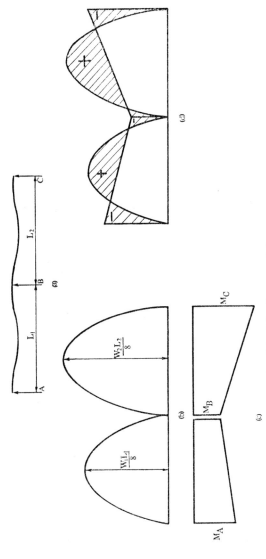

Fig. 5.6. The theorem of three moments.

(a) Dimensions and loads on two interior spans L_1 and L_2.
(b) Isostatic bending moments.
(c) Hyperstatic bending moments.
(d) The combined bending-moment diagram of the continuous beam.

These moments will probably be different, so that we derive next the general equations for the end slopes, due to two unequal restraining moments M_A and M_B. The equivalent load for the purpose of determining the slope, u, varies from M_A/EI to M_B/EI, and the reactions due to this uniformly varying load (obtained by taking moments about each support in turn) are

and

$$R_A = \theta_A = (2M_A + M_B)L_1/6EI$$

$$R_B = \theta_B = (2M_B + M_A)L_1/6EI$$

(5.8)

These are also the slopes at A and B due to the combined action of the restraining moments M_A and M_B in the span L_1.

To these we now add the slope due to the uniformly distributed load on simple supports (from eqn 5.6). Consequently the slope at B at the end of the span L_1 is

$$\theta_{B1} = \frac{2M_B + M_A}{6EI} L_1 + \frac{w_1 L_1^3}{24EI}$$

These two slopes are the same because of the continuity of the beam at B, but viewed from one span the slope is upwards, and from the other, downwards, so that

$$\theta_{B1} = -\theta_{B2}$$

This gives the *Theorem of Three Moments*, published by Clapeyron, a French mathematician, in 1857.

$$M_A L_1 + 2M_B(B_1 + L_2) + M_C L_2 = -\tfrac{1}{4}(w_1 L_1^3 + w_2 L_2^3) \quad (5.9)$$

Example 5.1. A beam carries a live load of 24 kN/m and a dead load of 12 kN/m. The beam is continuous over three spans as shown in Fig. 5.7. Determine the magnitude of the maximum negative and positive moments.

(a) Consider all spans loaded (dead and live load).

From the 'Theorem of Three Moments' we have fixing moments as follows:

For span L_1 and L_2, $M_A = 0$

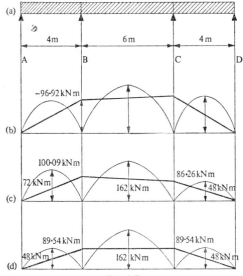

Fig. 5.7.

(a) Loading diagram.
(b) Bending-moment diagram. All spans loaded.
(c) Bending-moment diagram. Adjacent spans loaded.
(d) Bending-moment diagram. Central span loaded.

Therefore

$$0 + 2M_B(4 + 6) + M_C(6) = -\tfrac{1}{4}[(36 \times 4) \times 4^2 + (36 \times 6) \times 6^2]$$

or,

$$20M_B + 6M_C = -2520 \text{ kNm}$$

For span L_2 and L_3, $M_D = 0$

$$M_C \times 6 + 2M_C(6 + 4) + 0 = -\tfrac{1}{4}[(36 \times 6) \times 6^2 + (36 \times 4) \times 4^2]$$

or

$$6M_B + 20M_C = -2520 \text{ kNm}$$

Solving for M_B and M_C gives

$$M_B = -96 \cdot 92 \text{ kNm}$$
$$M_C = -96 \cdot 92 \text{ kNm}$$

(b) Consider live load on adjacent spans L_1 and L_2 as above.

For spans L_1 and L_2,

$$20M_B + 6M_C = -2520 \text{ kNm}$$

For spans L_2 and L_3,

$$6M_B + 20M_C = -\tfrac{1}{4}[(36 \times 6) \times 6^2 + (24 \times 4) \times 4^2]$$

$$= -2328 \text{ kNm}$$

Solving for M_B and M_C gives

$$M_C = -86\cdot37 \text{ kNm}$$

$$M_B = -100\cdot09 \text{ kNm}$$

(c) Consider live load on mid span (L_2) only, as above.

For spans L_1 and L_2,

$$20M_B + 26M_C = -\tfrac{1}{4}[(24 \times 4) \times 4^2 + (36 \times 6) \times 6^2]$$

$$= -2328 \text{ kNm}$$

For spans L_2 and L_3,

$$6M_B + 20M_C = -2328 \text{ kNm}$$

Solving gives

$$M_B = M_C = 89\cdot54 \text{ kNm}$$

From Fig. 5.7b, c and d, it can be seen that the maximum positive moment occurs in the central span and has a value of 72·46 kNm, the maximum negative moment being 100·09 kNm. In the case of a reinforced concrete beam or a built-up or plated steel section it would be necessary to determine the maximum positive moment in spans L_1 or L_3. This would be obtained by removing the live load from span L_2 and proceeding as above.

Table 5.3 gives the bending moment coefficients for uniformly distributed loads and for concentrated loads at mid-span (which

Table 5.3
Continuous beams.
Bending moment coefficients for dead loads (assuming all spans are loaded):
$M = $ coefficient $\times WL$.

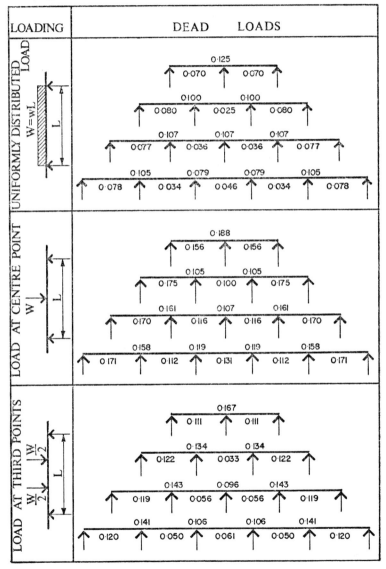

gives approximately the worst condition for a moving load). In addition it lists the bending moments due to concentrated loads at third points, which covers the most common reactions exerted by secondary beams on primary beams (see Fig. 1.21).

We must allow for two further variations. The live load can cover the whole or any part of the floor. Evidently this introduces too many variations, and in buildings we usually simplify the problem by assuming that the live load either covers the entire span, or does not cover any part of the span. From eqn 5.9 it is evident that the highest restraining moments result when the load covers both spans, and this gives the largest negative moments. On the other hand, the positive moments are greatest when the restraining moments are lowest (see Example 5.1). We therefore normally consider two conditions:

(i) alternate spans covered by the live load;
(ii) adjacent spans covered by the live load.

The dead load must, by definition, cover all spans. In continuous beams, the bending moments due to a live load may therefore be higher than the bending moments due to a dead load of the same magnitude (Table 5.4).

Since continuity is particularly common in concrete construction, we must also make some allowance for inelastic deformation. The high peak moments at the supports are not realised in concrete structures [5.5], because some redistribution of stress occurs on account of inelastic deformation. Some concrete codes [5.3] therefore allow a reduction in the negative moments by 15% provided this amount is added to the positive moments.

The bending moment coefficients for beams up to five spans, which are obtained from the Theorem of Three Moments with the above adjustments, are given in Tables 5.3 and 5.4.

For beams continuous over a large number of spans, the variation is slight, and building codes frequently quote coefficients for exterior supports, the first interior support, and all other interior supports, and similarly for end spans and interior spans. An interior span of a very long continuous beam is, of course, identical to a built-in beam.

Table 5.4
Continuous beams.
Bending moment coefficients for live loads (assuming either alternate or adjacent spans are loaded, whichever gives the higher result): $M = coefficient \times WL.$

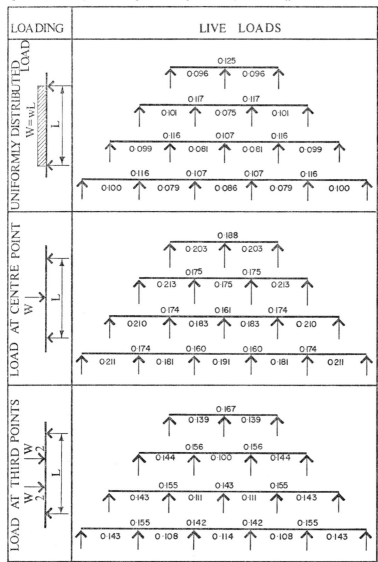

5.4. Rigid Frames and Flat Plates

The theory of continuous beams has played the same part in the design of concrete-frame buildings as the isostatic theory did from an earlier date in the design of steel-frame buildings. The tabulated bending moment coefficients can be used for beams with equal spans, and the solution can be obtained with only a little more work by solving the Theorem of Three Moments. The shear force distribution is altered only slightly by the continuity, and its effect is generally ignored in shear calculations, except at the first interior support.*

Some allowance must, however, be made for the bending moments induced in columns, particularly on the exterior of the frame. The British Concrete Code [5.2] has long included a provision whereby the moment at the ends of the beam is distributed to the columns in the proportion which the column stiffness (EI) bears to the sum of the stiffness terms for the beams and columns meeting at that point, *i.e.* the column is designed for a moment

$$M = \frac{(EI)_{column}}{\Sigma (EI)}$$

in addition to the vertical load.

Just as the growing use of concrete construction gave a special impetus to the theory of hyperstatic beams, so a number of factors combined to promote the use of a more precise theory for rigid frames. The first of these is the difficulty of working out stresses due to horizontal loads (earthquake forces, wind on high buildings) by any other method. The second is the growing popularity of rigid portals, particularly in welded steel, instead of the older isostatic frames (see Fig. 4.21). Rigid frames can be produced with symmetrically sloping roofs, north- (or south-) light roofs, or monitor roofs (Figs. 5.8 and 5.9). They give a neater appearance without a false ceiling, and eliminate most of the ledges on which dust accumulation in industrial buildings can provide a health or safety

---

* The restraining moments produce a shear force which equals $(M_A - M_B)/L$. At the first interior support, the difference between adjacent support moments is greatest, an increase of about 15% in the isostatic shear force is often made. Otherwise isostatic values suffice for checking shear.

hazard. In addition they give a greater clear height inside for the same outside dimensions. There is no particular advantage in using three-pinned welded steel portals, which need more material and labour.

The most important is probably the introduction of the flat-plate reinforced concrete floor, which rests directly on the columns without supporting beams. The floors are much more flexible than beam-supported floors, and the columns tend to be stiffer, so that the concept of a continuous floor pin-jointed to supporting columns is no longer tenable.

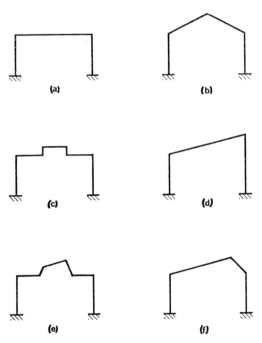

Fig. 5.8.   Rigid frames as single bay roof structures.
(a) Flat roof.
(b) Gabled roof.
(c) Monitor roof (subtropical zone).
(d) North (south) light roof (subtropical zone).
(e) Monitor roof (temperate zone).
(f) North light roof (temperate zone).

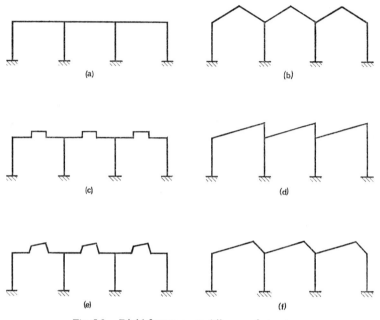

Fig. 5.9. Rigid frames as multibay roof structures.
(a) Flat roof.
(b) Gabled roof.
(c) Monitor roof (subtropical zone).
(d) North (south) light roof (subtropical zone).
(e) Monitor roof (temperate zone).
(f) North light roof (temperate zone).

The oldest method for the design of rigid frames, dating from 1870, is based on the minimum-energy principle (see Chapter 7). The problem can be solved, as in the Theorem of Three Moments, by equating the slopes of the members meeting at a rigid joint (see Section 5.3).

Both these methods produce a large number of simultaneous equations (as many as there are redundancies), and they are laborious without the aid of computers. Using only a slide rule or small calculating machine, it is simpler to consider each beam on its own in the first place, and then distribute the unbalanced moments to the columns.

5.5. THE MOMENT DISTRIBUTION METHOD

The moment distribution method, proposed by Hardy Cross in 1930, obtains the result by successive approximation, and it can be taken to the accuracy required for a final design, or left at a lower stage of distribution for a preliminary analysis. Apart from a careful layout of the arithmetic pattern, and care in the sign convention, it calls for no special skill; the routine calculations can therefore be performed by semi-skilled persons.

All the joints of a frame are initially assumed clamped. Each joint is then released in turn, and the out-of-balance moments are distributed until the residual is sufficiently small. We can obtain the extent of the distribution from eqn 5.8 by clamping the support B, and thus making $\theta_B = 0$. This gives

$$\theta_B = (2M_B + M_A)L/6EI = 0$$

and the carry-over moment due to a moment M_A at A, produces a carry-over moment at a clamped support B

$$M_B = -\tfrac{1}{2}M_A \tag{5.10}$$

The procedure is best illustrated by a simple example.

Example 5.2. Determine the negative bending moments at all supports for the beam shown in Fig. 5.10. The second moment of area is constant.

The first step is to determine the distribution factors at each joint. We have:

Joint	Member	Relative stiffness (I/L)	Distribution factor
A	AB	—	1·0
B	BA	1/6	9/15 = 0·6
	BC	1/9	6/15 = 0·4
C	CB	1/9	9/18 = 0·5
	CD	1/9	9/18 = 0·5
D	DC	Fixed	0

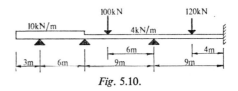

Fig. 5.10.

The second step is to determine the moments at each support assuming all joints fixed.

(a) Cantilever:

Moment $= 10 \times 3^2/2 = 45$ kNm

(b) Span AB:

Uniformly distributed load:

Fixed end moment $= WL^2/12$

$\text{FEM}_A = \text{FEM}_B = 10 \times 6^2/12 = 30$ kNm

(c) Span BC:

Uniformly distributed load:

$\text{FEM}_B = \text{FEM}_C = 4 \times 9^2/12 = 27$ kNm

Point load:

$$\text{FEM}_C = \frac{45 \times 3^2 \times 6}{9^2} = 30 \text{ kNm}$$

$$\text{FEM}_B = \frac{45 \times 6^2 \times 3}{9^2} = 60 \text{ kNm}$$

(d) Span CD:

Uniformly distributed load:

$\text{FEM}_C = \text{FEM}_D = 4 \times 9^2/12 = 27$ kNm

Point load:

$\text{FEM}_D = 81 \times 4 \times 5^2/9^2 = 100$ kNm

$\text{FEM}_C = 81 \times 5 \times 4^2/9^2 = 80$ kNm

Fixed end bending moments	M_{cant}	M_{AB}	M_{BA}	M_{BC}	M_{CB}	M_{CD}	M_{DC}
Uniformly distributed load	45	30	30	27	27	27	27
Point load				60	30	80	100
Σ	45	30	30	87	57	107	127

The third step is to draw the beam roughly to scale and record the distribution factors and fixed end moments at the various joints. All moments are recorded with the sign convention applicable to the convention used—in this case clockwise moments are positive. The next step is to release each joint in turn. Where there is an unbalanced moment at the joint, the release will allow rotation to take place, which will be absorbed by the various members in proportion to their stiffness. This bending moment (balancing) will be of opposite sign to the original unbalanced value. On completion of the balancing operation at all joints a line is drawn to indicate the end of this stage, and half the balancing moment is transferred to the joint at the far end of the member. This operation will result in further unbalanced moments at the various joints and the above procedure is repeated until the difference is no longer significant.

Support	A		B		C		D
Distribution factors	1·0	0·6	0·4	0·5	0·5	0	
FEM	+45	−30	+30	−87	+57	−107	+127
Balance	—	−15	+34·2	+22·8	+25	+25	—
Distribute		+17·1	−7·5	+12·5	+11·4	—	+12·5
Balance		−17·1	−3·0	−2·0	−5·7	−5·7	—
Distribute		−1·5	−8·55	−2·85	−1·0	—	−2·85
Balance		+1·5	+6·9	+4·60	+0·5	+0·5	—
Distribute		+3·45	+0·75	+0·25	+2·3	—	+0·25
Balance		−3·45	−0·6	−0·4	−1·15	−1·15	—
Distribute		−0·3	−1·7	−0·6	−0·2	—	−0·6
Balance		+0·3	+1·4	+0·9	+0·1	+0·1	—
Final bending moment in	+45	−45	+51·9	−51·8	+88·3	88·3	+136·3
kNm	45		51·8		88·3		136·3

Example 5.3. The frame shown (in Fig.5.11) is unsymmetrical both in terms of geometry and loading; it carries a horizontal wind load at eaves level. Determine the bending moments for which the frame must be designed.

A frame of this nature is normally analysed separately for gravity and wind loads. Using superposition, the various bending moments

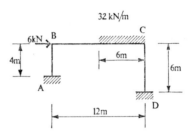

Member	Relative Values of I
AB	1
BC	2
CD	1.5

Fig. 5.11.   Loading diagram. Ratio of moments of inertia $I_{AB} = 1$, $I_{BC} = 2$, $I_{CD} = 1·5$.

are combined to give the worst design cases for the members. Where wind is present this load or its resulting bending moment is reduced to a static dead load equivalent to make allowance for the increase in stress allowed for wind in the various codes of practice.

(a) Consider gravity loads only:

Distribution factors

Joint	Member	Relative stiffness	Distribution factor
A	AB	Fixed	0
B	BA	$I/L = 1/4$	$6/10 = 0·6$
	BC	$I/L = 2/12 = 1/6$	$4/10 = 0·4$
C	CB	$I/L = 2/12 = 1/6$	$4/10 = 0·4$
	CD	$I/L = 1·5/6 = 1/4$	$6/10 = 0·6$
D	DC	Fixed	0

Fixed end moments:
Member BC:

$$M_B = 5/192 \times 32 \times 12^2 = 120 \text{ kNm}$$

$$M_C = 11/192 \times 32 \times 12^2 = 264 \text{ kNm}$$

This first moment distribution (see Fig. 5.12) will produce an unbalanced shear the value of which is given by

$$(+54 + 108)/4 + (-90 - 180)/6 = -4.5 \text{ kN}$$

Since no horizontal force has been considered in this moment distribution, correcting moments must be added to the columns to bring the internal shear to zero.

It can be shown [5.4] that for a frame of this type the applied correcting moments must vary as stiffness/length, *i.e.* in the ratio of $1/4^2$ to $1.5/6^2$, or in the ratio of 2 to 3. Arbitrary moments in the ratio of 20 and 30 kNm are used in this instance (see Fig. 5.13).

The unbalanced shear produced by these correcting moments is

$$(21.99 + 13.75)/4 + (15.62 + 11.24)/6 = 13.4 \text{ kNm}$$

The required shear, however, is $+4.5$ kNm and by simple proportion the correcting moments must be multiplied by factor of $4.5/13.4$ or 0.33.

	Arbitrary correcting moments	$\times 0.33$
M_{AB}	$+21.89$	$+7.2$
M_{BA}	$+13.75$	$+4.5$
M_{CD}	$+11.24$	$+3.7$
M_{DC}	$+15.62$	$+5.2$

These moments must be added to those obtained from the first moment distribution to give

	Correcting moment (kNm)	First moment distribution (kNm)	Final moment (kNm)
M_{AB}	$+7.2$	$+54$	$+61.2$
M_{BA}	$+4.5$	$+108$	$+112.5$
M_{CD}	$+3.7$	-180	-176.3
M_{DC}	$+5.2$	-90	-84.4

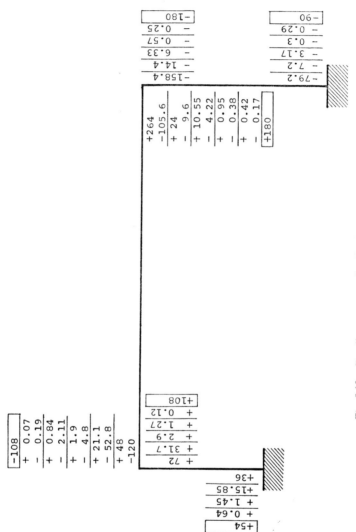

Fig. 5.12. Bending moment distribution neglecting sidesway.

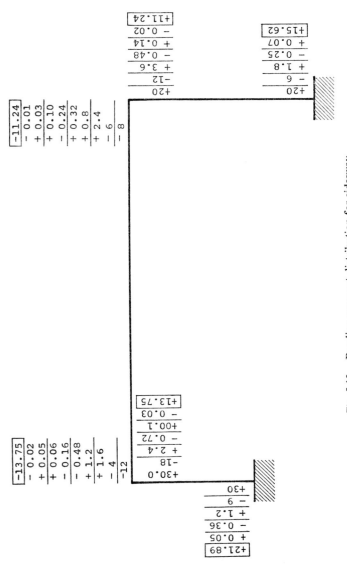

Fig. 5.13.   Bending moment distribution for sidesway.

(b) Consider now the horizontal wind load:

The arbitrary correcting moments applied above produced a horizontal shear of $+13\cdot4$ kN. A shear of -6 kN is, however, required. Therefore the moments must be multiplied by a factor of $-6/13\cdot4$ or $-0\cdot44$.

	Arbitrary correcting moment	$\times(-0\cdot44)$
M_{AB}	$+21\cdot89$	$-9\cdot64$
M_{BA}	$+13\cdot75$	$-6\cdot05$
M_{CD}	$+11\cdot24$	$-4\cdot95$
M_{DC}	$+15\cdot60$	$-6\cdot86$

These moments are reduced to their static dead load equivalent and combined with the gravity loads to produce the worst design condition for each member, due attention being given to the sign of such moment.

Chapter 6

The Virtual Displacement Method of Calculating Deformations

In this chapter we introduce the principle of virtual displacements, a generalised method which can be used to determine deformations of structures as well as in the analysis of hyperstatic structures. It forms the basis for many computerised methods, however, it is still used in the preliminary analysis of unusual structures.

6.1. The Principle of Virtual Displacements

The principle of virtual displacements is one of the most useful tools in structural analysis. Here, we shall be using it to determine the deformations of structures and to analyse hyperstatic structures; more comprehensive treatments are given elsewhere [6.1, 6.2]. It is also known as the virtual work method and is sometimes referred to as the virtual load or unit load method.

The principle may be stated as:

For any system of forces in equilibrium the total work done by all the forces is equal to zero for any arbitrary, virtual displacement of that system.

The principle can be seen to apply, intuitively, by examining the structure shown in Fig. 6.1. Remember that for forces the work done

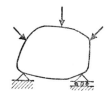

Fig. 6.1. Generalised structure.

157

is the product of the force and the distance moved in the direction of the force; if we give this structure any arbitrary vertical displacement the work done by the vertical components of the forces must be zero since $\Sigma V = 0$ for vertical force equilibrium and all the forces will have undergone the same displacement, say d, thus $\Sigma Vd = 0$ must also hold. Similarly, we may show that any arbitrary horizontal displacement or any arbitrary rotation must also produce zero work if $\Sigma H = 0$ and $\Sigma M = 0$, the equations of equilibrium for horizontal forces and moments. The reason why the principle is associated with virtual displacements is that the displacements need not actually occur, it is sufficient to conceive of them and if they did occur then the total work would be zero.

The principle may seem somewhat trivial, however, we will show its power in the remainder of this chapter. It can be used to derive the equations of equilibrium, Clapeyron's Three Moment Theorem (see Section 5.3) and the moment distribution method (see Section 5.5). In most of what follows the crucial consideration is that of distinguishing between the equilibrium system and the displacement system through which the equilibrium system moves.

The displacements need not be a gross movement of the kind discussed in relation to Fig. 6.1, they could be internal to the structure such as we need to consider in calculating the elastic deformation of frames. If we are considering internal displacements then there will be internal work, W_i, as well as external work, W_e. We could restate the principle as:

For any system of forces in equilibrium the sum of the internal and external work done by all the forces is equal to zero for any arbitrary, virtual displacement of that system,
i.e.

$$W_i + W_e = 0$$

6.2. Deformations of Trusses

In order to determine the deformation of trusses we can use the principle as follows: choose a simple equilibrium system of forces and move it through the actual displacements caused by the real loads, and then use the condition of zero total work to determine the displacement we desire.

The external work done by our equilibrium system can be simply calculated. The internal work calculation needs some discussion. Let F_1 be the forces in the truss due to be equilibrium system; these forces move through the elongations of the respective members caused by the real loads. The deformations of the members can be determined from

$$d = \frac{F_1 L}{EA}$$

where F_1 = force in member, L = length of member, E = elastic modulus, A = area of member.

If we let F_0 be the forces in the members due to the real loads, the internal work is given by

$$W_i = -\sum F_1 d$$

$$= -\sum \frac{F_1 F_0 L}{EA}$$

Supposing we choose as our equilibrium system a unit load at the point we wish to determine the deflection (Δ). Then, according to the principle, since the external work will be the unit load moving through the actual external displacement, Δ (the reactions do not move):

$$1 \times \Delta = \sum \frac{F_0 F_1 L}{EA} \qquad (6.1)$$

Eqn 6.1 can be used to calculate the deflection at any point in a truss.
    The procedure can be summarised:

1. Calculate member deformations (d) due to real loads (this requires an analysis of the truss).
2. Place a unit load at the point we wish to determine the deflection, in a suitable direction.
3. Calculate member forces (F_1) of real structure due to the unit load (this is the equilibrium system).
4. Determine total work by summing internal work and external work. This gives a single equation in the required deflection.

Example 6.1. Determine the vertical deflection at C for the truss shown in Fig. 6.2.

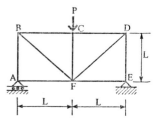

Fig. 6.2.   Truss used in Example 6.1.

The calculations can best be carried out in a table.

Member	F_0 $(\times P)$	F_1	d $\left(\times \dfrac{PL}{EA}\right)$	$F_1 d$ $\left(\times \dfrac{PL}{EA}\right)$
AB	−0·50	−0·50	−0·50	0·25
BC	−0·50	−0·50	−0·50	0·25
CD	−0·50	−0·50	−0·50	0·25
DE	−0·50	−0·50	−0·50	0·25
EF	0	0	0	0
FA	0	0	0	0
BF	0·71	0·71	1·00	0·71
DF	0·71	0·71	1·00	0·71
CF	−1·00	−1·00	−1·00	1·00

$$\Sigma F_1 d = 3\cdot42 \frac{PL}{EA}$$

Internal work $W_i = -\Sigma F_1 d$, where F_1 is the force system in the truss shown in Fig. 6.2 due to a unit vertical load at C (see Fig. 6.3).

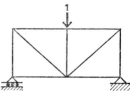

Fig. 6.3.   Unit load placed at the point where deflection is to be determined for the truss in Fig. 6.2.

External work due to a unit load at C:

$$W_e = 1 \times \Delta_C$$

$$\therefore \qquad 1 \times \Delta_C = \sum F_1 d$$

$$\Delta_C = 3{\cdot}42 \frac{PL}{EA}$$

Example 6.2. Determine the horizontal deflection at A of the truss shown in Fig. 6.4a.

The internal work can be calculated by determining the member displacements as before. The equilibrium system to be moved

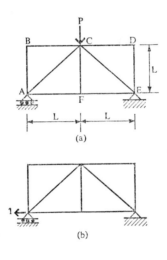

(a)

(b)

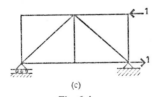

(c)

Fig. 6.4.

(a) Truss used in Example 6.2.
(b) Unit load applied at the point where deflection is to be determined.
(c) Couple applied to member whose rotation is to be determined.

through these displacements is caused by a horizontal unit load at A (Fig. 6.4b) as this will introduce Δ_A, the horizontal deflection at A into the work equation.

Calculate the internal work:

Member	F_0 $(\times P)$	F_1	d $\left(\times \dfrac{PL}{EA}\right)$	$F_1 d$ $\left(\times \dfrac{PL}{EA}\right)$
AB	0	0	0	0
BC	0	0	0	0
CD	0	0	0	0
DE	0	0	0	0
EF	0·50	1·00	0·50	0·50
FA	0·50	1·00	0·50	0·50
AC	−0·71	0	−1·00	0
CE	−0·71	0	−1·00	0
CF	0	0	0	0

$$\Sigma F_1 d = 1\cdot00 \frac{PL}{EA}$$

External work due to unit horizontal load at A:

$$W_e = 1 \times \Delta_A$$

$$\therefore \qquad \Delta_A = 1\cdot00 \frac{PL}{EA}$$

We can also determine the rotations of truss members using the principle. To determine rotations we need to introduce the rotation, θ, into the work equation. Consider a single member shown in Fig. 6.5 loaded by a couple, the work done by the couple is

$$W = 1 \times L \times \theta$$

Fig. 6.5. Couple applied to single member whose rotation is to be determined.

We can, therefore, use as our equilibrium system a couple produced by placing opposing unit loads at the ends of the member whose rotation we wish to calculate.

Example 6.3. Determine the rotation of member DE of the truss shown in Fig. 6.4a.

Place a couple onto member DE as shown in Fig. 6.4c, the forces produced by this couple are the F_1 forces. We can now calculate the internal work as before:

Member	F_0 $(\times P)$	F_1	d $\left(\times \dfrac{PL}{EA}\right)$	$F_1 d$ $\left(\times \dfrac{PL}{EA}\right)$
AB	0	0	0	0
BC	0	0	0	0
CD	0	−1·00	0	0
DE	0	0	0	0
EF	0·50	0·5	0·50	0·25
FA	0·50	0·5	0·50	0·25
AC	−0·71	−0·71	−1·00	0·71
CE	−0·71	0·71	−1·00	−0·71
CF	0	0	0	0

$$\Sigma F_1 d = 0.50 \frac{PL}{EA}$$

The external work due to this couple is:

$$W_e = 1 \times L \times \theta$$

$$\therefore \quad L\theta = 0.50 \frac{PL}{EA}$$

$$\theta = 0.50 \frac{P}{EA} \text{ rad}$$

6.3. Hyperstatic Trusses

The principle can be used to analyse hyperstatic trusses. Consider the truss in Fig. 6.6a which is the same as the truss in Fig. 6.4a with the addition of member BF, hence, it is indeterminate in one degree.

We can use the principle of superposition and treat the system as if it were composed of two loads as shown in Fig. 6.6b where X is the unknown force in BF; this was achieved by cutting member BF to make the truss statically determinate. The unit force in the cut member BF is a self-equilibrating force system and we can use it to calculate the deformation of the two cut ends with respect to each

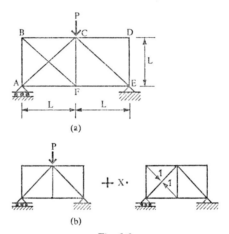

(a)

(b)

Fig. 6.6.

(a) A hyperstatic truss.
(b) The truss in (a) is equivalent to the sum of the isostatic truss on the left plus X times the truss on the right.

other (Δ). But, in reality, there is no displacement there, so the external work done by the unit load must be zero. With this information we generate an equation in X and hence can determine its value. Once we have the value of X we can finish the analysis of the truss.

The procedure may be summarised as:

1. Cut redundant member to produce a statically determinate structure.
2. Compute forces, F_0, in modified structure under the original load system.
3. Compute the member displacements of the modified structure,

$$d = \frac{F_0 L}{EA}$$

4. Let the magnitude of force in the cut member be X. Note that the force system in the frame associated with X constitutes a set of forces in equilibrium and calculate these forces for $X = 1$.

5. Hence, the total force in each member is given by

$$F_{total} = F_0 + XF_1$$

6. The external work will be zero, hence

$$W_i = -\sum F_1 d_{total} = -\sum F_1 F_{total} \frac{L}{EA}$$

$$= -\sum F_1(F_0 + XF_1)\frac{L}{EA} = 0$$

$$\therefore \qquad X = -\frac{\Sigma F_1 F_0(L/EA)}{\Sigma F_1{}^2(L/EA)} \qquad (6.2)$$

and F_{total} can now be determined.

Example 6.4. Analyse the structure shown in Fig. 6.6a.
Choose member BF as the redundant member:

Member	F_0 ($\times P$)	F_1	$F_0 F_1 \dfrac{L}{EA}$ $\left(\times \dfrac{PL}{EA}\right)$	$F_1{}^2 \dfrac{L}{EA}$ $\left(\times \dfrac{L}{EA}\right)$	XF_1 ($\times P$)	F_{total} ($\times P$)
AB	0	−0·71	0	0·5	−0·19	−0·19
BC	0	−0·71	0	0·5	−0·19	−0·19
CD	0	0	0	0	0	0
DE	0	0	0	0	0	0
EF	0·50	0	0	0	0	0·50
FA	0·50	−0·71	−0·35	0·5	−0·19	0·31
AC	−0·71	1·00	−0·71	1·00	0·26	0·45
CE	−0·71	0	0	0	0	−0·71
CF	0	−0·71	0	0·5	−0·19	−0·19
BF	0	1·00	0	1·00	1·26	0·26

$$\sum \frac{F_0 F_1 L}{EA} = -1·06 \qquad \sum \frac{F_1{}^2 L}{EA} = 4·00$$

From eqn 6.2:

$$X = \frac{1·06(PL/EA)}{4·00(L/EA)}$$

i.e.

$$X = 0·26P$$

Hence, the remaining two columns of the table can be filled out and the forces in the original structure determined. If we desired we could now compute the deflections of the truss in Example 6.4 by the method outlined earlier.

The same concepts can be used to analyse trusses that have more than one redundant (*i.e.* are statically indeterminate in more than one degree).

The procedure for a truss with n redundants may be summarised as:

1. Cut n redundant members to produce a statically determinate structure.
2. Calculate forces (F_0) in modified structure under the original load system.
3. Let the unknown forces X_i ($i = 1, \ldots, n$) act at each cut. With $X_1 = 1$ and all the remaining $X_i = 0$, calculate the forces F_1 in all the members of the modified structure.
4. Repeat step 3 by letting each $X_i = 1$ in turn with remaining $X_i = 0$ and hence calculate the forces F_i in the modified structure.
5. The forces in the real structure can be found from

$$F_{\text{total}} = F_0 + X_1 F_1 + X_2 F_2 + \cdots + X_n F_n$$

6. The total elongation of each member is

$$d_{\text{total}} = F_{\text{total}} \frac{L}{EA}$$

7. The magnitudes of X_i are determined from the requirement that the relative displacement at each cut is zero, *i.e.* $W_e = 0$. This leads to n simultaneous equations in X_i. Let Δ_{ij} be the displacement of cut i due to load j, then for the above condition we can write

$$\Delta_{10} + X_1 \Delta_{11} + X_2 \Delta_{12} + \cdots + X_n \Delta_{1n} = 0$$
$$\Delta_{20} + X_1 \Delta_{21} + X_2 \Delta_{22} + \cdots + X_n \Delta_{2n} = 0$$
$$\cdots \cdots \cdots \cdots \cdots \cdots \cdots \cdots \cdots \cdots \cdots \cdots \cdots$$
$$\Delta_{n0} + X_1 \Delta_{n1} + X_2 \Delta_{n2} + \cdots + X_n \Delta_{nn} = 0 \qquad (6.3)$$

where Δ_{ij} can be calculated from

$$\Delta_{ij} = \sum F_i F_j \frac{L}{EA}$$

Example 6.5. Analyse the truss shown in Fig. 6.7a, if all members have a constant E and all chord members have an area 65 cm^2 and all web members an area of 37·5 cm^2 (except EF which has an area of 32·5 cm^2).

This truss has two redundants. Select members AE and EB as redundants to be cut. Figure 6.7b shows the modified structure loaded by the original load system, by a unit load at cut 1 and a unit load at cut 2 with X_1 and X_2 being the unknown forces, respectively.

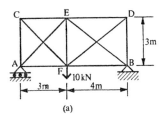

(a)

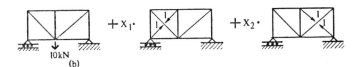

(b)

Fig. 6.7.
(a) Truss used in Example 6.5. It has two redundants.
(b) The sum of these trusses is equivalent to the truss in (a).

From eqn 6.3, for this problem:

$$\Delta_{10} + X_1\Delta_{11} + X_2\Delta_{12} = 0$$

$$\Delta_{20} + X_1\Delta_{21} + X_2\Delta_{22} = 0$$

i.e.

$$\sum F_1 F_0 \frac{L}{EA} + X_1 \sum F_1{}^2 \frac{L}{EA} + X_2 \sum F_1 F_2 \frac{L}{EA} = 0$$

$$\sum F_2 F_0 \frac{L}{EA} + X_1 \sum F_1 F_2 \frac{L}{EA} + X_2 \sum F_2{}^2 \frac{L}{EA} = 0$$

We can calculate F_0, F_1, F_2 and the respective member lengths and tabulate them below, as before.

Member	L	L/A	F_0	F_1	F_2	$F_1{}^2L/A$	F_1F_2L/A	$F_2{}^2L/A$	F_0F_1L/A	F_0F_2L/A
AF	3	0·046	0	−0·71	0	0·023	0	0	0	0
BF	4	0·062	0	0	−0·80	0	0	0·040	0	0
CE	3	0·046	−5·7	−0·71	0	0·023	0	0	0·186	0
DE	4	0·062	−5·7	0	−0·80	0	0	0·040	0	0·282
AC	3	0·046	−5·7	−0·71	0	0·023	0	0	0·186	0
EF	3	0·093	0	−0·71	−0·60	0·046	0·040	0·033	0	0
DB	3	0·046	−4·3	0	−0·60	0	0	0·016	0	0·119
CF	4·25	0·113	8·1	1·00	0	0·113	0	0	0·915	0
EA	4·25	0·113	0	1·00	0	0·113	0	0	0	0
EB	5	0·133	0	0	1·00	0	0	0·133	0	0
DF	5	0·133	7·1	0	1·00	0	0	0·133	0	0·945
						$\Sigma = 0·341$	$\Sigma = 0·040$	$\Sigma = 0·395$	$\Sigma = 1·287$	$\Sigma = 1·346$

Therefore

$$1{\cdot}287 + 0{\cdot}341X_1 + 0{\cdot}040X_2 = 0$$

$$1{\cdot}346 + 0{\cdot}040X_1 + 0{\cdot}395X_2 = 0$$

and

$$X_1 = -3{\cdot}3 \text{ kN}$$

$$X_2 = -3{\cdot}1 \text{ kN}$$

6.4. DEFORMATIONS OF BEAMS

Methods for calculating deformations of beams have already been mentioned in Chapter 5. We shall briefly examine here the use of the virtual displacement principle to determine the same deformations. As we shall see in Section 6.6 we can apply the principle to determine deformations of structures in which those deformations are due to a combination of stresses.

In order to utilise the principle with beams we must go back to our concepts of work. Since beams carry their loads by moments we need to be able to calculate the work done by moments. Work is done by moments when they rotate through an angle, say θ. We can, therefore, apply the principle to beams in an analogous manner to trusses, *i.e.* letting the moments caused by a unit load rotate through the rotations of the actual structure caused by the real loads. Since the moments and the unit load are an equilibrium system the total work done will be zero. The internal work done by these moments M_1, in an infinitesimally small part of beam undergoing the rotation, $d\theta_0$, due to the actual loads, is given by

$$dW_i = -M_1\,d\theta_0$$

The relative rotation of two ends of an infinitesimally small part of a beam is given by (see Section 5.1)

$$d\theta = \frac{M}{EI}\,dx$$

therefore

$$dW_i = -\frac{M_0 M_1}{EI} dx$$

i.e.

$$W_i = -\int_0^L \frac{M_0 M_1}{EI} dx$$

and the external work can be calculated as before.

Example 6.6. Determine the deflection at the end of a cantilever due to a concentrated load at the end (Fig. 6.8a).

Firstly, calculate the moments (M_0) due to the real loads (Fig. 6.8b).

$$M_0 = Px$$

Now apply a unit load at the end, hence, the moments due to this unit load are given by (Fig. 6.8c).

$$M_1 = -1x$$

$$\therefore \qquad W_i = -\int_0^L \frac{Px^2}{EI} dx$$

$$= -\frac{PL^3}{3EI}$$

The external work is given by the unit load moving through the deflection at the end

$$W_e = 1 . \Delta$$

Now

$$W_e + W_i = 0$$

$$\therefore \qquad \Delta = \frac{PL^3}{3EI}$$

which is the same as the relationship in Table 5.1.

For isostatic, straight, prismatic beams the use of tables obviates the need for calculating deflections and rotations. However, when the beam is not straight or does not have a uniform cross-section then the principle can be utilised to determine these deformations.

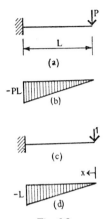

Fig. 6.8.
(a) Cantilever beam used in Example 6.6.
(b) Moments (M_0) due to original loads.
(c) Unit load placed at point where deflection is required and the resulting moments, M_1.

Example 6.7. Determine the deflection at the end of the cantilever shown in Fig. 6.9.

This type of situation often occurs in plated steel beams in which flange plates are added to increase the strength and stiffness of a beam. Applying the same procedure as before the only difference is

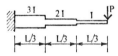

Fig. 6.9. Cantilever with variable moment of inertia used in Example 6.7.

that we have to consider the beam in three sections $-x = 0$ to $L/3$, $x = L/3$ to $2L/3$ and $x = 2L/3$ to L

$$M_0 = -Px \qquad x = 0 \text{ to } L/3$$

$$M_0 = -Px \qquad x = L/3 \text{ to } 2L/3$$

$$M_0 = -Px \qquad x = 2L/3 \text{ to } L$$

Similarly with M_1.

$$\therefore \quad W_i = -\left(\int_0^{L/3} \frac{Px^2}{EI}\, dx + \int_{L/3}^{2L/3} \frac{Px^2}{2EI}\, dx + \int_{2L/3}^{L} \frac{Px^2}{3EI}\, dx \right)$$

$$\therefore \quad = \frac{PL^3}{3EI}\left(\frac{1}{27} + \frac{7}{54} + \frac{19}{81} \right)$$

$$= 0 \cdot 134 \frac{PL^3}{EI}$$

The deflection of any structural system composed of elements in bending can be determined in this manner. For example the deflection at the top pin of the three-pin portal of Fig. 4.21 could be determined by combining the moments previously calculated with those produced by placing a unit vertical load at the top pin.

Example 6.8. Determine the horizontal deflection at C of the parabolic arch shown in Fig. 6.10 if the moment of inertia varies inversely with the cosine of the slope of the arch.

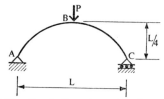

Fig. 6.10.   Parabolic arch used in Example 6.8.

The equation of the arch is given by

$$y = x \frac{(L - x)}{L}$$

with the origin at A.

The moment of inertia at any point is given by

$$I = \frac{I_0}{\cos \theta}$$

$$= I_0 \frac{ds}{dx}$$

where ds is the distance along the arch.

Apply a unit horizontal inward load at C to obtain the M_1 moments

$$\therefore \qquad 1 \times \Delta_c = \int_0^L M_0 M_1 \frac{ds}{EI}$$

$$= \int_0^L M_0 M_1 \frac{dx}{EI_0}$$

$$= -2 \int_0^{L/2} \frac{P}{2} . x . y . \frac{dx}{EI_0}$$

Substituting for y, we get

$$\Delta_c = -\frac{P}{LEI} \int_0^{L/2} (x^2 L - x^3) \, dx$$

$$= -\frac{5PL^3}{192EI}$$

the negative sign means that deflection is outwards.

6.5. HYPERSTATIC BEAMS

Chapter 5 has already discussed some of the techniques available to analyse hyperstatic beams. Here, we will show the use of the principle first by a simple example and then by applying it to a parabolic arch. Just as for hyperstatic trusses we use the principles of superposition and compatibility. The approach is to release the redundants, calculate the displacements at the releases due to the original loads on the modified structure, then apply the redundants as unit actions on the modified structure and determine the displacements at the releases due to them. By equating the sum of these to zero we can calculate the redundants.

Example 6.9. Analyse the propped cantilever shown in Fig. 6.11a.

It will be sufficient to determine the vertical reaction at the prop, for once that is known the remaining reactions can be solved by the equations of equilibrium. Choose this vertical reaction as the redundant value X, and the structure is now shown in Fig. 6.11b.

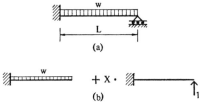

Fig. 6.11.
(a) Propped cantilever used in Example 6.9.
(b) Modified isostatic beam plus unit load at the redundant.

We could use the principle to determine the deflections of the modified structure due to the original load acting downwards and that due to the unit load upwards. However, through the use of Table 5.1 we can bypass this phase. Thus,

$$\Delta_0 = \frac{WL^3}{8EI} \qquad \text{where } W = wL$$

$$\Delta_1 = -\frac{L^3}{3EI}$$

From compatibility, since there is no deflection at the prop, we have

$$\Delta_0 + X\Delta_1 = 0$$

i.e.

$$X = \tfrac{3}{8}W$$

Example 6.10. Analyse the parabolic arch shown in Fig. 6.12a. The moment of inertia varies inversely with the cosine of the slope of the arch.

Note that this is the same as the arch for Example 6.8 with the exception that there is no roller at the right-hand support. Treat the horizontal reaction at this support as the redundant, hence the modified structure is exactly the same as the one used in Example 6.8. The horizontal deflection of the modified structure due to original loads have been calculated as

$$\Delta_0 = -\frac{5PL^3}{192EI_0}$$

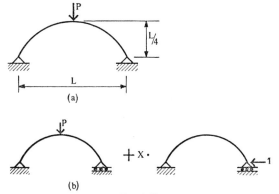

Fig. 6.12.
(a) Two-pin parabolic arch used in Example 6.10.
(b) Modified isostatic arch plus unit load at the redundant.

Now we need to calculate the deflection due to the unit load at the right hand support (Fig. 6.12b).

$$1 \times \Delta_1 = \int_0^L \frac{M_1^2 \, \mathrm{d}x}{EI_0}$$

$$= 2 \int_0^{L/2} \frac{y^2 \, \mathrm{d}x}{EI_0}$$

Using the equation for y given previously

$$\Delta_1 = \frac{2}{L^2 EI_0} \int_0^{L/2} (x^2 L^2 - 2x^3 L + x^4) \, \mathrm{d}x$$

$$= \frac{L^3}{30EI_0}$$

Since $\Delta_0 + X\Delta_1 = 0$,

$$X = 0 \cdot 78P$$

6.6. Deformations Due to Combined Actions

For the analysis of deformations and forces of structures which combine a variety of actions the virtual displacement method is a most useful hand method. So far we have looked at deformations due to axial forces and bending moments separately, let us examine an example in which these two actions combine to produce the deformation of the structure.

Example 6.11. Determination the vertical deflection at C for the structure shown in Fig. 6.13a. The tie has an area of A_t and the beam a moment of inertia of I and an area of A_b.

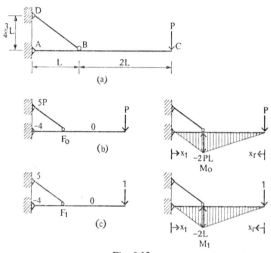

Fig. 6.13.
(a) Tied cantilever used in Example 6.11.
(b) The forces, F_0, and moments, M_0, due to original loads.
(c) The forces (F_1) and moments (M_1) due to unit load at the point where deflection is required.

Here we need to consider the contribution to the deflection of both the axial deformation of the tie (DB) and the bending and axial deformations of the beam (AC). To determine the deflection at C we need to calculate the moments and axial forces in the structure due to the original loads (*i.e.* M_0 and F_0) and then the moments and axial forces due to a unit load at C (*i.e.* M_1 and F_1).

From the virtual displacement principle we can write

$$1 \times \Delta_C = \int \frac{M_0 M_1}{EI} \, \mathrm{d}x + \sum \frac{F_0 F_1 L}{EA}$$

Figure 6.13b shows the actions due to the real loads and Fig. 6.13c shows the actions due to the unit load at C.

Treating axial deformations first:

Member	F_0 $(\times P)$	F_1	$\dfrac{L}{EA}$ $\left(\times \dfrac{L}{E}\right)$	$\dfrac{F_0 F_1 L}{EA}$ $\left(\times \dfrac{PL}{EA}\right)$
AB	-4	-4	$\dfrac{1}{A_b}$	$\dfrac{16}{A_b}$
BC	0	0	$\dfrac{2}{A_b}$	0
DB	5	5	$\dfrac{1 \cdot 25}{A_t}$	$\dfrac{31 \cdot 2}{A_t}$

Therefore, the contribution due to axial forces is

$$\sum \frac{F_0 F_1 L}{EA} = \frac{L}{E}\left(\frac{16}{A_b} + \frac{31 \cdot 2}{A_t}\right)$$

Now, we can calculate the contribution due to the moments, the integral can be best evaluated if we use different origins for each section of the beam (Fig. 6.13b and c),

i.e.

$$\int \frac{M_0 M_1}{EI}\, \mathrm{d}x = \int_0^L \frac{M_0 M_1}{EI}\, \mathrm{d}x_L + \int_0^{2L} \frac{M_0 M_1}{EL}\, \mathrm{d}x_R$$

$$= \frac{1}{EI}\int_0^L (-2Px_L)(-2x_L)\, \mathrm{d}x_L$$

$$+ \frac{1}{EI}\int_0^{2L} (-Px_R)(-1x_R)\, \mathrm{d}x_R$$

$$= \frac{4PL^3}{EI}$$

∴

$$\Delta_C = \frac{L}{EA_t}\left(\frac{16A_t}{A_b} + 31 \cdot 2\right) + \frac{4PL^3}{EI}$$

Note that if the area of the beam is very large compared to the area of the tie, which would normally be the case, the first term in the bracket could be neglected.

6.7. Deformations Due to Shear, Torsion and Temperature

So far we have been examining the deformations produced by both axial forces and bending moments, the most common actions in building frames. We now want to look at the effects of other actions. Although *shear forces* exist in virtually all loaded beams their effects on deformations are small, however, they can be easily calculated using the principle. We can develop an expression for the work done by the shear forces in a similar manner to those we developed for axial forces and bending moments.

Consider an element of a beam shown in Fig. 6.14 under the

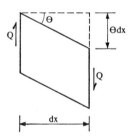

Fig. 6.14.   Beam element undergoing rotation, θ, due to the shear force Q.

action of shear forces, Q. As the beam deforms the work done by the shear force is simply

$$dW_i = -Q\theta \, dx$$

Now we need to let the shear forces, Q_1, due to a unit load move through the displacements caused by the original loads. Since the internal shear forces and the unit load are an equilibrium system the total work done will be zero.

Now

$$\theta \, dx = \alpha \frac{Q \, dx}{GA} *$$

Where α is a form factor that is dependent on the shape of the section (for a rectangular section it is 1·2, a circular section 1·11, a steel beam section it is approximately the gross area divided by the web area and for a tube it is 2), G is the shear modulus of the material and A is the area of the section. Hence, the internal work can be determined from

$$W_i = -\int \alpha \frac{Q_0 Q_1}{GA} \, dx$$

and the deflection at some point due to shear deformations given by

$$1 \times \Delta = \int \alpha \frac{Q_0 Q_1}{GA} \, dx$$

Example 6.12. Determine the deflection at the end of a cantilever due to a concentrated load (P) at its end, include both shearing and bending deformations.

The bending deformation contribution has already been determined in Example 6.6 as

$$\Delta_{\text{bending}} = \frac{PL^3}{3EI}$$

The original load (P) produces a uniform shear of P throughout a cantilever, *i.e.* $Q_0 = P$; a unit load also produces a uniform shear of unity, *i.e.* $Q_1 = 1$.

$\therefore$

$$\Delta_{\text{shear}} = \int_0^L \alpha \frac{P \times 1}{EA} \, dx$$

$$= \alpha \frac{PL}{GA}$$

$\therefore$

$$\Delta_{\text{total}} = \frac{PL^3}{3EI} + \alpha \frac{PL}{GA}$$

---

* The derivation of this expression can be found in most text-books on the Strength of Materials, *e.g.* Reference [4.2].

If we give E, G, I and A realistic values we can see the contributions of each. Assume we have a rectangular cross-section, *i.e.* $\alpha = 1.2$, with $E = 200$ GPa, $G = 80$ GPa, $I = 200 \times 10^6$ mm^4 and $A = 10^4$ mm^2; then

$$\Delta = P(8.35 \times 10^{-9}L^3 + 1.5 \times 10^{-9}L)\ \text{m}$$

If L is around 1 m then the shear contribution is around 15%; if L is 0.5 m then the shear contribution rises to over 40% of the total. If, as is more commonly the case for the values given, L is above 2 m then the shear contribution drops below 5% and may be neglected.

The effects of *torsional moments*, which occur when we have out of plane loads such as in balcony beams, can also be computed by the principle. The derivation of the work expressions parallels that for bending moments. If we let T be torsional moment and J the torsion constant of the cross sections then we have, for internal work caused by a unit load

$$W_i = -\int \frac{T_0 T_1}{GJ}\,dx$$

hence, the deflection can be calculated from

$$W_e + W_i = 0$$

i.e.

$$1 \times \Delta = \int \frac{T_0 T_1}{GJ}\,dx$$

For cylindrical sections J is equal to the polar moment of inertia. The torsion constant for other cross-sections is more complicated, however, suitable accuracy can be achieved if the relationships in Fig. 6.17 are used.

Example 6.13. Determine the deflection at the end of the bent bar shown in Fig. 6.15a.

Situations like this can occur in the design of unusual staircases. It is obvious the section BC will experience a bending moment and section AB a torsional moment and the deflection at C will be the sum of these two. Figure 6.15b shows the M_0 and T_0 systems due to

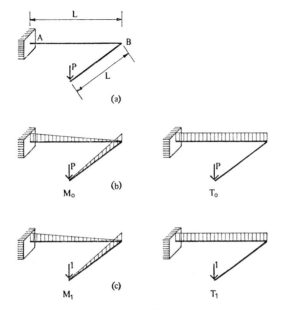

Fig. 6.15.
(a) Bent bar used in Example 6.13.
(b) The bending moments (M_0) and torsional moments (T_0) due to the original load.
(c) The bending moments (M_1) and torsional moments (T_1) due to a unit load at the point where deflection is to be determined.

the original load and Fig. 6.15c the M_1 and T_1 systems due to a unit load at C.

The internal work done by moving the actions due to the unit load at C through the deformations due to the original load is given by

$$W_i = -\left(\int_A^B \frac{T_0 T_1}{GJ}\,\mathrm{d}x + \int_B^C \frac{M_0 M_1}{EI}\,\mathrm{d}x + \int_A^B \frac{M_0 M_1}{EA}\,\mathrm{d}x\right)$$

$$= -\left(\frac{1}{GJ}\int_0^L PL^2\,\mathrm{d}x + \frac{1}{EI}\int_0^L Px^2\,\mathrm{d}x + \frac{1}{EI}\int_0^L Px^2\,\mathrm{d}x\right)$$

$$= -PL^3\left(\frac{1}{GJ} + \frac{2}{3EI}\right)$$

From $W_e + W_i = 0$ we get

$$1 \times \Delta_C = PL^3 \left(\frac{1}{GJ} + \frac{2}{3EI} \right)$$

We can use the principle to analyse hyperstatic beams involving torsional moments as the next example shows.

Example 6.14. Determine the vertical reaction at C on the bent beam of Fig. 6.16a.

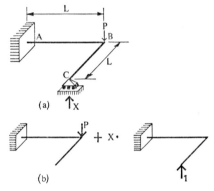

Fig. 6.16.
(a) Hyperstatic bent beam used in Example 6.14.
(b) Modified isostatic structure plus unit load at the redundant.

This beam has one redundant, choose as the redundant the vertical reaction at C (X) (Fig. 6.16b). Determine the deflections at C of the modified structure due to the original load (Δ_0) and due to a unit load at C (Δ_1) and use the compatibility condition of zero actual deflection to calculate X. Since

$$\Delta_0 - X\Delta_1 = 0$$

Δ_0 is the same as the deflection of a simple cantilever, we have already used the principle to determine this as

$$\Delta_0 = \frac{PL^3}{3EI}$$

We have already determined an expression for Δ_1 using the principle in Example 6.13. Hence

$$\frac{PL^2}{3EI} - XL^3\left(\frac{1}{GJ} + \frac{2}{3EI}\right) = 0$$

$$X = \frac{P}{3EI[(1/GJ) + (2/3EI)]}$$

The relationship between X and P shows that when the effect of torsion is neglected the reaction at C is $0.50P$, however when torsion is included it is less than that. If the section is in concrete with a square cross-section, we can show that

$$G = \frac{E}{2.5}$$

and (see Fig. 6.17)

$$J \approx 1.71$$

$$X = 0.27P$$

i.e. only one half of the previous value.

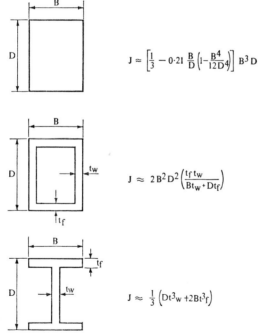

$$J \approx \left[\frac{1}{3} - 0.21\,\frac{B}{D}\left(1 - \frac{B^4}{12D^4}\right)\right] B^3 D$$

$$J \approx 2B^2 D^2\left(\frac{t_f\,t_w}{Bt_w + Dt_f}\right)$$

$$J \approx \frac{1}{3}\left(Dt^3_w + 2Bt^3_f\right)$$

Fig. 6.17.   Torsion constants for various sections.

We can include the effects of *temperature changes* on the deformations of structures. This is done by using as the displacement system the deformations due to the temperature changes and letting the equilibrium system caused by the unit load move through it to produce internal work.

Example 6.15. Determine the deflection of point C of the truss used in Example 6.1 if the top chord members only are subjected to a rise in temperature of t; the coefficient of thermal expansion of the members is c.

We can follow the working of Example 6.1 with the exception that the internal displacements are not due to the force P but to the temperature change as shown in the table below,

Member	d ($\times cLt$)	F_1	F_1d ($\times cLt$)
AB	0	−0·50	0
BC	1·00	−0·50	−0·50
CD	1·00	−0·50	−0·50
DE	0	−0·50	0
EF	0	0	0
FA	0	0	0
BF	0	0·71	0
DF	0	0·71	0
CF	0	−1·00	0

$$\Sigma F_1d = -1\cdot00 \times cLt$$

$$\therefore \qquad 1 \times \Delta_C = -cLt$$

i.e. there is an upward movement at C.

Similarly, we can calculate the deformations of structures composed of beams due to temperature changes. We can include the effects of *wrong dimensions* in the same manner. For hyperstatic structures *elastic foundations* can be included in the analysis by choosing as a redundant the vertical reaction at that point and instead of setting the deflection due to the load on the modified structure plus X times the deflection due to the unit load to zero, set it equal to kX where k is the spring or settlement factor of the foundations.

6.8. Prestressed Trusses

Sometimes trusses have chords prestressed to increase their stiffness. These structures can be analysed as demonstrated in the following example. It should be pointed out that in this book we have been considering only linear or first-order analyses in which deflections are small. To gain an accurate picture of the behaviour of prestressed structures we generally need to include second-order effects.

Example 6.16. Determine the value of the prestress in the lower chord of the truss shown in Fig. 6.4a for there to be zero deflection under the load.

First we need to determine the deflection due to the load. This is done using the virtual displacement principle following the procedure demonstrated in Example 6.1. The results are tabulated below:

Member	F_0 $(\times P)$	F_1	d $\left(\times \dfrac{L}{EA}\right)$	$F_1 d$ $\left(\times \dfrac{PL}{EA}\right)$
AB	0	0	0	0
BC	0	0	0	0
CD	0	0	0	0
DE	0	0	0	0
EF	0·50	0·50	0·50	0·25
FA	0·50	0·50	0·50	0·25
AC	−0·71	−0·71	−1·00	0·71
CE	−0·71	−0·71	−1·00	0·71
CF	0	0	0	0

$$\sum F_1 d = 1 \cdot 92 \frac{PL}{EA}$$

Now we need to determine the upward deflection at C due to a prestress of X in the bottom chord.

The F_0 system is simply the forces in the lower chord, the F_1 system is caused by an upward unit force at C.

Member	F_0 $(\times X)$	F_1	d $\left(\times \dfrac{L}{EA}\right)$	$F_1 d$ $\left(\times \dfrac{XL}{EA}\right)$
AB	0	0	0	0
BC	0	0	0	0
CD	0	0	0	0
DE	0	0	0	0
EF	$-1\cdot00$	$-0\cdot50$	$-1\cdot00$	$0\cdot50$
FA	$-1\cdot00$	$-0\cdot50$	$-1\cdot00$	$0\cdot50$
AC	0	$0\cdot71$	0	0
CE	0	$0\cdot71$	0	0
CF	0	0	0	0

$$\sum F_1 d = 1\cdot00 \frac{XL}{EA}$$

For zero deflection at C these two deflections must be the same, i.e.

$$1\cdot92 \frac{PL}{EA} = 1\cdot00 \frac{XL}{EA}$$

$$\therefore \qquad\qquad X = 1\cdot92P$$

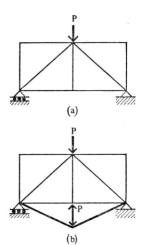

Fig. 6.18.

(a) Simple truss.

(b) Truss in (a) with the addition of sagging prestressed members providing an upward force equivalent to P, hence balancing the load.

An alternative method of increasing the stiffness of trusses is to borrow some of the concepts of prestressed concrete design in particular that of *load-balancing* [6.3], in which the idea is to produce an equal and opposite force to the load through the use of further truss elements which are prestressed. Figure 6.18a shows the simple truss of Fig. 6.4a, by the addition of three members, the two sagging members being prestressed to produce a load equal to P in the vertical member (Fig. 6.18b), we can produce a situation in which there is zero deflection under load. The value of the prestress required is a function of the sag.

These concepts can be extended for the analysis of prestressed beams with sagging truss members and also guyed and suspended buildings.

The principle of virtual displacement represents a generalised approach to the analysis of structures. It is particularly useful in the preliminary analysis of unusual structures although it has been virtually replaced by computer based techniques, many of which are derived from the concepts of the principle, for detailed analysis even of relatively simple frames.

Chapter 7

Computer-Based Methods of Analysis and Design

In this chapter we discuss the two methods of matrix analysis of building frames—the flexibility method and the stiffness method. We show their derivation from basic structural principles of equilibrium and compatibility. We then go on to provide guidelines on the utilisation of computer programs for frame analysis. The chapter concludes with an examination of the application of computers to the design of building frames.

7.1. INTRODUCTION

The digital computer has had a significant effect on many aspects of modern life and structural analysis has been affected to such a degree that the design of the modern building frame is almost entirely dependent on the computer. In the past twenty years structural analysis has been revolutionised by the introduction of *matrix methods* of analysis. These are methods which employ the ability of the computer to be programmed to perform matrix manipulations extremely efficiently. The basis of these methods is still the solution of the equations of equilibrium and compatibility. Part of this chapter is devoted to an introduction to the two methods of formulating structural analysis problems for computer solution through the use of matrices. For the reader who wishes to follow this particular topic beyond the introduction up to the point of being able to implement the techniques on a computer a number of excellent textbooks exist and he is referred to these [B7, B8, 7.1, 7.2].

Although matrix methods of analysis have virtually superseded hand methods for hyperstatic structures, there is still interest in the use of iterative methods such as moment distribution because they can be used on small computers and in some instances can be more efficient than matrix formulations [7.3]. Today it is rare for the designer of building frames to write or even to commission the writing of his own analysis program. He uses programs from service bureaux or ones he has purchased. For readers interested in developing their own programs, an excellent introduction to the general problem of how to formulate engineering problems in suitable computable terms can be found in Reference [7.4]. Now that computer-based methods of analysis have become accepted both by designers and also by regulatory or checking authorities, attention is being turned to the use of the computer in structural design. Initial work on its use in member selection has resulted in a number of relatively cheap programs for this purpose. The newest applications of the computer are in the direction of optimum design, *i.e.*, given an objective and some constraints on the variables, what value should the variables take to maximise or minimise the objective. The variables could be member sizes or even shape of structure. This is the subject of Chapter 13.

7.2. Matrices

A *matrix* is a convenient way of grouping together numbers or symbols arranged in some related manner. Normally this grouping only makes sense if the matrix is to be manipulated. Thus, these computer-based methods of analysis derive their name from the way in which we present the equations to be solved, *i.e.* in matrix form. We shall briefly mention the various types of matrix here; more details may be found in standard texts [7.5].

Let us look at the equations generated in Example 6.5, these could be re-written as

$$a_{11}X_1 + a_{12}X_2 = c_1$$
$$a_{21}X_1 + a_{22}X_2 = c_2$$

and in matrix form as

$$\begin{bmatrix} a_{11} & a_{12} \\ a_{21} & a_{22} \end{bmatrix} \times \begin{bmatrix} X_1 \\ X_2 \end{bmatrix} = \begin{bmatrix} c_1 \\ c_2 \end{bmatrix}$$

where we use the square brackets to indicate that it is a matrix. We could write this in a shorthand as

$$\mathbf{A} \times \mathbf{X} = \mathbf{C}$$

(we shall use bold capital letters to denote a matrix). Thus

$$A = \begin{bmatrix} a_{11} & a_{12} \\ a_{21} & a_{22} \end{bmatrix}$$

$$X = \begin{bmatrix} X_1 \\ X_2 \end{bmatrix}$$

$$C = \begin{bmatrix} c_1 \\ c_2 \end{bmatrix}$$

or more generally

$$A = \begin{bmatrix} a_{11} & a_{12} \cdots a_{1n} \\ a_{21} & a_{22} \cdots a_{1n} \\ \cdot & \cdot \\ \cdot & \cdot \\ \cdot & \cdot \\ a_{m1} & \cdots\cdots a_{mn} \end{bmatrix}$$

We can now say that A is a matrix with m rows and n columns, its general term is a_{ij}, where i indicates the row and j the column of its location.

The size of the matrix is called its *order*.

Types of matrices include:

1. *Square matrix—$m = n$*

$$A = \begin{bmatrix} a_{11} & a_{12} \cdots a_{1m} \\ a_{21} & & \cdot \\ \cdot & & \cdot \\ \cdot & & \cdot \\ \cdot & & \cdot \\ a_{m1} & \cdots\cdots a_{mm} \end{bmatrix}$$

2. *Column matrix*—$n = 1$

$$A = \begin{bmatrix} a_{11} \\ a_{21} \\ . \\ . \\ . \\ a_{m1} \end{bmatrix}$$

3. *Symmetrical matrix*—$a_{ij} = a_{ji}$
   This means that $m = n$

4. *Unit matrix*—$a_{ij} = 1$ for $i = j$ and zero elsewhere

$$I = \begin{bmatrix} 1 & 0 & 0 & 0 & 0 \\ 0 & 1 & 0 & 0 & 0 \\ 0 & 0 & 1 & 0 & 0 \\ 0 & 0 & 0 & 1 & 0 \\ 0 & 0 & 0 & 0 & 1 \end{bmatrix}$$

5. *Transpose of a matrix*—the transpose of **A** is another matrix, **B**, where

$$B = A'$$

sometimes written as A^T, in which

$$b_{ij} = a_{ji}$$

i.e. if

$$A = \begin{bmatrix} a_{11} & a_{12} & a_{13} \\ a_{21} & a_{22} & a_{23} \end{bmatrix}$$

then

$$A' = \begin{bmatrix} a_{11} & a_{21} \\ a_{12} & a_{22} \\ a_{13} & a_{23} \end{bmatrix}$$

Matrix addition is carried out by adding corresponding elements which also means that the two matrices must be of the same order,

$$\begin{bmatrix} a_{11} & a_{12} \\ a_{21} & a_{22} \end{bmatrix} + \begin{bmatrix} b_{11} & b_{12} \\ b_{21} & b_{22} \end{bmatrix} = \begin{bmatrix} (a_{11} + b_{11}) & (a_{12} + b_{12}) \\ (a_{21} + b_{21}) & (a_{22} + b_{22}) \end{bmatrix}$$

which may be written as

$$\mathbf{A} + \mathbf{B} = \mathbf{C}$$

i.e.

$$c_{11} = a_{11} + b_{11}$$

$$c_{21} = a_{21} + b_{21}$$

$$c_{12} = a_{12} + b_{12}$$

$$c_{22} = a_{22} + b_{22}$$

Scalar multiplication is the multiplication of a matrix by a single constant, each element is multiplied by the same scalar.

$$s \times \begin{bmatrix} a_{11} & a_{12} \\ a_{21} & a_{22} \end{bmatrix} = \begin{bmatrix} sa_{11} & sa_{12} \\ sa_{21} & sa_{22} \end{bmatrix}$$

Matrix multiplication is the multiplication of a matrix by another matrix to produce a third matrix. The product

$$\mathbf{A} \times \mathbf{B} = \mathbf{C}$$

may be achieved using the following rule:

The element in row i and column j of the product may be obtained by multiplying each element in row i of matrix $\mathbf{A}$ by the corresponding elements of column j of matrix $\mathbf{B}$ and adding the products.

This is only possible if the number of columns in $\mathbf{A}$ equals the number of rows in $\mathbf{B}$.

e.g.

$$\begin{bmatrix} a_{11} & a_{12} \\ a_{21} & a_{22} \end{bmatrix} \times \begin{bmatrix} b_{11} & b_{12} \\ b_{21} & b_{22} \end{bmatrix} = \begin{bmatrix} a_{11}b_{11} + a_{12}b_{21} & a_{11}b_{12} + a_{12}b_{22} \\ a_{21}b_{11} + a_{22}b_{21} & a_{21}b_{12} + a_{22}b_{22} \end{bmatrix}$$

Therefore

$$\begin{bmatrix} 1 & 0 & 5 & 3 \\ 2 & -1 & 0 & -3 \end{bmatrix} \times \begin{bmatrix} 4 & 1 & -2 \\ 0 & 3 & 2 \\ -1 & 3 & 1 \\ 6 & 0 & 5 \end{bmatrix} = \begin{bmatrix} 17 & 16 & 18 \\ -10 & -1 & -21 \end{bmatrix}$$

Matrix inversion. The inverse or reciprocal of a matrix is needed to solve the set of equations represented by

$$A \cdot X = C$$

i.e.

$$X = A^{-1}C$$

where A^{-1} is the inverse of A and

$$A^{-1} \times A = I$$

The various methods of inverting matrices are not developed here; suffice to note that for a matrix to have an inverse it must be square. The efficiency of this inversion plays an important role in the efficiency of structural analysis computer programs.

7.3. The Flexibility Method

The flexibility method, also known as the force or action method, can be used to analyse hyperstatic structures; we shall first introduce it and then discuss its major disadvantage in terms of using it as the basis for a computerised method. We have already used the concepts of the flexibility method in Chapter 6 when we were analysing hyperstatic trusses and beams. The basis of this method may be summarised as:

Determine the degree of indeterminancy of the structure and release a corresponding number of redundants to produce a released statically determinate structure and hence calculate the resultant deformation discontinuities caused by the absence of the redundants. The redundants are then replaced to restore compatibility and the resultant compatibility equations are solved to determine the redundant actions.

To demonstrate the application of the flexibility method let us examine the beam in Fig. 7.1a. This structure is two-fold indeterminate and, hence, we need to release two redundants. The selection of redundants plays an important role in this method. We shall select the two redundants marked X_1 and X_2 respectively to produce the released structure shown in Fig. 7.1b. The loads acting on the released structure cause displacements as shown in Fig. 7.1c, Δ_1 corresponds to the displacement at X_1 and Δ_2 to the one at X_2. We now need to apply the redundants to the released structure one by one.

When $X_1 = 1$, Fig. 7.1d, we get displacements at both B and C and can denote the one at B by f_{11} and at C by f_{12}. The first subscript

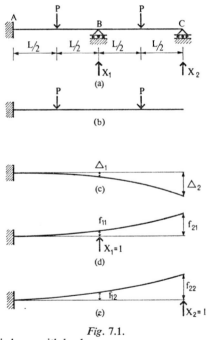

Fig. 7.1.
(a) Hyperstatic beam with loads.
(b) Loads applied to released structure.
(c) Displacements caused by loads applied to released structure.
(d) The flexibility coefficients due to unit load at X_1.
(e) The flexibility coefficients due to unit load at X_2.

indicates which redundant is acting, the second the location of the deformation. These are termed *flexibility coefficients*. Similarly, Fig. 7.1e shows the flexibility coefficients for $X_2 = 1$.

We can now write a set of equations which relate to the compatibility of deformation at B and C for the real structure, since the displacements in the real structure at these points are zero we get

$$\Delta_1 + f_{11}X_1 + f_{12}X_2 = 0$$
$$\Delta_2 + f_{21}X_1 + f_{22}X_2 = 0 \qquad (7.1)$$

These equations are comprised of three parts: the displacement due to the loads, the displacement due to the first redundant X_1 and the displacement due to the second redundant X_2. The superposition of all these displacements gives the actual displacements which are zero. Of course if the actual displacements were not zero we would have non-zero terms on the right-hand side.

The above equations can be written in matrix form as

$$\mathbf{D} + \mathbf{FX} = 0 \qquad (7.2)$$

where $\mathbf{D}$ is the matrix of displacements of the released structure due to the loads, *i.e.*

$$\mathbf{D} = \begin{bmatrix} \Delta_1 \\ \Delta_2 \end{bmatrix}$$

and $\mathbf{F}$ is the flexibility matrix of the released structure corresponding to the redundants

$$\mathbf{F} = \begin{bmatrix} f_{11} & f_{12} \\ f_{21} & f_{22} \end{bmatrix}$$

and

$$\mathbf{X} = \begin{bmatrix} X_1 \\ X_2 \end{bmatrix}$$

The redundants can now be determined from eqn 7.2 as

$$\mathbf{X} = -\mathbf{F}^{-1}\mathbf{D} \qquad (7.3)$$

where $\mathbf{F}^{-1}$ is the inverse of the flexibility matrix. Once $\mathbf{F}$ and $\mathbf{D}$ are known $\mathbf{X}$ can be calculated and hence the structure can be analysed fully.

Example 7.1. Determine the redundants in Fig. 7.1a.

First, we need to calculate **D**, assume that EI is constant throughout. These displacements can be determined by considering the beam in Fig. 7.1c and by the use of the virtual displacement method or through the use of tables [7.6].

The deflections of a cantilever with an intermediate point load (Fig. 7.2) are given by

$$\text{(A to B)} \quad y = \frac{P}{6EI}(-a^3 + 3a^2 L - 3a^2 x)$$

$$\text{(B to C)} \quad y = \frac{P}{6EI}[(x - b)^3 - 3a^2(x - b) + 2a^3]$$

Hence

$$\Delta_1 = \frac{5}{48} \cdot \frac{PL^3}{EI} + \frac{7}{12} \cdot \frac{PL^3}{EI} = \frac{11}{16} \cdot \frac{PL^3}{EI}$$

$$\Delta_2 = \frac{11}{48} \cdot \frac{PL^3}{EI} + \frac{81}{48} \cdot \frac{PL^3}{EI} = \frac{92}{48} \cdot \frac{PL^3}{EI}$$

Therefore

$$\mathbf{D} = \frac{PL^3}{48EI} \cdot \begin{bmatrix} 33 \\ 92 \end{bmatrix}$$

The flexibility matrix can be calculated from its elements

$$f_{11} = \frac{L^3}{3EI}$$

$$f_{12} = \frac{5L^3}{6EI}$$

$$f_{21} = \frac{5L^3}{6EI}$$

$$f_{22} = \frac{8L^3}{3EI}$$

Note that $f_{ij} = f_{ji}$ (Maxwell's theorem), *i.e.* it is symmetrical. Hence

$$\mathbf{F} = \frac{L^3}{6EI} \cdot \begin{bmatrix} 2 & 5 \\ 5 & 16 \end{bmatrix}$$

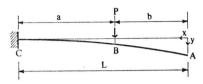

Fig. 7.2. Simple cantilever with point load.

The inverse of this flexibility matrix is given by

$$\mathbf{F}^{-1} = \frac{6EI}{7L^3} \begin{bmatrix} 16 & -5 \\ -5 & 2 \end{bmatrix}$$

Note that the inverse of the flexibility matrix is also symmetrical. We can now determine **X**:

$$\mathbf{X} = -\frac{6EI}{7L^3} \begin{bmatrix} 16 & -5 \\ -5 & 2 \end{bmatrix} \times \frac{PL^3}{48EI} \cdot \begin{bmatrix} 33 \\ 92 \end{bmatrix} = \frac{P}{56} \cdot \begin{bmatrix} 68 \\ 19 \end{bmatrix}$$

Hence

$$X_1 = +\frac{68}{56}P$$

and

$$X_2 = +\frac{19}{56}P$$

It can be seen from the above example that the flexibility matrix is a property of the released statically determinate structure only, whilst the displacement matrix (**D**) can be derived from the real loads and the released structure.

Example 7.2. Determine the redundants of the truss shown in Fig. 6.7a.
Let us choose as the redundants the forces in members AE and EB. We need to calculate **D**, the displacements in the cut members due to the loads acting on the released truss produced by cutting

members AE and EB. These can be calculated using the virtual displacement method (see Example 6.5)

$$\Delta_1 = 1.287 \frac{1}{E}$$

$$\Delta_2 = 1.346 \frac{1}{E}$$

Therefore,

$$\mathbf{D} = \frac{1}{E} \begin{bmatrix} 1.287 \\ 1.346 \end{bmatrix}$$

Now we need to determine the flexibility matrix, the elements of this matrix, f_{ij} can be calculated from the deformations at i due to unit action at j.
Therefore

$$f_{11} = 0.341 \frac{1}{E}$$

$$f_{12} = 0.040 \frac{1}{E}$$

$$f_{21} = 0.040 \frac{1}{E}$$

$$f_{22} = 0.395 \frac{1}{E}$$

Hence

$$\mathbf{F} = \frac{1}{E} \begin{bmatrix} 0.341 & 0.040 \\ 0.040 & 0.395 \end{bmatrix}$$

and

$$\mathbf{F}^{-1} = E \begin{bmatrix} 2.97 & -0.30 \\ -0.30 & 2.56 \end{bmatrix}$$

The redundants can now be found

$$\mathbf{X} = -\mathbf{F}^{-1} . \mathbf{D}$$

$$= -E \begin{bmatrix} 2\cdot97 & -0\cdot30 \\ -0\cdot30 & 2\cdot56 \end{bmatrix} \frac{1}{E} \begin{bmatrix} 1\cdot287 \\ 1\cdot346 \end{bmatrix}$$

$$= \begin{bmatrix} -3\cdot3 \\ -3\cdot1 \end{bmatrix}$$

$$X_1 = -3\cdot3 \text{ kN}$$

$$X_2 = -3\cdot1 \text{ kN}$$

So far we have been looking at the problem of determining the redundants of a hyperstatic structure, however, in analysis we are primarily interested in *reactions* and *member end-actions*. These are the resultant actions at the ends of a member when it is considered to be isolated from the remainder of the structure. Although we can find these once we know the value of the redundants we can also extend this method so that this information is calculated in parallel with the calculations for the redundants. The development of the calculation procedure follows closely that for the determination of redundants. We can at the same time also calculate the *deformations of the structure at the joints*, if we wish to determine the deformation at a point in the structure which does not occur at the junction of two or more members we can treat that point as a fictitious joint.

To demonstrate this additional phase let us go back to the beam shown in Fig. 7.1a and let us suppose that not only do we wish to determine the redundants but also the reactions at the fixed end, the member end-actions and the deformations at the supports. It should be noted that in a beam of this kind only the rotations at joints B and C are of interest. Let us use the matrix **R** to represent the reactions, the matrix **A** to represent the end-actions and the matrix **U** to represent the deformations.

Example 7.3. Determine the reactions, end-actions and joint displacements of the beam in Example 7.1.

The beam is redrawn in Fig. 7.3a showing the reactions and joint

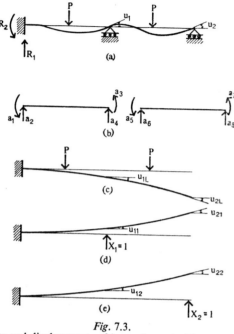

Fig. 7.3.
(a) Reactions and displacements of beam shown in Fig. 7.1a.
(b) End-actions to be determined.
(c) Displacements due to loads on released structure.
(d) Displacements of released structure due to unit load at X_1.
(e) Displacements of released structure due to unit load at X_2.

deformations. Whilst Fig. 7.3b shows the end-actions for the two spans of the beam.

Just as we used the principle of superposition to develop eqn 7.1 so we can use it here. The reactions of the hyperstatic structure are the sum of the reactions of released structure due to the loads and the reactions of the released structure due to the redundants. Thus,

$$r_1 = r_{1L} + r_{11}X_1 + r_{12}X_2$$

where r_{1L} is the reaction at 1 in the released structure due to the load, and r_{ij} is the reaction at i due to a unit load at the redundant j. This may be generalised to

$$\mathbf{R} = \mathbf{R}_L + \mathbf{R}_x \cdot \mathbf{X}$$

For our example

$$R = \begin{bmatrix} r_1 \\ r_2 \end{bmatrix}$$

$$R_L = \begin{bmatrix} r_{1L} \\ r_{2L} \end{bmatrix}$$

$$R_x = \begin{bmatrix} r_{11} & r_{12} \\ r_{21} & r_{22} \end{bmatrix}$$

In a similar manner we can write general expressions for end-actions

$$A = A_L + A_x \cdot X$$

For our example

$$A = \{a_1 \quad a_2 \quad a_3 \quad a_4 \quad a_5 \quad a_6 \quad a_7 \quad a_8\}^*$$

$$A_L = \{a_{1L} \quad a_{2L} \quad a_{3L} \quad a_{4L} \quad a_{5L} \quad a_{6L} \quad a_{7L} \quad a_{8L}\}$$

$$A_x = \begin{bmatrix} a_{11} & a_{12} \\ a_{21} & a_{22} \\ a_{31} & a_{32} \\ a_{41} & a_{42} \\ a_{51} & a_{52} \\ a_{61} & a_{62} \\ a_{71} & a_{72} \\ a_{81} & a_{82} \end{bmatrix}$$

Similarly for joint displacements,

$$U = U_L + U_x \cdot X$$

* We shall use braces { } to indicate a column matrix.

For our example,

$$\mathbf{U} = \begin{bmatrix} u_1 \\ u_2 \end{bmatrix}$$

$$\mathbf{U}_L = \begin{bmatrix} u_{1L} \\ u_{2L} \end{bmatrix}$$

$$\mathbf{U}_x = \begin{bmatrix} u_{11} & u_{12} \\ u_{21} & u_{22} \end{bmatrix}$$

Continuing with our example, we can use the equations of statics to determine the relevant matrices for the calculation of the reactions

$$\mathbf{R}_L = \begin{bmatrix} 2P \\ 2PL \end{bmatrix}$$

$$\mathbf{R}_x = \begin{bmatrix} -1 & -1 \\ -L & -2L \end{bmatrix}$$

The end-actions are the shears and moments; by statics

$$\mathbf{A}_L = \{2PL \quad 2P \quad -PL/2 \quad -P \quad PL/2 \quad P \quad 0 \quad 0\}$$

$$\mathbf{A}_x = \begin{bmatrix} -L & -2L \\ -1 & -1 \\ 0 & L \\ 1 & 1 \\ 0 & -L \\ 0 & -1 \\ 0 & 0 \\ 0 & 1 \end{bmatrix}$$

The joint displacement component matrices can be calculated using the virtual displacement principle. Remember that u_{iL} is the deformation at point i due to the loads on the released structure and u_{ij} is the deformation at point i due to unit load at point j.

Thus, from Fig. 7.3c

$$U_L = \frac{PL^2}{2EI}\begin{bmatrix} 2\cdot25 \\ 2\cdot50 \end{bmatrix}$$

and from Fig. 3.7d and e

$$U_x = \frac{L^2}{2EI}\begin{bmatrix} -1 & -3 \\ -1 & -4 \end{bmatrix}$$

Earlier we found **X**—the redundants

$$\mathbf{X} = \frac{P}{56}\begin{bmatrix} 68 \\ 19 \end{bmatrix} = P\begin{bmatrix} 1\cdot21 \\ 0\cdot34 \end{bmatrix}$$

Therefore, the reactions are given by

$$\mathbf{R} = \begin{bmatrix} 2P \\ 2PL \end{bmatrix} + \begin{bmatrix} -1 & -1 \\ -L & -2L \end{bmatrix} \times P\begin{bmatrix} 1\cdot21 \\ 0\cdot34 \end{bmatrix}$$

$$= \begin{bmatrix} 0\cdot45P \\ 0\cdot11PL \end{bmatrix}$$

i.e. the vertical reaction at the left support is $0\cdot45P$ whilst the moment reaction is $0\cdot11PL$. The reactions can be checked simply by statics. The end-actions are given by

$$\mathbf{A} = \begin{bmatrix} 2PL \\ 2P \\ -PL/2 \\ -P \\ PL/2 \\ P \\ 0 \\ 0 \end{bmatrix} + \begin{bmatrix} -L & -2L \\ -1 & -1 \\ 0 & L \\ 1 & 1 \\ 0 & -L \\ 0 & -1 \\ 0 & 0 \\ 0 & 1 \end{bmatrix} \times P\begin{bmatrix} 1\cdot21 \\ 0\cdot34 \end{bmatrix}$$

$$= \{0\cdot11PL \quad 0\cdot45PL \quad -0\cdot16PL \quad 0\cdot55P \quad 0\cdot16PL \quad 0\cdot66P \quad 0 \quad 0\cdot34P\}$$

And the two rotations by

$$
\mathbf{U} = \frac{PL^2}{2EI}\begin{bmatrix} 2\cdot25 \\ 2\cdot50 \end{bmatrix} + \frac{L^2}{2EI}\begin{bmatrix} -1 & -3 \\ -1 & -4 \end{bmatrix} \times P\begin{bmatrix} 1\cdot21 \\ 0\cdot34 \end{bmatrix}
$$

$$
= \frac{PL^2}{EI}\begin{bmatrix} 0\cdot010 \\ -0\cdot035 \end{bmatrix}
$$

i.e. u_1 is clockwise whilst u_2 is anti-clockwise.

It is possible partially to automate the flexibility method by automatically assembling the flexibility matrix of the released structure from the flexibility sub-matrices of the individual members. The joint displacements of the released structure due to the loads can be represented by

$$
\mathbf{U}_L = \mathbf{F}_m \cdot \mathbf{A}_L
$$

where $\mathbf{F}_m$ represents the individual member flexibilities. For example, for a member with axial-force end-actions $\mathbf{F}_m = [L/EA]$ whilst $\mathbf{A}_L = [P]$, hence

$$
\mathbf{U}_L = \left[\frac{L}{EA}\right] \cdot [P]
$$

Therefore, the displacements of the released structure corresponding to the redundants due to the loads will be given by

$$
\mathbf{D} = \mathbf{A}'_x \cdot \mathbf{F}_m \cdot \mathbf{A}_L
$$

Where $\mathbf{A}'_x$ is the transpose of $\mathbf{A}_x$, needed to allow the multiplication. Note that this formulation can easily be derived from the expressions of the virtual displacement method

$$
\left(\Delta = \int \frac{M_0 M_1}{E}\,\mathrm{d}x \text{ or } \Delta = \sum \frac{P_0 P_1 L}{EA}\right)
$$

We can re-write eqn 7.3 as

$$
\mathbf{X} = -\mathbf{F}^{-1}\mathbf{A}'_x\mathbf{F}_m\mathbf{A}_L
$$

Furthermore the *overall* or *assembled flexibility matrix* (**F**) may be conceived as the matrix of displacements of the released structure corresponding to the redundants due to unit values of the redundants, *i.e.*

$$F = A'_x F_m A_x$$

Hence

$$X = -(A'_x F_m A_x)^{-1} A'_x F_m A_L \tag{7.4}$$

In other words the redundant may be calculated from the member end-actions and the unassembled or member flexibilities.

The member flexibilities represent the deformations of a member due to unit end-actions on that member. Consider the member shown in Fig. 7.4a subjected to three end-actions (A) as shown, the resultant deformations (U) are given (see Fig. 7.4b) by

$$\begin{bmatrix} u_1 \\ u_2 \\ u^3 \end{bmatrix} = \begin{bmatrix} \dfrac{L}{EA} & 0 & 0 \\ 0 & \dfrac{L^3}{3EI} & -\dfrac{L^2}{2EI} \\ 0 & -\dfrac{L^2}{2EI} & \dfrac{L}{EI} \end{bmatrix} \times \begin{bmatrix} a_1 \\ a_2 \\ a_3 \end{bmatrix}$$

Therefore, for a member subjected to axial force only, as in trusses

$$F_m = \begin{bmatrix} \dfrac{L}{EA} \end{bmatrix}$$

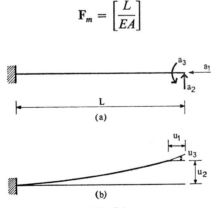

Fig. 7.4.
(a) Member subjected to end-actions.
(b) Deformations due to end-actions.

For a member subjected to shear forces and bending moments only, as in beams or frames neglecting axial effects,

$$\mathbf{F}_m = \begin{bmatrix} \dfrac{L^3}{3EI} & -\dfrac{L^2}{2EI} \\[3ex] -\dfrac{L^2}{2EI} & \dfrac{L}{EI} \end{bmatrix}$$

For a complete structure with n members

$$\mathbf{F}_m = \begin{bmatrix} f_{m1} & 0 \cdots 0 & 0 \\ 0 & f_{m2} & \cdots 0 \\ . & & . \\ . & & . \\ . & & . \\ 0 & \cdots\cdots\cdots & f_{mn} \end{bmatrix}$$

With this formulation it is possible to extend the analysis in a simple and coherent manner to include several load cases and the calculation of displacements at any or all joints.

Example 7.4. Determine the forces in the members of the truss shown in Fig. 7.5a. Assume all members have the same L/EA.

1. Select as redundants the forces in the downward sloping bars.
2. Construct the unassembled flexibility matrix

$$\mathbf{F}_m = \dfrac{L}{EA} \begin{bmatrix} 1 & 0 & 0 & 0 & 0 & 0 & 0 & 0 & 0 & 0 \\ 0 & 1 & 0 & 0 & 0 & 0 & 0 & 0 & 0 & 0 \\ 0 & 0 & 1 & 0 & 0 & 0 & 0 & 0 & 0 & 0 \\ 0 & 0 & 0 & 1 & 0 & 0 & 0 & 0 & 0 & 0 \\ 0 & 0 & 0 & 0 & 1 & 0 & 0 & 0 & 0 & 0 \\ 0 & 0 & 0 & 0 & 0 & 1 & 0 & 0 & 0 & 0 \\ 0 & 0 & 0 & 0 & 0 & 0 & 1 & 0 & 0 & 0 \\ 0 & 0 & 0 & 0 & 0 & 0 & 0 & 1 & 0 & 0 \\ 0 & 0 & 0 & 0 & 0 & 0 & 0 & 0 & 1 & 0 \\ 0 & 0 & 0 & 0 & 0 & 0 & 0 & 0 & 0 & 1 \end{bmatrix}$$

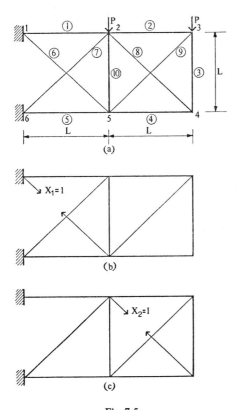

Fig. 7.5.

(a) Hyperstatic truss used in Example 7.4. Circled numbers refer to members, other numbers refer to joints.

(b) Released structure subject to a unit load at X_1.

(c) Released structure subject to a unit load at X_2.

3. Determine the matrix of member end-actions **A** due to unit loads at the redundants, Fig. 7.5b and c

$$\mathbf{A}_x = \begin{bmatrix} -0\cdot71 & 0 \\ 0 & -0\cdot71 \\ 0 & -0\cdot71 \\ 0 & -0\cdot71 \\ -0\cdot71 & 0 \\ 1 & 0 \\ 1 & 0 \\ 0 & 1 \\ 0 & 1 \\ -0\cdot71 & -0\cdot71 \end{bmatrix}$$

4. Determine the matrix of member end-actions due to loads

$$\mathbf{A}_L = P\{3 \quad 1 \quad 0 \quad 0 \quad -1 \quad -2\cdot82 \quad 0 \quad -1\cdot41 \quad 0 \quad 1\}$$

5. Determine $\mathbf{F} = \mathbf{A}'_x \mathbf{F}_m \mathbf{A}_x$

$$\mathbf{A}'_x \mathbf{F}_m =$$
$$\frac{L}{EA} \begin{bmatrix} -0\cdot71 & 0 & 0 & 0 & -0\cdot71 & 1 & 1 & 0 & 0 & -0\cdot71 \\ 0 & -0\cdot71 & -0\cdot71 & -0\cdot71 & 0 & 0 & 0 & 1 & 1 & -0\cdot71 \end{bmatrix}$$

$$\mathbf{A}'_x \mathbf{F}_m \mathbf{A}_x = \frac{L}{EA} \begin{bmatrix} 3\cdot5 & 0\cdot5 \\ 0\cdot5 & 4\cdot0 \end{bmatrix}$$

$$= \mathbf{F}$$

$$\therefore \quad (\mathbf{A}'_x \mathbf{F}_m \mathbf{A}_x)^{-1} = \frac{EA}{L} \begin{bmatrix} 0\cdot291 & -0\cdot036 \\ -0\cdot036 & 0\cdot255 \end{bmatrix}$$

6. Determine $\mathbf{A}'_x \mathbf{F}_m \mathbf{A}_L$
   We have already calculated $\mathbf{A}'_x \mathbf{F}_m$; hence

$$\mathbf{A}'_x \mathbf{F}_m \mathbf{A}_L = \frac{PL}{EA} \begin{bmatrix} -4\cdot95 \\ -2\cdot83 \end{bmatrix}$$

7. Hence determine $\mathbf{X}$

$$\mathbf{X} = (\mathbf{A}'_x \mathbf{F}_m \mathbf{A}_x)^{-1} \mathbf{A}'_x \mathbf{F}_m \mathbf{A}_L$$

$$= \frac{EA}{L} \begin{bmatrix} 0 \cdot 291 & -0 \cdot 036 \\ -0 \cdot 036 & 0 \cdot 255 \end{bmatrix} \times \frac{PL}{EA} \begin{bmatrix} -4 \cdot 95 \\ -2 \cdot 83 \end{bmatrix}$$

$$= P \begin{bmatrix} -1 \cdot 34 \\ -0 \cdot 54 \end{bmatrix}$$

i.e. $X_1 = -1 \cdot 34P$ in the direction opposite to the one assumed
$X_2 = -0 \cdot 54P$ also in the opposite direction to the one assumed

8. The member forces can now be found from

$$\mathbf{A} = \mathbf{A}_L + \mathbf{A}_x \cdot \mathbf{X}$$

$$= P \begin{bmatrix} 3 \\ 1 \\ 0 \\ 0 \\ -1 \\ -2 \cdot 82 \\ 0 \\ -1 \cdot 41 \\ 0 \\ 1 \end{bmatrix} + \begin{bmatrix} -0 \cdot 71 & 0 \\ 0 & -0 \cdot 71 \\ 0 & -0 \cdot 71 \\ 0 & -0 \cdot 71 \\ -0 \cdot 71 & 0 \\ 1 & 0 \\ 1 & 0 \\ 0 & 1 \\ 0 & 1 \\ -0 \cdot 71 & -0 \cdot 71 \end{bmatrix} \times P \begin{bmatrix} -1 \cdot 34 \\ -0 \cdot 54 \end{bmatrix}$$

$$= P\{3 \cdot 95 \quad 1 \cdot 38 \quad 0 \cdot 38 \quad 0 \cdot 38 \quad -0 \cdot 05 \quad -4 \cdot 16 \quad -1 \cdot 34$$
$$-1 \cdot 95 \quad -0 \cdot 54 \quad 2 \cdot 33\}$$

Summary of the Flexibility Method
1. Select the redundants ($\mathbf{X}$) to make the structure, on their release, statically determinate.
2. Determine the member flexibilities based on the member actions and construct the unassembled flexibility matrix ($\mathbf{F}_m$).

3. Determine the end-action matrices of the released structure due to loads (A_L) and redundants (A_x).
4. Determine the reaction matrices of the released structure due to loads (R_L) and redundants (R_x).
5. Determine X from eqn 7.4.
6. Hence, determine the member end-actions (A), the reactions (R) and the displacements (U).

The main disadvantage of the flexibility method as the basis for a computerised analysis technique is that there is no simple way of determining which redundants to release, as their choice can significantly affect the amount of work required to achieve the solution. It is for this reason that virtually all computer-based analysis programs utilise the stiffness method which we shall consider next. However, for hand calculations involving simple structures, the flexibility method leads to an easier formulation of the problem.

7.4. The Stiffness Method

The stiffness method, also known as the displacement or equilibrium method, can be conceived of as the inverse of the flexibility method. Whereas in the flexibility method we released all redundants, in the stiffness methods we *add* restraints to fix all the degrees of freedom. The restraints are released to restore equilibrium. The resulting equilibrium equations are solved for the unknown displacements, hence the remainder of the analysis can be carried out.

To demonstrate the application of the stiffness method let us examine the beam in Fig. 7.1, reproduced in Fig. 7.6a. This structure has two degrees of freedom (at the joints)—it can rotate at B and C. If we included axial effects then we would have to add two further degrees of freedom, namely the horizontal translations of joints B and C. In this method we apply restraints at joints to prevent all joint displacements (Fig. 7.6b) producing a *restrained structure*. The restrained structure is now acted upon by the loads to produce end-actions equivalent to the end-actions of built-in beams, A_L.* These

---

* Note that here and in the following derivation that we are using the same notation as for the flexibility method but with an inverted meaning.

actions correspond to **U** the unknown joint displacements and can be found for various load conditions from Table 5.2. Just as in the flexibility method we applied unit values of the unknowns to determine the flexibility coefficients, in a similar manner we apply unit displacements at the unknown displacements to determine stiffness coefficients. Thus, a unit displacement at u_1, consisting of a unit rotation at B, will generate s_{11} and s_{12} (Fig. 7.6c). Whilst a unit

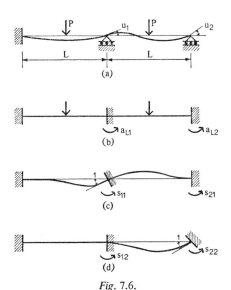

Fig. 7.6.
(a) Two-span beam used in the development of the stiffness method.
(b) Restrained structure produced by fixing all joints.
(c) Stiffness coefficients due to a unit rotation at u_1.
(d) Stiffness coefficients due to a unit rotation at u_2.

rotation at C will generate s_{21} and s_{22} (Fig. 7.6d). These stiffness coefficients are the couples produced at the joints due to the unit rotations. By superposition we can write

$$a_{L1} + s_{11}u_1 + s_{12}u_2 = 0$$

$$a_{L2} + s_{21}u_1 + s_{22}u_2 = 0$$

If there exist moments at the joints being considered then the right hand side of these equations will not be zero; for generality let us include them, they are the actions in the original structure corresponding to the unknown joint displacements, A_u. Thus, these actions are made up of the actions in the restrained structure, corresponding to the unknown joint displacements, the actions due to the loads, the actions due to the displacement u_1 in the restrained structure and the actions due to the displacement u_2.

The above equations can be written in matrix form as

$$A_L + SU = A_u \qquad (7.5)$$

where A_L is the matrix of actions in the restrained structure, corresponding to the unknown joint displacements, due to the loads, *i.e.*

$$A_L = \begin{bmatrix} a_{L1} \\ a_{L2} \end{bmatrix}$$

and S is the stiffness matrix for the unknown joint displacements

$$S = \begin{bmatrix} s_{11} & s_{12} \\ s_{21} & s_{22} \end{bmatrix}$$

The stiffness coefficients for a unit rotation are the end-actions of a built-in beam subject to the unit rotation at one end. They can be easily determined for the virtual displacement method and are shown in Fig. 7.7; these are called *member stiffnesses*.

Fig. 7.7.   Stiffness coefficients of a single member subjected to a unit rotation at one end. These form the member-stiffness matrix.

The determination of the unknown joint displacements can now be carried out from eqn 7.5 by making U the subject of the equation, *i.e.*

$$U = S^{-1}(A_u - A_L) \qquad (7.6)$$

where S^{-1} is the inverse of the stiffness matrix. Once S, A_u and A_L are known, U can be calculated and the structure can be analysed fully.

Example 7.5. Determine the joint displacements at B and C of the beam in Fig. 7.6a.

First we need to fix all joints as shown in Fig. 7.6b and then determine A_u and A_L. Since there are no actions in the original structure corresponding to these displacements

$$A_u = \begin{bmatrix} 0 \\ 0 \end{bmatrix}$$

A_L (see Fig. 7.6b) can be determined from Table 5.2

$$A_L = PL \begin{bmatrix} 0 \\ -0.125 \end{bmatrix}$$

The joint stiffness s_{ij} (Fig. 7.6c and d) can be calculated using the member stiffnesses of Fig. 7.7. For a unit rotation at B moments are caused at B in each of the members coming to B, their value is $4EI/L$ hence,

$$s_{11} = \frac{4EI}{L} + \frac{4EI}{L} = \frac{8EI}{L}$$

This unit rotation at B causes a moment of $2EI/L$ at C, hence

$$s_{21} = \frac{2EI}{L}$$

Similarly,

$$s_{12} = \frac{2EI}{L}$$

and

$$s_{22} = \frac{4EI}{L}$$

All of these are considered positive, taking as our sign convention that anti-clockwise moments are positive. Therefore,

$$S = \frac{EI}{L} \begin{bmatrix} 8 & 2 \\ 2 & 4 \end{bmatrix}$$

and

$$S^{-1} = \frac{L}{EI} \begin{bmatrix} 0.143 & -0.071 \\ -0.071 & 0.286 \end{bmatrix}$$

Using eqn 7.6 we get

$$\mathbf{U} = \frac{L}{EI}\begin{bmatrix} 0{\cdot}143 & -0{\cdot}071 \\ -0{\cdot}071 & 0{\cdot}286 \end{bmatrix} \times \left\{ \begin{bmatrix} 0 \\ 0 \end{bmatrix} - PL\begin{bmatrix} 0 \\ -0{\cdot}125 \end{bmatrix}\right\}$$

$$= \frac{PL^2}{EI}\begin{bmatrix} -0{\cdot}009 \\ +0{\cdot}036 \end{bmatrix}$$

which, within slide rule accuracy, is the same result we arrived at in Example 7.3.

We can now determine the member end-actions and the reactions in a manner paralleling that for the flexibility method, by superposition of the actions caused by the loads on the restrained structure and the actions caused by unit displacements at the joints in the restrained structure multiplied by the value of those displacements. For member actions we get

$$\mathbf{A} = \mathbf{A}_L + \mathbf{A}_v\mathbf{U} \tag{7.7}$$

In order to allow for actions in members at joints which are not to be released we have to use another term $(\mathbf{A}_v)$ for the end actions caused by unit displacements.

Similarly, the reactions may be obtained from

$$\mathbf{R} = \mathbf{R}_L + \mathbf{R}_v\mathbf{U} \tag{7.8}$$

where $\mathbf{R}$ is the matrix of reactions in the original structure, $\mathbf{R}_L$ is the matrix of reactions in the restrained structure due to the loads (except those occurring at the unknown displacements) and $\mathbf{R}_v$ is the matrix of reactions in the restrained structure due to unit displacements.

Example 7.6. Determine the member end-actions and the reactions for the beam in Example 7.5.

The four reactions $(\mathbf{R})$ are shown in Fig. 7.8a and the eight member end-actions are shown in Fig. 7.8b. From the restrained structure of Fig. 7.6b the $\mathbf{A}_L$ and $\mathbf{R}_L$ can simply be determined as

$$\mathbf{A}_L = \{0{\cdot}125PL \ 0{\cdot}5P \ -0{\cdot}125PL \ 0{\cdot}5P \ 0{\cdot}125PL \ 0{\cdot}5P \ -0{\cdot}125PL \ 0{\cdot}5P\}$$

and

$$\mathbf{R}_L = \{0{\cdot}125PL \ \ 0{\cdot}5P \ \ 1{\cdot}0P \ \ 0{\cdot}5P\}$$

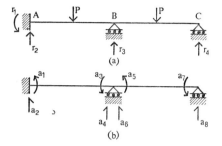

(a)

(b)

Fig. 7.8.
(a) The beam used in Example 7.6 showing the four reactions.
(b) The eight member end-actions to be calculated.

The $\mathbf{A}_v$ and $\mathbf{R}_v$ matrices can be determined from Fig. 7.6c and d
and from Fig. 7.7. For example a_{v11} is the moment at A in member
AB due to the unit rotation at B, hence, $a_{v11} = 2EI/L$. Also, a_{v21}
is the shear at A due to the unit rotation at B, hence, $a_{v21} = 6EI/L^2$.
Therefore,

$$\mathbf{A}_v = \frac{EI}{L^2} \begin{bmatrix} 2L & 0 \\ 6 & 0 \\ 4L & 0 \\ -6 & 0 \\ 4L & 2L \\ 6 & 6 \\ 2L & 4L \\ -6 & -6 \end{bmatrix}$$

and

$$\mathbf{R}_v = \frac{EI}{L^2} \begin{bmatrix} 2L & 0 \\ 6 & 0 \\ 0 & 6 \\ -6 & -6 \end{bmatrix}$$

Hence,

$$
\mathbf{A} =
\begin{bmatrix}
0{\cdot}125PL \\
0{\cdot}5P \\
-0{\cdot}125PL \\
0{\cdot}5P \\
0{\cdot}125PL \\
0{\cdot}5P \\
0{\cdot}125PL \\
0{\cdot}5L
\end{bmatrix}
+ \frac{EI}{L^2}
\begin{bmatrix}
2L & 0 \\
6 & 0 \\
4L & 0 \\
-6 & 0 \\
L & 2L \\
6 & 6 \\
2L & 4L \\
-6 & -6
\end{bmatrix}
\times \frac{PL^2}{EI}
\begin{bmatrix}
-0{\cdot}009 \\
0{\cdot}036
\end{bmatrix}
$$

$$\mathbf{A} = \{0{\cdot}11PL \quad 0{\cdot}45P \quad -0{\cdot}16PL \quad 0{\cdot}55P \quad 0{\cdot}16PL \quad 0{\cdot}66P \quad 0 \quad 0{\cdot}34P\}$$

and

$$
\mathbf{R} =
\begin{bmatrix}
0{\cdot}125PL \\
0{\cdot}5P \\
1{\cdot}0P \\
0{\cdot}5P
\end{bmatrix}
+ \frac{EI}{L^2}
\begin{bmatrix}
26 & 0 \\
6 & 0 \\
0 & 6 \\
-6 & -6
\end{bmatrix}
\times \frac{PL^2}{EI}
\begin{bmatrix}
-0{\cdot}009 \\
0{\cdot}036
\end{bmatrix}
$$

$$\mathbf{R} = \{0{\cdot}11PL \quad 0{\cdot}45P \quad 1{\cdot}21P \quad 0{\cdot}34P\}$$

Both of these results agree with those determined by the flexibility method in Example 7.3.

Member stiffnesses form the basis of the stiffness method, these stiffnesses are a function not only of the type of action possibly experienced by the member but also the degrees of freedom at its ends. A beam element can experience both rotation, as shown in Fig. 7.7, and translation, as shown in Fig. 7.9. Members which

Fig. 7.9. The stiffness coefficients for a beam undergoing translation only.

experience axial forces have a member stiffness matrix which consists of one element only

$$s_m = \frac{EA}{L}$$

Members which act in three dimensions may also experience bending in two directions as well as torsional moments and suitable member stiffness matrices may be developed for these.

The most common member in building frames is one subjected to both axial forces and bending action. If such a member is allowed both to rotate and to translate one end with respect to the other we can derive its stiffness matrix. The member stiffness matrix can be written as

$$A = S_m U$$

the displacements are shown in Fig. 7.10 and the result written as

$$
\begin{bmatrix} a_1 \\ a_2 \\ a_3 \\ a_4 \\ a_5 \\ a_6 \end{bmatrix}
=
\begin{bmatrix}
\dfrac{4EI}{L} & \dfrac{6EI}{L^2} & \dfrac{2EI}{L} & -\dfrac{6EI}{L^2} & 0 & 0 \\[2ex]
\dfrac{6EI}{L^2} & \dfrac{12EI}{L^3} & \dfrac{6EI}{L^2} & -\dfrac{12EI}{L^3} & 0 & 0 \\[2ex]
\dfrac{2EI}{L} & \dfrac{6EI}{L^2} & \dfrac{4EI}{L^2} & -\dfrac{6EI}{L^2} & 0 & 0 \\[2ex]
-\dfrac{6EI}{L^2} & -\dfrac{12EI}{L^3} & -\dfrac{6EI}{L^2} & \dfrac{12EI}{L^3} & 0 & 0 \\[2ex]
0 & 0 & 0 & 0 & \dfrac{EA}{L} & -\dfrac{EA}{L} \\[2ex]
0 & 0 & 0 & 0 & -\dfrac{EA}{L} & \dfrac{EA}{L}
\end{bmatrix}
\times
\begin{bmatrix} u_1 \\ u_2 \\ u_3 \\ u_4 \\ u_5 \\ u_6 \end{bmatrix}
$$

It is possible to automate the stiffness method by first referring the member stiffnesses of inclined members to a global co-ordinate system by a transformation matrix and building up the joint-stiffness matrix for the structure from the member-stiffness sub-matrices in a manner analogous to the development of the structure-flexibility matrix in Section 7.3.

Fig. 7.10.   The six displacements (*u*) corresponding to the six possible end-actions
(*a*). These are used to generate the member-stiffness matrix.

7.5. COMPUTER-BASED ANALYSIS OF BUILDING FRAMES

The stiffness method is most commonly used in computer-based
structural analysis because the restrained structure can be automatically produced by fixing all the joints.

Computer programs for the analysis of structures are readily
available. These programs can be generally broken into five stages
[B8, 7.2, 7.7].

1. *Assembly of Structure Data*
    (i) structure parameters
    (ii) elastic moduli
    (iii) joint co-ordinates
    (iv) member properties
    (v) joint restraints

2. *Generation and Inversion of Stiffness Matrix*
    (i) generation of stiffness matrix from member-stiffness sub-
    matrices
    (ii) inversion of stiffness matrix

3. *Assembly of Load Data*
    (i) actions applied at joints
    (ii) actions at ends of restrained members due to loads

4. *Generation of Load Matrices*
    (i) equivalent joint loads may be determined from member
    end-actions
    (ii) combined joint loads may be determined from equivalent
    joint loads and the actions applied at joints

5. *Calculation of Results*

Through the use of eqns 7.6, 7.7 and 7.8 all the required results can be calculated:

(i) joint displacements
(ii) member end-actions
(iii) reactions

The entire process of structural design using the computer in analysis is exemplified in the flow chart of Fig. 7.11.

General purpose computer programs, *i.e.* ones that will analyse any general structure, tend to be less efficient than special programs written for the analysis of specific structural forms, particularly when we include the data preparation time. Often the cost of data preparation and data input and output will exceed the computing cost of the analysis. Chapter 11 includes several discussions on the criteria for the selection of suitable computer programs for the analysis of building frames.

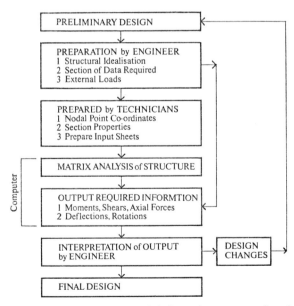

Fig. 7.11.   The flowchart for structural design using computer-based analysis.

Data output via *computer graphics* provides a simple and useful means of checking the geometry of the input data and for obtaining an overall qualitative appreciation of the results (Fig. 7.12). It is a relatively simple matter to write a computer program which will take the building frame geometry and output moments, shears, axial forces and deflections and produce graphical plots of them. However, at the time of writing the cost of these plots can be comparable to the computing cost of the analysis.

The *acceptance of computer-based analysis*, whether by the building designer or by some regulatory authority when the computer program was written by a third party, has been the subject of some investigation [7.8] and guidelines have been developed. They can be grouped under four general headings [7.9]:

1. *Information Supplied by the Designer About the Problem*
A statement of the design criteria used and a diagram showing the loading conditions and the structure assumed.

2. *Information Required on the Computer Program*
   (i) description of problems to be solved by the program
   (ii) theory of analysis, including references
   (iii) assumptions made in the program
   (iv) design constants used in the program
   (v) storage requirements

3. *Verification of the Computer Program*
   (i) computer solution of test problems
   (ii) check of solution against an alternative method

4. *Input/Output and Data Requirements*
   (i) guide to input/output (users' manual)
   (ii) reprinting of all input data by program

7.6. COMPUTER-BASED DESIGN OF BUILDING FRAMES

With the computer being utilised to analyse building frames its use is being extended into the area of the design of these frames. Most of the computer programs developed for structural design are iterative in nature, however, optimum design concepts are being

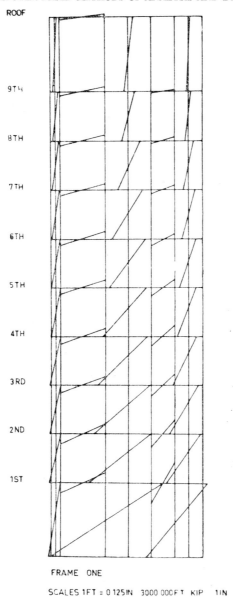

FRAME ONE

SCALES 1FT = 0 125IN   3000 000F T KIP   1IN

Fig. 7.12.   A computer-produced graphical plot of the moments in a building frame.

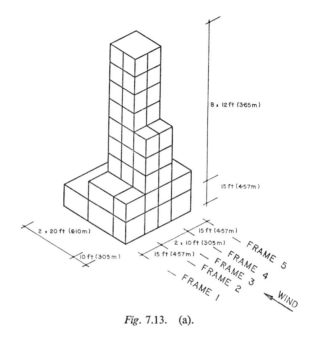

Fig. 7.13. (a).

applied; these are discussed in Chapter 13. Iterative structural design computer programs [7.10–15] generally follow the procedure given below:

1. the designer selects the structural form and the structural configuration that satisfies the requirements of the overall design problem;
2. he enters this information and any special loading requirements into the system, which probably consists of a series of programs;
3. the system performs a load distribution to determine member loads;
4. the system then performs a preliminary design to determine section sizes;
5. the system then performs an analysis based on the preliminary design of the sections;
6. the system then checks the suitability of the sections based on pre-defined criteria;
7. the system then re-designs the sections as necessary;

INPUT DATA

DIMENSIONS   50 FT DEEP × 50 FT WIDE × 9 STOREYS HIGH

STOREY HEIGHTS   TOP 12 FT GRND 15 FT OTHERS 12 FT

SPACING OF FRAMES   1 AT 15 FT, 2 AT 10 FT, 1 AT 15 FT

BAY SIZES   2 FRAMES FRAMES 1 AND 5 HAVE 3 BAYS 10,20,20 FT
            3 FRAMES FRAMES 2,3 AND 4 HAVE 4 BAYS 10,10,10,20 FT

SHEAR WALLS   1 FRAME FRAME 3 HAS A WALL 20 FT WIDE

STARTING 10.0 FT IN FROM
THE FRONT STARTING IN STOREY 1 ENDING IN STOREY 3 I=333.33
FT4 A=10.0 FT2
FRONT SETBACK   10 FT WITH 4 STOREYS ABOVE

BACK SETBACK   20 FT WITH 8 STOREYS ABOVE

LEFT SETBACK   15 FT WITH 7 STOREYS ABOVE

RIGHT SETBACK 15 FT WITH 7 STOREYS ABOVE

MISSING INTERIOR COLUMN FRAME 3 STOREY 9 COLUMN 3

DEAD LOADING VERTICAL   100 PSF

LIVE LOADING VERTICAL   100 PSF

WIND SPEED   70 MPH

END OF DATA

(b).

Fig. 7.13. A problem-oriented language for input of information to an automated structural-design program reduces the need to rely on formats and
provides the user with a concise method of presenting data.
(a) Structure to be described.
(b) Description of structure in a problem-oriented language. (Note that the
complete geometry of this nine-storey building including specification of
shear walls is given in thirteen statements.)

8. if sections have been changed the system returns to 5 (the analysis)
and repeats procedures 5 to 8 until there is no change in section
size; at that point the final design has been reached.

Such a system (Fig. 7.13) would be considered as a fully automated design system. With suitable design rules to determine the

STOREY   SELECTED MEMBER SIZES   FRAMES 1 & 5

```
         ┌--- 1005.025 ---┬--- 1206.027 ---┐
  2      │                │                │
      606│016         606│020          606│016
         ├--- 805.017 ---┼--- 1406.030 ---┼--- 1406.030 ---┐
  1      │                │                │                │
      606│016         606│020          606│020          606│016
```

STOREY   SELECTED MEMBER SIZES   FRAMES 2 & 4

```
                         ┌--- 805.017 ---┬--- 805.017 ---┐
  9                      │               │               │
                      606│016         606│016         606│016
                         ├--- 805.017 ---┼--- 805.017 ---┤
  8                      │               │               │
                      606│016         606│020         606│016
                         ┌--- 805.017 ---┼--- 805.017 ---┤
  7                      │               │               │
                      606│016         606│020         606│016
                         ├--- 805.017 ---┼--- 805.017 ---┤
  6                      │               │               │
                      606│016         606│020         606│016
             ┌--- 805.017 ---┼--- 805.017 ---┼--- 805.017 ---┤
  5          │               │               │               │
          606│016         606│020         606│020         606│016
             ├--- 805.017 ---┼--- 805.017 ---┼--- 805.017 ---┤
  4          │               │               │               │
          606│016         606│020         808│031         606│016
             ├--- 805.017 ---┼--- 805.017 ---┼--- 805.017 ---┤
  3          │               │               │               │
          606│016         606│020         808│031         606│016
             ├--- 805.017 ---┼--- 805.017 ---┼--- 805.017 ---┤
  2          │               │               │               │
          606│016         606│020         808│031         606│016
             ├--- 805.017 ---┼--- 805.017 ---┼--- 1406.030 ---┼--- 1406.034 ---┐
  1          │               │               │               │                │
          606│020         808│031         808│031         808│031         808│031
```

Fig. 7.14.

STOREY   SELECTED MEMBER SIZES   FRAME 3

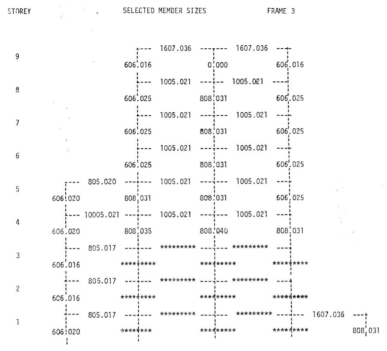

Fig. 7.14.   The resultant design of the various frames of the structure described in Fig. 7.13.

Notation: The steel section sizes are designated by *ddwwmmm*, where *dd* is the depth (in inches), *ww* the width (in inches) and *mmm* the weight per unit length (pounds per foot). Thus, 1406.030 represents a beam of depth 14 in, width 6 in and weight per ft of 30 lb. Where a shear wall occurs it is designated by a series of asterisks.

section sizes in the preliminary design only two to four iterations are required to produce the final design for buildings composed of frames with beam and column members. Considerable work has gone into developing *problem-oriented languages* to place at the front of such systems so that the designer may use the language of the problem to input the data rather than a set of fixed rules relating to the location of the numerical values of the data (Fig. 7.14). In addition, interaction with the computer is being obtained through the use of graphics consoles or terminals which allow the user to communicate directly with the system [7.16–18].

Chapter 8

Buckling

In this chapter we examine a problem quite different to the ones relating to either strength or stiffness that we have been considering so far. That problem is buckling or stability. Firstly, we derive the equations for column buckling and for the buckling of individual members. After a brief discussion of the problems associated with local and torsion buckling we go on to examine the buckling of frames. Here, we derive a graphical method for the simple and rapid buckling analysis of a variety of frames. The utility of this method is demonstrated through examples which show its application both to the design of frames against buckling and to the checking of frames to ensure that frames designed for both strength and stiffness will not fail in buckling.

8.1. COLUMN BUCKLING

The formula published by Leonard Euler in 1744 for the buckling of very slender elastic columns is the oldest structural formula still in use today. It is interesting to note that this complicated problem was solved half a century before the simple theory of bending.*

The mathematical difficulty of the buckling theory, by the standards of engineering education in the early 19th century, was one reason why it did not find ready acceptance in England, where simple empirical formulae persisted to the end of the 19th century. Secondly, Euler's theory deals with the buckling of perfectly elastic columns, and thus gives a load-bearing capacity higher than that of actual structural columns which deform partly elastically, and partly

---

* Any theoretical discussion of buckling problems necessarily involves the use of mathematics which is unfamiliar to some architects. The results derived in this chapter can, however, be used without following the derivations of the formulae. The latter are printed in small type which may be omitted without loss of continuity.

plastically, during buckling. The Euler formula thus represents the upper bound which is reached only if the column remains fully elastic during buckling.

It is perfectly possible for a column to buckle elastically without structural damage (Fig. 8.1) provided the material has a high strength in relation to its elasticity (as in spring steel), and provided the

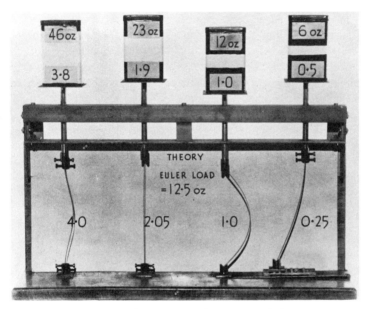

Fig. 8.1. Elastic column buckling. (From left to right: Built-in column; column built-in at one end and pinned at the other; pin-jointed column; cantilever column.) The columns are loaded by a depth of lead-shot equal to the white band. *Architectural Science Laboratory, University of Sydney.*

column is sufficiently slender (thin in relation to its length). Buckled columns are employed deliberately, *e.g.* in some load control devices and instruments, because a small increase in load produces a large deflection. The *elastic instability* caused by buckling constitutes structural failure, even if no structural damage results.

Buckling seriously reduces the strength of some compression members. We derived in Section 4.3 the load-bearing capacity of tension or compression members based on the strength of the material. Tension members can only fail by direct overstressing, and consequently a material, such as steel, which has equal strength on tension and compression (see Section 3.6) is used more advantageously in tension. A material, such as concrete, which has low tensile strength, is used more advantageously in compression; particularly as concrete members are usually of massive thickness in relation to their length so that buckling is not a serious problem.

Since steel structures cannot be built without compression members, buckling must be considered as a secondary effect in architectural design. Occasionally it must be considered for long concrete columns, for masonry walls, or for thin concrete shells. Buckling is a primary design factor in aircraft structures, where very thin columns and shells are employed to save weight. Most of the recent work on buckling has therefore been done by aeronautical engineers.

8.2. THE EULER AND THE RANKINE FORMULAE

Let us consider a slender elastic column simply supported at both ends, as for example the second from the right shown in Fig. 8.1. The column buckles perfectly elastically at a load P_e, called the Euler load.

Let us further assume that the column deflects sideways by a distance a at the centre (Fig. 8.2). We will now consider a point, which is a distance x above the centre point and has a sideways deflection y relative to the centre point.

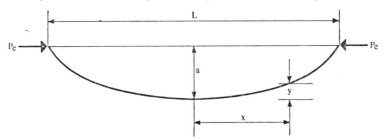

Fig. 8.2.   Euler's theory of the elastic buckling of pin-jointed columns.

From eqn 5.4 the deflection

$$y = \int \int \frac{M}{EI} \, dx \, dx$$

so that

$$\frac{d^2 y}{dx^2} = \frac{M}{EI}$$

Because of the sideways deflection the column is subjected to a bending moment which increases towards the centre point. At the point (x, y)

$$M = P_e(a - y)$$

Putting $k^2 = P_e/EI$ for convenience in writing down the following equations we obtain a linear differential equation

$$\frac{d^2y}{dx^2} + k^2(y - a) = 0$$

whose solution* is

$$y = A \sin kx + B \cos kx + a \tag{8.1}$$

where A and B are constants of integration, which must be determined from the boundary conditions. These are:

(i) at $x = 0$, the sideways deflection $y = 0$, which gives $B = -a$.
(ii) at $x = 0$, the slope $dy/dx = 0$

Differentiating eqn 8.1

$$\frac{dy}{dx} = Ak \cos kx - Bk \sin kx$$

Equating this to zero, we get $A = 0$.
Substituting boundary conditions (i) and (ii) into eqn 8.1

$$y = a(1 - \cos kx)$$

(iii) The third boundary condition is that at the ends $x = -\frac{1}{2}L$ and $y = a$, which gives

$$a \cos \tfrac{1}{2}kL = 0$$

This is satisfied either when $a = 0$, which means that no buckling occurs because there is no sideways deflection, or when

$$\cos \tfrac{1}{2}kL = 0$$

The cosine is zero when $\frac{1}{2}kL$ is $\frac{1}{2}\pi, \frac{3}{2}\pi, \frac{5}{2}\pi$, etc., and elastic stability can be attained in the laboratory when the load is increased above the first buckling mode until the second buckling mode is reached. In building construction this is impractical, since the structure collapses as soon as the first buckling mode is reached.

$$\tfrac{1}{2}kL = \tfrac{1}{2}\pi$$

and the Euler load

$$P_e = \pi^2 EI/L^2 \tag{8.2}$$

It is convenient to express the Euler load in terms of the *slenderness ratio*, L/r.

In this expression the *radius of gyration* $r = (I/A)^{\frac{1}{2}}$, where I is

---

* See any mathematics book which covers the elementary theory of differential equations.

the second moment of area and A is the cross-sectional area of the column. Thus, for a circular reaction $r = \frac{1}{4}D$, where D is the diameter. For a square section $r = d/\sqrt{12}$, where d is the side of the square. For a rectangular section also $r = d/\sqrt{12}$, where d is the length of the shorter side of the rectangle, if the section is not restrained from failing in the direction of least depth.

The *effective length* (L) is the length of an equivalent column, pin-jointed at the ends. In a built-in column (Fig. 8.3b) the half-length of the pin-jointed column, $\frac{1}{2}L$, repeats itself four times in the

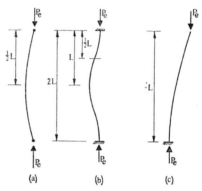

Fig. 8.3. Effective length of Euler columns. A built-in column 8 m long, a pin-jointed column 4 m long and a cantilever column 2 m long all have the same strength in buckling if the material and the cross-section are the same.

geometry of the deformed shape, and a 8 m built-in column thus has the same Euler load as a 4 m pin-jointed column of the same cross-section and material. Similarly a cantilever column had only one curve corresponding to the half-length of the pin-jointed column, and a 2 m cantilever column thus has the same Euler load as a 4 m pin-jointed column or a 8 m built-in column of the same cross section and material.

In practice columns are never fully built in, but a rigid connection or a heavy floor slab can exercise appreciable restraint. At the other end of the scale, architectural columns are never cantilevered, but in light single-storey construction there may be considerable freedom of sideway. The effective lengths of columns with various degrees of restraint are generally laid down in building codes for steel, aluminium and concrete construction, and they vary from 0·7L for firmly restrained columns to 1·5L for columns with freedom of sidesway.

Equation 8.2 may be expressed in terms of the slenderness ratio L/r as an Euler stress

$$f_e = \frac{P_e}{A} \pi^2 (r/L)^2 \qquad (8.3)$$

where π is the circular constant 3·1416. It follows that the Euler load P_e and the Euler stress f_e are independent of the strength of material, since the yield stress, proof stress or ultimate stress do not appear in the equations. It is, however, dependent on the modulus of elasticity (E) of the material.

From eqn 4.4 the limiting short column load and stress

$$f_s = \frac{P_s}{A} = f_y \qquad (8.4)$$

where f_y is the limiting stress, *i.e.* the yield stress for mild steel, the proof stress for aluminium alloys and high-tensile steels, and the crushing stress for concrete. The short column stress is independent of the modulus of elasticity.

Buckling is a problem mainly in metal columns, because concrete columns usually have low slenderness ratios. The limiting stress of both iron and aluminium can be increased by several hundred per cent through suitable alloying, heat-treatment or cold-working; but none of these improvements in strength appreciably alter the modulus of elasticity (see Section 3.4). Buckling is therefore a particular problem with high-strength alloys. Furthermore it is a more serious problem in aluminium alloys, because E is only 69 GPa (10×10^6 lb/in^2), as compared with 200 GPa (30×10^6 lb/in^2) for steel.

The Euler and the short-column formulae, eqns 8.3 and 8.4, are plotted in Fig. 8.4. For low slenderness ratios the Euler load is not reached, because the material fails at a lower stress. For very high slenderness ratios the column buckles elastically in accordance with the Euler theory, provided it is perfectly straight and perfectly concentrically loaded; if the load is removed, the column recovers

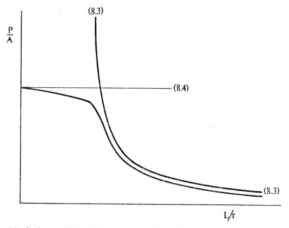

Fig. 8.4. Variation of buckling stress (f) with slenderness ratio (L/r). The straight line for f_s (8.4) represents the short-column failure, which is independent of the modulus of elasticity. The hyperbola for f_e (8.3) represents the Euler load which is independent of the strength of the material. The actual buckling strength falls below both curves. The Rankine curve corresponds to

$$\frac{1}{f} = \frac{1}{f_s} + \frac{1}{f_e}.$$

elastically. In practice columns in architectural structures have much lower slenderness ratio, and the material is therefore damaged if the column buckles. The stress at failure then falls below the Euler curve. The Euler formula is still widely used, particularly in American structural codes.

There are several empirical, semi-empirical and theoretical formulae which allow for the simultaneous failure by buckling and by overstressing. The best of the semi-empirical formulae is the one proposed by Professor W. J. M. Rankine in the late 19th century.

The Rankine formula takes the short-column and the Euler equations as the limiting values for zero and infinite slenderness ratios, and then uses a simple interaction, which gives the Rankine column load (P).

$$\frac{1}{P} = \frac{1}{P_s} + \frac{1}{P_e} \qquad (8.5)$$

This is shown as the lower curve on Fig. 8.4.

8.3. The Perry and the Secant Formulae

A more sophisticated approach, used in many modern building codes, allows for the inevitable imperfections of practical columns. Even with very high slenderness ratios the Euler load can be reached only if the column is perfectly straight and perfectly concentrically loaded. The problem of elastic instability has some resemblance to that of gravitational instability; a needle can be balanced on its point if it is plumbed so perfectly that the centre of gravity is directly above the point, but this is almost impossible in practice.

Instead of allowing for both the inevitable lack of straightness and the inevitable eccentricity of loading (both geometrically very slight imperfections which, however, produce substantial reductions in strength) current column formulae assume either one of these imperfections only, with an allowance for the other. The British and Australian steel codes employ the Perry formula, which assumes that the column is initially slightly curved, and its departure from straightness is given by

$$y_0 = c_0 \cos \pi x/L$$

where c_0 is the lack of straightness at the centre of the column, and y_0 the lack of straightness at a distance x from the centre (Fig. 8.5).

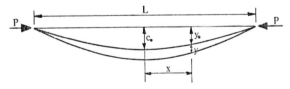

Fig. 8.5.   Elastic buckling of initially curved columns (*Perry formula*).

At a point (x, y) the bending moment is then

$$M = -P(y_0 + y)$$

where P is the buckling load according to the Perry formula.

Following the method used in Section 8.2, we obtain the differential equation

$$\frac{d^2y}{dx^2} + k^2(y + c_0 \cos \pi x/L) = 0$$

where $k^2 = P/EI$.

The solution is

$$y = A \sin kx + B \cos kx + \frac{k^2 c_0 \cos \pi x/L}{\pi^2/L^2 - k^2}$$

The constants of integration A and B are obtained from the boundary conditions: $y = 0$ for $x = +\frac{1}{2}L$ and for $x = -\frac{1}{2}L$, which gives $A = B = 0$. Hence

$$y = \frac{Pc_0}{P_e - P} \cos \pi x/L$$

since $P = k^2 EI$ and the Euler load (from eqn 8.2) $P_e = \pi^2 EI/L^2$. The total deflection

$$y + y_0 = \left(\frac{P}{P_e - P} + 1\right) c_0 \cos \pi x/L$$

which has a maximum value at $x = 0$ (where the cosine $= 1$).

$$y_{max} = P_e c_0/(P_e - P)$$

The maximum bending moment

$$M_{max} = P y_{max} = PP_e c_0/(P_e - P)$$

The maximum compressive stress occurs on the concave side of the column It is the sum of the stress due to bending (My_c/I) (where y_c is the distance of most stressed compressive part of the column from its neutral axis), and the direct compressive stress, P/A.

$$f_{max} = \frac{PP_e c_0 y_c}{(P_e - P)I} + \frac{P}{A}$$

The maximum compressive stress at failure $f_{max} = f_y$, the yield proof, or crushing stress. The Euler stress $f_e = P_e/A$ and the maximum average stress in the column according to the Perry formula $f = P/A$. Introducing the term $\eta = c_0 y_c A/I$, we get

$$f_y = \frac{ff_e \eta}{f_e - f} + 1 \qquad (8.6)$$

The maximum average stress at buckling is therefore

$$f = \frac{1}{2}[f_y + (\eta + 1)f_e] - \{\frac{1}{4}[f_y + (\eta + 1)f_e]^2 - f_y f_e\}^{\frac{1}{2}} \qquad (8.7)$$

The ratio $\eta = c_0 y_c/r^2$ depends on the quality of the fabricating methods, which determine the curvature c_0, and the cross-sectional dimensions c_0 and r (the radius of gyration $= (I/A)^{\frac{1}{2}}$). It is determined from experimental data and is of the order $\eta = 0 \cdot 003 L/r$.

In the Secant formula, which is frequently used in American steel and aluminium codes, the initial imperfection is assumed to be a small eccentricity of loading (ε) (Fig. 8.6).

The bending moment at a point (x, y) is therefore

$$M = P(\varepsilon + a - y)$$

and the differential equation

$$\frac{d^2y}{dx^2} + k^2(\varepsilon + a - y) = 0$$

where $k^2 = P/EI$.

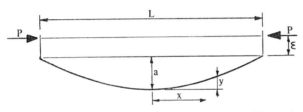

Fig. 8.6. Elastic buckling of eccentrically loaded columns (*Secant formula*).

The solution is

$$y = A \sin kx + B \cos kx + \varepsilon + a$$

Since the deflection $y = 0$ for $x = 0$, and the slope $dy/dx = 0$ for $x = 0$, we obtain (by a similar procedure as in Section 8.2).

$$y = (\varepsilon + a) \cdot (1 - \cos kx)$$

Since the sideways deflection $y = a$ for $x = \frac{1}{2}L$, we obtain from these three boundary conditions

$$\varepsilon + a = \varepsilon \sec \tfrac{1}{2}kL = \varepsilon \sec [\tfrac{1}{2}L(P/EI)^{\frac{1}{2}}]$$

The maximum bending moment at $x = 0$

$$M = P(\varepsilon + a)$$

and the maximum compressive stress

$$f = \frac{P}{A} + \frac{M}{I} y_c = \frac{P}{A}(1 + My_c/r^2)$$

where y_c is the distance of the most stressed compressive part of the column from the neutral axis, and r is the radius of gyration.

The secant formula is obtained by combining the last three equations. The maximum compressive stress at failure $f = f_y$, the yield, proof or crushing stress.

$$f_y = \frac{P}{A} \{1 + \eta' \sec [\tfrac{1}{2}L(P/EI)^{\frac{1}{2}}]\} \tag{8.8}$$

and the maximum average stress at buckling, $f = P/A$, is obtained by solving this equation. Since the buckling load P occurs both inside and outside the secant term, direct solution is not possible, and the Perry formula has the advantage of convenience, because the simple quadratic equation permits a direct answer.

The secant formula can be used for columns in which there is a deliberate eccentricity of loading, as well as for columns which are nominally concentrically loaded. The term $\eta' = \varepsilon y_c/r^2$ is then determined experimentally. For conventional structural steelwork η' is approximately 0·25.

8.4. Local Buckling and Torsion Buckling

A column whose overall stability is satisfactory, may still fail by local buckling if it is composed of very thin material (Fig. 3.14d). Hot-rolled or extruded steel and aluminium sections are generally designed to avoid local buckling; but the effect must be considered in sections cold-rolled from sheet metal and in tubes [8.4, 8.5]. Local buckling could occur in channel-, Z- or box-sections, and in circular tubes.

The relevant slenderness ratio is (width of side/sheet thickness). Local buckling does not depend on the length of the column, only on the shape of the cross-section. The theory [8.2] is beyond the scope of this book. Manufacturers of light-gauge steel and of aluminium sections supply design charts to check local buckling.

The shape of the section is also important in torsion buckling. Hot-rolled steel sections buckle sideways before torsional instability occurs; but the effect must be checked in aluminium and in light-gauge steel columns. The theory [8.2] is beyond the range of this book, and practical design is normally based on charts supplied by manufacturers of aluminium and light-gauge steel sections. Torsional instability was the ultimate cause of the spectacular failure of the Tacoma Narrows Bridge [8.8]. The stability of a column can be controlled by providing restraints in one direction, *e.g.* by a wall or sheet attached to a column. Sideways buckling can then occur only at right angles to the direction of restraint, and a deep narrow section is used to advantage. The wall may not, however, provide sufficient restraint to stop torsion buckling. Evidently the most economical section to resist buckling is a circular tube, and a square tube is almost as good. It has the material in the cross-section at the greatest distance from the axis, and thus offers the most favourable conditions against buckling sideways in two perpendicular directions and also against torsion buckling. The section reaches its useful limit when the material becomes so thin that local buckling occurs before overall buckling. In aircraft design saving in weight is more important than saving in material or fabrication cost, and design for least weight is generally based on equalising the limits of the various stability criteria [8.6].

8.5. BUCKLING OF BEAMS

Buckling is only a secondary design criterion for beams; but several distinct buckling modes must be considered. Since the bending moment places part of the beam into compression, we have to consider the buckling of the compression flange in the design of all metal beams. Because of the restraint exercised by the tension flange, danger of instability failure is much less than in columns, and elaborate calculations are unnecessary. Most structural codes require that the maximum permissible compressive flexural stress be reduced as the slenderness ratio increases, in accordance with some simple empirical formula.

If a beam is made too deep and narrow, there is a danger of *lateral buckling* under the action of the flexural compression. A very small restraining force prevents lateral buckling; alternatively the remedy is to use a wider section. In steel structures lateral buckling is unlikely, except in tied arches where restraints are difficult to provide [8.7]. In aluminium beams the lateral stability may need checking.

Local buckling can occur in the compression flanges of beams,

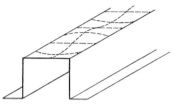

Fig. 8.7.   Local buckling in beams. This is crinkling caused by the flexural
compression, and is independent of the overall length.

just as it can occur in columns. It is a possible cause of stability
failure in cold-rolled steel and aluminium sections (Fig. 8.7), and can
be stopped by rolling in corrugations which reduce the slenderness
ratio (Fig. 8.8). The spacing of rivets or bolts also effects local
buckling.

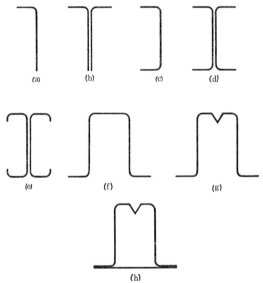

Fig. 8.8.   Prevention of local buckling by corrugations and lips. Local buckling
of light-gauge sheet-metal sections can be prevented by cold-rolling a more
effective shape, which reduces the local slenderness ratio.
(a)–(d) Shapes imitating hot-rolled steel:
(a) Angle; (b) T-section; (c) Channel; (d) I-section.
(e)–(h) New shapes:
(e) Stiffened I-section; (f) Top-hat; (g) Corrugated top-hat; (h) Boxed top-hat.

Web buckling is caused by the diagonal compressive component of the shear force. Most metal beams, including plate girders assembled from hot-rolled sections, require stiffeners so as to reduce the effective length of the web in diagonal compression.

8.6. BUCKLING OF FRAMES

The fundamentals of frame buckling are the same as for column buckling although it is often convenient to provide the explanation in other terms. Take a frame where axial forces are dominant; as the load is increased there comes a stage when the energy lost by the loads deflecting is the same in magnitude but opposite in sense to the energy stored in the members undergoing the same deformations. At this load the frame becomes unstable because there are an infinite number of equilibrium positions; this load is called the *critical load*. As we have seen in Section 8.2 the effect of axial compression in a member is to reduce its stiffness (conversely that of axial tension is to increase its stiffness). This fact allows us to explain the buckling phenomenon of frames in another manner: the critical load of a frame is that load which reduces member stiffnesses to the extent that the joint stiffness of the frame becomes zero and any slight disturbance causes the frame to buckle.

There are a variety of methods available for determining critical loads. One method, well suited to computer solution, is to form the stiffness matrix of the structure and, by an iterative routine, the critical load is determined as that load which makes the matrix singular [8.12]. A number of methods based on a modified moment distribution have been developed [8.13, 8.14], also a direct method is now available [8.15]. As well as these there are a number of books that deal with the general problem of buckling [8.2, 8.11, 8.16, 8.17].

It is proposed to examine two methods of determining critical loads of frames. In the first method we need to be able to determine the joint stiffnesses in order to equate them to zero. The effect of an axial load on a member is to reduce its stiffness [8.18]; what we need to do is to determine the relationship between stiffness and axial load and the carry-over effect from one joint to another (see Section 5.5). Let us examine the single member shown in Fig. 8.9, where s, the restrained stiffness, is the bending moment required to produce unit rotation at end 1, and c the carry-over factor,

i.e.

$$M_{12} = sk_1$$

and

$$M_{21} = sck_1$$

where

$$k_1 = \frac{EI}{l}$$

Fig. 8.9. Single member acted upon by an axial force, restrained at end 1.

The equation of the bending moment at any point is, from equilibrium,

$$EI \frac{d^2y}{dx^2} + Py = sck_1 - s(1 + c)k_1 \frac{x}{l}$$

The general solution to this differential equation is

$$y = \frac{sk_1}{Pl} [cl - (1 + c)x] + A \cos \frac{\pi x}{l} (\rho)^{\frac{1}{2}} + B \sin \frac{\pi x}{l} (\rho)^{\frac{1}{2}}$$

where

$$\rho = \frac{P}{P_e}$$

and P_e, the Euler buckling load is given by eqn 8.2. The constants A and B can be found from the end condition, $y = 0$ at $x = 0$ and at $x = l$. The value of c can be determined from the end condition $\theta = dy/dx = 0$ at $x = l$, therefore,

$$c = \frac{\alpha - \sin \alpha}{\sin \alpha - \alpha \cos \alpha} \tag{8.9}$$

where

$$\alpha = l \left(\frac{P}{EI}\right)^{\frac{1}{2}} = \pi(\rho)^{\frac{1}{2}}$$

Similarly, s can be determined from the end condition $\theta = dy/dx = 1$ at $x = 0$, therefore

$$s = \frac{(1 - \alpha \cot \alpha)\alpha/2}{\tan \alpha/2 - \alpha/2} \tag{8.10}$$

Values of s, c and sc have been tabulated [8.10] and are graphed in Fig. 8.10 in terms of ρ. These functions are called the *stability functions*. For ρ negative P is tension and α is imaginary so that the trigonometric functions in the expressions for s and c need to be replaced by hyperbolic equivalent functions. Similar stability functions can be derived for the situation where both ends are free to rotate, obviously the stiffness (s) will be reduced. This *reduced stiffness* (s'') has also been graphed in Fig. 8.10. As would be expected $s'' = 0$ when $\rho = 0$, *i.e.* at the critical load for a pin-ended strut.

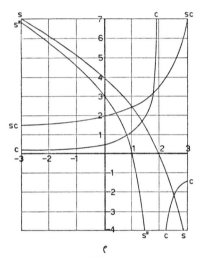

Fig. 8.10.   Graphs of stability functions s, c, sc and s''.

Example 8.1. Determine the critical load of the frame in Fig. 8.11 assuming it is restrained from sidesway motion; the moment of inertia of the members is constant throughout.

Since the sidesway has been restrained the action at joints 2 and 3 is the same and the critical load can be determined by examining joint 3 alone. The stiffness of this joint is given by

$$s_3 = sc_{32} + s_{34}$$

Since the frame is symmetrical, there will be no axial force in member 32, *i.e.* $\rho_{32} = 0$. Hence, $sc_{32} = 2$ from Fig. 8.10. For the joint stiffness to be zero s_{34} must be equal but opposite to sc_{32}, *i.e.*

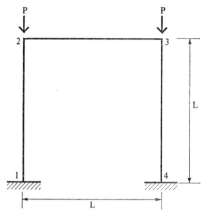

Fig. 8.11.   Frame for Example 8.1.

$s_{34} = -2$. Again, going to Fig. 8.10 we get for this value of s, $\rho = 2\cdot55$, hence $P_c = 2\cdot55P_e$. The critical load of the frame is $2\cdot55$ times the Euler buckling load of the column.

Example 8.2. Determine the critical load of the frame in Example 8.1 if the bases are pinned.

A similar procedure as above yields the following relationship for the stiffness of joint 3.

$$s_3 = sc_{32} + s''_{34}$$

so that s''_{32} must be -2 for the joint stiffness to vanish. With this value of s'' we enter Fig. 8.10 and obtain $\rho = 1\cdot31$. The critical load for this frame is $1\cdot31$ times the Euler buckling load of the column.

Most cases, however, are not as simple as the above two examples: when sidesway is introduced, or when the structure is multi-storey and/or multi-bay, there is considerable numerical labour even with modified techniques [8.13]. The problem, of course, is still the same, that of determining a load which makes the stiffness of the structure, obtained from joint stiffnesses, zero. Switzky and Wang [8.15] have developed a new technique for the direct determination of critical loads on frames with minimal effort. To a large extent the remainder of this chapter is drawn from their paper.

The method uses the *Langrangian Multipliers* [8.20, 8.21] to minimise the weight of the frame subject to stability constraints. Thus, given the loads, we can design the frame for stability and conversely, given the frame design, we can check for stability. The Langrangian multipliers method can be stated in the following terms. Suppose we wish to minimise an objective function (W) (*e.g.* weight) which is a function of several unknown variables (Z_i) as well as known geometric and material parameters. Furthermore, there exists a stability function, $s = 0$, relating the critical load to the known and unknown geometry and material parameters. Using this method, the problem is solved by noting that the partial derivatives of the objective function, plus a constant (λ) times the zero constraint condition (the stability equation), with respect to any of the variables is identically equal to zero at the minimum value of the objective function, *i.e.*

$$\frac{\partial(W + \lambda s)}{\partial Z_i} = 0$$

$$\frac{\partial W}{\partial Z_i} + \lambda \left(\frac{\partial s}{\partial Z_i}\right) = 0$$

and

$$\lambda = -\left(\frac{\partial W}{\partial Z_i}\right) \Big/ \left(\frac{\partial s}{\partial Z_i}\right)$$

or

$$\frac{\partial W}{\partial Z_j} = \left(\frac{\partial W}{\partial Z_i}\right) \left(\frac{\partial s}{\partial Z_j}\right) \Big/ \left(\frac{\partial s}{\partial Z_i}\right) \tag{8.11}$$

Equation (8.11), together with the stability equation provides enough information to solve for the unknown parameter and the constant (λ), Switzky and Wang simplified the problem by setting it up in terms of non-dimensional unknowns which permit easier differentiation of the W and s functions.

The weight of a rectangular frame can be expressed as

$$W = N_h A_h \cdot h + N_g A_g \cdot g \tag{8.12}$$

where N is the number of members, A is the cross-sectional area, h is the column height, g is the girder length, h and g as subscripts refer to column and girder respectively.

The area of an I-shaped beam can be related to its moment of inertia through a constant [8.22],

$$I = kA^2 \tag{8.13}$$

Substitute for A in eqn 8.12 from eqn 8.13

$$W = N_h \cdot h \left\{\frac{I_h}{k}\right\}^{\frac{1}{2}} + N_g \cdot g \left\{\frac{I_g}{k}\right\}^{\frac{1}{2}} \tag{8.14}$$

To turn this equation into a non-dimensional form divide throughout by $N_g \cdot h^2$ and multiply throughout by $(E/P)^{\frac{1}{2}}$ where E is the elastic modulus and P the axial load in the columns. To take account of the different boundary conditions we introduce a constant (f) in the non-dimensional form of (f/f). Equation 8.14, therefore, becomes

$$\left\{\frac{Wk^{\frac{1}{2}}E^{\frac{1}{2}}}{h^2 N_g P^{\frac{1}{2}}}\right\} = \left\{\frac{N_h}{f \cdot N_g}\right\} \left\{\frac{f^2 E I_h}{Ph^2}\right\}^{\frac{1}{2}} + \left\{\frac{g^3}{f^2 h^3}\right\}^{\frac{1}{2}} \left\{\frac{f^2 E I_g}{hgP}\right\}^{\frac{1}{2}} \tag{8.15}$$

If we let

$$\varphi = \frac{1}{f}\alpha = \frac{h}{f}\left(\frac{P}{EI_h}\right)^{\frac{1}{2}}$$

$$\beta = \frac{N_h}{fN_g}$$

$$\zeta = \frac{f^2EI_g}{hgP}$$

and

$$\mu = \frac{Wk^{\frac{1}{2}}E^{\frac{1}{2}}}{h^2N_gP^{\frac{1}{2}}}$$

(8.16)

then eqn 8.15 can be re-written as

$$\mu = \frac{\beta}{\varphi} + \left\{\frac{g^3}{f^2h^3}\right\}^{\frac{1}{2}}\zeta^{\frac{1}{2}}$$ (8.17)

Now all stability equations of rectangular frames [8.2, 8.6] can be written in the generic form

$$S = \chi + \tau = 0$$ (8.18)

where

$$\chi = \frac{hI_g}{pgI_h} = \left(\frac{1}{p}\right)\left\{\frac{f^2EI_g}{ghP}\right\}\left\{\frac{h^2P}{f^2EI_h}\right\} = \frac{\zeta\varphi^2}{p}$$ (8.19)

τ is a function of φ only; p is a constant defined by the boundary conditions (see Table 8.1). The stability equations are set up as explained previously in this section. Substituting for χ from eqn 8.19 in eqn 8.18 and dividing by φ^2/p yields

$$s = \zeta + \frac{p\tau}{\varphi^2} = 0$$ (8.20)

and

$$\zeta = -\frac{p\tau}{\varphi^2}$$ (8.21)

We are now in a position to apply the Langrangian multiplier method to the weight function μ and the stability function (s) of eqns 8.17 and 8.20

i.e.

$$\frac{\partial u}{\partial \zeta} = \left(\frac{\partial u}{\partial \varphi}\right)\left(\frac{\partial s}{\partial \zeta}\right)\bigg/\left(\frac{\partial s}{\partial \varphi}\right)$$

$$\frac{1}{2}\left(\frac{g^3}{f^2h^3}\right)^{\frac{1}{2}}\zeta^{-\frac{1}{2}} = \frac{-\beta/\varphi^2}{(p/\varphi^2)(2\zeta\varphi/p) + (p/\varphi^2)(\partial\tau/\partial\varphi)}$$ (8.22)

Rearranging eqn 8.22 and substituting for χ from eqn 8.19 and letting

$$G = \left\{\frac{2N_h}{p^{\frac{1}{2}}N_g}\right\}^{\frac{2}{3}},$$

yields

$$\eta = G\left(\frac{h}{g}\right) = \frac{[2\tau - \varphi(\partial\tau/\partial\varphi)]^{\frac{2}{3}}}{\chi^{\frac{1}{3}}}$$ (8.23)

Note that the functions χ, ζ and η can all be evaluated as transcendental function of φ.

Table 8.1

Correlation chart of structure with relevant figure. Values for p and f are given.

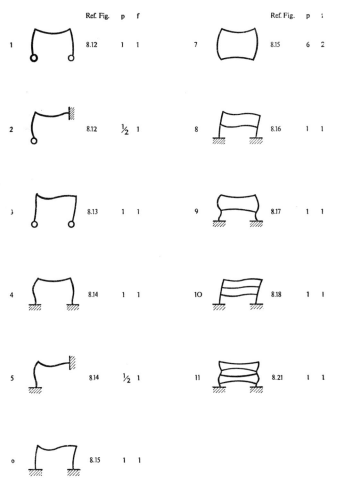

	Ref. Fig.	p	f		Ref. Fig.	p	:
1	8.12	1	1	7	8.15	6	2
2	8.12	½	1	8	8.16	1	1
3	8.13	1	1	9	8.17	1	1
4	8.14	1	1	10	8.18	1	1
5	8.14	½	1	11	8.21	1	1
6	8.15	1	1				

Stability analysis requires the solution of φ in eqn 8.18 with a given χ. This, however, is extremely difficult; with a given φ it is a simple matter to calculate χ. It is therefore possible to graph χ versus φ for a series of given φ. Once the graph is available it becomes equally simple to determine φ for a given χ as the converse. Figures 8.12 to 8.21 are non-dimensional semi-log plots of the column stability parameter (φ) versus the stiffness ratio (χ), the girder parameter (ζ), and the length ratio (η). The graphs are based on eqns 8.12, 8.21 and 8.23.

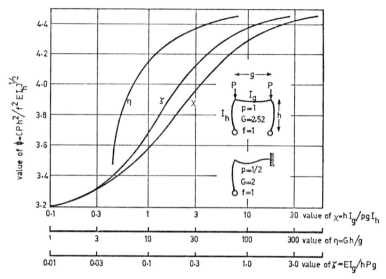

Fig. 8.12.   Hinged rectangular frame with no sidesway (after Switzky & Wang [8.15]).

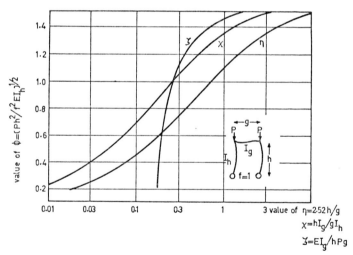

Fig. 8.13.   Hinged rectangular frame with sidesway (after Switzky & Wang [8.15]).

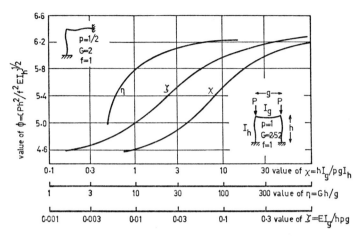

Fig. 8.14. Clamped rectangular frame with no sidesway (after Switzky & Wang [8.15]).

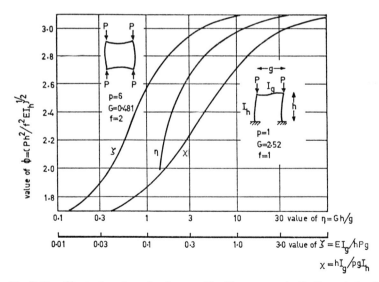

Fig. 8.15. Clamped rectangular frame with sidesway or elastically restrained column (after Switzky & Wang [8.15]).

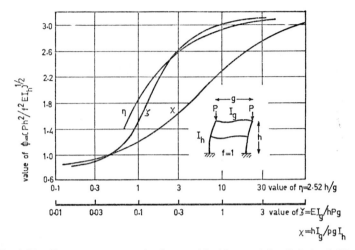

Fig. 8.16.   Two-storey rectangular frame with sidesway (after Switzky & Wang [8.15]).

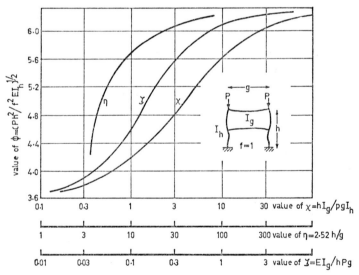

Fig. 8.17.   Two-storey rectangular frame with no sidesway (after Switzky & Wang [8.15]).

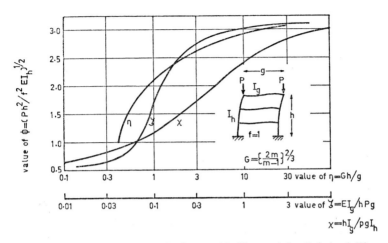

Fig. 8.18.   Three-storey rectangular frame with sidesway (after Switzky & Wang [8.15]).

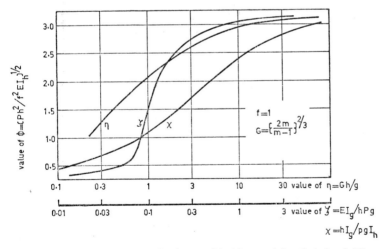

Fig. 8.19.   Five-storey rectangular frame with sidesway (after Switzky & Wang [8.15]).

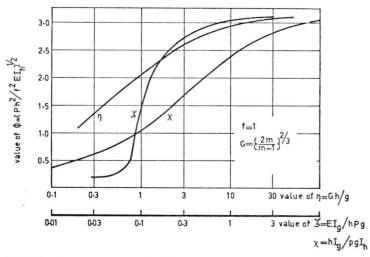

Fig. 8.20.   Ten-storey rectangular frame with sidesway (after Switzky & Wang [8.15]).

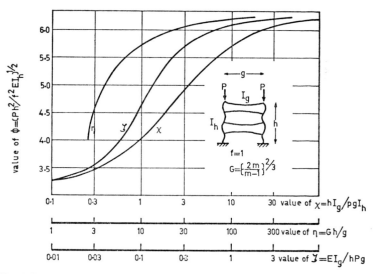

Fig. 8.21.   Multi-storey rectangular frame with no sidesway (after Switzky & Wang [8.15]).

In the figures and in the table m is defined as the number of column members (N_h) divided by the number of stories (n)

i.e.
$$m = \frac{N_h}{n} \qquad (8.24)$$

The design requires the solution of φ and ζ from eqns 8.21 and 8.23 with given η or in some cases a solution φ given η. In both analysis and design the use of the graphs leads to a simple and rapid solution.

Analysis using the graphs: In analysis the problem is given the frame geometry and the beam and column inertias determine the critical load. The procedure is as follows:

1. Determine appropriate number for the given boundary conditions from Table 8.1.
2. Determine p and f from Table 8.1.
3. Calculate
$$\chi = \frac{h I_g}{p g I_h}$$
4. Enter the appropriate graph at χ and determine corresponding φ.
5. Calculate the critical load
$$P = \frac{f^2 \varphi^2 E I_h}{h^2}$$

Example 8.3. Check the critical load calculated in Example 8.2.

1. From Table 8.1 the appropriate Ref. Fig. is 8.12.
2. From Table 8.1
$$p = 1$$
$$f = 1$$
3. $\qquad\qquad h = g = l$
$$I_h = I_g = I$$
$\therefore \qquad\qquad \chi = 1$

4. From Fig. 8.12 at $\chi = 1$, $\varphi = 3.58$
$$P = \frac{1 \times 3.58^2 E I}{l^2} = 12.8 \frac{E I}{l^2}$$
$$P = 1.3 \frac{\pi^2 E I}{l^2} = 1.3 P_e$$

This agrees with the previous result.

Example 8.4. Determine the critical load of the frame examined in Example 8.3 if sidesway is allowed.

1. From Table 8.1 the appropriate Ref. Fig. is 8.13.
2. From Table 8.1

$$p = 1$$
$$f = 1$$

3.
$$h = g = l$$
$$I_h = I_g = I$$
$$\chi = 1$$

4. From Fig. 8.13 at $\chi = 1$, $\varphi = 1.32$

$$P = \frac{1 \times 1.32^2 EI}{l^2} = 1.75 \frac{EI}{l^2}$$

$$P = 0.177 P_e$$

Compare this load with the critical load determined previously when sidesway was prevented.

Example 8.5. Analyse, in terms of stability, a rigid frame with pinned columns and no restraint against sidesway. The columns are $305 \times 165 \times 54$UB, with $I_h = 116.86 \times 10^6$ mm^4, the beam is a $305 \times 165 \times 46$UB with $I_g = 99.24 \times 10^6$ mm^4. The column height is 3.05 m, the span is 6.1 m.

1. From Table 8.1, the appropriate Ref. Fig. is 8.13.
2. From Table 8.1

$$p = 1$$
$$f = 1$$

3.
$$h = 3.050 \text{ m}$$
$$g = 6.100 \text{ m}$$
$$\chi = \frac{3.05 \times 116.86 \times 10^6}{1 \times 6.10 \times 99.24 \times 10^6} = 0.59$$

4. From Fig. 8.13 at $\chi = 0.59$, $\varphi = 1.23$

$$P = \frac{1 \times 1.23^2 \times 200 \times 10^9 \times 116.86 \times 10^{-8}}{3.05^2} = 3801 \text{ kN}$$

Thus, the buckling load of the frame is in excess of the carrying capacity of the columns as it would produce a stress in the column well above yield stress.

Example 8.6. Examine the critical load for the frame of Fig. 8.22 when sidesway is prevented and then when sidesway is permitted, $I_h = 1 \cdot 5 I_g$.

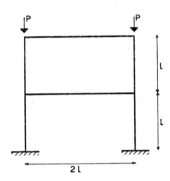

Fig. 8.22.   Frame for Example 8.6.

For the no sidesway condition:

1. From Table 8.1 the appropriate Ref. Fig. is 8.17.
2. From Table 8.1

$$p = 1$$
$$f = 1$$

3. $$g = h = 2l$$
$$I_h = 1 \cdot 5 I_g$$
$$\chi = 1 \cdot 5$$

4. From Fig. 8.17 at $\chi = 1 \cdot 5$, $\varphi = 4 \cdot 4$

$$P = \frac{1 \times 4 \cdot 4^2 E I_h}{(2l)^2} = 4 \cdot 85 \frac{E I_h}{l^2} \left(= 19 \cdot 4 \frac{E I_h}{h^2} \right)$$

$$P = 0 \cdot 49 P_e$$

For sidesway permitted

1. From Table 8.1 the appropriate Ref. Fig. is 8.16.

2. $p = 1$

                                 $f = 1$

3. $\chi = 1 \cdot 5$

4. From Fig. 8.16 at $\chi = 1 \cdot 5$, $\varphi = 2 \cdot 45$

$$P = \frac{1 \times 2 \cdot 45^2 \times EI_h}{(2l)^2} = 1 \cdot 5 \frac{EI_h}{l^2} \left(= 6 \cdot 0 \frac{EI_h}{h^2} \right)$$

$$P = 0 \cdot 152 P_e$$

As can be seen it is the sidesway condition which determines the critical load.

Design Using the Graphs

The design proceeds as follows if h, g and P (working load times a safety factor) are given and we wish to determine I_g and I_h:

1. Determine appropriate figure number for the given boundary conditions from Table 8.1.
2. Determine f and G from the table.
3. Calculate η from eqn 8.23.
4. Enter the appropriate graph at η and determine the corresponding φ. With this value of φ determine its corresponding ζ.
5. The inertias can be obtained from

$$I_h = \frac{h^2 P}{f^2 E^2 \phi^2} \tag{8.25}$$

$$I_g = \frac{\zeta h g P}{f^2 E} \tag{8.26}$$

Example 8.7. Design a single storey steel rigid frame with fixed bases and no restraint against sidesway to carry a load of 420 kN (210 kN times a safety factor of two). The height of the columns is 7·620 m, the rafter spans 6·100 m.

1. From Table 8.1 the appropriate Ref. Fig. is 8.15.
2. From Table 8.1

$$f = 1$$

$$G = 2\cdot52$$

3. $$\eta = G\left(\frac{h}{g}\right) = 2\cdot52(7\cdot62/6\cdot10) = 3\cdot14$$

4. From Fig. 8.15 at $\eta = 3\cdot14$, $\phi = 2\cdot69$ and hence $\zeta = 0\cdot129$.

5. $$I_h = \frac{h^2 P}{f^2 E^2 \phi^2} = \frac{7\cdot62^2 \times 420 \times 10^3}{1^2 \times 200 \times 10^9 \times 2\cdot69^2}$$

$$= 16\cdot85 \times 10^{-6} \text{ m}^4$$

$$= 16\cdot85 \times 10^6 \text{ mm}^4$$

Use $152 \times 152 \times 30$UC, $I = 17\cdot42 \times 10^6$ mm^4, $A = 3820$ mm^2

$$\frac{P}{A} = \frac{420 \times 10^3}{38\cdot2 \times 10^{-6}} = 110 \text{ MPa}$$

$$I_g = \frac{\gamma hg P}{f^2 E} = \frac{0\cdot129 \times 7\cdot62 \times 6\cdot10 \times 420 \times 10^3}{1^2 \times 200 \times 10^9}$$

$$= 12\cdot59 \times 10^{-6} \text{ m}^4$$

$$= 12\cdot59 \times 10^6 \text{ mm}^4$$

Use $152 \times 152 \times 23$UC, $I = 12\cdot63 \times 10^6$ mm^4.

It can be seen that this is a direct method of design which is very easy to use. The required ratio of inertias of beams to columns can be found from eqns 8.25 and 8.26 which, when re-written, become

$$P = \frac{EI_h f^2 \phi^2}{h^2} \quad \text{and} \quad P = \frac{EI_g f^2}{\zeta hg} \quad \text{respectively.}$$

Equating them yields

$$\frac{I_g}{I_h} = \zeta \phi^2 \left(\frac{g}{h}\right) \tag{8.27}$$

Example 8.8. Determine the required ratio of inertias, beam to column for the frame in Fig. 8.22 on the basis of stability alone.

1. From Table 8.1 the appropriate Ref. Fig. is 8.16.
2. From Table 8.1:

$$f = 1$$

$$G = 2\cdot52$$

3. $\eta = 2\cdot52(\times 1) = 2\cdot52$

4. From Fig. 8.16 at $\eta = 2\cdot52$, $\phi = 2\cdot5$ and hence $\zeta = 0\cdot252$. From eqn 8.27

$$\frac{I_g}{I_h} = 0\cdot252 \times 2\cdot5^2 \left(\frac{2l}{2l}\right) = 1\cdot57$$

A situation occurs frequently in the design of rigid frames for stability when not only h, g and P are given but also the moment of inertia of the beam, which has been proportioned on the basis of bending. In this situation the procedure is as follows:

1. As before.
2. As before, only f needs to be determined.
3. Calculate ζ from eqn 8.26.
4. Enter appropriate graph at ζ and determine corresponding ϕ.
5. I_h is obtained as before.

Example 8.9. If the frame in Fig. 8.23 requires a beam section of $305 \times 165 \times 46UB$, $I_g = 99\cdot24 \times 10^6$ mm^4 to carry the moments, design the column section if P is 444 kN.

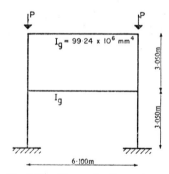

Fig. 8.23. Frame for Example 8.9.

1. From Table 8.1 the appropriate Ref. Fig. is 8.16.
2. From Table 8.1, $f = 1$.

3. $$\zeta = \frac{f^2 E I_g}{hgP} = \frac{1 \times 200 \times 10^9 \times 99\cdot24 \times 10^{-6}}{6 \times 6 \times 444 \times 10^3} = 1\cdot24$$

4. From Fig. 8.16 at $\gamma = 1\cdot24$, $\phi = 2\cdot95$.

5. $$I_h = \frac{6^2 \times 444 \times 10^3}{1^2 \times 200 \times 10^9 \times 2\cdot95^2} = 9\cdot18 \times 10^{-6} \text{ m}^4$$

$$= 9\cdot18 \times 10^6 \text{ mm}^4$$

Use $152 \times 152 \times 23$UC, $I = 12\cdot63 \times 10^{-6}$ mm^4 (minimum available).

In most cases the stiffness of the beam required to carry the bending moments is sufficiently high to produce a restraint at the column ends which is nearly equal to the fully clamped condition.

Example 8.10. Design suitable beam and column sections for buckling for the idealised 20 storey building shown in Fig. 8.24.

1. From Table 8.1 the appropriate figure is Fig. 8.21 since unsymmetrical buckling is not possible.

2. $$p = 1$$
$$f = 1$$
$$G = 2\cdot52$$

3. $$\eta = 2\cdot52(60/12) = 12\cdot6$$

4. From Fig. 8.21 at $\eta = 12\cdot6$, $\phi = 5\cdot8$ and $\zeta = 0\cdot126$.

5. In *steel*
$$I_h = \frac{60^2 \times 4400 \times 10^3}{1^2 \times 200 \times 10^9 \times 5\cdot8^2} = 2354 \times 10^{-6} \text{ m}^4$$

$$= 2354 \times 10^6 \text{ mm}^4$$

$$I_g = \frac{0\cdot126 \times 60 \times 12 \times 4400 \times 10^3}{1^2 \times 200 \times 10^9} = 1996 \times 10^{-6} \text{ m}^4$$

$$= 1996 \times 10^6 \text{ mm}^4$$

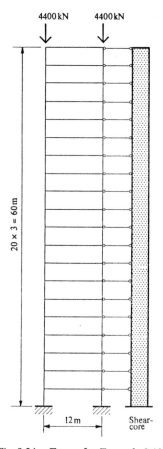

Fig. 8.24.   Frame for Example 8.10.

Now the beam section is much too large for bending purposes, so choose a beam with $I_g = 1400 \times 10^6 \, \text{mm}^4$ and select another column section compatible with this.

$$\zeta = \frac{1^2 \times 200 \times 10^9 \times 1400 \times 10^{-6}}{12 \times 60 \times 4400 \times 10^3} = 0.086$$

From Fig. 8.21 the corresponding value of ϕ is 4.5.

i.e.

$$I_\mathrm{h} = \frac{60^2 \times 4400 \times 10^3}{1^2 \times 200 \times 10^9 \times 4\cdot 52} = 3911 \times 10^{-6}\ \mathrm{m}^4$$
$$= 3911 \times 10^6\ \mathrm{mm}^4$$

This latter solution uses considerably more material than the former and obviously both should be examined for strength and stiffness as well.

In *concrete* the initial solution becomes

$$I_\mathrm{h} = 23\,540 \times 10^6\ \mathrm{mm}^4$$
$$I_\mathrm{g} = 19\,960 \times 10^6\ \mathrm{mm}^4$$

if $E_\mathrm{c} = 20$ GPa. Thus, the column could be 0·400 m × 0·400 m and the beam 1·000 m × 0·300 m, again the solution should be examined for strength and stiffness.

In all the structures we have been considering we have replaced the loads by equivalent concentrated loads acting directly on the columns. In doing this we have eliminated the bending moments due to those loads. The effect of these moments on the critical load of the frame depends on whether the buckling mode is symmetrical or unsymmetrical [8.23] to [8.25]. The buckling load is decreased when the no-sway condition applies under the action of the moments due to the load. There is generally no decrease when sway occurs.

Chapter 9

The Plastic Theory of Steel Structures

Having previously considered elastic design of steel structures, we now examine the principles governing their plastic design. Consideration is first given to statically determinate, or isostatic structures, and then to statically indeterminate, or hyperstatic structures. The plastic design (ultimate strength) of concrete structures is discussed in Chapter 10.

9.1. FUNDAMENTAL CONCEPTS

The idea of designing a structure against collapse is by no means new. The builders of medieval cathedrals certainly used the principle in evolving their structures. In modern times the principle has been commonly used in aircraft design. Plastic design is the collapse method applied to mild steel structures. Thus, the plastic theory is concerned with *strength* and not stiffness and it is here that its main advantage as well as its main disadvantage lies.

Elastic design concentrates on strength and stiffness; by limiting stresses and deformations it attempts to control both factors. However, it will be shown that there is no direct relation between stresses required to cause failure of a member and load required to cause collapse of a structure. Failure of a structure is defined to occur in the elastic design process when the stress at any point in the structure reaches the yield stress, that structure being subjected to the working load times a safety factor.

Let us examine the load required to cause yielding and then the load required to cause collapse of two beams: one simply supported, the other fixed at both ends. Figure 9.1 shows the load–deflection curve for these beams. As the load is increased on the simply supported beam there comes a time when the external fibres at the point of maximum moment reach yield stress, the load required to cause this is designated W_y. As the load is increased the material will

260

deform more rapidly and deflections will increase at a greater rate. Although there is a slight increase in load carrying capacity above W_y, this increase is accompanied by large deflections. For the built-in beam, as the load is increased, a load (W_y) is reached which causes the external fibres at the point of maximum moment to attain the yield stress. As the load is further increased the beam will continue to

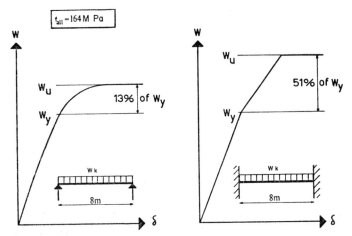

Fig. 9.1.   Load–deflection curves to collapse for a simply supported and a fully restrained beam.

deflect at a greater rate than before but not at an ever-increasing rate as occurred with the simply supported beam. We know that built-in beams have three points where the moment diagrams peak (see Section 5.2), one at each end and one at the centre. As the load is increased the sections at each end yield until finally the whole section has yielded. Elsewhere the structure is still elastic and will continue to carry load until yielding commences at the third point of peak moment. When sufficient zones of yielding have been formed the structure collapses with a load W_u.

We can now compare the ratio of collapse load to that required to initiate yielding in both cases. For the simply supported beam this ratio is 113%, whilst for the built-in beam it becomes 151%. This example illustrates a number of important points—there is no direct relation between the load required to cause yielding and the load required to cause collapse of a structure; the elastic design theory does not provide a constant factor of safety against collapse; and the plastic design method is most advantageous in structures that are hyperstatic.

Let us examine another aspect of the plastic design method. Consider the three-bar structure shown in Fig. 9.2, all have the same

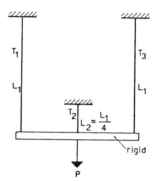

Fig. 9.2.　Three-bar statically-indeterminate structure.

cross-sectional area (A). The state of the elastic stresses cannot be determined by the equations of equilibrium alone since the structure is hyperstatic so we have to consider continuity to generate the required equations (see Chapter 5). The *elastic analysis* proceeds as follows: from symmetry it can be seen that

$$T_1 = T_3$$

and from equilibrium

$$2T_1 + T_2 = P \tag{9.1}$$

Since the horizontal bar is rigid the deflections of the three bars will be the same, *i.e.*

$$\Delta L_1 = \Delta L_2$$

or

$$\frac{T_1 L_1}{AE} = \frac{T_2 L_2}{AE} \tag{9.2}$$

since

$$L_1 = 4L_2$$

$$T_2 = 4T_1 \tag{9.3}$$

substituting from eqn 9.3 into eqn 9.1 we get

$$P = 1 \cdot 5T_2$$

Since bar 2 is the most heavily loaded, yielding will commence there. The maximum load becomes

$$P_y = 1 \cdot 5 f_y A$$

where f_y is the yield stress.

The *plastic analysis* proceeds as follows: even though bar 2 has yielded the structure will not collapse because we are left with a two bar structure plus an upward force of $f_y A$. This situation continues until the outer two bars yield. Each yields at a load of $f_y A$. Therefore, the total load required to cause collapse becomes

$$P_u = \underset{\substack{\text{from} \\ \text{bar 2}}}{f_y A} + \underset{\substack{\text{from bars} \\ \text{1 and 3}}}{2f_y A}$$

i.e.

$$P_u = 3f_y A \qquad (9.4)$$

The reason for the simplicity of the calculation of the collapse load is that the continuity or the indeterminacy due to continuity need not be considered. We have obtained the collapse load (eqn 9.4) by assuming that all bars are stressed to the yield point and by using the equations of equilibrium (eqn 9.1). In other words, *the collapse load is an isostatic quantity*. It can be calculated directly when the cross sections of the members and the yield stress of the steel are known. It does not require a previous analysis of the elastoplastic behaviour of the structure. The collapse load is therefore independent of imperfections such as incorrect lengths of members, residual stresses and foundation movement. The isostatic nature of the collapse load makes it much easier to calculate than the load required to cause yielding (the elastic failure load).

The reasons for the use of the plastic theory of design are that the elastic theory does not produce consistent safety factors and does not adequately describe the overall behaviour of a structural system. Furthermore, the elastic theory assumes that nowhere in the structure must the yield stress of the material be reached. However, in practice there are many factors that contribute towards a violation of this criterion, *e.g.* residual stresses, stress concentrations and 'lack-of-fit' stresses. By-products of the plastic design method are generally simpler computations and lighter structures.

A number of comprehensive books dealing with plastic design are available [B.11, 9.1–5].

9.2. The Simple Plastic Theory of Bending

The property of steel that makes the plastic theory applicable is *ductility* [9.6], *i.e.* the ability of a material to undergo inelastic deformation. The stress–strain curve for mild steel is shown in Fig. 9.3a. It consists of an elastic region, a plastic region and a strain-hardening region. Between the elastic and plastic regions are the upper and lower yield points. This curve is idealised to produce an elasto-plastic material with a stress–strain curve as shown in Fig. 9.3b, *i.e.* the upper and lower yield points and the effect of strain-hardening are neglected. The latter provides a reserve of strength above that computed when the strains become large although the

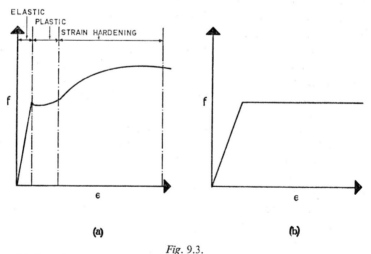

Fig. 9.3.
(a) Stress–strain curve for mild steel.
(b) Idealised stress–strain curve for an elasto-plastic material.

critical strains at the collapse load will rarely exceed 1·5% [B.11, p. 6].

Fundamental to the behaviour of frames in the plastic range is the formation of plastic hinges. Before we examine plastic hinges, let us first consider bending in the plastic range. Consider the stress and strain behaviour of a beam cross section as it is loaded beyond its

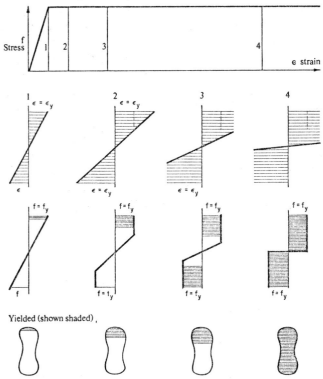

Fig. 9.4. Bending of a beam section beyond the elastic range to produce a plastic moment.

elastic limit. Figure 9.4 shows the stress–strain curve for the material, the stress and strain distributions and the distribution of yielding across the cross-section. As the load reaches the load required to cause yielding, shown as point 1 in the figure the strain (ε) throughout are less than the yield strain (ε_y) except at the extreme fibre where the strain is the yield strain—similarly for stresses. No part of the cross-section has yielded. As the load is increased (point 2) the strains near the extremities of the cross-section are greater than the yield strain; the stresses, however, cannot exceed the yield stress (f_y) so that the triangular stresses block is truncated by a rectangular section where the stresses equal the yield stress. In this region the section has yielded and can carry no further load. It simply carries the load required to cause yielding of that section. As we load to point 3 strains continue to increase and the area of the cross-section where the stresses have reached the yield stress increases as does the amount of the cross-section which can carry no further load. Thus, any increase in load must be carried by the unshaded portions of the section. There will come a stage at which the section will carry no further load (point 4) where the strains throughout the cross-section are above the yield strain (theoretically there will always be a portion near the neutral axis of the section where the strains are less than yield but this has a very small effect and can be ignored). At the same time the entire section will have yielded with the yield stress being reached throughout. The moment required to cause this is called the *plastic moment* and is designated by M_p.

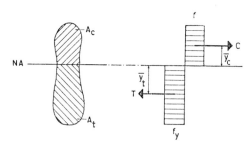

Fig. 9.5. Cross-section of beam with stress distribution upon reaching the plastic moment.

Let us examine the situation when we have reached the plastic moment in more detail. Figure 9.5 shows the cross-section with its accompanying stress distribution at this stage. The moment of resistance of the section must balance the applied moment M_p. The resisting moment is generated by the sum of the moments produced by the forces above and below the neutral axis. Since the stress block is rectangular the compressive and tensile forces (C and T) are:

$$C = f_y A_c$$

$$T = f_y A_t$$

where A_c and A_t are the areas in compression and tension respectively. From horizontal equilibrium

$$C = T$$

i.e.

$$f_y A_c = F_y A_t$$

∴

$$A_c = A_t = A_p \qquad (9.5)$$

Equation 9.5 defines the position of the neutral axis and hence the distances to the centroids of the compressive and tensile stress blocks ($\bar{y}_c$ and $\bar{y}_t$). The equation for the resisting moment can be written as

$$M_p = C\bar{y}_c + T\bar{y}_t$$
$$= f_y(A_c \cdot \bar{y}_c + A_t \cdot \bar{y}_t)$$

or as

$$M_p = f_y \cdot Z_p \qquad (9.6)$$

where Z_p is the *plastic modulus* of the section. (Equation 9.6 is the same as eqn 4.11.) Substituting from eqn 9.5 into eqn 9.6 we can write an expression for the section modulus as

$$Z_p = A_p(\bar{y}_c + \bar{y}_t) \qquad (9.7)$$

where A_p is the area of half the cross-section.

Example 9.1. Derive the expression for the plastic modulus of a rectangular cross-section.

Consider the rectangular cross-section shown in Fig. 9.6.

$$Z_p = A_p(\bar{y}_c + \bar{y}_t)$$

$$= b \cdot \frac{d}{2}\left(\frac{d}{4} + \frac{d}{4}\right)$$

$$Z_p = \frac{bd^2}{4}$$

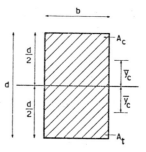

Fig. 9.6.   Rectangular cross-section.

The elastic modulus of a rectangular cross-section is

$$Z = \frac{bd^2}{6}$$

We can see that the plastic modulus is 50% larger than the elastic modulus for this shape section.

Example 9.2. Determine the plastic modulus of the universal (wide flange) beam shown in Fig. 9.7.

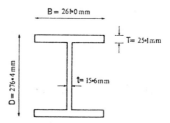

Fig. 9.7.   Universal (wide flange) beam.

Substituting into eqn 9.7

$$Z_p = B \cdot T \cdot (D - T) + \tfrac{1}{2}(D - 2T) \cdot t \cdot \left(\frac{D - 2T}{2}\right)$$

$$= 261 \cdot 0 \times 25 \cdot 1 \times 251 \cdot 3 + 0 \cdot 5 \times 226 \cdot 2 \times 15 \cdot 6 \times 113 \cdot 1$$

$$Z_p = 1 \cdot 846 \times 10^6 \text{ mm}^3$$

The *shape factor* is a measure of the available capacity between the moment required to cause yield in the extreme fibres and the plastic moment. Thus the shape factor (γ) is

$$\gamma = \frac{M_p}{M_y} = \frac{Z_p}{Z} \tag{9.8}$$

Example 9.3. Determine the shape factor for a rectangular section.
From Example 9.1 we have

$$Z_p = \frac{bd^2}{4}$$

$$Z = \frac{bd^2}{6}$$

$$\gamma = \frac{Z_p}{Z} = \frac{bd^2}{4} \Big/ \frac{bd^2}{6}$$

$$= 1 \cdot 5$$

Example 9.4. Determine the shape factor of the section in Example 9.2.
The elastic modulus of the section shown in Fig. 9.7 can either be determined from tables or calculated directly. In both cases it becomes

$$Z = 1620 \times 10^3 \text{ mm}^3$$

The shape factor, therefore, becomes

$$\gamma = \frac{Z_p}{Z} = \frac{1846}{1620}$$

$$= 1 \cdot 13$$

This is a typical figure for I-shaped sections.
As pointed out previously, fundamental to the plastic behaviour of structures is the *plastic hinge*. Let us examine the moment–rotation

characteristics of a beam with a rectangular cross-section. The rotation per unit length (φ) for moments less than the moment required to cause yielding (M_y) is given by

$$\varphi = \frac{M}{EI}$$

and at the point of yielding

$$\varphi_y = \frac{M_y}{EI} \qquad (9.9)$$

Figure 9.8 shows stress-block and strain diagram for the situation

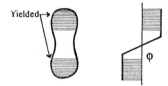

Fig. 9.8.   Cross-section of beam with strain distribution when section is partly plastic and partly elastic.

when the section is partly plastic and partly elastic, equivalent to point 3 in Fig. 9.4. It can be seen that

$$\varphi = \frac{\varepsilon_y}{y_0}$$

$$= \frac{f_y}{E y_0}$$

i.e.

$$y_0 = \frac{f_y}{E\varphi} \qquad (9.10)$$

where y_0 is the distance from the neutral axis to the extreme fibre still not yelded.

Now the moment of resistance is made up of two components:

the moment due to the plastic portion and that due to the elastic portion. This moment can be written as

$$M = f_y(Z_p + Z)$$

$$= f_y \left[2 \cdot b \left(\frac{d}{2} - y_0 \right) \left(\frac{d}{4} + \frac{y_0}{2} \right) + \frac{b \cdot (2y_0)^2}{6} \right]$$

plastic   elastic

$$= f_y b \left\{ \frac{d^2}{4} - \frac{y_0^2}{3} \right\} \tag{9.11}$$

Substituting for y_0 from eqn 9.10 into eqn 9.11 yields

$$M = f_y b \left\{ \frac{d^2}{4} - \frac{f_y^2}{3E^2\varphi^2} \right\} \tag{9.12}$$

Now, from eqn 4.10 for a rectangular section with the maximum stress f_y, the moment can be written as

$$M_y = \frac{f_y bd^2}{6} \tag{9.13}$$

Dividing eqn 9.12 by eqn 9.13 to put it into a non-dimensional form and substituting from eqn 9.9 yields

$$\frac{M}{M_y} = \frac{3}{2} \left[1 - \frac{1}{3} \left\{ \frac{\varphi_y}{\varphi} \right\}^2 \right] \tag{9.14}$$

for $\varphi > \varphi_y$.

The M–φ relationship represented by eqn 9.14 has been drawn up in Fig. 9.9. There is one important observation that can be drawn from this curve. Even though the plastic moment has been reached the member continues to rotate at a constant restraining moment M_p. This is the plastic hinge which can therefore be defined as a yielded section of a beam which acts as if it were hinged with a constant restraining moment M_p.

In Section 9.1 we stated that the ratio of collapse load to that required to cause yielding for a built-in beam was of the order of 1·5.

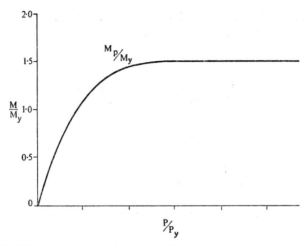

Fig. 9.9.   Moment–curvature graph for a rectangular cross-section.

However, the shape factor for most rolled beam sections is only around 1·15 so that the increase in load-carrying capacity is not simply derived from the available capacity above the moment required to cause first yield. Another of the advantages of taking structures into the plastic range is their ability to *redistribute moments* when in this range. It is a consequence of the formation of the plastic hinges and contributes most to the increase in load-carrying capacity. Consider the built-in beam shown in Fig. 9.10a loaded by a distributed load of W and examine its behaviour as the load is increased. As the load is increased the point is reached when the maximum moment, which occurs at the ends and is equal to $WL/12$, equals the plastic moment of the section M_p and a plastic hinge forms at both ends (Fig. 9.10b). The beam now acts like a simply supported beam with a constant restraining moment M_p at both ends. This beam can carry further load. The load increase, now, is accompanied by an increase in the moment at the centre but not at the ends and the point is reached when the central moment equals the plastic moment and the beam can carry no further load (Fig. 9.10c). The reason why no further load can be carried is that the beam has been transformed into a *mechanism* and a small increase in load produces very large deflections and collapse.

The load (W_y) required to cause first yield is (from Fig. 9.10d) given by

$$\frac{W_y L}{8} = \frac{3}{2} M_y$$

or

$$W_y = \frac{12 M_y}{L} \tag{9.15}$$

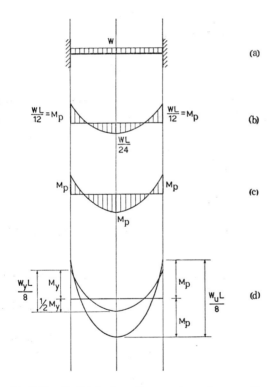

Fig. 9.10.   Redistribution of moment carrying capacity.
(a) Built-in beam with uniform load.
(b) Initial plastic hinges form at supports.
(c) Central moment reaches plastic moment.
(d) Loads for first yield (W_y) and collapse load (W_u).

The load at collapse (W_u) is given by

$$\frac{W_u L}{8} = 2M_p$$

or

$$W_u = \frac{16M_p}{L} \tag{9.16}$$

From eqns 9.15 and 9.16

$$\frac{W_u}{W_y} = \frac{4}{3} \frac{M_p}{M_y} = \frac{4}{3}$$

taking a shape factor of 1·13

$$\frac{W_u}{W_y} = 1·51$$

which is the figure we had at the beginning of the chapter. This increase in load carrying capacity above the load required to cause yield was achieved through a redistribution of the moments from the normal distribution in the elastic range.

9.3. UPPER AND LOWER BOUNDS

It has been seen that for collapse to occur three conditions must be satisfied simultaneously:

1. *the mechanism condition:* the ultimate load is reached when a mechanism forms;
2. *the equilibrium condition:* equilibrium of forces and moments must apply;
3. *the plastic moment condition:* the moments in the beam or frame must nowhere be greater than the plastic moment.

The equivalent conditions in elastic analysis are:

continuity must be satisfied everywhere;
equilibrium must be satisfied everywhere; and nowhere must the moments be greater than the yield moment.

There are two basic methods of plastic analysis and design of steel structures. The reason why there are two methods can be found in the fact that usually it will not be possible to satisfy all three conditions in one operation. One method assumes a mechanism and uses the equilibrium equations to determine the collapse load. This method does not directly take cognisance of the plastic moment condition. The other method uses a moment diagram which has all the moments less than or equal to the plastic moment and which satisfies equilibrium. This method does not directly take cognisance of the mechanism condition. The former method is called the

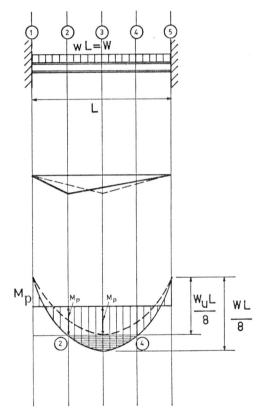

Fig. 9.11.   Demonstration of the upper-bound theorem.

mechanism or kinematic method and the latter the *statical or equilibrium method.*

Two theorems are available which provide bounds for both methods—when both theorems are satisfied then the solution is correct. These theorems are called the upper- and lower-bound theorems.

The upper-bound theorem states [B.11]: *a load computed on the basis of an assumed mechanism will always be greater than or at best equal to the correct collapse load.* This can be seen in Fig. 9.11, for an assumed mechanism other than the correct one for the built-in beam shown, the moments at the centre would be greater than M_p and this is not possible without reinforcing the beam, indicating that the collapse load calculated on the basis of the assumed mechanism must be greater than the actual collapse load. The upper-bound theorem forms the basis of the *mechanism method* of plastic design.

In its most elementary form the mechanism method consists of successively considering all possible collapse mechanisms. The load corresponding to each mechanism can be determined using the equilibrium equations of the virtual-displacement theorem (see Section 6.1). According to the upper bound theorem the lowest load obtained in this manner is the collapse load.

Example 9.5. If the beam in Fig. 9.12a is made of a section with a plastic moment (M_p) determine the collapse load (W).

Using the mechanism method we need to investigate the possible mechanism shown in Fig. 9.12b, c and d. The plastic hinges are located at points of maximum moment.

Consider the mechanism shown in (b). Suppose at the collapse load it is allowed to move through a small virtual displacement. If the rotation at point 4 is called θ, then the resultant geometry can be defined in terms of θ. Since the beam is in equilibrium we can apply the virtual displacement method (see Chapter 6). The external work is the work done by the loads at points 2 and 3 travelling through δ_2 and δ_3 respectively where

$$\delta_2 = 3 \times 2\theta$$

and

$$\delta_3 = 3 \times \theta$$

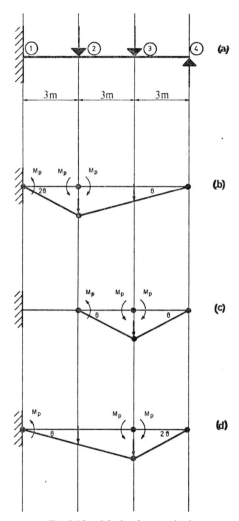

Fig. 9.12. Mechanism method.
(a) Beam for Example 9.5.
(b), (c), (d) possible mechanisms.

The total external work becomes

$$W_e = W \times 3 \times 2\theta + W \times 3 \times \theta$$

Section 2   Section 3

$$= 9 \times W \times \theta \tag{9.17}$$

The internal work is the work done by the plastic moments rotating through their respective angles. The total internal work becomes

$$W_i = M_p \times 2\theta + M_p \times 3\theta$$

Section 1   Section 2

$$= 5 \times M_p \theta \tag{9.18}$$

Equating the expressions for work in eqns 9.17 and 9.18 yields

$$9W\theta = 5M_p\theta$$

$$W = 0\cdot55M_p \tag{a}$$

The same technique applied to the mechanism shown in (c) gives

$$W_e = W \times 3\theta$$

Section 3

$$W_i = M_p \times \theta + M_p 2\theta$$

Section 2   Section 3

$$= 3M_p\theta$$

and equating work

$$W = 1\cdot0M_p \tag{b}$$

Similarly for the mechanism in Fig. 9.12d

$$W_e = W \times 3\theta + W \times 6\theta$$

$$\text{Section 2} \quad \text{Section 3}$$

$$= 9W\theta$$

$$W_i = M_p\theta + M_p3\theta$$

$$\text{Section 1} \quad \text{Section 3}$$

$$= 4M_p\theta$$

and equating work

$$W = 0.44M_p \tag{c}$$

Comparing the three results in eqns (a), (b) and (c) shows that the mechanism in Fig. 9.12d produced the lowest collapse load. Since all possible mechanisms have been examined the collapse load for the beam is $W = 0.44M_p$.

The correct location of the plastic hinges is a prior requirement of the mechanism method. Incorrect locations simply produce loads greater than the correct collapse load. Hinges can form at points of maximum moment which occur at the ends of members, under concentrated loads, and at the position of zero shear in members subjected to distributed loads. At joints where two members meet, the plastic hinge forms in the weaker member. At joints where more than two members meet, plastic hinges may form at the ends of each member. The position of the plastic hinge in a member subjected to distributed loads depends on the values of the end moments.

Example 9.6. Determine the positions of plastic hinges in the beam shown in Fig. 9.13.

One plastic hinge is going to occur at the built-in support because there is a peak moment there. At least one other hinge is required to turn this beam into a mechanism; this hinge will occur somewhere under the distributed load. It will occur at a point x from the left-hand support at the lowest value of $W = W_u$. We can therefore

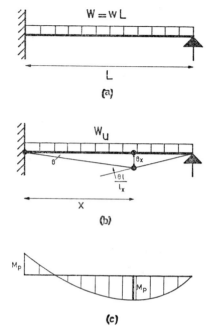

Fig. 9.13.   Determination of the position of plastic hinges for distributed loads.

determine the value of x by obtaining an expression for W in terms of M_p and determining its minimum.

Figure 9.13c shows the beam at the collapse load; applying the equilibrium condition through the virtual displacement principle we get

$$\tfrac{1}{2}W_u\theta_x = M_p\theta + M_p\frac{\theta x}{l-x}$$

$$W_u = \frac{4M_p l}{x(l-x)} - \frac{2M_p}{l-x}$$

differentiating the above equation yields

$$\frac{\partial W_u}{\partial x} = -\frac{4M_p l^2}{x^2(l-x)^2} + \frac{8M_p x l}{x^2(l-x)^2} - \frac{2M_p}{(l-x)^2}$$

equating this equation to zero and solving will yield the value of x.

$$\frac{\partial W_u}{\partial x} = 0 = -2l^2 + 4xl - x^2$$

i.e.

$$x = 0 \cdot 586l$$

The *lower-bound theorem* states [B.11]: *a load computed on the basis of an assumed equilibrium moment diagram in which the moments are nowhere greater than the plastic moment is less than or at best equal to the correct collapse load.* This can be seen in Fig. 9.14; for an

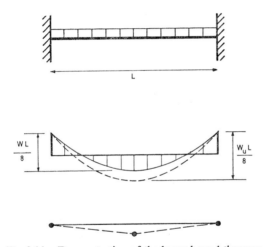

Fig. 9.14.   Demonstration of the lower-bound theorem.

assumed moment diagram based on a load W, in which the plastic moments have been reached at the ends but not at the centre, the load is less than the collapse load since an increase in load is required to produce sufficient hinges to turn the structure into a mechanism. The lower-bound theorem forms the basis of the *statical method* of plastic design.

In its most elementary form the statical method consists of determining equilibrium-moment diagrams for which there is a corresponding mechanism.

Example 9.7. Determine the collapse load of the beam in Example 9.5 using the lower-bound theorem.

The beam is redrawn in Fig. 9.15a. The aim, using the lower bound theorem, is to draw an equilibrium moment diagram in which the moments nowhere exceed the plastic moment but which has sufficient plastic hinges to produce a mechanism. Figure 9.15b

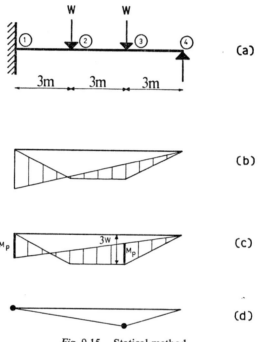

Fig. 9.15. Statical method.
(a) Beam for Example 9.7.
(b), (c) Equilibrium-moment diagram.
(d) Corresponding mechanism.

shows an equilibrium moment diagram, since the beam requires only two further hinges to form a mechanism, we examine the moment diagram for the two points where hinges are most likely to occur; these are points 1 and 3 as the moment diagram peaks there.

Figure 9.15c is the same moment diagram redrawn so that the moments at 1 and 3 are equal. The simply supported beam moment at 3 is $3W$; the same height can be represented by $M_p + \frac{1}{3}M_p$, *i.e.*

$$3W = 1\cdot33M_p$$

$$W = 0\cdot44M_p$$

This is the value obtained in Example 9.5. The corresponding mechanism is shown in Fig. 9.15d.

The upper- and lower-bound theorems can be combined to yield a new theorem. The load which satisfies both theorems at the same time is the collapse load. This can be expressed in the *combined theorem* which states: *a load computed on the basis of an equilibrium*

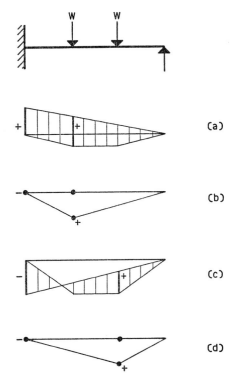

Fig. 9.16. Combined theorem—two possible moment diagrams (a) and (c) with corresponding mechanisms (b) and (d).

moment diagram, in which the magnitude of the bending moment equals the plastic moment in a sufficiently large number of sections to produce a mechanism with plastic hinges in these sections, is the collapse load if the sign of the bending moment at these sections corresponds to the sense of the hinge rotation of the mechanism. The combined theorem is more difficult to apply than the upper- and lower-bound theorems and care should be taken to see that the signs of the bending moments at plastic hinges correspond to the sign of the rotation of the hinges.

Consider again the beam of Example 9.5 (Fig. 9.12). There are two possible equilibrium-moment diagrams with their corresponding mechanisms. These are shown in Fig. 9.16a–d. For the moment diagram shown in Fig. 9.16a the corresponding mechanism (Fig. 9.16b) has a negative rotation at the built-in end although the moment diagram is positive at that point—the load computed from this will therefore not be the collapse load. For the moment diagram shown in Fig. 9.16c the corresponding mechanism, Fig. 9.16d, has the same sign rotations at the hinges as does the moment diagram. The load computed from this will be the collapse load. This diagram of course corresponds with both Figs. 9.12d and 9.15.

9.4. DESIGN OF SIMPLE HYPERSTATIC STRUCTURES

In elastic design a safety factor is applied to the allowable stress which limits its value to a percentage of the yield stress (defined failure stress). In plastic design a factor is applied to the collapse load for the same reasons (see Section 2.4), this factor is called the *load factor* and is denoted by λ. The *working load* is multiplied by the load factor to obtain the *factored load* and the structure is designed, for strength, by considering the factored load as the load which will cause collapse.

The procedure for *design using the statical method* is as follows:

1. Determine the working loads, multiply these by the load factor to obtain the factored loads.
2. Turn the structure into an isostatic structure by setting the redundants to zero.

3. Draw the bending moment diagram of the isostatic structure due to the factored loads.
4. Draw the bending moment diagram of the isostatic structure loaded by the redundants.
5. Draw the actual bending moment diagram by superimposing the above two diagrams, the values of the redundants being drawn to satisfy the plastic moment and mechanism conditions of Section 9.3. (This can be achieved by noting the number of plastic hinges required to cause the structure to collapse. One for a simply supported beam, plus one for each redundant. Check the positions of the maximum moments and scale the bending moment diagram due to the redundants to make the values of the maximum moments equal in magnitude. These maximum moments are the plastic moments.)
6. Measure or calculate the plastic moment, divide by the yield stress to obtain the required plastic modulus. Select the appropriate structural section from tables.

The use of the statical method for the design of simple hyperstatic structures is best illustrated by an example.

Example 9.8. Design a suitable section for strength for the two span beams shown in Fig. 9.17 if $\lambda = 1.75$ and $f_y = 250$ MPa.

1. Factored load $= \lambda \times$ Working load

$$= 1.75 \times 200 = 350 \text{ kN}$$

2. Choose the moment at the centre support as the redundant and hence turn the continuous beam into two simply supported beams.
3. Figure 9.17a shows the bending moment diagram of the isostatic structure due to the factored loads.
4. Figure 9.17b shows the bending moment diagram due to the redundant.
5. Figure 9.17c shows these two diagrams superimposed with the value of the redundant moment scaled so that at two points the maximum moments are equal. This occurs under load 1 and at the centre support. Figure 9.17d shows the corresponding mechanism.

6. In order to calculate the value of the plastic moment it should be
noted that under load 1 the value of the redundant moment has
reduced to one-third, *i.e.*

$$1050 = M_p + 0.33M_p$$
$$M_p = 789.5 \text{ kNm}$$
$$Z_p = 789.5/250$$
$$= 3.150 \times 10^6 \text{ mm}^3$$

Use 610 × 229UB, 113 kg/m

$$Z_p = 3.283 \times 10^6 \text{ mm}^3$$

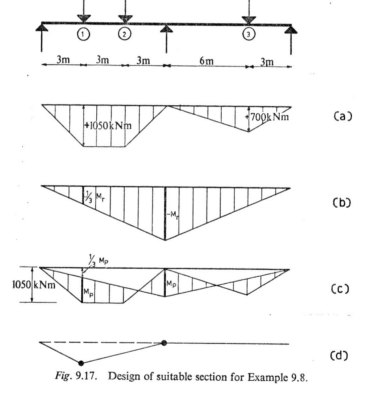

Fig. 9.17.   Design of suitable section for Example 9.8.

The location of points of maximum moment and hence hinges due to *distributed loads* can often be difficult. The position depends on the values of the moments at the ends of the member and can be found using the virtual displacement principle as in Example 9.6. The position may also be readily determined from charts [9.4, 9.7]. Figure 9.18 shows the position and value of the maximum moment on a propped cantilever with a uniformly distributed load.

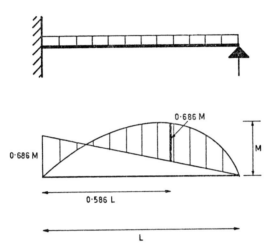

Fig. 9.18.   Position and value of maximum moment on a propped cantilever with a uniformly distributed load.

Example 9.9. Design suitable beams for the beam shown in Fig. 9.19. The spans are to collapse simultaneously and $\lambda = 1\cdot75, f_y = 250$ MPa.

1. Factored load $= 1\cdot75 \times 20 = 35$ kN/m

   and
$$1\cdot75 \times 180 = 315 \text{ kN}$$

2. Choose moments at supports as redundants; this turns the continuous beam into three simply supported beams.
3. Figure 9.19a shows the bending moment diagram of the isostatic structure due to the factored loads.
4. Figure 9.19b shows the bending moment diagram due to the redundants.

5. Figure 9.19c shows the two diagrams superimposed. Consideration must be given to the numerical values of the bending moments to determine which bay will have the weaker section at a support; for the plastic moment at a support is the plastic moment of the weaker section at that support.

6. Examine, firstly, the right-hand span as this has the smallest isostatic moment. Assuming that the centre span will have a stronger section (this will be checked later), then

$$M_{p4} = M_{p5} = \tfrac{2}{3} \times 472 \cdot 5 = 315 \text{ kNm}$$

7. Examining the left-hand span since it has the next lowest isostatic moment, again assuming the centre span will have a stronger section, then

$$M_{p1} = M_{p2} = 0 \cdot 686 \times 630 = 432 \cdot 2 \text{ kNm}$$

8. Check now to see that the centre span does require a stronger section

$$M_{p3} = 886 - \tfrac{1}{2}(M_{p2} + M_{p4})$$
$$= 512 \cdot 4 \text{ kNm}$$

The original assumption was correct. We can now calculate the required plastic modulus and hence the section for each span.

9. Centre span:
$$Z_{rep} = 512 \cdot 4/250$$
$$= 2 \cdot 040 \times 10^6 \text{ mm}^3$$

Use 553 × 165UB, 82 kg/m
$$Z_p = 2 \cdot 051 \times 10^6 \text{ mm}^3$$

10. Left-hand span:
$$Z_{rep} = 432 \cdot 2/250$$
$$= 1 \cdot 720 \times 10^6 \text{ mm}^3$$

Use 533 × 165UB, 73 kg/m
$$Z_p = 1 \cdot 776 \times 10^6 \text{ mm}^3$$

11. Right-hand span:
$$Z_{rep} = 315/250$$
$$= 1 \cdot 260 \times 10^6 \text{ mm}^3$$

Use 457 × 152UB, 60 kg/m
$$Z_p = 1 \cdot 284 \times 10^6 \text{ mm}^3$$

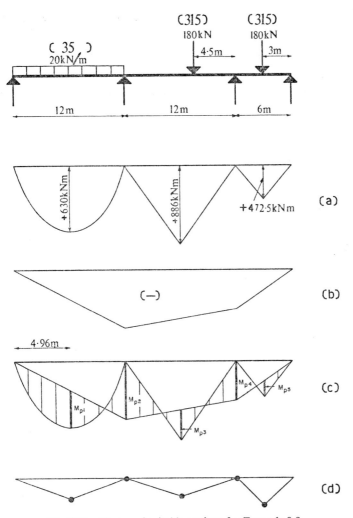

Fig. 9.19. Design of suitable sections for Example 9.9.

The procedure for *design using the mechanism method* is as follows:

1. Determine the working loads, multiply these by the load factor to obtain the factored loads.
2. Determine location of possible plastic hinges (these will generally be under concentrated loads, at joints and at points of zero shear).
3. Select possible mechanisms.
4. Solve the equilibrium equation for each mechanism to check for the largest plastic moment which becomes the design plastic moment and the corresponding mechanism is the actual collapse mechanism.
5. Draw the bending moment diagram, if necessary to check that nowhere have the plastic moments been exceeded.
6. Determine the required plastic moment from the design plastic moment.

Example 9.10. Design a suitable section for the beam shown in Fig. 9.20, if $\lambda = 1{\cdot}75$ and $f_y = 250$ MPa.

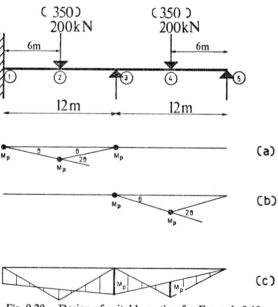

Fig. 9.20. Design of suitable section for Example 9.10.

1. Factored load $= 1.75 \times 200 = 350$ kNm.
2. There are four possible locations of hinges; these have been numbered 1 to 4.
3. There are only two possible mechanisms shown in Fig. 9.20a and b.
4. Applying the virtual displacement principle to mechanism (a), by equating external work with internal work

$$350 \times 6\theta = M_p(\theta + 2\theta + \theta)$$

i.e.

$$M_p = 525 \text{ kNm}$$

Similarly, mechanism (b) yields

$$350 \times 6\theta = M_p(\theta + 2\theta)$$

i.e.

$$M_p = 700 \text{ kNm}$$

Thus, mechanism (b) is the collapse mechanism with a plastic moment of 700 kNm.

5. The bending moment diagram corresponding to the collapse mechanism is shown in Fig. 9.20c.

6. $$Z_{rep} = 700/250$$

$$= 2.800 \times 10^6 \text{ mm}^3$$

Use 610 × 229UB, 110 kg/m

$$Z_p = 2.877 \times 10^6 \text{ mm}^3$$

9.5. Design of Rigid Frames

In order to be able to design rigid frames we need to be able to recognise the possible positions of plastic hinges and hence the type of mechanism formed. It is convenient to give different modes of

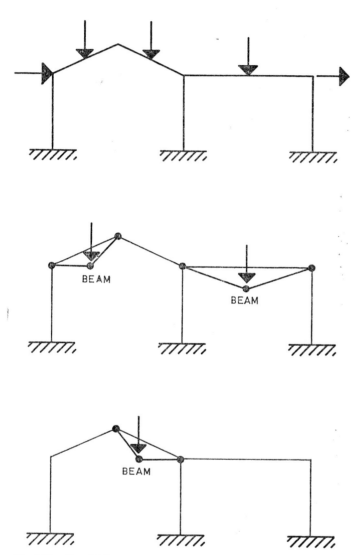

Fig. 9.21.   Possible mechanisms of a rigid frame (see also facing page).

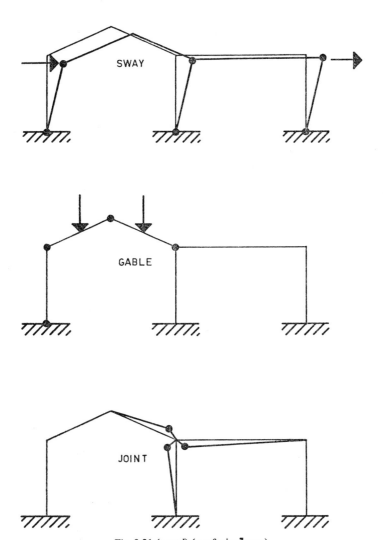

Fig. 9.21 (*contd*) (see facing page).

failure different names. Figure 9.21 shows a typical rigid frame with the different types of *independent mechanisms*:

>*beam* mechanism—due to point load or distributed loads along a member
>
>*sway* mechanism—sidesway of entire frame
>
>*gable* mechanism—spreading of the column tops with respect to base
>
>*joint* mechanism—forms at the junction of three or more members.

It is possible to combine independent mechanisms to produce composite mechanisms.

It is important when using the mechanism method to design to be able to ascertain the *number of independent mechanisms*. This can be determined from the following equation

$$N = P - R \qquad (9.19)$$

where N is the number of possible independent mechanisms, P is the number of possible plastic hinges, R is the number of redundants.

A structure with R redundants will require R plastic hinges to make it isostatic and the formation of one more hinge will make it unstable so that for a structure with P possible plastic hinges the number of independent mechanisms will be that number less the number of plastic hinges needed to form to make the structure isostatic. In the mechanism method of design, to determine the largest plastic moment, it is necessary to investigate all the independent mechanisms and then to examine those mechanisms with large values of plastic moment to see whether they can be combined to produce an even higher value.

Let us now look at the procedure for the design of a rectangular frame. At this stage a number of effects will be neglected; these are the effects due to shear and axial force and stability.

Example 9.11. Design a suitable uniform section for the rigid frame shown in Fig. 9.22 using the mechanism method if $\lambda = 1.75$ and $f_y = 250$ MPa with $\lambda = 1.40$ for wind loads or combination of loads including wind loads.

There are two loading cases to be considered.

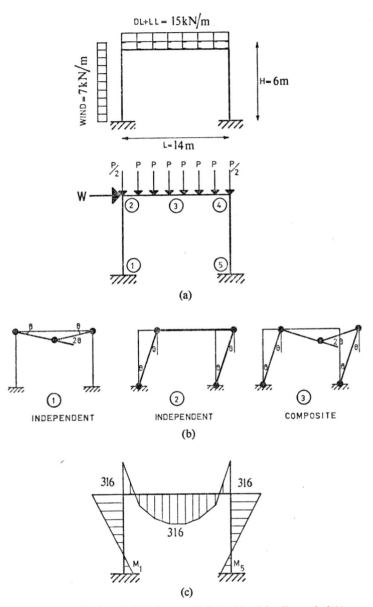

(a)

(b)

(c)

Fig. 9.22.   Design of rigid frame with lateral load for Example 9.11.

Loading case I

$$DL + LL \qquad \lambda = 1\cdot75$$

$$w_I = 15 \times 1\cdot75 = 26\cdot25 \text{ kNm}$$

with the purlins at 2 m centres the load on each purlin (P) (except for the purlins above the columns which carry $P/2$) will be

$$P = 2 \times w = 52\cdot5 \text{ kN}$$

Loading case II

$$DL + LL + \text{Wind} \qquad \lambda = 1\cdot40$$

$$P = 42 \text{ kN}$$

and replace the horizontal distributed wind load by an equivalent concentrated load (W), which produces equal work, at the top of the column

$$w_{II} = 7\cdot0 \times 1\cdot4 = 9\cdot8 \text{ kN/m}$$

$$W = \frac{w_{II} \times H \times H/2}{H} = 29\cdot4 \text{ kN}$$

The structure with these loads on it is shown in Fig. 9.22a.

There are five possible locations of plastic hinges labelled in the above figure and the structure has three redundants; substituting these values into eqn 9.12 yields two independent mechanisms. Since there are only two independent mechanisms there can only be one composite mechanism. These are shown in Fig. 9.22b. Consider, firstly, *loading case I* and solve the equilibrium equation for mechanism 1 as the other mechanisms cannot occur for this loading case since it is symmetrical.

Mechanism 1

$$M_p \times (\theta + 2\theta + \theta) = P\frac{\theta L}{7}(1 + 2 + 3)2 = 1\cdot72P\theta L$$

$$M_p = 0\cdot43PL = 316 \text{ kNm}$$

Similarly, for *loading case II*, mechanism 2 and 3 since obviously mechanism 1 will produce a lower plastic moment.

Mechanism 2

$$M_p(\theta + \theta + \theta + \theta) = W \times \theta \times H$$

$$M_p = 0.25WH = 44.1 \text{ knm}$$

Mechanism 3

$$M_p(\theta + 2\theta + 2\theta + \theta) = W \times \theta \times H + 1.72P\theta L$$

$$M_p = 0.17WH + 0.29PL = 200.5 \text{ knm}$$

The highest plastic moment is due to load case I and equals 316 kNm. Now, draw the bending moment diagram to check that nowhere has the plastic moment been exceeded. Figure 9.22c shows the bending moment diagram. We know that for a rigid frame for symmetrical vertical loading the moment at the base is half the moment at the knee, so that $M_1 = 158$ kNm and nowhere are the moments greater than the plastic moment.

The *selection of the section* proceeds as for the beams designed previously

$$Z_{reg} = 316/250 = 1.260 \times 10^6 \text{ mm}^3$$

Use 457 × 152UB, 60 kg/m

$$Z_p = 1.284 \times 10^6 \text{ mm}^3$$

Example 9.12. Design the frame of Example 9.11 using the statical method, taking it as pinned at the base.

Use can be made of the factored loads derived previously. Figure 9.23a shows the isostatic structure produced when the redundant, one horizontal reaction, are removed. We now draw the isostatic bending moment diagram. For single-bay frames it is often easier to treat the frame as a beam with possible plastic hinges at joints. The isostatic bending moment diagram is superimposed on the moment diagram of the redundants.

This is shown for loading case I (see Fig. 9.23b), in which it can be seen that maximum moments occur at points 1, 2 and 3. With plastic hinges at these points there would be a beam mechanism in the

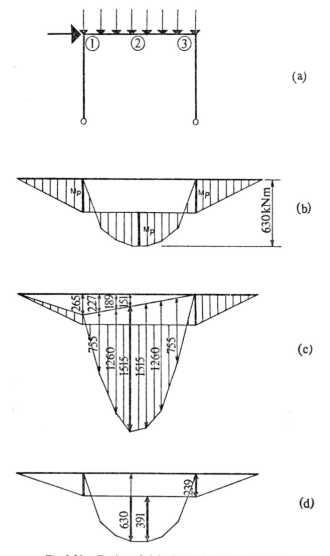

Fig. 9.23.   Design of rigid frame for Example 9.12.

rafter. The value of the plastic moment can be determined from the fact that $2M_p$ equals the maximum isostatic moment

$$2M_p = 630 \text{ kNm}$$

$$M_p = 315 \text{ kNm}$$

One point of interest can be noted here: the controlling factor in the plastic design of rigid frames by the statical method is the magnitude of the range of moments in the isostatic bending moment diagram between the maximum positive and negative peaks.

Applying the procedure just outlined to loading case II, results in the combined moment diagram shown in Fig. 9.23c. Since the range of moments of the isostatic moments is less than that for the first loading case, this case is not critical and the design plastic moment becomes 315 kNm.

Select the required section to satisfy this moment

$$Z_{rep} = 315/250 = 1 \cdot 260 \times 10^6 \text{ mm}^3$$

Use 406 × 178UB, 67 kg/m

$$Z_p = 1 \cdot 343 \times 10^6 \text{ mm}^3$$

It is possible, with the information available, to produce a design with different sections for the column and rafter. If we increase the size of the rafter section to say a 533 × 165UB, 66 kg/m with a plastic modulus of $1 \cdot 562 \times 10^6$ mm^3 and a plastic moment of resistance of 391 kNm. The required moment capacity of the column can be determined from Fig. 9.23d as 239 kNm

$$Z_{rep} = 239/250 = 9 \cdot 50 \times 10^5 \text{ mm}^3$$

Use 381 × 152UB, 52 kg/m

$$Z_p = 9 \cdot 59 \times 10^5 \text{ mm}^3$$

In the original design the total mass of steel was 1560 kg in the revised design 1562 kg per frame. Whilst the revised design is not more economical, it does show the flexibility of choice of sections.

Whilst uniform section throughout is often sufficient for preliminary design, for a detailed design different section sizes almost always prove more economical, especially for multi-bay frames. The next example demonstrates the method of determining the ratio of section sizes before the final analysis takes place.

Example 9.13. Design a two-bay rigid frame which has a wall height of 5 m, one bay spans 12 m and the other 18 m. The loads to be supported are 1·5 kPa vertical dead plus live load and 0·8 kPa horizontal wind load, the frames are spaced at 6 m centres. $\lambda = 1·75$ for dead and live loads and 1·40 for wind loads; $f_y = 250$ MPa.

Figure 9.24 shows the frame

$$DL + LL = 1·5 \times 6 = 9 \text{ kN/m}$$

$$\text{Wind} = 0·8 \times 6 = 4·8 \text{ kN/m}$$

Factored loads

loading case I:

$$DL + LL = 1·75 \times 9 = 15·75 \text{ kN/m}$$

loading case II:

$$DL + LL = 1·40 \times 9 = 12·6 \text{ kN/m}$$

$$\text{Wind} = 1·40 \times 4·8 = 6·72 \text{ kN/m}$$

In problems like this the mechanism method is more suitable because of the difficulty in drawing the bending moment diagrams. Next, determine the number of independent mechanisms, using eqn 9.19.

$$P = 7, \quad R = 3, \quad N = 4$$

see Fig. 9.24.

Loading case I

Three mechanisms are possible with this load, two beam mechanisms (beams BD and DF) and one joint mechanism (at joint D).

Consider the beam mechanism in span BD, Fig. 9.24e.

$$M_{p1}(\theta + 2\theta + \theta) = \frac{(DL + LL)12^2}{4} \theta$$

$$M_{p1} = \frac{(DL + LL)12^2}{16} = 141·75 \text{ kNm}$$

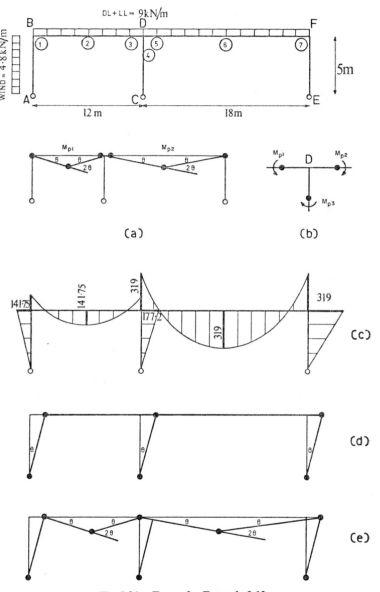

Fig. 9.24.   Frame for Example 9.13.

Similarly, for the beam mechanism in span DF, Fig. 9.24a

$$M_{p2} = \frac{(DL + LL)18^2}{16} = 319 \text{ kNm}$$

for these two beams to have the same plastic hinge at D their plastic moduli should be in the ratio of M_{p1}/M_{p2}. This means that the plastic modulus of the section for beam DF should be 2·25 times that for beam BD. Examine the joint mechanism at D (Fig. 9.24b).

$$M_{p3} = M_{p1} - M_{p2}$$
$$= M_{p1}(1 - 2·25) = -1·25M_p$$

i.e. the plastic modulus of the centre column should be 1·25 times that for beam BD

$$M_{p3} = 177·2 \text{ kNm}$$

The bending moment diagram is drawn (Fig. 9.24c) to check the plastic moment condition.

Loading case II

So far three of the four independent mechanisms have been examined. The remaining independent mechanism is the sway mechanism shown in Fig. 9.24d; this can be shown not to be critical. However, there is a composite mechanism obtained by adding together all the above, that should be examined (Fig. 9.24e). A reasonable assumption is that the beam hinges from midspan

$$M_{p1}\theta(2 + 2) + M_{p2}\theta(2 + 2) = (DL + LL)12 \times \tfrac{12}{4}\theta$$

$$+ (DL + LL) \times 18 \times \tfrac{18}{4}\theta$$

$$+ (\text{Wind})5 \times \tfrac{5}{4}\theta$$

Noting that $M_{p2} = 2·25M_{p1} = M_p$ the above equation becomes

$$13M_p = 1516·4$$

$$M_p = 116·64 \text{ kNm}$$

The bending moment diagram for this composite mechanism can be drawn to check that it satisfies the plastic moment condition.

It can be seen that loading case I is the design load. Sections are selected as follows:

Beam B-D $\left.\begin{matrix} \\ \end{matrix}\right\}$ $Z_{\text{rep}} = 141{\cdot}75/250 = 5{\cdot}60 \times 10^5 \text{ mm}^3$
Column A-B

Use 305 × 127UB, 42 kg/m

$$Z_p = 6{\cdot}09 \times 10^5 \text{ mm}^3$$

Beam D-F $\left.\begin{matrix} \\ \end{matrix}\right\}$ $Z_{\text{rep}} = 319/250 = 1{\cdot}200 \times 10^6 \text{ mm}^3$
Column F-E

Use 406 × 152UB, 67 kg/m

$$Z_p = 1{\cdot}323 \times 10^6 \text{ mm}^3$$

Column D-C $Z_{\text{rep}} = 177{\cdot}2/250 = 7{\cdot}00 \times 10^5 \text{ mm}^3$

Use 356 × 171UB, 45 kg/m

$$Z_p = 7{\cdot}71 \times 10^5 \text{ mm}^3$$

Gable frames are designed in the same manner as are rectangular frames using either the statical method or the mechanism method. The former being favoured for single and two-bay frames.

Charts have been developed to assist in the design of single span rigid frames. The charts and formulae can be derived using the mechanism method of analysis. Figure 9.25 gives the moments and reactions at collapse load of pinned-base gable frames and Fig. 9.26 for fixed-base gable frames. Note that these charts and formulae can be used for rectangular frames as these are simply a special gable frame with zero rise in the rafter. These reduce the effort of design to a minimum.

Other charts are available [9.8] for multi-bay frames.

Example 9.14. Design the gable frame shown in Fig. 9.27 using the design charts; $\lambda = 1{\cdot}75$ for dead and live load and $1{\cdot}40$ for wind loads; $f_y = 250$ MPa.

Loading case I
Factored loads

$$DL + LL = 1{\cdot}75 \times 4{\cdot}0 = 7 \text{ kN/m}$$

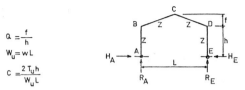

$$Q = \frac{f}{h}$$

$$W_u = wL$$

$$c = \frac{2\,T_u h}{W_u L}$$

$T_u h =$ MOMENT OF TOTAL HORIZONTAL LOADING T_u ABOUT A
$Z =$ PLASTIC MODULUS

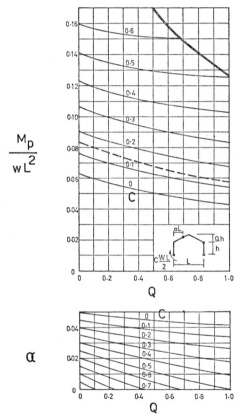

Fig. 9.25.   Design chart for moments and reactions at collapse load of pinned base gable frames (after Reference [9.8]).

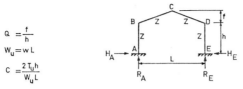

$Q = \dfrac{f}{h}$

$W_u = wL$

$C = \dfrac{2T_u h}{W_u L}$

$T_u h =$ MOMENT OF TOTAL HORIZONTAL LOADING T_u ABOUT A

$Z =$ PLASTIC MODULUS

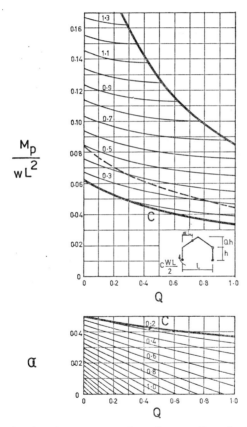

Fig. 9.26.   Design chart for moments and reactions at collapse load of fixed base gable frames (after Reference [9.8]).

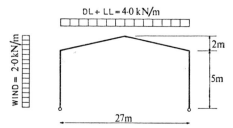

Fig. 9.27.   Gable frame for Example 9.14.

Use the chart in Fig. 9.25

$$Q = 2/5 = 0.4$$

$$C = 0$$

from the chart

$$\frac{M_p}{WL^2} = 0.052$$

$$M_p = 7 \times 27 \times 27 \times 0.052 = 265 \text{ kNm}$$

Loading case II
  Factored loads

$$DL + LL = 1.40 \times 4.0 = 5.6 \text{ kN/m}$$

$$Wind = 1.40 \times 2.0 = 2.8 \text{ kN/m}$$

Equivalent point load for wind

$$T_u = \frac{2.8 \times 7 \times 7/2}{5} = 13.7 \text{ kN}$$

$$W_u = (DL + LL) \times 27 = 151.2 \text{ kN}$$

$$Q = 0.4 \text{ from above}$$

$$C = \frac{2 \times 13.7 \times 5}{151.2 \times 60} = 0.0151$$

from the chart, since C less than 0·14 wind loading is not critical and the design plastic moment is 265 kNm

$$Z_{rep} = 265/250 = 1·061 \times 10^6 \text{ mm}^3$$

Use 406 × 178UB, 54 kg/m

$$Z_p = 1·046 \times 10^6 \text{ mm}^3$$

Axial load in a member, subject at the same time to bending has two effects:

1. It reduces the plastic moment that the member can carry.
2. It increases the possibility of failure by buckling.

Although its effect is generally not important for single storey frames lightly loaded (*i.e.* without snow load) it does become increasingly important in multi-storey frames.

In the elastic range of behaviour the stress diagram of a symmetrical shape subjected to both axial force (P) and bending moment (M) can be resolved into two parts as shown in Fig. 9.28a. When this section becomes fully plastic, primarily due to the moment, the neutral axis remains in the same position and the resultant stress diagram can be represented by two parts as shown in Fig. 9.28b where the axial load is assumed to be carried by the central portion of the section. If the axial load produced complete yielding over the cross-section, the section would have no resistance to bending, call this load P_y. Let the reduced plastic moment capacity corresponding to an axial load of P be M'_p, then the ratio of M'_p/M_p, for a symmetrical shape, can be expressed in terms of P/P_y.

Figure 9.29 shows hatched the envelope of M'_p/M_p versus P/P_y for a variety of symmetrical rolled steel sections. The heavy line represents a lower limit of probable variation. This line can be expressed by the formulae

$$M'_p/M_p = 1·18(1 - P/P_y) \quad \text{for } P/P_y > 0·15 \qquad (9.20)$$

$$M'_p/M_p = 1·0 \qquad\qquad \text{for } P/P_y < 0·15 \qquad (9.21)$$

This assumes that stability is not a governing factor.

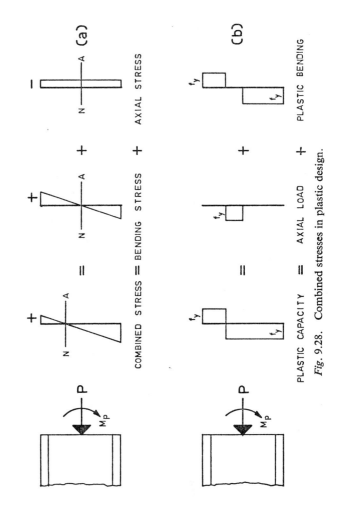

Fig. 9.28.   Combined stresses in plastic design.

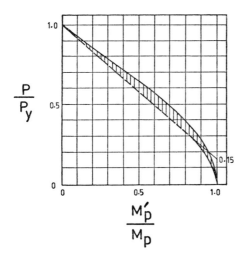

Fig. 9.29. Reduction of plastic moment capacity due to axial forces.

Example 9.15. Check the design of Example 9.14 for axial force effects in the columns due to vertical load only.

The vertical reaction at the base is 94·5 kN (half the total vertical load). The axial yield load of the section chosen 406 × 178UB, 54 kg/m is

$$P_y = f_y A = 250 \times 68\cdot3 = 17\,075 \text{ kN}$$

$$P/P_y = 94\cdot5/17\,075 = 0\cdot006 < 0\cdot15$$

Therefore, column design is satisfactory with this section. None of the frames designed in the previous examples need to be altered when the effect of the axial loads in the columns is considered.

9.6. OTHER DESIGN CONSIDERATIONS

Shear stresses, like axial stresses, when occurring in conjunction with the plastic moment tend to reduce the plastic-moment capacity of the section. This reduction is small and can be ignored for rolled sections subjected to normal loadings in normal spans. The effect of the shear-stress should be allowed for when the mean-web shear stress exceeds one third of the yield stress in tension.

The reduction in the plastic modulus for a symmetrical I-section with a web thickness (t) and an overall depth (D) is given by [9.9]:

$$\text{Reduction} = \frac{rtD^2}{4} \qquad (9.22)$$

where

$$r = 1 - \left(1 - \frac{3q^2}{fy^2}\right)^{\frac{1}{2}}$$

q = factored shear stress

Since the plastic method of design is based on strength alone, checks must be made to ensure that the stiffness criteria are satisfied. *Deflections* in the structure at the point of collapse may be readily determined. Deflections at working load may be determined exactly by an elastic analysis either by any of the classical methods or by matrix methods (see Chapter 7). This assumes that under working load no plastic hinges are formed. Since the plastic method is best suited to frames where strength rather than stiffness is the criterion, so that deflections become secondary considerations, the following method provides approximate values for deflections at working load. In essence it consists of computing the deflection at the point of collapse and dividing this value by the load factor.

i.e.

$$\delta_w = \delta_u/\lambda \qquad (9.23)$$

where δ_u = deflection at collapse load
δ_w = deflection at working load.

Whilst this method does not produce the exact result it is an upper bound solution.

It is assumed that the structure has the idealised stress–strain curve shown in Fig. 9.3b and that apart from the plastic hinge point the member retains its original flexural rigidity. The deflection at the collapse load is computed on the assumption that one particular hinge is the last to form turning the structure into a mechanism. The deflection calculations are carried out on the assumption that each hinge is the last to form; the correct deflection at collapse is the maximum value obtained from the various trials. These deflections may be calculated simply using the principle of virtual displacements.

The collapse mechanism for the structure is derived and the moments M_0 at collapse are determined. Using the equations derived in Chapter 6, the deflection at a particular point is

$$\delta = \int \frac{M_0 M_1}{EI}\, dx + \sum M_1\theta \qquad (9.24)$$

where θ = rotation of plastic hinge

M_1 = bending moment due to unit load in equilibrium structure.

Equation 9.24 must include all members and all hinges. The choice of a suitable equilibrium structure becomes important insofar as it can reduce the amount of calculation required. It is often desirable to generate this structure by putting real hinges at the points where plastic hinges are going to form, except for the last hinge. It then becomes unnecessary to calculate hinge rotations and the right-hand term in eqn 9.24 vanishes and the equation now becomes

$$\delta_u = \int \frac{M_0 M_1}{EI}\, dx \qquad (9.25)$$

Example 9.16. Determine the expression for the maximum deflection at collapse of a uniformly loaded, fixed-ended beam.

The beam is shown in Fig. 9.30, load W, span L. The hinges, at collapse, form at the ends first and then at the centre. The bending moment diagram at collapse (the 'M_0' system) is shown in Fig. 9.30a with $M_p = WL^2/16$. Since the loading is symmetrical the maximum deflection will occur at the centre. We can produce an equilibrium structure by inserting hinges at both ends producing a simply supported beam. Following the procedure outlined in Section 6.1, the deflection at the centre is determined by placing a unit load at that point in the equilibrium structure. This and the resulting M_1 moment diagram are shown in Fig. 9.30b and c.

Substituting into eqn 9.25

$$\delta_u = 2\int_0^{\frac{1}{2}L} \frac{1}{EI}\left(-\frac{WL^2}{16} + \frac{WLx}{2} - \frac{Wx^2}{2}\right)(\tfrac{1}{2}x)\, dx$$

$$= \frac{WL^4}{192EI} = \frac{M_p L^2}{12EI}$$

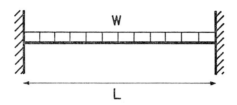

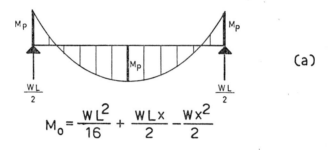

$$M_0 = \frac{WL^2}{16} + \frac{WLx}{2} - \frac{Wx^2}{2}$$

(a)

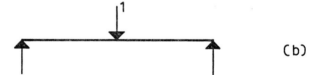

(b)

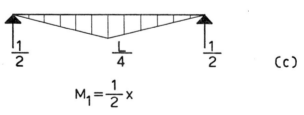

$$M_1 = \frac{1}{2}x$$

(c)

Fig. 9.30.   Beam for Example 9.16.

Compare this with the value for deflection under elastic conditions of $WL^4/384EI$; the deflection at the point of collapse is double that under elastic loads. In most cases no plastic hinges form at working load, however, the above method is not suited to the calculation of the exact deflection at working load.

In all of the frames examined it has been assumed that *stability* is not the governing criterion. For the situation where working loads do not cause any plastic hinges (as is generally the case) the frame can be examined for buckling using the procedures outlined in Section 8.6. If the stability criteria are satisfied at working load it does not necessarily mean that the frame will not buckle at either collapse load or at some load between working load on a fully elastic structure and a load less than the collapse load on a partially plastic structure. Whilst considerable work has been done on the inelastic stability of single storey frames [9.10–12] very little work has been carried out on multi-storey inelastic frame buckling [9.13]. In these buildings it is thought that the cladding acts as bracing, increasing the frame stiffness and reducing the likelihood of buckling.

Lateral stability and local buckling of beams need to be considered in plastic design just as in elastic design (see Sections 8.3 and 8.4 as well as References [9.14–17]). Since plastic design methods assume completely rigid joints the design of the *connections* can become important. There are three principal design requirements for connections in this context:

1. *strength*: the connection must be designed to develop an adequate plastic moment capacity (equal, at least, to that of the weaker member).
2. *stiffness*: although not very important it is desirable that the stiffness be at least equal to that of the members being connected.
3. *rotation capacity*: the connection must be designed to achieve the necessary rotation after a plastic hinge has formed. This rotation is required to assure hinge behaviour and is a reserve of ductility of the connection after the plastic moment has been reached. Design guides may be found in References [B11, 9.18–21].

Chapter 10

Masonry and Concrete Structures

In this chapter we consider those aspects of the design of masonry, and concrete structures which differ specifically from those of steel structures. We first examine the design of masonry, and specifically brick, structures which are made much taller than traditional masonry structures because their resistance to wind loading is analysed in accordance with engineering principles. We then look at the advantages which have traditionally commended masonry and concrete structures, namely their fire and sound resisting properties.

Next we derive the principal formulae for the design of reinforced and prestressed concrete structures in accordance with the old-established elastic theory, and then we repeat the procedure for the more recent ultimate-strength theory.

We briefly consider the various types of concrete slabs, especially the important flat plate construction, and also the use of precast concrete panels. Finally we look briefly at the problems created by non-structural deformations.

10.1. STRUCTURAL MASONRY

For 7000 years, masonry construction has been a system commonly used to house and serve man. Over this time a considerable amount of knowledge about this technology should have been recorded. Unfortunately, this was not done. For example, brick has been used as a compression material, yet there is no internationally recognised column formula which adequately describes the buckling characteristics of a brick wall or column. The same is true for other masonry materials. The lack of structural design consensus regarding masonry cannot be attributed to a dearth of research. On the contrary, there is a wealth of excellent research data in existence throughout the world.

Compression testing of masonry began in this country with work

314

done at Watertown Arsenal in 1882. But the fact remains that, although the world's literature is replete with individual research papers, there are only two books in English which describe the structural properties of masonry . . . . The scarcity of literature in English on masonry structural systems can be partly attributed to the fact that until only recently unit masonry was considered an architectural material rather than an engineering structural system.

Franklin B. Johnson [10.1, *p.* 7]

The basic principle in structural masonry construction is that the load-bearing walls are designed to act in compression (with sometimes a nominal tensile stress allowed). In order to achieve this condition the architect and engineer must work closely together at the preliminary planning stages since the shape of the building and the location of walls play a paramount part. Unlike steel or reinforced concrete (or reinforced masonry), normal masonry walls rely on the form of the structure to ensure that the design conditions are

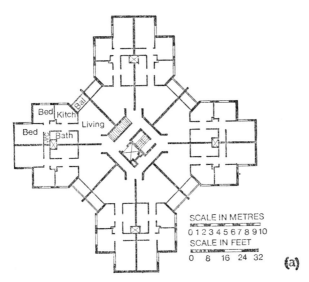

Fig. 10.1a.   Plan of typical floor of loadbearing construction: Kingsway Gardens, Western Australia; Krantz and Sheldon—architects; G. Katewa and Partners—structural engineers.

achieved; increasing a wall thickness will not always solve the problem. Figure 10.1 shows a number of plans for typical load-bearing masonry construction. Because the structure delineates cellular spaces, masonry construction has found its greatest application in flat and apartment buildings and to a lesser extent in hotels and motels. Buildings up to 20 storeys have been constructed in un-reinforced masonry.

The method of design for *vertical loads* is simply to calculate the total loads per foot run applied by the flooring, the self-weight of the wall and the live load, and sum these at each floor level. Walls carrying floors of unequal spans and external walls will be eccen-trically loaded. However, if an effective eccentricity is calculated, making the assumption that these eccentricities only apply on the

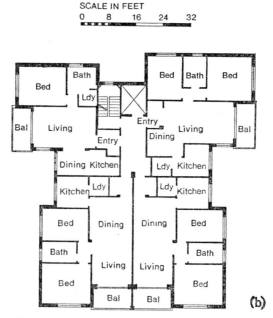

Fig. 10.1b. Plan of typical floor of loadbearing construction: Chiswick, New South Wales; Gabor Lukacs—architect; A. Fekete—structural engineer.

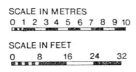

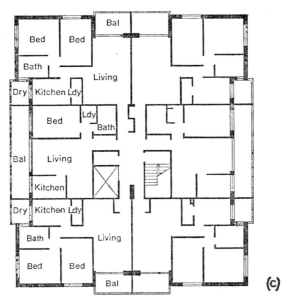

(c)

Fig. 10.1c. Plan of typical floor of loadbearing construction: Eastlakes, New South Wales; Stephen Gergely—architect; A. Fekete—structural engineer.

floor being considered, then in the more critical lower parts of the building, the effect on the strength of brick required is negligible, especially as a 25 % increase in permissible stress due solely to bending is allowed in most codes. Having arrived at a loading, it is simple to convert this into brick strength and mortar mix by reference to the permissible stress and slenderness reduction factors published in codes [10.2–8].

In the *design for wind* the commonly accepted method is to treat the building as a vertical cantilever. The amount of wind moment taken by each wall is in proportion to its second moment of area; this assumes that the horizontal forces will distribute themselves to the stiffest members. Each individual wall is then designed to carry its share of the wind moment together with its vertical load. It is desirable that the resultant stress diagram produce no tension. However, it is not uncommon to allow up to 20% of the wall to exhibit tension under these conditions provided the stress block is adjusted to allow for the resulting increase in compression by ignoring the tensile triangle and making the area of the compression triangle equal to the total load on the wall (Fig. 10.2).

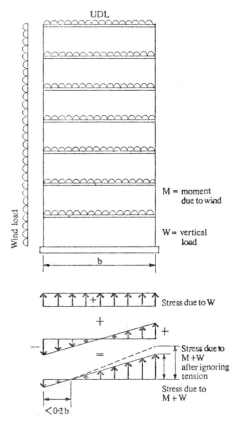

Fig. 10.2.   Stress diagrams on a loadbearing wall due to vertical loads (W) and wind moment (M) with the effect of ignoring tension shown.

The American Structural Clay Products Institute has published computer programs which can be used to analyse the effects of lateral wind loads parallel to walls utilising the lumped stiffness concept mentioned earlier [10.9]: this program has been added to include the torsional effects of a non-uniform distribution in the stiffness of walls [10.10]. A further computer program is available for vertical dead- and live-load analysis [10.11]. All of these programs are based on approximate models of the behaviour of these structures—they fail to account for axial shortening of columns, and more importantly frame action. Furthermore, little cognisance seems to be taken in design of such problems as the effects of deflections of slabs on the cracking of external walls, the interaction of walls and slabs generally, and shear in walls [10.12].

A set of typical calculations [10.2] in accordance with British Standard CP111 [10.3] is shown below. The layout of a standard floor of a 15 storey high building is indicated in Fig. 10.3. There are four 1-bedroom flats per floor, arranged symmetrically about the centre line. The floors are 127 mm (5 in) thick *in situ* concrete flat slabs. A feature of this particular design is the slenderness of the load-bearing walls. Apart from two piers in the entrance hall area and a short length of external wall, all the internal structural walls are 171 mm (6¾ in) thick using Calculon bricks and the external walls are 229 mm (9 in) wide sandfaced V-bricks laid in stretcher bond. The outcome of using such slender walls is that less than 8 % of the gross floor area is taken up with structural walls; a very low proportion for such a building.

Loads

(i) roof load—dead load = 4·3 kPa (90 lb/ft²)
           live load = 0·9 kPa (20 lb/ft²)

(ii) floor load—dead load = 4·3 kPa (90 lb/ft²)
           live load = 1·9 kPa (40 lb/ft²)

(iii) self weight—Calculon (plastered both sides) = 3·6 kPa
                                          (75 lb/ft²)

           V-brick (plastered one side)   = 3·6 kPa
                                          (75 lb/ft²)

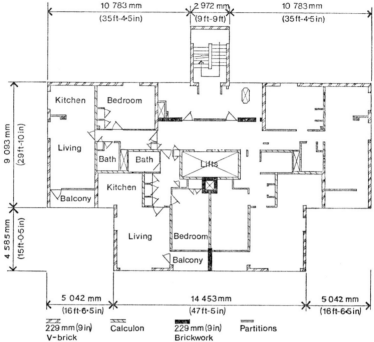

Fig. 10.3.   Plan of building used in typical calculations (after Reference [10.2]).
Borough High Street, London Borough of Southwark. Ronald Hardy—architect.
Jenkins and Potter—consulting engineers.

Load Capacity of Brickwork

(i) V-brick (external walling), storey height 2·65 m (8·67 ft), effective
thickness 229 mm (9 in), giving a slenderness ratio of

$$\frac{(2\cdot65 \times 1000) \times 0\cdot75}{229} = 8\cdot68$$

From the Code [10.3] the reduction factor for concentric
loading is 0·89.

Permissible stresses:

41 000 kPa (6000 lb/in^2) bricks (1:1:6 mortar) = 2100 kPa
$$(305 \text{ lb/in}^2)$$

41 000 kPa (6000 lb/in^2) bricks (1:$\frac{1}{4}$:3 mortar) = 2900 kPa
$$(420 \text{ lb/in}^2)$$

Thus, permissible loads per ft run of V-brick wall with 41 000 kPa (6000 lb/in²) bricks:

$$1:1:6 \text{ mortar} = 2100 \times 0\cdot229 \times 0\cdot89 = 430 \text{ kN/m run}$$
$$(29\ 300 \text{ lb/ft})$$

$$1:\tfrac{1}{4}:3 \text{ mortar} = 2900 \times 0\cdot229 \times 0\cdot89 = 590 \text{ kN/m run}$$
$$(40\ 400 \text{ lb/ft})$$

(ii) 171 mm (6¼ in) Calculon (internal walling), storey height 2·64 m (8·67 ft) effective thickness 171 mm giving a slenderness ratio of

$$\frac{(2\cdot64 \times 1000) \times 0\cdot75}{171} = 11\cdot58$$

The reduction factor for this wall is 0·78.
Permissible stresses (p) and permissible loads (P) calculated as above:

34 500 kPa (5000 lb/in²) bricks

1:1:6 mortar $p = 1800$ kPa (270 lb/in²),

$$P = 250 \text{ kN/m run } (17\ 000 \text{ lb/ft})$$

1:¼:3 mortar $p = 2500$ kPa (360 lb/in²),

$$P = 330 \text{ kN/m run } (22\ 700 \text{ lb/ft})$$

48 300 kPa (7000 lb/in²) bricks

1:¼:3 mortar $p = 3300$ kPa (480 lb/in²),

$$P = 440 \text{ kN/m run } (30\ 300 \text{ lb/ft})$$

68 900 kPa (10 000 lb/in²) bricks

1:¼:3 mortar $p = 4500$ kPa (660 lb/12²),

$$P = 600 \text{ kN/m run } (41\ 700 \text{ lb/ft})$$

Wind Calculations
The distribution of the walls assumed to carry the wind load in two orthogonal directions is shown in Fig. 10.4. The total moment

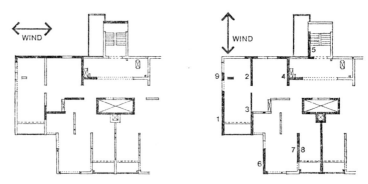

Fig. 10.4. Layout of walls taking wind loads on a typical floor (after Reference [10.2]).

due to a wind load of 670 Pa (14 lb/ft^2) acting on the long face of the building is calculated to be 10 700 kN m (7·89 × 10^6 lb ft). As described earlier, the wind moment is distributed between the walls in proportion to their second moment of area (moment of inertia, I). Where walls form complex sections that are stronger than single walls, this additional stiffness is usually calculated. Small walls having a low moment of inertia are generally ignored. The calculation for this distribution is often performed by computer. A summary for the distribution of the wind moment in the long direction is shown below; the building is symmetrical in this direction.

Wall no.	No. off	Total I (m^4)	Distributed moment (kN)	Moment on one wall (kN)
1	2	4·833	1 478	732
2	2	2·244	680	339
3	2	3·711	1 125	563
4	2	3·703	1 125	563
5	2	1·674	515	258
6	2	1·062	325	163
7	2	1·191	366	183
8	1	16·408	5 030	5 030

The height of the building is 34·5 m (113 ft) above the two entrance floors.

Design of Calculon Wall No. 7:

Length of wall $= 3.43$ m $(11.25$ ft$)$ $I = 0.596$ m^4 $(69$ ft$^4)$

Wind moment from above table $= 184$ kN m $(135\ 000$ lb ft$)$

Span of floor on wall $= 3.51$ m $(11.5$ ft$)$

$\therefore$ load per metre run for each floor $= 3.51 \times (4.3 + 1.9)$

$$21.76 \text{ kN } (15.09 \text{ kN ex live load})$$

Reactions from beam in slab, bearing on end with loads of 1.34 kPa $(28$ lb/ft$^2)$ of floor at leeward end, is 208 kN $(46\ 700$ lb$)$ and reaction at windward end with load of 0.81 kPa $(17$ lb/ft$^2)$ of floor is 89 kN $(20\ 000$ lb$)$ at just below first floor level (Fig. 10.5).

When taking into account wind on a wall, the uplift at one end can be as critical as the compression at the other. Therefore, one should take live load plus dead load at the leeward end, but dead load, only, at the windward end. Then the uniform load at ground floor level (12 floors plus roof above):

with live load $= 18.49 + (12 \times 21.76) + (34.5 \times 3.6)$

$$= 404 \text{ kN/m run } (27\ 670 \text{ lb/ft})$$

without live load $= 15.09 + (12 \times 15.09) + (34.5 \times 3.6)$

$$= 320 \text{ kN/m run } (21\ 920 \text{ lb/ft})$$

Taking moments about the centre of gravity of the wall for the loads shown in Fig. 10.5:

$$M = 208 \times \frac{3.43}{2} - 89 \times \frac{3.43}{2} + 404 \times \frac{3.43^2}{8}$$

$$- 320 \times \frac{3.43^2}{8} + 183.033$$

$$= 356.720 - 152.635 + 594.127 - 470.596 + 183.033$$

$$= 510.65 \text{ kN m } (361\ 000 \text{ lb ft})$$

Total vertical load:

$$W = 208 + 89 + 404 \times \frac{3.43}{2} + 320 \times \frac{3.43}{2}$$

$$= 1539 \text{ kN } (346\ 000 \text{ lb})$$

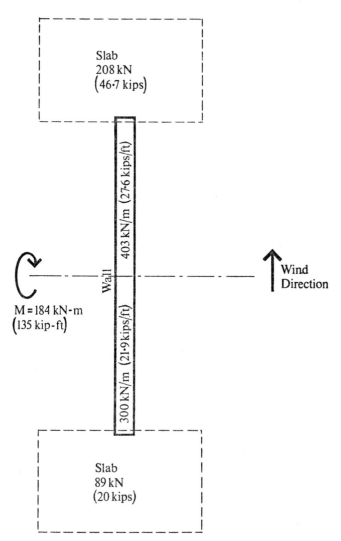

Fig. 10.5.   Loading diagram on Wall 7 (after Reference [10.2]).

Then, the stresses at the ends of the wall, given by

$$f = \frac{M}{A} \pm \frac{M}{Z}$$

where A = wall area

Z = section modulus $\{I/(\text{wall length}/2)\}$

$$\therefore \quad f = \frac{1539}{3\cdot43 \times 0\cdot171} \pm \frac{510\cdot65}{0\cdot596} \times \frac{3\cdot43}{2}$$

$$= 2623\cdot90 \pm 1469\cdot40$$

$$= 4093\cdot30 \text{ and } 1154\cdot50 \text{ kPa}$$

or

$$f = 699\cdot95 \text{ and } 197\cdot42 \text{ kN/m run (48 000 and 13 500 lb/ft)}$$

The permissible load on 68 900 kPa (10 000 lb/in²) Calculon bricks using $1:\frac{1}{4}:8$ mortar = 598 + 150 (25% wind allowance) = 748 kN/m (51 250 lb/ft) run so that this strength brick and mortar should be used. By checking the stresses at other levels, and with reference to the permissible loads above, the brick strengths throughout the building can be obtained. In conclusion the design engineer states that with the wind blowing on the short side, the resisting walls are not symmetrical about the centre line. In a building with *in situ* concrete floors, it is problematical what effect this has on stresses, but in this case no account was taken of composite action and this was regarded as a sufficient safeguard of overstress due to possible torsion.

Structural masonry can be reinforced in regions of tensile stress which can occur in beams, columns and walls. The behaviour of *reinforced masonry* is quite similar to reinforced concrete (see Section 10.3). However, the orthogonal anisotropic nature of masonry causes some differences. Over-reinforced masonry beams are more brittle than over-reinforced concrete beams, and the relative magnitudes of shear, tensile and compressive strength are somewhat different from those of reinforced concrete [10.12]. The design of reinforced masonry is based on the same assumptions as in reinforced concrete.

Prestressing is usually associated with concrete construction yet records show that post-tensioned brickwork was successfully employed over 140 years ago for part of the Thames Tunnel Project [10.13]. Since then, however, progress has been slow and it has been only in the last decade that prestressing has again been applied to masonry. Most of the applications have been for beams and floors [10.14, 10.15]; more recently the use of prestressed masonry walls has been suggested as a means not only of controlling tension in walls but also of allowing the walls of cellular structures to be interrupted and completely cut off to provide a break in spatial arrangements below them [10.16].

Non-structural factors which favour the use of structural masonry as a constructional material include its high sound absorption, its fire resistance, its thermal layers, its high thermal insulation, its durability and the lack of the need for maintenance.

10.2. Concrete in Fireproof and Soundproof Construction

Structural safety (see Section 2.8) has been improved so much that the collapse of a building in peacetime due to structural failure is a newsworthy event. Destruction of buildings by fire, on the other hand, is a daily occurrence. It is therefore inevitable that protection of the structure against fire is becoming an increasingly important design factor.

The problem goes back to the earliest days of urban settlement. Alberti [10.17] wrote in the 15th century:

I am entirely for having the roofs of temples arched, as well because it gives them greater dignity, as because it makes them more durable. And indeed I know not how it happens that we shall hardly meet any one temple whatsoever that has not fallen into the calamity of fire . . . Caesar owned that Alexandria escaped being burnt, when he himself took it, because its roofs were vaulted.

The stone vault of the Gothic cathedrals also had this function of protecting the timber roof above against fire. In 1212 King John passed an ordinance requiring alehouses in the City of London to be built of stone, presumably because they constituted an abnormal occupancy as far as fire protection was concerned; but even in stone buildings the floors and roofs were generally of timber until the 19th century, when the industrial revolution made iron available in quantity. Unlike timber, iron and steel do not burn, but they lose their strength above approximately 400°C. In a major building fire the temperature of 400°C is reached within 10 min and a temperature of 1000°C is reached within two hours. Only ceramics retain their strength at this temperature (see Section 3.3) and natural stone, brick and concrete are therefore the principal fireproof materials. Clay tiles were frequently used as fire-protection for structural steel-work in the early 19th century, and it was largely on the evidence of their inadequate performance in the fire following the San Francisco earthquake of 1906 [10.19] that concrete became accepted as the best material for the fire-protection of steel frames.

Since the structural steel frame originated in the United States in the late 19th century, the three great fires of Chicago (1871, estimated damage £76 million—$190 million), Baltimore (1904, estimated damage £60 million—$150 million) and San Francisco (1906, estimated damage £160 million—$400 million) had a profound influence on future policy.

Small fires are still commonplace, and disastrous conflagrations occur from time to time. Tremendous destruction was caused by fires due to enemy action during the World War 1939–45, e.g. in London, Dresden and Hiroshima. Even in peacetime serious fires have not been eliminated, for instance in Istanbul in 1954 a fire caused damage estimated at £71 million ($178 million) in a single day.

The design of buildings in relation to fire is discussed in another title in this series [1.8]; it may be sufficient to state here that reinforced concrete columns are generally required to have at least 40 mm ($1\frac{1}{2}$ in) cover as a protection against rusting of the steel, and that 40 mm of cover over the reinforcement gives fire protection for $1\frac{1}{2}$ hours under most conditions.

The early high-rise buildings were built with a steel frame, as reinforced concrete had evident limitations for very high buildings because concrete has a lower compressive strength than steel (see Section 1.3). With improved quality control, however, the strength of concrete has risen and the load factor has been reduced (see

Section 2.8). The economic limit has increased accordingly, and today in some countries, such as Australia, reinforced concrete is cheaper for tall buildings than structural steel, and is used for the tallest buildings (250 m, 770 ft).

The large size of reinforced concrete columns has become less important with the development of new concepts for framing tall buildings (see Chapter 11) which eliminate interior columns.

In North America steel columns protected against fire by lightweight ceramics, such as vermiculite, are normally used for tall buildings, and the saving in weight over solid concrete protection is an obvious and incontestable advantage. The resulting saving in cost is partly dependent on local fire-regulations, and in some countries the economic advantage is with reinforced concrete.

Higher standards of sound insulation have been another factor in favour of reinforced concrete, particularly in low-cost construction where non-structural insulation is often lacking. Structural failure and failure by fire are unmistakable faults; it is harder to determine when sound insulation is inadequate, and many people have accepted low standards for lack of comparison. Noise is particularly obnoxious in residential accommodation and a structural concrete floor 175 mm (7 in) thick provides excellent sound insulation. The value of sound-insulated floors is greatly increased when air conditioning eliminates the leakage of sound through open windows in summer.

Airborne noise can be stopped only by a massive barrier, and the relatively high weight of a structural concrete floor therefore provides good insulation, without additional treatment or cost. Impact noise is less disturbing in apartments; it can be attenuated partly by the concrete barrier and partly by a carpet or a floating-floor finish.

The British Code of Practice CP 114:1969, which is still in use, is basically an elastic code; ultimate-strength clauses are framed in pseudo-elastic terms. The British Code of Practice CP 110:1972 [5.2] deletes all reference to the elastic design of sections, but uses elastic methods for the design of frames. In one respect this new British code is ahead of the current American and Australian codes; it uses a *partial safety factor for load*, γ_f, in conjunction with a *partial safety factor for strength*, γ_m. Thus dead loads have a lower safety factor than superimposed loads, and steel has a lower safety factor than concrete. This is evidently more realistic and ultimately more economical than the older American formulae reproduced in Chapter 2 (eqns 2.6 to 2.8). The current American Code [5.1] is also a code using ultimate-strength design for reinforced-concrete sections and elastic design for the design of the frame; however, elastic design of reinforced-concrete sections is still admitted as an alternative method. The Australian Code [5.3] is in the process of transition from a basically elastic code to one in which ultimate strength is the normal basis for the design of reinforced concrete sections. The authors' treatment is in accordance with the American Code [5.1] as it is the one most widely understood.

There are differences in the notation. The notation used in CP 114: 1969 (which differs from that used in earlier British codes) has been revised in CP 110:1972. It is now much nearer to the well-established American notation, but there are still differences. The authors have therefore decided to use a compromise, simplified notation embodying features known from the American, British and Australian notations, and hope this will be generally intelligible.

The changeover to the metric *Système International* has not brought the unity which had been expected. The British codes CP 110 and CP 114 use N/mm^2 for stresses and kN/mm^2 for moduli of elasticity. The new Australian codes use MPa (which is the same as MN/m^2) for stresses and GPa (equal to GN/m^2) for moduli of elasticity. Recent publications of the American Society for Testing Materials have used conversions to MN/m^2 and GN/m^2. The authors have used MPa and GPa as a reasonable compromise, with conversion to lb/in^2.

It is not, of course, proposed that this chapter should cover the design of reinforced-concrete frames. There are several excellent British and American text-books dealing with the subject in detail and in accordance with the national code; the position in Australia is less fortunate. The authors propose to confine themselves to examining the background of the theory of reinforced concrete design as it relates to building frames. They have included elastic design, partly because it is still used in some codes, and partly because it is relevant to a consideration of serviceability limit-states, *e.g.* deflection and cracking.

Examples have not been used. Because of the differences in

national practices mentioned, they might, in this condensed treatment, confuse rather than illuminate.

A_s cross-sectional area of steel

b width of section

C resultant compressive force in section

d effective depth of section, *i.e.* depth to centroid of reinforcement

d_c depth of compression steel

e_c, e_s strain in concrete, steel

e_y steel strain at which yield commences

e'_c, e'_s ultimate strain of concrete, steel

E_c, E_s modulus of elasticity of concrete, steel

f_c, f_s service stress in concrete, steel

f_y yield or proof stress of steel

f'_c, f'_s ultimate strength of concrete, steel

j lever-arm ratio (length of lever arm/effective depth) at the working load

j' lever-arm ratio at the ultimate load

k, k' neutral axis depth ratio at the working, at the ultimate, load

K balanced design coefficient at the working load $(= M/bd^2)$ at the moment which produces the maximum permissible stresses simultaneously in the steel and the concrete

K' balanced design coefficient at the ultimate load $(= M'/bd^2)$ when the steel just reaches the stress f_y and the concrete the stress f'_c

M bending moment, resistance moment at the working load

M' ultimate resistance moment

p steel ratio $= A_s/bd$

p_0 balanced steel ratio, corresponding to design coefficients K and K' above

P column load

t thickness of flange of T-beam

T resultant tensile force in section

α, β, γ constants of the ultimate-stress block for concrete (see Fig. 10.12)

The following symbols are used additionally for prestressed concrete:

A cross-sectional area of concrete

M_G bending moment due to the self-weight of the prestressed
        concrete beam

P prestressing force

Z section modulus of concrete section

ε eccentricity of prestressing force

10.3. THE ELASTIC THEORY OF REINFORCED-CONCRETE DESIGN

We noted in Section 4.7 that the simple theory of bending is not strictly isostatic, since it involves assumptions on the elastic and inelastic deformation of the material in the beam. In reinforced concrete we have the additional complication of dealing with two materials. In the early years of this century, when the elastic theory of reinforced concrete design was developed [10.20], some exceedingly complicated equations were produced. Some of these still appeared in books reprinted in the 1940s. The problem is, however, more apparent than real, because we can make a number of simplifying assumptions which make little difference to the economy or the safety of the structure.

The first of these is to ignore the tensile strength of the concrete (Fig. 10.6). Since the tensile strength of concrete is only $\frac{1}{10}$ of its

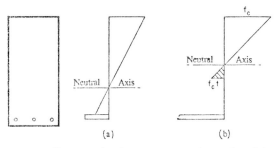

Fig. 10.6. The tensile strength of concrete may be neglected in reinforced concrete beams.
(a) Stress distribution at low loads before the concrete cracks.
(b) Stress distribution at working loads.

compressive strength (see Section 3.5), the error is less than 1%. We are now left with a compressive force in the concrete, and a tensile force in the steel. The ratio of steel reinforcement in concrete slabs and rectangular beams generally is sufficiently low to produce a failure which is initiated by the plastic deformation of the steel (see Section 10.5). The tensile force is $f_s A_s$ (where f_s is the maximum permissible tensile stress in the steel and A_s is its cross-sectional area). The resistance moment (Fig. 10.7) of the section is therefore

$$M = f_s A_s jd \tag{10.1}$$

where j depends on the percentage of steel, but in practice lies between 0·8 and 0·9. Its exact value may be calculated or read from design tables or charts (*e.g.* Reference 10.21).

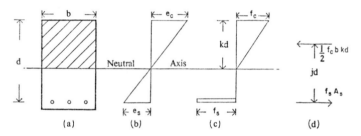

Fig. 10.7.   Resistance moment of rectangular concrete sections.
(a) Dimensions of section.
(b) Strain distribution.
(c) Stress distribution.
(d) Resistance moment.

Equation 10.1 is valid as long as the ratio of steel to concrete is less than the *balanced steel ratio* (p_0). This is defined as the ratio at which the maximum permissible stresses in the steel and the concrete are reached simultaneously.

In elastic design the balanced steel ratio (p_0) is much lower than in design based on ultimate strength, and indeed it is common practice to design rectangular beams and slabs with a balanced steel ratio. We must therefore consider this limitation in more detail.

Since plane sections remain plane (see Section 4.7), the ratios of the maximum concrete strain and the strain in the steel (Fig. 10.7b)

$$\frac{e_c}{e_s} = \frac{kd}{d - kd}$$

In the elastic range stress is proportional to strain

$$e_c = \frac{f_c}{E_c} \quad \text{and} \quad e_s = \frac{f_s}{E_s}$$

Calling the ratio of the moduli of elasticity of steel and concrete

$$n = \frac{E_s}{E_c} \quad \text{(modular ratio)}$$

$$\frac{nf_c}{f_s} = \frac{kd}{d - kd} \tag{10.2}$$

and the neutral axis depth ratio

$$\frac{kd}{d} = k = \frac{nf_c}{nf_c + f_s}$$

which varies from 0·3 to 0·6, depending on the maximum permissible steel and concrete stresses.

The resultant compressive force acts at the centre of gravity of the triangular stress-block (Fig. 10.7c), i.e. at a depth $\frac{1}{3}kd$, and the lever arm ratio

$$\frac{jd}{d} = j = 1 - \tfrac{1}{3}k = \frac{1 - \tfrac{1}{3}nf_c}{nf_c + f_s}$$

which, as previously mentioned, lies for practical combinations of maximum permissible stresses between 0·8 and 0·9, and is frequently taken as 0·85.

Equating the horizontal forces in Fig. 10.7d

$$\tfrac{1}{2}f_c bkd = f_s A_s = f_s p_0 bd$$

and substituting from eqn 10.2, the balanced steel ratio

$$p_0 = \frac{kf_c}{2f_s}$$

(where p_0 and f_s are the maximum permissible concrete and steel stresses). This ratio can vary from 0·004 to 0·04, and consequently includes the practical range of economical reinforcement. In practice it also represents the upper limit to the amount of steel in the section. If a steel ratio higher than p_0 is employed, the resistance moment can be increased only by lowering the depth of the neutral axis. This increases the area of the triangle ($\frac{1}{2}f_c kd$) but reduces the length of the lever arm (jd) and reduces the steel strain (e_s) and consequently the steel stress (f_s). Even quite a small increase in the bending moment therefore increases the steel area (A_s) appreciably, because the tensile force in the steel ($f_s A_s$) must balance the force in the concrete ($\frac{1}{2}f_c bkd$). An impractically high steel area (A_s) is soon reached, and p_0 is therefore the economical upper limit to the steel ratio.

At the steel ratio p_0, the resistance moment, from eqn 10.1 is

$$M = f_s p_0 bd \cdot jd = Kbd^2 \qquad (10.3)$$

where $K = f_s p_0 j$ is a design constant for any combination of maximum permissible stresses f_c and f_s.

One great advantage of reinforced concrete lies in the interaction of the floor slab and the ribs on which it is supported. The structure is cast in one piece and the slab is thus a load-carrying structural member in one direction, and also contributes to the strength of the supporting beam at right angles (see also Section 10.9). As a further simplification we neglect the compressive stresses in the concrete rib, since the neutral axis is usually close to the base of the slab, the compressive stresses are low in a rib which is also much smaller in width than the flange, and the error is less than 5%, and on the safe side (Fig. 10.8).

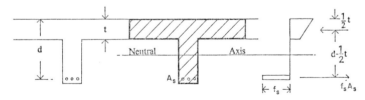

Fig. 10.8.   Resistance moment of reinforced concrete T-beams.

We may then make a further approximation by assuming that the compressive force acts half-way down the slab; also the error is on the safe side and less than 5%. In T-beams there is a relatively large amount of concrete in the slab, by comparison with the reinforcement in the ribs, so that failure is invariably initiated by plastic deformation of the steel. Consequently

$$M = f_s A_s (d - \tfrac{1}{2}t) \tag{10.4}$$

Since concrete structures are normally continuous over the supports (see Section 5.3), the slab of a ribbed floor becomes the tensile (and therefore cracked) zone over the columns or primary beams. The rib does not provide a sufficient amount of concrete for the negative support moment, and we therefore introduce compression reinforcement (Fig. 10.9) to avoid deepening or widening of the section where this is architecturally unacceptable. We can divide the resulting section into two parts, the first being a rectangular beam with tension reinforcement only; this has a resistance moment (see eqn 10.3)

$$M_1 = Kbd^2$$

and, from eqn 10.1, a steel area

$$A_{s1} = \frac{M_1}{f_s jd}$$

The remainder of the resistance moment

$$M_2 = M - M_1$$

is provided by the rest of the tension reinforcement and the entire compression reinforcement

$$M_2 = f_s A_{s2}(d - d_c)$$

The problem of the elastic design of reinforced concrete beams can therefore be reduced to terms which are only slightly more complicated than those for structural steel [10.29–31].

In this context, reinforced concrete has one advantage over steel.

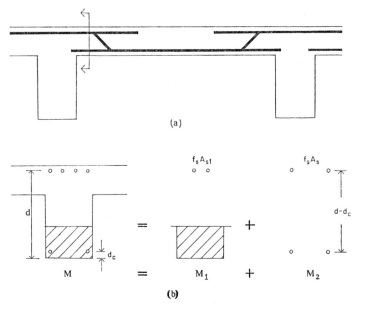

Fig. 10.9.   Concrete beams with compression steel.

(a) The need for compression steel arises from the negative moments over the
supports, where the slab is in tension, and compressive concrete area is
therefore small.

(b) The resistance moment can be divided into two parts: one comprises the
concrete in compression and a part of the tension steel (A_{s1}), the other
the entire compression steel and the remainder of the tension steel (A_{s2}).

The stiffness of the section, which figures so prominently in rigid-
frame calculations, is dependent almost entirely on the dimensions
of the concrete, since the steel occupies at most a few percent of the
cross-sectional area. The strength, on the other hand, is largely
dependent on the amount of steel. It is therefore possible to introduce
a direct element into the elastic design of hyperstatic concrete
structures which is lacking in rigid frames of structural steel. We can
modify the strength of the structure after our first check, within
certain limits, by altering the amount of reinforcement. If we do not
alter the overall dimensions of the concrete, the rigid frame analysis
is not affected.

The only reinforced sections whose elastic analysis cannot be reduced, even approximately, to simple terms are those subject to combined bending and compression. Since all external columns of rigid frames are subject to bending, this is a common problem. It is generally solved in practice by the use of tables and design charts to avoid evaluating the complex equations [10.21].

Although concentrically columns can easily be solved by elastic equations, it has been common practice for many years, to design them by ultimate strength, even when the rest of the structure was elastically designed. The problem is discussed in Section 10.8.

10.4. THE ELASTIC THEORY OF PRESTRESSED-CONCRETE DESIGN

The object of prestressing simple concrete beams is to introduce compressive stresses into those parts of the beam where tension occurs under load. If the concrete is entirely in compression under load, its low tensile strength is no longer important and full advantage can be taken of the high compressive strength of concrete. Prestressed concrete beams are therefore free from cracks under the action of the working loads (Fig. 10.10). Against this we must set the cost of the prestressing operation.

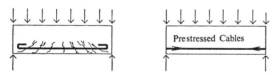

Fig. 10.10. Reinforced concrete cracks under working loads, prestressed concrete cracks only under an overload. The steel stress in reinforced concrete is limited to 230 MPa (33 500 lb/in^2) to avoid excessive cracking. The use of high tensile steel in prestressed concrete saves steel, but not necessarily money.

The most advantageous stress distribution is obtained if the concrete just reaches the maximum permissible compressive stress at the bottom face under the action of the eccentric prestressing force and the weight of the beam, and at the top face under the full load (Fig. 10.11). In each case the stress at the opposite face is nil under the same loads, or sometimes a small tensile stress may be permitted

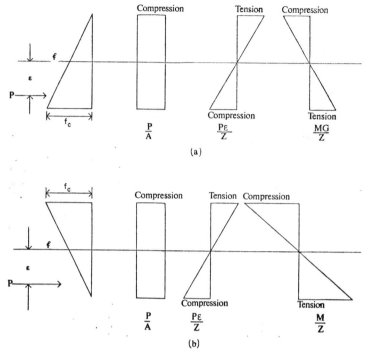

Fig. 10.11. Simply supported prestressed concrete beams are isostatic since P and M and both independent variables.

(a) Beam under the action of its dead weight and the prestress.

(b) Beam carrying the full working load.

P = prestressing force; ε = eccentricity of prestressing force; M_G = bending moment due to the self-weight of the beam; M = bending moment due to the full working load; f_c = maximum permissible concrete stress; A = cross sectional area of the concrete; Z = section modulus of the concrete (which is identical for the top and bottom in a symmetrical section).

[10.22–24]. Under the action of prestress and dead weight the stresses are:

at the top

$$0 = \frac{P}{A} - \frac{P\varepsilon}{Z} + \frac{M_G}{Z}$$

and at the bottom

$$f_c = \frac{P}{A} + \frac{P\varepsilon}{Z} - \frac{M_G}{Z}$$

(10.5)

Under the action of the full load the stresses are:

at the top
$$f_c = \frac{P}{A} - \frac{P\varepsilon}{Z} + \frac{M}{Z}$$

and at the bottom
$$0 = \frac{P}{A} + \frac{P\varepsilon}{Z} - \frac{M}{Z}$$

(10.6)

The steel stress does not enter into these equations, but the area of steel must be sufficient to provide the prestressing force P. Since the concrete does not crack under the action of the working loads, there is no restriction on the maximum permissible steel stress as there is in reinforced concrete, where stresses in excess of 350 MPa (50 750 lb/in^2) are not normally permitted, to limit the size of the cracks (which get wider as the steel extends). It is possible to use economically a maximum permissible steel stress of 1000 MPa (145 000 lb/in^2) and this results in a great steel saving. High-strength steel is more expensive than reinforcing steel, but the tensile force is provided more economically by a small area of high strength steel.

The use of high strength steel is not merely desirable on economic grounds, it is also essential because of the inelastic deformation of the concrete. Concrete shrinks approximately 3×10^{-4} mm per millimetre during curing and hardening, and the prestressing steel contracts by an equal amount. Taking the modulus of elasticity of steel as 200 GPa (29×10^6 lb/in^2), we lose $3 \times 10^{-4} \times 200 \times 10^9$ = 60 MPa (8700 lb/in^2) due to shrinkage alone. This is too high a proportion of the maximum permissible stress of normal reinforcing steel (about 140 MPa), but it is only a small percentage of the stress permissible in high tensile steel. A further loss occurs when the concrete creeps under the action of the permanently acting prestressing force (see Section 3.5). Even with high tensile steel there is a loss of prestress due to shrinkage and creep of about 15%, and the prestressing force P in eqn 10.6 is therefore about 15% less than the P in eqn 10.5.

10.5. The Ultimate-Strength Theory for Concrete Structures

Although the elastic theory of reinforced concrete design was developed almost a century later than the elastic theory of iron and steel structures, the discussion of its ultimate strength preceded the development of the plastic theory of steel structures. This is due to the fact that the behaviour of steel at the service stress closely approximates to that of an elastic material, whereas that of concrete evidently does not (see Section 3.5).

The earliest inelastic theories for reinforced concrete design aimed to modify the classical elastic theory to allow for the non-linear relation between stress and strain in concrete under the action of the working loads, and attention therefore concentrated on the exact shape of the stress–strain diagram. When simple relations, such as the second-order parabola, proved inadequate, more complex curves like the fifth-degree parabola and the ellipse were used, and the resulting theories involve very complex mathematics. At least twenty-four inelastic theories for reinforced concrete design were published between 1914 and 1949 [10.25, 10.26].

The development of a satisfactory ultimate strength theory for steel structures demonstrated that the exact shape of the diagram was unimportant. The problem can be solved if the area contained under the stress–strain curve and the centre of gravity of this area are known. Both can be established by experiment, without knowing the actual shape of the curve.

The general shape of the concrete stress–strain diagram determined from experiments [10.27] is shown in Fig. 10.12. When test piece is loaded rapidly, i.e. the test is completed within one hour, the concrete deforms mainly elastically at low loads; the diagram departs slightly from proportionality due to a small amount of creep under rapid loading. At higher loads the curvature increases more sharply due to the formation of micro-cracks until it reaches the maximum stress, after which the stress falls off with increasing strain. Crushing occurs when the strain reaches its ultimate value (e'_c). The maximum stress ($\gamma F'_c$) is generally slightly less than the crushing strength obtained in the standard cylinder compression test (see Section 3.6). The curve can also be derived from the rheological model shown in Fig. 3.13. The early part of the diagram results from the elastic deformation of the springs and the creep of the dashpots. When the springs reach their brittle strength, and break one after the other with increasing strain, the deformation of the model increases more rapidly, and eventually the number of springs

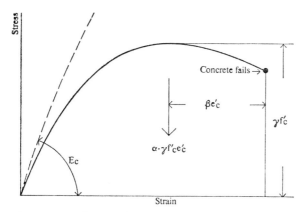

Fig. 10.12. General shape of the concrete stress–strain diagram.
f'_c = cylinder crushing strength of the concrete; e'_c = ultimate strain for concrete; E_c = modulus of elasticity of concrete; α, β, γ are constants.

becomes so small that the load on the model must be reduced. Finally we reach the ultimate strain e'_c, when the last spring breaks.

The model therefore illustrates one important difference between the plastic theory of steel, which is based on the continuous reformation of atomic bonds during plastic deformation. Structural steel eventually breaks, but only when the strain reaches 200 to 300×10^{-3}. In concrete, on the other hand, micro-cracks occur at about 60% of the ultimate stress; these can only be repaired by chemical action over a period of many months, and the material fractures at a compressive strain of about $e'_c = 3 \times 10^{-3}$, or $\frac{1}{100}$ of the ultimate structural steel strain.

We need two further experimental constants. α is the ratio of the area contained under the curve to the enclosing rectangle, so that

$$\int_0^{e'_c} f_c \, de_c = \alpha \cdot \gamma f'_c \cdot e'_c \qquad (10.7)$$

and β defines the centroid of this curve (see Fig. 10.12). These four experimental constants in practice usually reduce to two, since three appear frequently as the ratio $\beta/\alpha\gamma$. This ratio varies only slightly, even with large variations of concrete strength. Hognestad [10.27] obtained for the ratio $\beta/\alpha\gamma$ 0·49 at 7 MPa (1000 lb/in²), 0·59 at 24 MPa (3500 lb/in²), and 0·65 at 48 MPa (7000 lb/in²).

10.6. THE ULTIMATE-STRENGTH THEORY FOR
REINFORCED-CONCRETE BEAMS

Although ultimate-strength formulae for reinforced concrete design have been used for several decades in Russia, their acceptance was much slower in Western Europe, America and Australia. Following publication of the Joint ASCE-ACI Committee Report [10.28] they were admitted as alternative design methods in America [5.1] and Australia [5.3], and they have since been admitted in Great Britain [5.2] for the design of reinforced concrete sections. This is not ultimate strength design in the full sense of the plastic theory of steel, but corresponds to the introduction of the plastic shape factor for steel sections, while determining moments by the elastic theory (see Section 10.9).

The use of ultimate strength equations for concrete sections subject to bending has, however, several advantages. The quadratic design equations of the elastic theory become linear, which is convenient. Compression steel can be used more economically, because its stress is no longer considered tied by the condition of equal elastic strains to the stress in the surrounding concrete.* Most important of all, loads can be individually factored (see Section 2.8 and the note prior to Section 10.3); since dead loads (which require only small load factors) are a comparatively high proportion of the total loads in most buildings, this can lead to substantial economies.

In ultimate-strength design, the tensile strength of the concrete is neglected (see Section 10.3). Furthermore, as in elastic design, it is assumed that plane sections remain plane (see Section 4.7); this may seem surprising in view of the extensive cracking at high loads, but it agrees sufficiently with experimental data if due allowance is made for the location of the cracks.

The failure of a reinforced concrete flexural member may be initiated either by crushing of the concrete (*primary compression failure*) or by the yielding of the steel (*primary tension failure*). Even

---

* The American Code has for many years permitted the compression re-inforcement to be stressed to the full maximum permissible steel stress, without considering the strains in the concrete surrounding the steel, and several other codes have since done the same. This is quite safe because of the redistribution of stress which occurs before failure, but it is contrary to elastic design assumptions.

in primary tension failure, however, the final collapse of the beam is due to crushing of the concrete (Fig. 10.13). When the steel yields, the resultant tensile force in the section

$$T = f_y A_s = f_y pbd \qquad (10.8)$$

(where $p = A_s/bd$ is the steel ratio)
can increase no further, since the steel strain increases at a constant yield stress. The moment of resistance can therefore be increased only by lengthening the lever arm, *i.e.* by a rise in the neutral axis. This

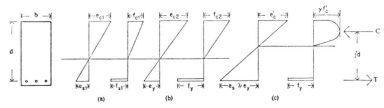

Fig. **10.13.** Primary tension failure of reinforced concrete beam with tension
reinforcement only.
(a) Elastic stage.
(b) Steel yields.
(c) Failure.
e_y = yield strain of steel; f_y = yield stress of steel; e'_c = ultimate concrete strain; f'_c = cylinder crushing strength of concrete.

causes a rapid increase in the steel *strain* (while the steel stress remains constant at the yield stress), and the concrete strain, until the ultimate concrete strain e'_c (about 3×10^{-3}) is reached, when the concrete is crushed.

With the notation shown in Fig. 10.13, the compressive force is then

$$C = \alpha \cdot \gamma f'_c \cdot bk'd \qquad (10.9)$$

For horizontal equilibrium, $C = T$, and from eqns 10.8 and 10.9 the neutral-axis depth-ratio at failure

$$k' = \frac{pf_y}{\alpha \gamma f'_c} \qquad (10.10)$$

The balanced steel ratio p_0 corresponds to the condition when the steel yields simultaneously with the crushing of the concrete, *i.e.*

when the steel strain e_y and concrete strain e'_c occur at the same load. The neutral axis depth is then (see Fig. 10.13c)

$$k' = \frac{e'_c}{e'_c + e_y} \qquad (10.11)$$

The value of e'_c is normally taken as 3×10^{-3}, and the value of $e_y = f_y/E_s$. The American Code [5.1] gives the constants α, β and γ in terms of an equivalent rectangular stress-block (Fig. 10.14). It

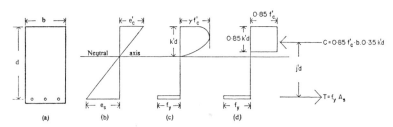

Fig. 10.14.   The equivalent rectangular stress block recommended by the American Concrete Code [5.1].
   (a) Dimensions of section.
   (b) Strain distribution.
   (c) Stress distribution.
   (d) Equivalent rectangular stress block.

recommends that the width of the rectangular stress-block be taken as $0.85f'_c$ (*i.e.* $\gamma = 0.85$), and the depth as $0.85k'd$ (*i.e.* $\alpha = 0.85$) up to values of $f'_c = 4000$ lb/in^2 (28 MPa), reducing by 0.05 for each 1000 lb/in^2 (7 MPa) above 4000 lb/in^2. This gives the position of the centroid as half the depth of the equivalent rectangle, *i.e.* $\beta = \frac{1}{2}\alpha = 0.425$. We can thus find p_0.

Using the American Code values, from eqn 10.10

$$p_0 = \frac{0.85^2 k' f'_c}{f_y} \qquad (10.12)$$

For $f_y = 250$ MPa (36 250 lb/in^2) and $E_s = 200$ GPa (29 000 000 lb/in^2), $e_y = 1.25 \times 10^{-3}$, and thus $k' = 0.707$.
   For $f'_c = 14$ MPa (2000 lb/in^2), $p_0 = 0.029$.
   For $f'_c = 24$ MPa (3500 lb/in^2), $p_0 = 0.049$.
   For $f'_c = 40$ MPa (5800 lb/in^2), $p_0 = 0.082$.

These values are much higher than those for elastic design, so that a primary compression failure is less likely than elastic calculations have suggested. This is fortunate, because a primary tension failure occurs slowly, and is accompanied by substantial cracking and deflection, while the steel extends gradually at the yield stress. By contrast, a primary compression failure occurs with little warning due to the brittle compression failure of the concrete. In order to ensure that the failure is always a primary tension failure, the American Code places an upper limit on the steel ratio of $0.75p_0$, as calculated above (Clause 10.3.2).

From Figs. 10.12 and 10.13, the length of the lever arm at failure is given by

$$j'd = d - \beta k'd = \left(1 - \frac{\beta}{\alpha\gamma} \frac{f_y}{f'_c} p\right) d$$

by substitution from eqn 10.10. The constants of the equivalent rectangular stress-block $\alpha = 0.85$, $\beta = 0.425$ and $\gamma = 0.85$, so that

$$j' = \frac{1 - 0.59pf_y}{f'_c} \tag{10.13}$$

The ultimate resistance moment is then

$$M' = Tj'd = f_y A_s j'd \tag{10.14}$$

The maximum permissible moment is obtained by dividing M' by the load factor (see Section 2.8).

This equation is identical with the elastic equation (10.1) except that j' is always slightly higher than j because the stress-block is linear in the elastic range and near-plastic at the ultimate strength. The economy of ultimate-strength design, as has been pointed out in Section 10.5, lies in the more discriminating use of load factors.

In the American Code the upper limit to the amount of tension steel is $0.75p_0bd$, and the moment is then

$$\begin{aligned} M' &= f_y \cdot 0.75p_0bdj'd \\ &= 0.75 \cdot 0.85^2 \cdot k'j'f'_c bd^2 \\ &= K'bd^2 \end{aligned} \tag{10.15}$$

Taking the specific case of $f_y = 250$ MPa and $f'_c = 24$ MPa:

$$k = 0.707, \quad j' = 0.70 \quad \text{and} \quad K' = 0.268f'_c$$

Any further increase in the bending moment for a section with given width b and effective depth d must be provided by compression steel. As in the case of elastic design (Fig. 10.9b) the section can be divided into two parts. The first part has a resistance moment

$$M_1 = K'bd^2$$

and requires a steel area

$$A_{s1} = \frac{M_1}{f_y j' d}$$

The remainder of the resistance moment

$$M_2 = M' - M_1$$

is provided by the rest of the tension reinforcement and the entire compression reinforcement

$$M_2 = f_y A_{s2}(d - d_c)$$

However, for a given section and a given bending moment an elastic design requires far more compression steel and less tension steel than a design based on ultimate strength.

The design of T-beams is also similar

$$M' = f_y A_s(d - \tfrac{1}{2}t)$$

However, many sections which are T-beams in elastic design become rectangular beams when ultimate-strength design is used, because the depth of the neutral axis is then less and it falls inside the flange.

10.7. THE ULTIMATE-STRENGTH THEORY FOR PRESTRESSED-CONCRETE BEAMS

We noted (see Fig. 10.11) that prestressed concrete is designed elastically to be wholly in compression, so that the neutral axis is near the top face (just inside or just outside the section) before the beam is loaded, and near the bottom face under full working load. The steel stress does not enter into the design directly; the prestressing force can be supplied by a small area of steel which is highly stressed, or by a larger area at a lower stress (although the latter would not be economical).

When the prestressed beam fails (Fig. 10.9), conditions are similar to those in a normal reinforced concrete beam at failure (see Fig. 10.13). Failure can occur only through crushing of the concrete or rupture of the steel. Because the high-tensile steel used in pre-stressed concrete has a much lower ultimate strain than normal reinforcing steel, primary compression failure is a possibility. However, consideration of all the problems associated with prestressed concrete design is beyond the scope of this book, and reference should be made to a specialist text [10.22, 10.23, 10.24]. We will confine ourselves to considering the more common case of primary tension failure (Fig. 10.15).

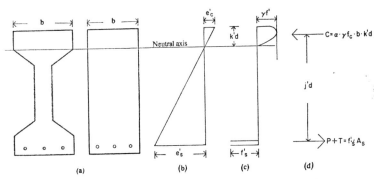

Fig. 10.15. Primary tension failure of prestressed concrete beam.
(a) Dimensions of section.
(b) Strain distribution.
(c) Stress distribution.
(d) Resistance moment
e'_s, f'_s = ultimate steel strain, stress; e'_c, f'_c = ultimate concrete strain, cylinder crushing strength; P = prestressing force.

As in the case of reinforced concrete, the resultant compressive force (see eqn 10.9)

$$C = \alpha \cdot \gamma f'_c \cdot bk'd$$

For horizontal equilibrium, this must equal the resultant tensile force in the section, which consists of the tensile force in the steel and prestressing force

$$P + T = f'_s A_s$$

The ultimate resistance moment

$$M' = Cj'd = (P + T)j'd$$

$$= f'_s A_s \left(\frac{1 - 0\cdot59pf'_s}{f'_c} \right) d \qquad (10.16)$$

Evidently this equation cannot be used to check the elastic design criterion, because it does not contain the prestressing force. For the normal case of primary tension failure, a beam with a low prestress has the same ultimate strength as one with a high prestress; but because of the low prestress the permissible service load is much smaller if cracking is to be avoided.

The reverse is also true: satisfactory elastic design does not guarantee an adequate load factor against failure. Let us consider the section shown in Fig. 10.16. If the beam carries a large dead load

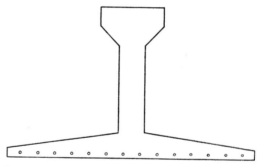

Fig. 10.16.   Prestressed concrete section which might have an inadequate load factor against failure.

and is highly prestressed, it may have an effective section for the elastic design conditions of eqn 10.5, because it provides a large area of concrete in the most highly stressed part of the compression zone (see Fig. 10.11). As soon as the neutral passes into the flange, however, the bottom concrete flange cracks, and ceases to make any contribution to the resistance moment. The entire tensile component of the resistance moment is thrown entirely on the steel; if this is already highly prestressed, the ultimate load may be reached with a relatively small increase in load.

It is therefore either necessary to design prestressed concrete sections by the elastic equations (10.5 and 10.6), and check them for ultimate strength as an additional, not an alternative, design criterion; or else to impose restrictions on the geometry of the sections to eliminate the possibility of either premature cracking or premature failure.

10.8. ULTIMATE STRENGTH OF REINFORCED-CONCRETE COLUMNS

Ultimate-strength design has been the basic design method for concentrically loaded reinforced concrete columns for three decades. Moreover, the elastic equations do not significantly enter into the consideration of the serviceability limit states.

When a column is loaded concentrically, the compressive strain in the concrete and the reinforcement is the same (see Section 4.3). Consequently the stresses in the concrete and the steel are, by Hooke's Law, related in proportion to the elastic moduli, and one of them cannot be stressed to its maximum permissible value without over-stressing the other; usually this means that the steel is used un-economically.

Let us now consider the deformation of the column beyond the elastic range (Fig. 10.17). The strains in both the concrete and the steel continue to increase, until the steel reaches the yield point. Further increase in the steel stress can occur only after strain-hardening, and before this is reached the column has failed. The compressive force in the steel therefore remains constant at $f_y A_s$ with increasing strain, while the compressive force in the concrete increases further until it reaches $\gamma f'_c A_c$. Although the column can be compressed a little further before the concrete crushing strain e'_c is reached, it can support no further increase in load, and the ultimate column load is therefore

$$P' = \gamma f'_c A_c + f_y A_s \tag{10.17}$$

In a building code which is otherwise framed in elastic terms, this is frequently written in terms of permissible loads and the maximum permissible concrete and steel stresses

$$P = f_c A_c + f_s A_s$$

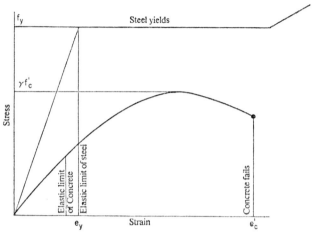

Fig. 10.17.   Relationship between stress and strain for steel and concrete in concentrically loaded column.

However, this is not an elastic formula, because elastic considerations require that the relation between the concrete and steel stresses be determined by their respective moduli of elasticity, in order to satisfy compatability of strains in accordance with Hooke's Law.

The ultimate strength design of eccentrically loaded columns is as complex as their elastic design. The elastic equations were traditionally solved by design charts which were, at the time, the most efficient method of dealing with complex equations of several variables. With the advent of digital computers, the ultimate strength problem has been more conveniently solved by computer printouts reproduced photographically. Although the tables are quite bulky [10.32], they are quicker to use and more accurate than charts.

10.9. RIGID FRAMES

The building codes discussed above [5.1–3] do not at present encourage the use of ultimate strength design for the design of complete concrete frames. Even when the cross-section of individual members is designed by ultimate strength (see Sections 10.5 to 10.8) the bending moments are normally calculated by one of the elastic methods discussed in Chapters 5 to 7. In principle the plastic theory described in Chapter 9 is equally applicable to reinforced concrete. However, it assumes a capacity for hinge rotation which concrete may not possess. In structural steel the atomic bonds reform continuously while the metal yields, and fracture occurs only at an ultimate strain of at least 100×10^{-3}.

Reinforced concrete is composed of two materials. The reinforcement deforms plastically like a structural steel section. The ultimate strain of concrete is, however, limited to between 2 and 6×10^{-3}, and the inelastic deformation at high loads results in damage to the micro-structure which can be repaired only by chemical action over long periods (see Sections 3.4 and 3.5). Plastic limit design can therefore be applied to reinforced concrete frames only if the first plastic hinge to form is still capable of resisting the full plastic moment at the load where the last hinge required by the collapse mechanism forms.

The existence of appreciable moment distribution was demonstrated almost 30 years ago [10.33]. Since then the problem has received world-wide attention, and extensive experimental data are available [10.34]. The degree to which concrete hinges can rotate has also been investigated [10.35]. Since beams fail in primary tension, and the neutral axis depth at failure is very small, a considerable amount of rotation is possible. Columns, which fail in primary compression, present a bigger problem because the plastic deformation of the reinforcement is not brought into play and ultimate rotation is small.

Complete redistribution of moments normally occurs in frames with only a few hyperstatic restraints, *e.g.* in single-bay single-storey frames, because the number of hinges required is correspondingly small. Furthermore, it is possible to design deliberately a frame in which all hinges form at exactly the same load, so that they do not need to sustain any substantial amount of rotation. This is much easier in reinforced concrete than in structural steel, because the resistance moment can be adjusted by varying the amount of reinforcement for different parts of the frame without altering the overall dimensions of the concrete cross-section. It should be noted, however, that as there is no moment redistribution in this case, the elastic and plastic analyses necessarily give the same answer.

10.10. Slabs and Plates

The general choice of the framing of concrete floor and roof slabs has already been mentioned in Section 1.6. The principal distinction is between slabs supported directly on the columns, which are discussed below, and slabs supported on beams, considered in this section. These again can be divided into those where the ratio of the span of the supporting beams is less than 1·5, which should be considered as spanning in both directions, and those where the ratio is above 2, which span in only one direction because the contribution made by the longer span is negligibly small (see Fig. 10.20). In the ratio of long/short span between 1·5 and 2 either one-way and two-way designs can be used economically.

Slabs spanning one way are designed as ordinary rectangular sections (see Section 10.3) with only nominal reinforcement in the longer direction (*i.e.* at right angles to the short, load-bearing span) to distribute the load and resist stresses caused by shrinkage and temperature movement (see Section 10.12).

Slabs spanning in two directions are designed to distribute the load partly to one and partly to the other pair of supporting beams, and the reinforcement is proportioned accordingly. This is a hyperstatic problem; each unit square of the slab forms part of a unit beam spanning between one pair of supporting beams, and also of another unit beam spanning at right angles. If the slab is designed elastically, the distribution of the load between the two spans is determined by the criterion that the element deflects by the same amount in both the spans of which it forms a part. Taking the centre span in each case (Fig. 10.18), the deflection of the common element at the centre of a rectangular slab simply supported on all four beams (see Table 5.1)

$$\frac{5}{384}\frac{w_xL_x^4}{EI} = \frac{5}{384}\frac{w_yL_y^4}{EI}$$

so that the ratio

$$\frac{w_x}{w_y} = \left(\frac{L_y}{L_x}\right)^4 \tag{10.18}$$

The bending moments $M_x = \frac{1}{8}w_xL_x^2$ and $M_y = \frac{1}{8}w_yL_y^2$ are then computed. The depth is determined by the larger bending moment

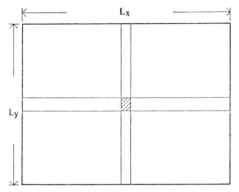

Fig. 10.18.   The unit square at the centre of a two-way slab forms part of the central strips spanning in both directions.

(this corresponds to the smaller span L which carries the bigger load), and the reinforcement is designed separately for the moments M_x and M_y in both directions at right angles.

This method, developed by F. Grashof in Germany in the 19th century, neglects the shear between the unit strips, and it requires in any case modification if the slab is not simply supported; most concrete slabs are continuous over intermediate supports, and partly restrained by walls at the edges.

The *theory of elastic plates* occupied the attention of European mathematicians throughout the late 18th and early 19th centuries. In 1876 the German physicist, G. R. Kirchhoff, published the elastic theory from which a number of solutions embodied in concrete codes are derived. The relation between the horizontal co-ordinates x and y, the elastic vertical deflection z, and the uniformly distributed load w is given [10.36] by the equation

$$\frac{\partial^4 z}{\partial x^4} + 2\frac{\partial^4 z}{\partial x^2\,\partial^2 y} + \frac{\partial^4 z}{\partial y^4} = \frac{w}{EI(1-\gamma^2)} \qquad (10.19)$$

where E = modulus of elasticity,
  I = second moment of area and
  γ = Poisson's ratio.

Over the beams the deflection is nil. When the slab is rigidly restrained the slope (dz/dx or dz/dy) is nil, and when the edge of the slab is free, the bending moment (d^2z/dx^2 or d^2z/dy^2) is nil. The solution has been tabulated for various boundary conditions, and subsequently adjusted for moment redistribution over the continuous supports (see Section 5.3). Tables based on this procedure were formerly included in the American Code dated 1965 [5.1], and are still given in the British and Australian Codes [5.2 and 5.3]. However, the equivalent frame method, discussed below, is now generally preferred, and it takes better account of the interaction of neighbouring panels and is less dependent on the range of available coefficients.

The Russian, the various Scandinavian, the Australian codes and the new British CP 110:1974 also permit the use of *ultimate strength design* for two-way slabs. Experiments on two-way reinforced concrete slabs have shown [10.37] that, at working loads, the stresses conform to those computed from Kirchhoff's theory of elastic plates; at higher loads there is considerable redistribution of moments, and failure occurs with a characteristic pattern of cracks which form a series of concentric curves on the compression face, and radiate towards the edges on the tension face. The cracks are generally very pronounced along the diagonals, and a good estimate of the ultimate load may be obtained by ignoring the effect of the remaining cracks and assuming that the slab at failure is converted into a mechanism through the yielding of the reinforcement along the lines of the major cracks. A theory based on these yield lines has been developed by K. W. Johansen [10.38] and elaborated by L. L. Jones and R. H. Wood [10.39] by including the membrane tension produced by the large deformation of the slab prior to failure.

Reference should be made to these publications for a detailed discussion of the *yield-line theory* (*i.e.* ultimate-strength theory) of slabs. The theory is mathematically much simpler than the elastic theory; but there are in most cases several alternative yield-line patterns to be considered. We will confine our attention to the simplest case of a square slab, simply supported at the edges and carrying a uniformly distributed load (Fig. 10.19). The slab is assumed to fail through yielding of the tension steel along the lines of the diagonals, causing rotation of the four triangular parts relative to one another, and turning the slab into a mechanism. The

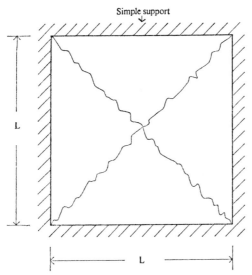

Fig. 10.19.   Yield-line theory for a square concrete slab, simply supported along the edges, carrying a uniformly distributed load.

parts of the slabs may be assumed to remain plane in view of the relatively much larger deflections caused by local curvature along the yield lines.

If the reinforcement is disposed uniformly across the slab in each direction so that the ultimate strength of any section, normal to the reinforcement is M' per unit width, the ultimate total load W' carried by the slab can be calculated by considering the equilibrium of any of the four triangular pieces. Taking moments about the edge of the slab:

$$\tfrac{1}{4}W' \cdot \tfrac{1}{3} \cdot \tfrac{1}{2}L = M' \cdot L$$

which gives the ultimate total load carried by the slab

$$W' = 24M' \tag{10.20}$$

From eqns 10.13 and 10.14

$$M' = f'_s A_s (1 - 0.59 p f'_s f'_c) d \tag{10.21}$$

where A_s is the area of reinforcement per unit width of slab in each direction; the 45° direction cosines for the steel area and the moment have been omitted for the sake of clarity, since they cancel one another out.

Having designed the concrete slab, either by the elastic theory or by ultimate strength, consideration must be given to the *load transmitted by the slab to the supporting beams*, so that the beams can be designed accordingly. The British and Australian Concrete Codes [5.2, 5.3], give a simple empirical rule (Fig. 10.20). Although this rule precedes the yield-line theory in point of time, the distribution evidently accords roughly with that to be expected at the ultimate load. Under elastic conditions the load transmitted depends largely on the relative stiffness of the beams and the slab [10.40].

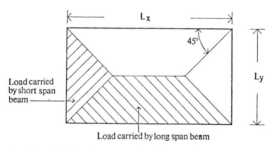

Fig. 10.20.   Load carried by the supporting beams of a two-way slab, according to Clause 314 b (iii) of the British Concrete Code [5.2].
    The bisection of the right angle in the diagram is an arbitrary rule, not based on theoretical or experimental evidence.

A *flat slab* is defined as a concrete slab carried directly on enlarged column heads without beams. The enlarged column heads reduce the shear stresses around the columns, and they are quite attractive in appearance for garages, warehouses and similar buildings. They are frequently used with thick slabs lightened by coffers (see Fig. 1.22) over comparatively large spans, so that the wide column spacing permits ample room for manoeuvring of vehicles.

Flat slabs were patented by Orlando Norcross in the United States in 1902, and the earliest design methods were purely empirical. The problem can be solved either by the theory of frames, or by the elastic eqn 10.19 with the appropriate boundary conditions. The latter solution, derived by H. M. Westergaard, over-estimates the moments, because of stress redistribution between adjacent panels (see Section 5.3), and a modified method, based on an experimental investigation by W. A. Slater [10.41] was first introduced into the American Code in 1925. It is still included, with minor modifications, in the current British and Australian concrete codes [5.2, 5.3]. The method was devised before a simple and accurate method of frame analysis had been perfected, and, although direct, it imposes a number of limitations on the ratios of depth to span, the variation in span between adjacent panels, the size of the openings, etc., because of the limited experimental data available.

Flat Plates, which are flat slabs without column heads generally fall outside the limitations imposed by the semi-empirical method based on the Westergaard–Slater investigation. When they came into use, in the 1940s, the moment distribution method had been perfected, and it was employed in preference to deriving new empirical coefficients for flat plates. Even in flat plates, the floors are stiffer than the columns, and it is sufficiently accurate to consider each floor with the columns above and below it, assuming the far end of the columns to be fixed (Fig. 10.21). Each unit is therefore relatively

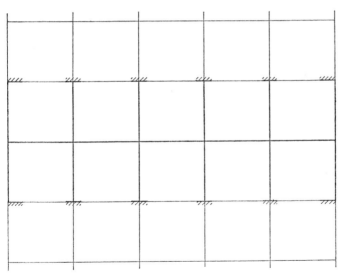

Fig. 10.21. Flat slabs and flat plates are sufficiently stiff in relation to the columns for the elastic frame analysis to assume that the far end of the columns is built in.

simple, so that moment-distribution calculations (see Section 5.5) are not unduly complex. It should be noted that each of the two frames at right angles to one another is considered to be carrying the full load. The frame is treated as a unit if a computer is used for the analysis (see Chapter 7), which is now the common method.

The flat plate floor requires only very simple formwork, and it is particularly economical when the soffit of the slab provides the finished ceiling. This implies that there is no false ceiling needed to accommodate service ducts, and that close column spacing is acceptable to avoid excessive creep deflection (see Section 3.5), which is due to the greater flexibility resulting from the absence of column heads. These conditions are frequently found in apartment buildings [10.42].

10.11. LOAD BALANCING

Although load balancing is a design method generally applicable to prestressed concrete beams and slabs (see Section 10.4), its most important architectural application is to flat plates. Because there are neither beams nor enlarged column heads to stiffen the floor structure, deflection is relatively high. It is not always convenient to use a close column spacing, and prestressing is then used to control creep deflection.

The elastic deflection due to the dead load could be compensated by building the slab with an upward camber. However, deflection due to creep occurs gradually (see Section 3.5) over a period of many months, and over-compensation can be as troublesome as under-compensation. As the deflection gradually increases, brittle finishes, brick and block partitions, are liable to crack and doors and windows may jam. Since creep is proportional to the elastic deflection, the problem may be eliminated by designing a flat slab which has zero deflection under its design load. Live loads are, by definition, removable, and it is best to balance the full dead load plus half the live load. The range of loading is then from one half of the live load below the balanced load, and one half of the live load above the balanced load.

The concept of load balancing, devised by T. Y. Lin [10.22], consists of shaping the prestressing cable to produce an upward bending moment which is exactly equal and opposite to the bending moment caused by the load to be balanced. For a slab carrying a uniformly distributed load w over a simply supported span L, the bending moment varies parabolically from 0 to $wL^2/8$; the prestressing cable is therefore given an eccentricity at midspan so that

$$P\varepsilon = \frac{wL^2}{8}$$

The cable is curved parabolically to reduce eccentricity to nil at the ends where the bending moment due to load is also nil (Fig. 10.22).

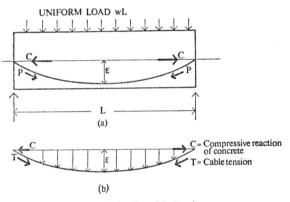

Fig. 10.22. Load balancing.

(a) The uniformly distributed load is balanced by a prestressing cable whose curvature closely follows the shape of the parabolic bending moment diagram.

(b) The prestressing tendon may thus be regarded as a suspension cable, with the concrete acting as the compressive anchorage to the cable.

10.12. Dimensional Stability and Cracking

Masonry materials develop cracks, due to thermal and moisture movement, which rarely cause structural failure, but may be very unsightly. Concrete shrinks irreversibly on setting, somewhat more if lightweight aggregate is used. Bricks often expand in the first few weeks after firing. In both, subsequent wetting and drying causes cyclic movement. All materials deform elastically on loading, expand on being heated and contract on being cooled.

Metals have a higher coefficient of thermal expansion, and timber has a higher rate of moisture movement. However, cracking is a particular problem in masonry, because of the low tensile strength of the materials and their brittle failure. One method of avoiding cracking is to insert movement joints in external walls and roofs at intervals of about 15 m (50 ft); if walls are required to resist shear, the joints must be suitably keyed to transmit the shear.

In concrete, reinforcement is normally used to bridge any likely crack, and to ensure that cracking is controlled to occur in the form of numerous hair cracks, instead of a few large ones, which are unsightly and are liable to allow the entry of moisture. Shrinkage and temperature reinforcement is therefore always provided in the form of small-diameter bars, closely spaced, so that they are properly bonded to the concrete.

10.13. INDUSTRIALISED MULTI-STOREY CONSTRUCTION

Tests have shown [10.43] that even multi-storey buildings can safely be erected from precast concrete load-bearing panels without a skeleton frame, and in Melbourne twenty-storey buildings of this type have been built without prestress, and thirty-storey buildings with the addition of vertical prestressing cables [1.19]. The use of precast panels obviates some of the problems of dimensional stability and cracking which are inherent in concrete cast in place, and in bricks laid in mortar. If the panels are precast, most of the shrinkage has taken place before they are erected. For large panels flexible jointing is generally needed, to allow for temperature and moisture movement. Attention should, however, be drawn to the serious structural damage which can result from internal blast (see Section 2.6).

Industrialised building with large concrete panels is an economic rather than a structural problem [10.45]. It has been most successful in Eastern Europe, where the planned economy provides a guaranteed large market, and in France, where a long pent-up demand for housing and a preference for high-density living has also created a market of adequate size.

The structural design [10.45] follows similar principles to that of load-bearing brick walls (see Section 10.1). Some of the early concrete wall units were designed to be handled and stacked lying flat; this produces large bending stresses during handling which do not occur after the wall unit is placed in position. Since the number of units is large, it is worthwhile to provide special handling gear to support wall units in the position and at the points where the load and reactions occur in the final structure. Handing stresses need not then be considered as a major design factor.

In Russia complete rooms, particularly bath-rooms and kitchens, have been precast as concrete boxes in the factory, and then taken to the site in one piece. There are practical difficulties in providing continuous bedding over the entire length of the supports for these large and heavy units, allowing for the fact that some warping is inevitable in precast concrete; furthermore the boxes have a great reserve in bending and torsional strength on account of the height and width of the room. A theory for designing the boxes as point-supported at the four corners has been developed by Drozdov [10.46].

Chapter 11

Behaviour of Building Frames

In Chapter 1 we briefly considered various structural systems for supporting loads; in this chapter we shall examine the behaviour of building frames under load and will comment on how they may be idealised so that they can be analysed by the techniques we have been discussing. Where applicable, we will provide design guides in the form of charts or tables to assist in the preliminary design of the structural system.

11.1. Introduction

The behaviour of small frames such as single storey rigid frames and the like is well understood in the areas of strength, stiffness and stability; however, as frames get larger (particularly taller) and more complex, many secondary factors which are normally neglected come to play an increasingly important role.

Most of the behavioural problems associated with building frames are connected with structures for tall buildings for in these structures the effects of lateral loads increase at a faster rate than the increase in height. In low buildings the interaction between the elements which make up the structure is often not very significant; also the need for a variety of elements does not manifest itself. In tall buildings the fundamental engineering problems relate to the method of carrying vertical and lateral loads, the method of vertical transportation, and the method of air-conditioning of the building and a successful engineering solution is always one in which these three aspects are harmoniously satisfied. The size and disposition of the lift core, the walls of which can be used for structural purposes, can have a significant effect on the structural system used. Sometimes, the structural system is such that no walling material other than the window glass is needed and, apart from having an effect on the cost of the wall, this also affects the cost of the air-conditioning system used. The location of lift zones with the accompanying mechanical floors, which cannot be used for office space, provides a freedom for the structural designer to utilise some of that space without interfering with rentable areas.

Of special interest in our examination of the behaviour of tall building frames is the method of achieving the required stiffness—the structural system and the factors which affects its stiffness—in particular the effects of member axial and shear stiffnesses. Once we have understood their behaviour we shall be in a position to look at various methods of approximate analysis.

11.2. DESIGN CRITERIA

The criteria for design of tall building frames include the primary considerations of:

strength—generally based on limiting stresses in individual members.

stability—stability of members is rarely a consideration but the stability of the building as a whole against overturning needs to be checked.

stiffness—lateral deformation of the structure under load.

For such frames other criteria are also important; these have been called the *serviceability criteria* [11.1]:

lateral deflection—this is the relative magnitude of the lateral displacement at the top of the building with respect to its height. The value for the limiting lateral deflection has been a subject for argument; however, figures between $\frac{1}{300}$ and $\frac{1}{800}$ are most often used [11.2].

ACI Committee 435 on allowable deflections recommends a deflection limit $\frac{1}{500}$ [11.3] stating that this criterion appears to have been satisfactory with respect to the following effects of sway under wind loadings:

(a) the stability of the individual columns as well as the structure as a whole;

(b) the integrity of the non-structural partitions and glazing;

(c) the comfort of the occupants of the building.

sway motion—the perception of lateral sway motion in buildings can produce undesirable psychophysical effects on the occupants; very little work has been carried out specifically with this problem in mind although the linear acceleration which causes the onset of sway perception in closed environments has been established [11.4, 11.5].

vertical deformation—relative vertical movements between exterior and interior structural elements caused either by differential thermal loads and differential axial deformations due to axial load and creep effects can cause severe distress [11.6, 11.7].

11.3. STRUCTURAL SYSTEMS

These have been mentioned in Chapter 1, but we shall review them here.

Frames

The frame is a structural system composed of linear elements which derives its behavioural characteristics from the rigidity of the joints which transfer moments. It is commonly used in relatively low buildings below twenty storeys, however, under unusual circumstances, it has been used in buildings of up to fifty storeys. Many building structures may be considered to be composed of plane frames in two directions. Figure 11.1 shows a typical framing plan for a multi-storey building in which the structure is composed of beams and columns rigidly connected. Figure 11.2 shows the elevation of one of the frames. Buildings composed of flat-slab or flat-plate

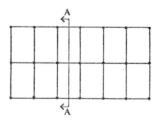

Fig. 11.1.   Typical framing plan of a multi-storey building composed of beams and columns.

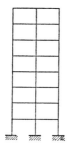

Fig. 11.2. Elevation of typical frame at section A-A in Fig. 11.1.

floor construction supported on columns without beams may also be treated as frames by taking an equivalent width of the floor as the beam.

Frames have proved to be an economic structural solution for relatively low buildings because the service core can be located independently of the structure and the architect has a high degree of freedom in how he expresses the facade of the building.

Shear Walls

As discussed in Chapter 1 structural walls are an outgrowth of the collecting together of the services into a core the walls of which are used structurally; these walls have such a high bending stiffness that if they are pierced with holes, we need to calculate their shear deformations if we want a true picture of the deflections, hence their name. Shear walls are generally surrounded by frames but are not always connected to them structurally as shown in Fig. 11.3. The

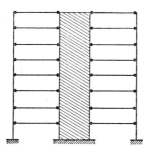

Fig. 11.3. Shear wall without structural interaction with surrounding frame.

reason for the hinge connection can be constructional as in prefabrication or to allow the external columns and core to move
vertically relative to one another without inducing stresses. The
stiffness of the wall alone is used to resist the lateral loads.

Interacting Frames and Shear Walls

Much more common is for the frames and shear walls to be
connected so that they interact and share the load carrying function.
As we shall see in Section 11.6, the effect of connecting the two is
greater than the simple addition of their respective stiffnesses. Interacting frame and shear-wall structures take many forms but in all
cases the core performs non-structural functions as well (Fig. 11.4);

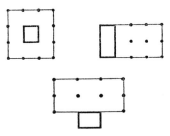

Fig. 11.4.   Some typical plans for interacting frame and shear-wall structures.

often the walls around a fire stair can be used to generate an additional
stiffness in long buildings (Fig. 11.5). Concrete buildings up to
seventy-five storeys have been built using this system. Construction-
ally, it has a number of advantages, as the core eliminates the need
for erection bracing and the external framing may be built rapidly to
provide two working surfaces.

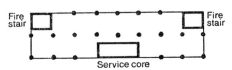

Fig. 11.5.   Additional shear walls may be provided by the use of stair wells in
long buildings.

'Top Hat' Interacting Frames and Shear Walls

Any increase in interaction between the frames and the shear walls increases the stiffness of the building; further interaction may be achieved by the use of a very stiff floor at the top (or elsewhere) which reduces the relative vertical deformations of the frames and walls [11.4]. Architecturally, this is only possible if the stiff floor occurs at mechanical service floors otherwise loss of rentable space results. This stiff floor can be achieved through the use of floor-height trusses or very deep beams (Fig. 11.6).

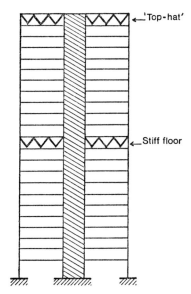

Fig. 11.6.   Increase of interaction between frame and shear wall can be achieved through the use of 'top-hats' or stiff floors.

Braced Facade (Tube)

In the interacting frame and shear wall system we were trying to get those elements furthest from the neutral axis to contribute to the lateral stiffness. This idea is extended to the point where all the structural elements are on the facade producing a perforated tube. The stiffness of the facade can be achieved in a number of ways, all of which are designed to transfer shear across the face and around

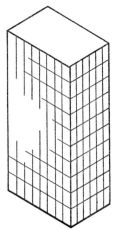

Fig. 11.7. A tube structure produced by closely spaced columns and stiff spandrel beams.

corners so the complete structure will act as a tube. One common method is to have closely spaced columns and stiff spandrel beams (Fig. 11.7); alternatively very deep spandrel beams without having closely spaced columns produce the same result. Another method is to use trusses in the plane of the facade such as shown in Fig. 1.17. Buildings of this type have been built higher than one hundred storeys in steel and to about fifty storeys in concrete.

Staggered Wall or Staggered Truss

This system uses storey-high beams or trusses which also act as walls spanning across a building to facade columns as shown in Fig. 11.8 [11.8].

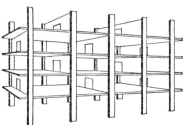

Fig. 11.8. A staggered wall (or truss) structural system. Note open spaces produced by the structure.

By staggering the location of these walls on alternate floors, large clear areas are created on each floor, although the floor slabs span only half the spacing, resting on the top of one and hung from the bottom of the next. Structures of this type have been designed in concrete and steel and in prestressed brickwork [11.9].

Panelised Construction

Panel systems derive their name from the load-bearing walls and floor panels that comprise their basic components. Wall panels are usually placed parallel to each other and run perpendicular to the face of the building. This results in cellular spaces (Fig. 11.9) such as

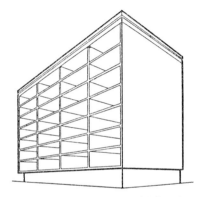

Fig. 11.9.   Panelised construction with facade removed.

might be used in hotels or multi-storey residential buildings. Panelised construction can be industrialised such that the panels can be mass-produced either in a factory or on site, if they are not *in situ* then particular attention must be paid to the joint design [11.10, 11.11]. Prefabricated panel buildings have been built to thirty-five storeys, and concrete buildings in which the action is primarily that of a panel building have been built much higher.

Suspended Construction

Suspended structural frames are composed of a central structural core, which also houses the services, a cantilever beam or plate system at the top of the core (and elsewhere) from which the hangers are suspended, Fig. 11.10. Apart from the obvious disadvantage that all the load must ultimately be carried by the core this system offers some constructional advantages. It can be used where the designer wants to change completely the structural layout of the super-structure from that of the basement areas, particularly where there are restrictions on the placement of structural supports due to obstructions such as railway tunnels, rivers and roads. Considerable increases in the speed of construction have been claimed for suspended construction.

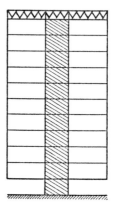

Fig. 11.10.   Suspended construction. The core acts as the vertical compressive and bending member with floors hung from it.

11.4. Behaviour of Frames

Behaviour Under Wind Loads

In frames over fifteen storeys the two main contributing effects on lateral deflection are those due to bending deformation in both beams and columns and to the axial deformation of the columns. This latter effect becomes predominant for slender frames. Figure 11.11 shows the deflection characteristics for a slender thirty-storey rigid frame; from this figure is evident the significant effect of the axial stiffness of the columns on the deflections and the deflected shape. In such frames this effect can be considerably more important than a change in column bending stiffness (Fig. 11.12).

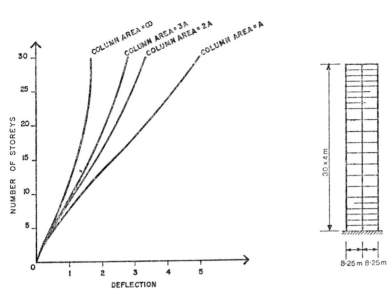

Fig. 11.11.   Effect of column axial stiffness on the lateral deflections of a 30-storey frame.

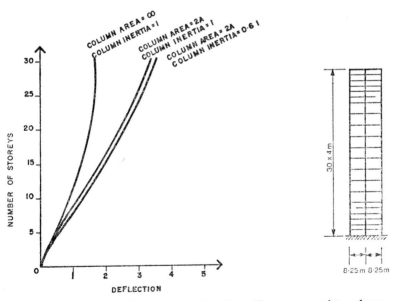

Fig. 11.12.   The small effect of column bending stiffness compared to column axial stiffness on the lateral deflections of a 30-storey frame.

Secondary considerations relating to lateral deflections include
the $P - \delta$ effect, the reduction in bending stiffness due to axial loads,
and shear deformation. The $P - \delta$ effect occurs when a frame deflects
laterally an amount δ so that an additional moment $P \cdot \delta$ is induced
due to the vertical load (P); this effect is negligible for all but the
slenderest frames [11.12]. The reduction of bending stiffness due to
axial loads can produce increases in lateral deflections, however, this
effect is also small unless the members are very slender, in which
case they do affect the stability of the frame. Shear deformations are
usually less than 5% of the total deflection for members made of

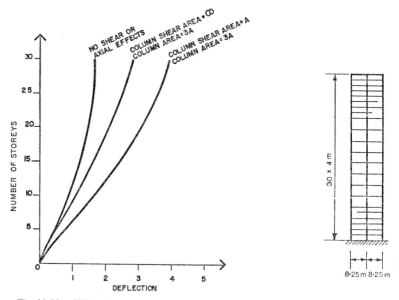

Fig. 11.13.   When the shear stiffness of the columns becomes *very* small then the
deflected shape changes (30-storey frame).

solid sections. If the effective shear area becomes small as can occur
in latticed steel columns, both the maximum deflection and the
deflected shape can be considerably altered; Fig. 11.13 shows this in
an exaggerated form.

As can be seen from the figures the idea that a frame deflects as a
large cantilever is inadequate to predict the behaviour of frames of

more than one bay in width. The reason for the deflected shape is closely tied to the axial stiffness of the columns and the propping action of these columns, an effect we shall also see in the behaviour of interacting shear walls and frames.

If the frame were to act as a simple cantilever then we would expect the windward columns to extend and the lee columns to compress an amount such that the floors remained plane, as this is an axiom of bending theory, if that were the case we would have these columns deforming many metres for the frame we have been discussing. Obviously, the axial stiffnesses of columns are such that they cannot deform these amounts, thus, the columns in tension provide a vertical tensile force at a distance from the neutral axis of the frame in the opposite direction to the load; similarly the columns in compression provide a vertical compressive force in the opposite direction to the load. These two forces produce a moment opposite to the moment of the load as shown in Fig. 11.14. This explains the importance of the column axial stiffness on the deflection of the

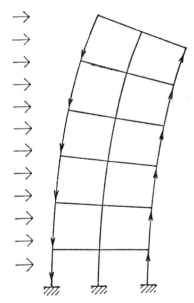

Fig. 11.14. Forces in columns produce a moment opposing the lateral load due to the axial stiffness of the columns.

frame; the effect is used to advantage in 'top-hat' structures which we examine in Section 11.7.

The moments, shears and axial forces in the members of frames due to lateral loads are affected by changes in column axial stiffness and shear stiffness.

Methods of Analysis

Analysis for member actions has always been simpler than for deformations. Moments, shears and axial forces due to vertical loads are easily determined floor by floor using moment distribution (Section 5.5). Analysis for lateral loads can be grouped into two categories: approximate methods and computer methods.

Approximate methods include the portal, cantilever, factor, equivalent column and substitute frame methods [11.13–15].

In the portal method, the following assumptions are made:

(i) there is a point of contraflexure at the centre of each beam;
(ii) there is a point of contraflexure at the centre of each column;
(iii) the total horizontal shear on each storey is divided between the columns of that storey in a manner such that each interior column carries twice as much shear as each exterior column.

This is the same as treating each storey and each bay as a separate portal frame, producing a series of statically determinate frames. The assumptions lead to geometric incompatibilities at the joints and more particularly to changes of geometry such as when a column is removed. Over ten to fifteen storeys it produces results significantly in error. The calculation of the deflection based on the results of the portal method is not satisfactory unless the effects of column axial deformations are included.

In the cantilever method the following assumptions are made:

(i) there is a point of contraflexure at the centre of each beam;
(ii) there is a point of contraflexure at the centre of each column;
(iii) the intensity of axial force in each column of a storey is proportional to the horizontal distance of that column from the centre of gravity of all columns of that storey.

This last assumption is arrived at by considering the entire frame to act as a cantilever beam; the errors introduced by this assumption should be clear from the previous discussion.

The equivalent-column and the substitute-frame methods lump the beams and columns together to produce a single column or frame; their usefulness is considerably limited. The usefulness of the approximate methods is limited to preliminary analysis; however, computer methods have superseded them even for this.

Computer methods of frame analysis are almost always based on the matrix methods developed in Chapter 7 which have been coded into computer programs [11.16–20].

Today it is very rare for the design engineer either to write a frame analysis program or to commission the writing of one as numerous general and specialised programs are available from computer bureaux, specialist software organisations ,universities and research institutions. However, great care must be exercised when selecting a particular program to analyse a building frame. It is more economic to use special purpose computer programs rather than general programs. For example, a program which will analyse any three-dimensional frame will, generally, be more costly to use to analyse a two-dimensional frame which is composed on vertical columns and horizontal floors, than a program which takes account of these conditions.

The *criteria for the selection of a computer program* would include:

(i) *axial deformation of columns*—as the discussion in this section has shown the effects of axial deformation of the columns cannot be neglected in lateral load analysis; if a program does not include this in the analysis then the results can be seriously in error.

    Care should be taken to eliminate axial effects when vertical dead loads are being considered since they occur incrementally during the construction of the building and not instantaneously as is assumed for lateral loads and, therefore, will not produce these axial deformations.

(ii) *ease of input*—the cost of analysing tall building frames has been reduced to such an extent that the cost of the engineer's time in preparing the input can far exceed the computing charges; it is here that special purpose programs can effect savings over general programs. The complete geometry of the frame shown in Fig. 11.2 can be specified in two cards—the first containing the bay widths, the second containing the floor heights; an alternative method to specify the geometry would be through the use of x and y co-ordinates, but this is obviously more lengthy. Similarly, if the beams in this frame are all the same in section properties, the input should be a single card. It can be worthwhile to write a routine which can be placed before the main program which reduces the amount of work the engineer needs to do to provide the information to the program.

(iii) *print-out of data*—it is essential that *all* the data supplied to the program for the analysis of a particular building be printed out to allow the user to check that his data has been correctly transmitted to the program and that it has been correctly interpreted.

(iv) *building analysis versus frame analysis*—does the program only handle single frames, if not, how are frame stiffnesses aggregated to produce the building stiffness? (This will be discussed in more detail below.)

 (v) *type of member*—can the program handle non-prismatic members (beams in particular); also, can it handle members other than beams and columns such as diagonals?

(vi) *error checks*—if there are errors in the data or in the processing, are there checks and is the user informed through error messages?

Structural Idealisation

Having conceived a structure and determined preliminary dimensions, the structure must be idealised in order to analyse it. The method of idealisation can have a significant effect on the results of the analysis. In buildings composed of frames a number of assumptions are often made to enable the structure to be analysed simply. The most common assumption made for many buildings is that the structure can be considered to be made up of individual frames which can be analysed as plane frames. This assumes that there will be no torsion on the building as a whole, although this is dependent on the degree of symmetry of the frame stiffnesses. Buildings which have a regular column grid such as the one in Fig. 11.15 can be analysed simply by making this assumption without loss of accuracy. This building is composed of three different frames although frames 2

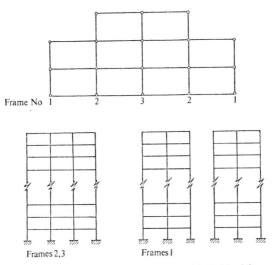

Frame No 1   2   3   2   1

Frames 2,3   Frames 1

Fig. 11.15.   Plan and elevations of building and individual frames.

and 3 have the same geometry. In buildings the floor is always concrete or steel sheet and concrete and, therefore, we may assume that it acts as an infinitely stiff diaphragm so that the horizontal deformation of each column on a floor is the same. Thus, our building now can be idealised to that shown in Fig. 11.16 in the main direction. Once it has been idealised to this point we are in a position to analyse it. There is no need to make these assumptions; we could analyse the building as a three-dimensional structure; the reasons for the high level of idealisation are that the engineer's

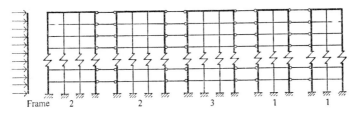

Frame   2   2   3   1   1

Fig. 11.16.   Structural idealisation of building in Fig. 11.15 achieved by connecting all frames together with 'links' which transfer deformations only. This method is the crux of building analysis by aggregating frames.

preparation time can be reduced and the difference in the cost of the analysis of this building analysed as a three-dimensional frame and as an idealised two-dimensional frame can be one order.*

When a structure is composed of a flat slab floor and columns we often take the 'column strip' as the effective width of the beam, ACI 318-63 [11.21] gives designers further guidance on this.

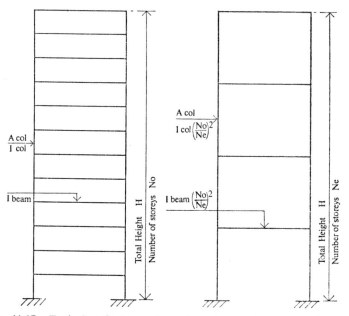

Fig. 11.17. Equivalent frame produced by reducing the number of storeys showing the reduction factors for area and moment of inertia.

The cost of analysis can be further reduced by idealising the building by reducing the number of floors while keeping the overall height the same, producing an equivalent building. The reduction ratios are shown in Fig. 11.17 [11.15]. The stiffness of the equivalent building is very close to the original but the strength characteristics

---

     * The computing cost of analysing the structure shown in Fig. 11.15 based on it being 30 storeys high using programs based on the same numerical techniques is $5 when the analysis is based on the above assumptions and $60 when analysed as a three-dimensional frame.

are not. Many computer programs have the size of the frame they
can analyse limited, not by a single parameter such as number of
storeys, but by a combination of number of storeys and number of
column lines such that a 50-storey, 10-bay frame may be its limit,
but it may still be capable of handling an 80-storey, 4-bay frame.

11.5. BEHAVIOUR OF SHEAR WALLS

Behaviour Under Wind Loads

Shear walls are normally of reinforced concrete although similar
structural effects may be produced with a braced steel bay. Under
the action of lateral load a single solid shear wall behaves as a
vertical cantilever. However, as we introduce holes into it (for lift
doors or lobbies) its behaviour becomes a little more complex because
it depends on the size and distribution of these openings. Generally,
these openings are one above the other and the behaviour of the wall
is not affected when the openings are small and when they are very
large we may treat the wall as two separate cantilevers; in between
we must include the effects of the beam stiffnesses joining the two
walls. A more detailed examination of these ranges will be carried
out below.

Methods of Analysis

Single and coupled shear walls may be analysed by the methods
of elasticity and matrix methods; an excellent summary of research
in this area can be found in [11.22].

The best known method of elasticity is the *continuum method* due
to Rosman [11.23, 11.24]. Briefly, the theory is derived as follows.
The individual connecting beams of stiffness I_b (Fig. 11.18) are
replaced by a continuous connection or by laminae. Under the action
of a horizontal load the walls deflect, inducing shear forces in the
laminae. If the laminae are considered to be cut at the middle of the
opening through their assumed points of contraflexure, then, by
considering their deformation, a second-order differential equation
for the laminae shears can be set up. The solution of this differential
equation for various boundary conditions (fixed base being of
importance) leads to those shears from which the moments and axial

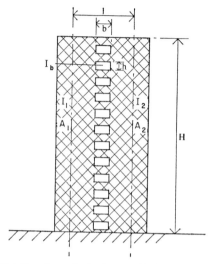

Fig. 11.18.   Notation for a single shear wall pierced with openings.

forces and hence the deformations can be determined. To analyse a system of coupled shear walls by this method can require very extensive calculation. It does appear that the parameter αH, where

$$\alpha^2 = \left(\frac{l^2}{I_1 + I_2} + \frac{1}{A_1} + \frac{1}{A_2}\right)\frac{12I_b}{hb^3}$$

(using notation of Fig. 11.17)
may be used to define the various regimes of behaviour. When $\alpha H \geq 13$ the wall may be considered as a simple cantilever; when $\alpha H < 1$ the wall may be considered as a series of separate cantilevers; for values in between, the walls must be considered as coupled shear walls and the effects of interaction produced by the beam stiffness needs to be accounted for in the analysis.

The above approach, apart from being subjected to a number of serious criticisms, has been superseded by *matrix methods* of analysis either by analysing the wall as a frame or through the use of finite elements [11.25]. The former is satisfactory for deformations and end-actions; the latter is used to determine deformations and stress distributions and will not be considered further.

Structural Idealisation

In idealising shear walls so that we may analyse them we can use the criteria established in relation to the effects of holes on the behaviour of the wall. The inclusion of shear deformation is not warranted unless the ratio of wall length to height is above 0·25. This can be shown as follows. Consider the wall as a cantilever with a point load; the bending and shear deformations at the end are given by

$$\delta_b = \frac{PL^3}{3EI} \quad \text{and} \quad \delta_s = \frac{PL}{GA_s}$$

where P = point load; L = span; E = elastic modulus; G = shear modulus; I = moment of inertia; A_s = shear area.

For a rectangular wall in concrete the ratios are $E/G = 2\cdot4$ and $I/A_s = 0\cdot1d^2$ (d = length of wall); therefore

$$\frac{\delta_s}{\delta_b} = \left(\frac{PL}{GA_s}\right) \bigg/ \left(\frac{PL^3}{3EI}\right)$$

$$= 0\cdot72 \left(\frac{d}{L}\right)^2$$

For ratios of (d/L) less than 0·25 the effect of shear deformation is less than 5% of the gross deformation and is usually neglected. If there are a number of small openings which reduce the effective shear area then shear deformations need to be taken into account.

Design Guide

Colaco [11.26] has presented a method of obtaining the preliminary dimensions of a shear wall in high rise concrete buildings for gravity and wind loads. The approach he used was to proportion the elements of the structure such that the wind forces do not control the design; hence, the structure is designed for gravity loads only. The type of shear wall considered is shown in Fig. 11.19, which also indicates the notation; it is assumed that there is no interaction between the wall and other walls or any surrounding frame.

The section properties of the wall are given by the following expressions.

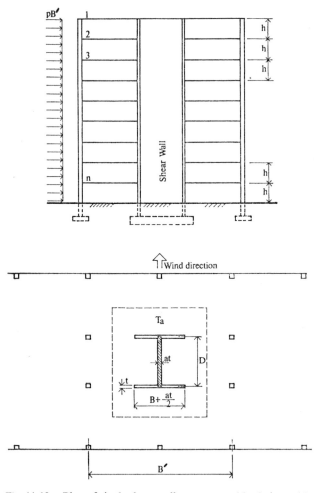

Fig. 11.19.   Plan of single shear-wall structure usd in design guide.

The area of each flange of the wall (A_f) is

$$A_f = \left(B + \frac{at}{2}\right) - at\left(\frac{t}{2}\right) = Bt$$

Hence, the area of the wall (A) is

$$A = 2Bt + atD$$

The moment of inertia of the cross-section (I_w) is

$$I_w = \frac{atD^3}{12} + 2A_f\left(\frac{D}{2}\right)^2$$

Hence

$$I_w = \frac{atD^3}{12} + \frac{BtD^2}{2}$$

The section modulus (Z_w) is then given approximately by

$$Z_w = \frac{I_w}{D/2}$$

Hence

$$Z_w = \frac{atD^2}{6} + BtD$$

The actions on the wall n floors below the roof, assuming that all floors are similar, are given by

$$P_u = n(T_a)(W_u)$$

and

$$M_w = \frac{(pB')(nh)^2}{2}$$

where P_u is the ultimate axial load on the wall at nth floor below roof

T_a is the tributary area for the wall for gravity loads

W_u is the ultimate gravity load on the wall per unit area per floor (including an estimate of the weight of the wall and live load reduction factors)

M_w is the design wind moment on the wall at nth floor below roof

p is the equivalent horizontal uniform design wind pressure per unit vertical surface area

h is the floor to floor height.

The approximate value for the axial design stress (F_a) according to ACI 318.63 [11.21] is given by

$$F_a = 0.40f'_c \quad (= 1.9 \times 0.21f'_c)$$

The ultimate axial stress in the wall (f_a) is given by

$$f_a = \frac{P_u}{t(2B + aD)}$$

The bending stress due to the wind moment (f_b) is given by

$$f_b = \frac{M_w}{Z_w} = \frac{pB'n^2h^2}{2Z_w}$$

If the wall is designed for gravity loads then we set $f_a = F_a$, hence

$$\frac{P_u}{t(2B + aD)} = 0.40f'_c \qquad \text{(i)}$$

For combined wind moment and axial load, assuming a gravity load factor of 1.6, we have

$$\frac{1.25}{1.6}f_a + 1.25f_b = 0.40f'_c$$

Hence,

$$f_b = 0.07f'_c$$

Substituting for f_b in the bending stress equation

$$Z_w = \frac{pB'n^2h^2}{0.14f'_c} \qquad \text{(ii)}$$

For control of lateral deflection of the building under wind forces using the recommendation of ACI Committee 435 [11.3] we will limit the deflection to 1/500 times the height of the building. Hence

$$0.002nh = \frac{pB'(nh)^4}{REI_w}$$

Where $R = 8$ for a wall with constant moment of inertia and $R = 6$ for a wall with a moment of inertia which tapers uniformly from I_w at the base to zero at the roof. For preliminary design assume $R = 7$.

We can now obtain the minimum moment of inertia required for deflection control.

$$I_w = \frac{71 \cdot 4 p B'(nh)^3}{E} \tag{iii}$$

Equations (i), (ii) and (iii) form the basis for the preliminary design. To facilitate the design, composite graphs are given in Figs. 11.20, 11.21, 11.22 for three different values of a, the ratio of the web thickness to the flange thickness.

For a trial value of t, the values P_u/tf'_c and Z_w/t are calculated from the graphs; for a chosen value of a, we obtain the values of B and D.

Example 11.1. Design a 10-storey shear wall structure based on the following design information:

Tributary area $(T_a) = 370$ m^2/floor (4000 ft^2/floor)
Ultimate gravity load $(W_u) = 12$ kPa (250 lb/ft^2) $= 12$ kN/m^2
Number of floors $(n) = 10$
Floor to floor height $(h) = 3 \cdot 050$ m (10 ft)
Wind load $(p) = 1 \cdot 435$ kPa (30 lb/ft^2) $= 1.438$ kN/m^2
Tributary width $(B') = 15 \cdot 200$ m (50 ft)
Concrete strength $(f'_c) = 27\,500$ kPa (4·9 $\times$ 10^3 lb/in^2)
Elastic modulus $(E) = 25 \times 10^6$ kPa (3640 $\times$ 10^3 lb/in^2)

At the base of the building, the ultimate axial load is

$$P_u = 10 \times 370 \times 12$$
$$= 44\,500 \text{ kN (10 000 kips)}$$

From eqn (ii) we get

$$Z_w = \frac{(1 \cdot 435 \times 15 \cdot 2) \times (10)^2 \times (3 \cdot 05)^2}{0 \cdot 14 \times 27\,500}$$
$$= 5 \cdot 27 \text{ m}^3 \text{ (322 000 in}^3\text{)}$$

From eqn (iii), we get

$$I_w = \frac{71 \cdot 4 \times (1 \cdot 435 \times 15 \cdot 2) \times (10)^3 \times (3 \cdot 05)^3}{25 \times 10^6}$$
$$= 1 \cdot 767 \text{ m}^4 \text{ (4·3 } \times 10^6 \text{ in}^4\text{)}$$

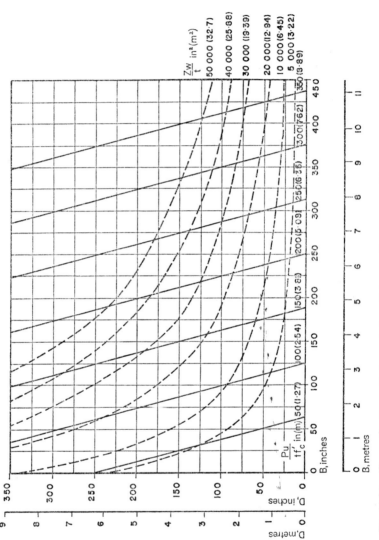

Fig. 11.20.   Curves for the preliminary design of shear-wall structures with $a = 0.5$ (after Colaco [11.26]).

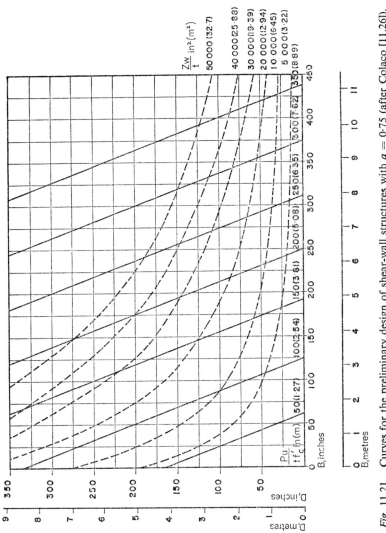

Fig. 11.21. Curves for the preliminary design of shear-wall structures with $a = 0.75$ (after Colaco [11.26]).

Begin with a trial value of $t = 305$ mm (12 in) and $a = 1·0$, then

$$\frac{Z_w}{t} = 17·28 \text{ m}^2 \ (26\ 900 \text{ in}^2)$$

$$\frac{P_u}{tf'_c} = \frac{44\ 500}{0·305 \times 27\ 500} = 5·31 \text{ m} \ (209 \text{ in})$$

From Fig. 11.22, for these values of Z_w/t and P_u/tf'_c read off $B = 5·330$ m (210 in) and $D = 2·660$ m (105 in). Hence

$$I_w = Z_w \frac{D}{2}$$

$$= 5·27 \times \frac{2·66}{2}$$

$$= 7·009 \text{ m}^4 > 1·767 \text{ m}^4$$

Try value of $t = 406$ mm (16 in) and $a = 1·0$, then

$$\frac{Z_w}{t} = 12·97 \text{ m}^2 \ (20\ 100 \text{ in}^2)$$

$$\frac{P_u}{tf'_c} = 3·96 \text{ m} \ (156 \text{ in})$$

Again, from Fig. 11.22 we can read off $B = 3·430$ m (135 in) and $D = 3·180$ m (125 in). Hence

$$I_w = 5·27 \times \frac{3·43}{2}$$

$$= 9·040 \text{ m}^4 > 1·780 \text{ m}^4$$

In general, planning requirements in relation to the core restrict the choice of the values for either B or D or sometimes both. If, in Example 11.1, the value of D is restricted to 2·280 m (90 in), then for $t = 305$ mm (12 in), $B = 7·110$ m (280 in) and for $t = 406$ mm (16 in), $B = 5·450$ m (215 in).

When wind *controls the design*, as is the case when D is restricted

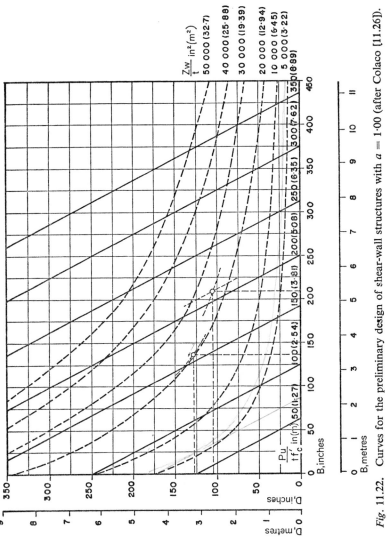

Fig. 11.22.   Curves for the preliminary design of shear-wall structures with $a = 1\cdot00$ (after Colaco [11.26]).

to values much below those for pure gravity design, we can use the same design guides with changed design equations; in this case

$$\frac{1\cdot25f_a}{1\cdot6} + 1\cdot25f_b = 0\cdot40f'_c$$

and

$$\frac{f_a}{1\cdot6} - f_b = 0$$

for there to be no tension in the wall under the combined load condition. We can obtain values for f_a and f_b in terms of f'_c from the equations; *i.e.*

$$f_a = 0\cdot256f'_c$$

$$f_b = 0\cdot16f'_e$$

Hence

$$\frac{P_u}{(2B + aD)} = 0\cdot256f'_c$$

and

$$Z_w = \frac{pB'n^2h^2}{0\cdot32f'_c}$$

which are the equivalent of eqns (i) and (ii) for gravity load design.

Example 11.2. Design the shear wall of Example 11.1 on the basis that wind controls the design.

The values of P_u and I_w remain the same as before, the required modulus now becomes

$$Z_w = 2\cdot310 \text{ m}^3 \text{ (141 000 in}^3\text{)}$$

With a trial value for $t = 305$ mm (12 in) and $a = 1\cdot0$

$$\frac{Z_w}{t} = 7\cdot6 \text{ m}^2 \text{ (11 800 in}^2\text{)}$$

The equivalent

$$\frac{P_u}{tf'_c} = \frac{44\,500}{0·305 \times 27\,500} \times \frac{0·40}{0·256}$$

$$= 8·25 \text{ m } (325 \text{ in})$$

From Fig. 11.22 read off $B = 9·780$ m (385 in) and $D = 0·890$ m (35 in). Hence

$$I_w = 2·310 \times \frac{0·89}{2}$$

$$= 1·028 < 1·780$$

i.e. deflection is the governing criterion.
Try a larger value of D, say $D = 1·270$ m (50 in). Hence

$$Z_w = \frac{I_w}{D/2}$$

$$= \frac{1·780}{1·27/2}$$

$$= 2·820 \text{ m}^3 \ (172\,000 \text{ in}^3)$$

$$\frac{Z_w}{t} = 9·2 \text{ m}^2 \ (14\,300 \text{ in}^2)$$

$$\frac{P_u}{tf'_c} = \text{as before}$$

Again, from Fig. 11.22, $B = 9·650$ m (380 in) for $D = 1·270$ m (50 in). Obviously, a solution on this basis will be more expensive than that derived in Example 11.1.

11.6. Behaviour of Interacting Frames and Shear Walls

Behaviour Under Wind Loads

Single shear walls are rarely used in isolation, rather they are connected to the surrounding frames to produce an interacting frame and shear-wall structure. The behaviour of such structures under

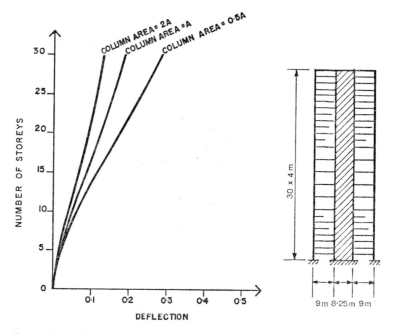

Fig. 11.23.   Effect of column axial stiffness on lateral deflections of a 30-storey interacting frame and shear-wall structure.

wind load is very similar to that of frames in that the lateral deflections are due to bending deformation in beams, columns and walls and the axial deformation of the columns. This latter effect is the predominant one for structures that are either very slender or have very stiff shear walls. Figure 11.23 shows the deflection characteristics of an interacting frame and shear-wall slender thirty-storey

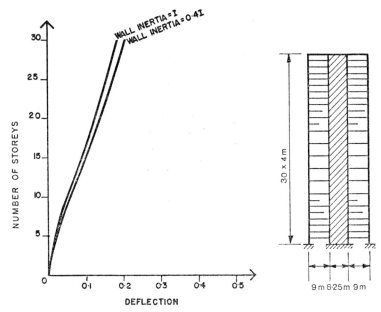

Fig. 11.24.   Effect of wall bending stiffness on lateral deflections of a 30-storey interacting frame and shear-wall structure. Note: compared with Fig. 11.23 these effects are much less.

structure. Again, the effect of column axial stiffness can be considerably more important than a change in shear-wall bending stiffness (Fig. 11.24).

Similar secondary considerations apply here as did to frames: the $P - \delta$ effect, the reduction in bending stiffness due to axial loads, and shear deformation, particularly when shear area becomes small.

The reason for the characteristic 'S' shape is the same as for frames, hence, the position of the wall in the frame is of importance. Because of the importance of the propping effect of the columns, the stiffness of the connecting beams plays an important part in the deflection characteristics of the structure.

Methods of Analysis

Approximate methods of analysis have been superseded by computer methods; Reference [11.1] contains a comparative summary of the more popular hand methods [11.15, 11.27–30]. Most of these hand methods are iterative and the normal procedure is to assume a shear distribution, calculate equilibrium and check for deformation compatibility; a process not only lengthy but prone to errors and convergence problems.

Computer methods similar to those used on frames are applicable to interacting frames and shear walls, as are the *criteria for selecting a computer program*. These would include, as before:

   (i) axial deformation of columns
  (ii) ease of input
 (iii) printout of data
 (iv) building analysis versus frame analysis
  (v) type of member
 (vi) error check

and in addition:

 (vii) *shear deformation*—the effects of shear deformations in columns and walls and possibly beams need to be included
(viii) *finite member size*—as members become larger it is no longer satisfactory to consider them as being concentrated along their centre lines. This applies to both beams and wall-columns, shear-wall widths can be larger than the clear-bay dimensions and must be accounted for. Failure to include this in the analysis can produce results seriously in error. Figure 11.25 shows the effect on deformations of assuming a zero column width for the frame we have been considering (in this example we have kept the clear-bay widths constant). As can be seen, the deformations so produced are completely erroneous. The maximum deflections are 58 mm (0·19 ft) including effects of column widths and 104 mm (0·34 ft) neglecting them. The respective base moments of the wall are 19 000 kN m (14 000 kip ft) and 27 000 kN m (20 000 kip ft) and the respective axial forces in the ground-floor columns are 2 300 kN (520 kips) and 2 850 kN (640 kips); the distribution of shear between the columns and wall at the base remains constant.

Alternatively, maintaining the centre-line dimensions without including column widths results in a reduction in stiffness of the beams because their effective lengths have been increased from that of column face to column face to centreline to centreline and the interaction between the columns and the wall is reduced. A similar effect, of less significance, is produced if deep beams are treated as if they were concentrated at their centreline. With the use of a computer there is very little effort required to include secondary effects [11.31].

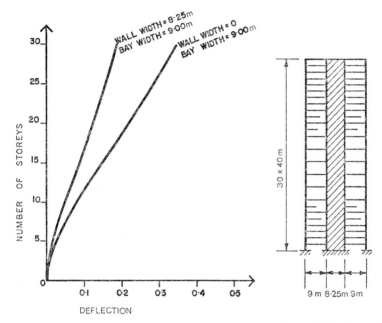

Fig. 11.25.   Effect of neglecting column and wall widths on lateral deflections of a 30-storey interacting frame and shear-wall structure.

Structural Idealisation

Similar concepts apply here as to frames and shear walls individually. Particular attention should be paid to assuming that the floor of a building may be treated as being infinitely stiff in its own plane so that the horizontal deformations of all elements on that floor are the same. Also, because of the high stiffness of a shear wall in relation to frames, care must be taken to assure that a reasonable degree of symmetry exists in the building in relation to the distribution of stiffnesses if a two-dimensional analysis is to be undertaken. Otherwise, the torsion in the columns due to the lack of symmetry will not be calculated.

Design Guide

Khan and Sbarounis [11.15] have presented an extensive set of charts in the form of influence curves to aid the designer. However, these curves do not include the effect of axial deformations in the columns or finite member size and hence should be used with care. In the cases of buildings less than twenty storeys in height, the effect of the above omissions is such that the charts can be used at the preliminary design stage. Their main advantage lies in their immediacy although any design office equipped with a computer terminal will have the same immediacy with a complete computer analysis.

In the ensuing charts the symbol S_s is used to denote the sum of the stiffnesses of the shear walls. Similarly, S_c represents the sum of the stiffnesses of the columns and S_b refers to the sum of the stiffnesses of the beams. The quantities S_s/S_c, the wall–column stiffness ratio and S_c/S_b, the column–beam stiffness ratio, refer to conditions at the first storey of the structure. These parameters give an indication of the relative stiffnesses of the frames and walls. For example, if $S_c/S_b = 1$, then we have an extremely stiff frame, whilst, if $S_c/S_b = 5$, then the frame is much more flexible. Similarly, if $S_s/S_c = 1000$, then we have extremely stiff walls, whilst if $S_s/S_c = 5$, then we have very slender walls.

A uniform wind load up the face of the building has been assumed.

Figures 11.26, 11.27 and 11.28 provide design guides in terms of the above parameters where:

Q_b is the total shear at the base of the structure
Q_{fx} is the shear in the frame at height x/H
Q_{tx} is the total applied shear at height x/H
Q_{wx} is the shear in the wall at height x/H
H is the total height of building.

This means that although the shear in the frame at a level is expressed as a fraction of the total base shear, the shear in the wall at a level is

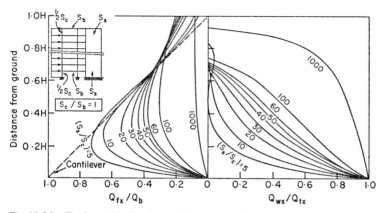

Fig. 11.26. Design guide for shears in interacting frames and shear walls for the ratio of the stiffness of columns to beams equal to 1. The shear taken by the frame at a particular level is expressed in terms of the shear at the base of the structure. The shear taken by the wall at a particular level is expressed in terms of the total shear at that level.

Note: This, and the ensuing figures, do not include axial deformation effects which play an important role in buildings above 20-storeys and affect the results for buildings above 10-storeys (after Khan and Sbarounis [11.15]).

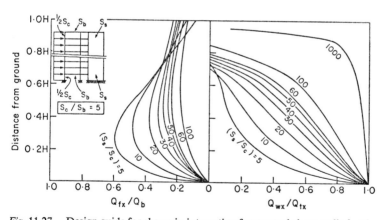

Fig. 11.27. Design guide for shears in interacting frames and shear walls for the ratio of the stiffness of columns to beams equal to 5 (after Khan and Sbarounis [11.15]).

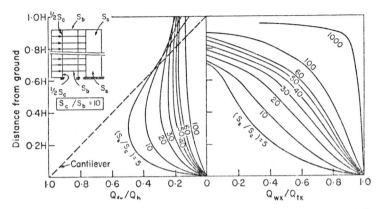

Fig. 11.28. Design guide for shears in interacting frames and shear walls for the ratio of the stiffness of columns to beams equal to 10 (after Khan and Sbarounis [11.15]).

expressed as a fraction of the total shear at that level. For example, given a stiff frame ($S_c/S_b = 1$) combined with a slender wall ($S_s/S_c = 5$) the shear carried by the wall at $0{\cdot}2H$ above ground is approximately 15 % of the total shear at that point (in which case it is hardly worth treating the wall as a separate entity and the whole structure could well be considered a frame). If we combined the same frame with a stiffer wall ($S_s/S_c = 100$) the shear now carried by the wall at 0·24 above the ground is approximately 75 % of the total shear at that level.

Khan and Sbarounis [11.15] have also produced charts for deflections of interacting frames and shear walls. Again these curves do not include the effects of axial deformations in the columns or finite member size. Figures 11.29, 11.30 and 11.31 contain the relative deflections of the same structures as shown in Figs. 11.26, 11.27 and 11.28. They are plotted in terms of distance from the ground and the ratio of deflection of the structure at any point divided by the free deflection of the shear wall at the top. This free deflection must first be computed separately before entering the charts to obtain the deflected shape of the structure.

All these charts can be used in design only if the shape and stiffness distribution of the structure are not too irregular. A suitable procedure is to estimate the storey shears in the frame from the

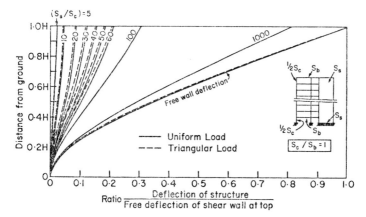

Fig. 11.29.   Design guide for deflections in interacting frames and shear walls for the ratio of the stiffness of columns to beams equal to 1. The deflection is expressed as a ratio of the free deflection of the shear at the top (after Khan and Sbarounis [11.15]).

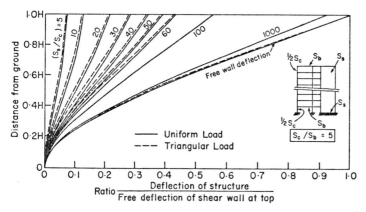

Fig. 11.30.   Design guide for deflections in interacting frames and shear walls for the ratio of the stiffness of columns to beams equal to 5 (after Khan and Sbarounis [11.15]).

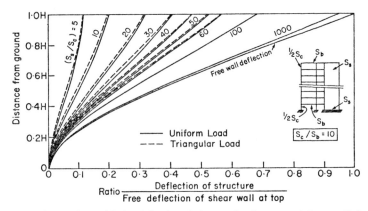

Fig. 11.31. Design guide for deflections in interacting frames and shear walls for the ratio of the stiffness of columns to beams equal to 10 (after Khan and Sbarounis [11.15]).

charts and the loads on the wall resulting from interaction by subtracting the estimated frame shears from the total shears. These loads can then be used to calculate the deflected shape of the wall. The calculated deflections can be compared with those estimated from the charts; if the results do not agree, then modifications to the load distribution need to be made. Because the curves in the charts were derived by making the frame and wall systems compatible at ten points, the wall–column stiffness ratio used to enter the charts should be computed by

$$\frac{S_s}{S_c} = \left[\frac{\Sigma \, (EI)_s}{\Sigma \, (EI)_c}\right] \left(\frac{10}{n}\right)^2 \qquad \text{(i)}$$

where n is the number of storeys in the structure. The quantities S_c and S_b used in the ratio S_c/S_b should be taken simply as the sum of the stiffnesses of the columns and beams respectively.

Once the deflected shape of the structure is known it can be used to distribute moments and shears to every member. At a column line that contains no shear walls, a set of fixed-end column moments obtained from the difference in storey deflection can be apportioned to all members by moment distribution. No sidesway correction is needed because the frame is in its final deflected shape.

If a shear wall is contained in a frame, it can be treated separately from the frame segment. With a known deflected shape and EI, the moment at any floor (i) can be obtained from

$$M_i = \left(\frac{EI_{si}}{h_i^2}\right)(\delta_{i+1} - 2\delta_i + \delta_{i-1})$$

where M_i is the moment at floor i
I_{si} is the moment of inertia of the wall at floor i
h_i is the storey height
δ_i is the deflection at floor i.

When interacting frames and shear walls are to be analysed, whether by the above method or by a computer matrix method, the question of the effective width of the floor slab to be used as the equivalent beam. Once the bay width (l), span (L) and column dimension (d) are known, guidance as to the effective width of the equivalent beam (l_e) can be found in Fig. 11.32.

Example 11.3. A 14-storey flat-plate structure, rectangular in plan, has nineteen bays of 3·510 m (11·5 ft) in the long direction and three bays of 6·100 m (20·0 ft) in the short direction. The first storey height is 3·960 m (13·0 ft), all the other floors have a height of 2·650 m (8·67 ft). The structure is supported on 72 columns and 6 shear walls. Given the design sizes below determine the frame shears under a uniform lateral load.

The average size of the columns in the first storey is 356 mm by 559 mm (14 in by 22 in), in the second storey 356 mm by 432 mm (14 in by 17 in) and in the fourteenth storey 356 mm by 356 mm (14 in by 14 in). The sums of the column moments of inertia in the first, second and fourteenth storeys respectively become 0·39 m⁴ (45·8 ft⁴), 0·24 m⁴ (28·8 ft⁴) and 0·096 m⁴ (11·1 ft⁴) and their respective stiffnesses (I/L) are 0·0985 (3·52), 0·0905 (3·32) and 0·0362 (1·28). The shear walls have constant cross-sections throughout the height of the structure. The sum of their moments of inertia is 21·95 m⁴ (2420 ft⁴). The slabs at all levels are 216 mm (8 in) thick. For this design, in each floor there are 49 spans of 6·100 m (20 ft) four 'link' spans of 3·660 m (12 ft) and four 'link' spans of 1·830 m

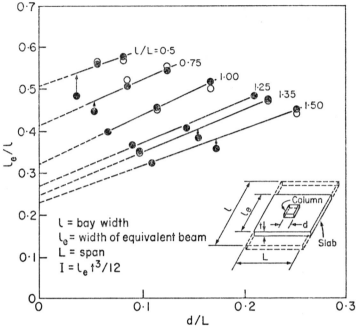

Fig. 11.32.   Effective width of equivalent beam of a flat-plate floor system for use in a frame analysis.

(6 ft). The 'link' spans are those that connect the walls with the surrounding frame (in their own plane).

At the first storey, the width to span and the column size to span ratios parallel to the short side of the building are

$$\frac{l}{L} = \frac{3 \cdot 510}{6 \cdot 100}$$

$$= 0 \cdot 575$$

and

$$\frac{d}{L} = \frac{0 \cdot 559}{6 \cdot 100}$$

$$= 0 \cdot 092$$

From Fig. 11.32, the width of the slab to be used as an equivalent beam, and its moment of inertia are

$$l_e = 0.57l$$

$$= 2.020 \text{ m } (6.6 \text{ ft})$$

$$I_b = \frac{2.020 \times 0.216^3}{12}$$

$$= 14.1 \times 10^{-4} \text{ m}^4 \ (0.163 \text{ ft}^4)$$

Similarly, the computed moment of inertia at the roof is 13.1×10^{-4} m^4 (0.151 ft^4).

In order to facilitate the use of the charts, the structure is subdivided into ten parts. The stiffnesses at the first and fourteenth storeys are used to obtain the values of S_c, shown in Column 2 of Table 11.1, at the ten points by linear interpolation.

Table 11.1

Distance from ground (1)	S_c $\times 10^{-2}$ (2)	S_b $\times 10^{-2}$ (3)	S_c/S_b (4)	S_s/S_c (5)	Q_{fx}/Q_b (6)	Storey (7)	Q_{fx}/Q_b (8)
1.0H						14	0.19
	3.75	1.46	2.6	107	0.19	13	0.21
0.9H						12	0.22
	4.47	1.48	3.0	90	0.22		
0.8H						11	0.24
	5.15	1.49	3.4	78	0.23		
0.7H						10	0.25
	5.86	1.51	3.9	69	0.25	9	0.26
0.6H						8	0.26
	6.54	1.52	4.3	62	0.26		
0.5H						7	0.26
	7.21	1.54	4.7	56	0.26	6	0.26
0.4H						5	0.24
	7.94	1.55	5.1	51	0.24		
0.3H						4	0.23
	8.64	1.56	5.5	47	0.22	3	0.21
0.2H							
	9.20	1.57	5.9	43	0.18	2	0.17
0.1H							
	9.90	1.58	6.3	27	0.10	1	0.07
0							

At the first floor the sum of beam stiffnesses is

$$S_b = 13 \cdot 1 \times 10^{-4} \left\{ \frac{49}{6 \cdot 100} + \frac{4}{3 \cdot 660} + \frac{4}{1 \cdot 830} \right\}$$

$$= 0 \cdot 0158 \ (0 \cdot 563)$$

and at the roof $S_b = 0 \cdot 0146 \ (0 \cdot 520)$. The values of S_b, shown in Column 3, were obtained by interpolation as before. The ratios of S_c/S_b shown in Column 4 were calculated using the previously tabulated values of S_b and S_c. The wall stiffness $S_s = 21 \cdot 95/2 \cdot 650 = 8 \cdot 28 \ (279)$ over the entire structure except the first storey where the floor height is $3 \cdot 960$ m ($13 \cdot 0$ ft), in which case $S_s = 5 \cdot 55 \ (189)$. From eqn (i) the stiffness ratio S_s/S_t for all storeys except the first is

$$\frac{S_s}{S_c} = \left(\frac{8 \cdot 28}{S_c} \right) \left(\frac{10}{14} \right)^2$$

$$= \frac{4 \cdot 21}{S_c}$$

and for the first

$$\frac{S_s}{S_c} = \frac{2 \cdot 79}{S_c}$$

These ratios are evaluated in Column 5. The values in Columns 4 and 5 are used to obtain the coefficients of Q_{fx}/Q_b by interpolating from the appropriate charts. For example, between levels $0 \cdot 6H$ and $0 \cdot 7H$, $S_s/S_c = 69$ and $S_c/S_b = 3 \cdot 9$. From Figs. 11.26 and 11.27 (ratios $S_c/S_b = 1$ and 5 respectively), the coefficients of Q_{fx}/Q_b (at $0 \cdot 65H$) are $0 \cdot 31$ and $0 \cdot 22$. Hence, for $S_c/S_b = 3 \cdot 9$ the interpolated coefficient is $0 \cdot 25$ as shown in Column 6. If the ten values in Column 6 are plotted midway between the subdivisions and a curve drawn joining them, then this curve can be subdivided into fourteen segments proportional to the storey heights of the structure. The shears from this curve at the mid-heights of the storeys are listed in Column 8.

The analysis can now be completed by first calculating the deflection of the shear wall due to the storey shear from

$$Q_{wx} = Q_{tx} - Q_{fx}$$

11.7. Behaviour of 'Top-hat' Interacting Frames and
Shear Walls

Behaviour Under Wind Loads

The use of stiff floors to provide a 'top-hat' increases the interaction between frames and shear walls locally so that the deflected
shape of the building under a wind load is quite different to that of
the same building without these high stiffness members (Fig. 11.33).
The parameters which control the lateral deformation are the same
as for frames with the additional consideration of the stiff floors.
The axial stiffness of the columns plays a predominant role. The

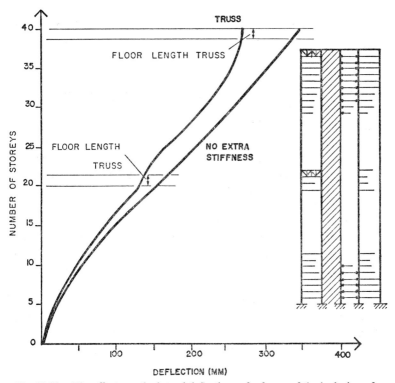

Fig. 11.33. The effects on the lateral deflections of a frame of the inclusion of a
'top-hat' and a stiff floor.

same secondary effects apply here as those noted in Section 11.6. Additionally, the shear deformation of the stiff floor may need to be included depending on how the stiffness is achieved.

Methods of Analysis

Although it is possible to make assumptions to allow an approximate analysis, because of the number of controlling parameters it is usual to examine the behaviour of these structures by the sort of computer programs we have discussed in Sections 11.5 and 11.6. Of particular importance in the requirements of the computer program is its ability to handle finite floor depths.

Structural Idealisation

The same concepts apply here as those for frames and interacting frames and shear walls aggregated to produce a complete building.

11.8. BEHAVIOUR OF BRACED-FACADE (TUBE) STRUCTURES

Behaviour Under Wind Loads

In the extreme case a braced-facade structure becomes a solid tube in which case under the action of wind loads its behaviour can be completely described by considering it to be an elementary cantilever. However, once we introduce openings into the faces which results in a facade braced with X's or more commonly a facade with stiff beams and columns then to treat it as a cantilever becomes inadequate, except as an approximation. This is due to the deformations of the beams and columns which results in a 'shear lag'. The effect of this is to increase the forces in the columns near the corners of the building and to decrease them near the centre of each face (Fig. 11.34). The shear lag is considerably reduced in buildings with braced facades. As a rough guide for closely spaced columns about 30% of the lateral deflection is due to column shortening in cantilever action of the tube whilst 70% is due to frame sway or racking which is not as efficient as a complete tube in which racking does not exist.

Because the floor system does not contribute to the lateral load

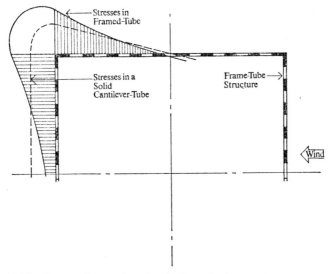

Fig. 11.34. Stresses due to shear lag in framed-tube structures compared to stresses in solid tube under the action of wind loads.

resistance it can be much shallower than in those forms of construction where it does contribute. Even though there are a large number of joints in the facade which are costly, there can be considerable savings because at the same time the structure forms the wall system and only windows need to be installed for the wall to be complete.

Methods of Analysis

As an *approximate method* we can commence by treating the entire structure as a tube, however, once we wish to progress beyond a shorthand method we cannot use this approximation for the reasons outlined above.

To gain a full appreciation of the behaviour of the structure *computer methods* are needed. Because of the three-dimensional behaviour of the structure it can be analysed by a space frame program. However, this can be very costly and we can make use of our understanding of the behaviour of the structure to treat it as a two-dimensional frame. The structural idealisation required will be treated below.

When choosing a computer program care must be taken to ensure that the input procedures take account of the very high degree of repetition associated with these buildings, in particular, geometrical and member property repetitions. Since the cost of data generation and preparation can far exceed the cost of computer processing this becomes very important.

Structural Idealisation

One method of turning a tube into a plane frame is to treat the columns on the windward and leeward faces as contributing only axial stiffness to the frames parallel to the load and neglect their bending stiffness at right angles to their own plane. Because of shear lag not all columns carry the same load as they would in a theoretical tube, the ones near the corners are more important, hence, instead of attaching half the columns to each of the frames the following guide is given [11.1]. The width of the windward/leeward frames which

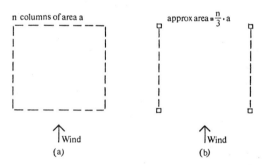

Fig. 11.35.
(a) Plan of framed-tube structure.
(b) Equivalent frames for wind analysis.

should be attached should be not more than (i) one half of the width of the frames parallel to the wind, (ii) one third of the width of the windward/leeward frames or (iii) 10% of the height of the building, whichever is the smallest (Fig. 11.35). This will produce axial forces in the end columns which can now be used in the analysis of the windward/leeward frames by treating them as shears at both edges, using the same program.

This idealisation has the advantage that there are many computer programs which can efficiently analyse frames although it does take two runs.

An alternative idealisation which normally requires that either a special program be written or a general purpose frame analysis program be used is not to assume what percentage of the windward/leeward frames contribute to the stiffness, but rather to rotate these frames about the corner into the same plane as the other frames and connect the two by constraints capable of transmitting only vertical shear. The lateral loads are then applied to the part of the idealised structure representing the frame parallel to the wind load. The part representing the frames perpendicular to the wind load is acted upon only by vertical shears transferred by the corner restraints [11.32, 11.33]. This idealised structure is shown in Fig. 11.36 and is conceptually the same as the one we idealised earlier.

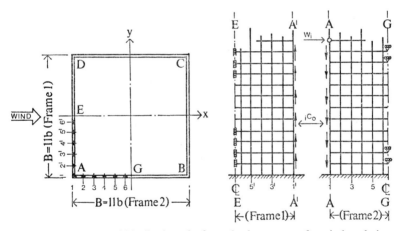

Fig. 11.36. Structural idealisation of a framed-tube structure for wind analysis.

Design Guide

Although tube structures have not been as extensively used as frames and shear walls (the first use was in 1961), Schwaighofer and Ast [11.34] have produced a set of tables to assist the design in the analysis of framed-tube buildings.

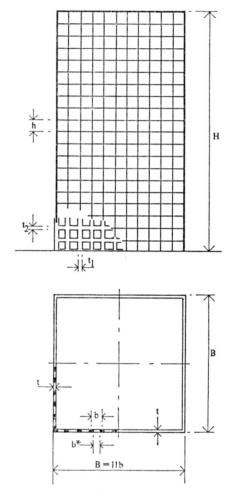

Fig. 11.37.   Plan and elevation of framed-tube structure with notation used in
the design guides.

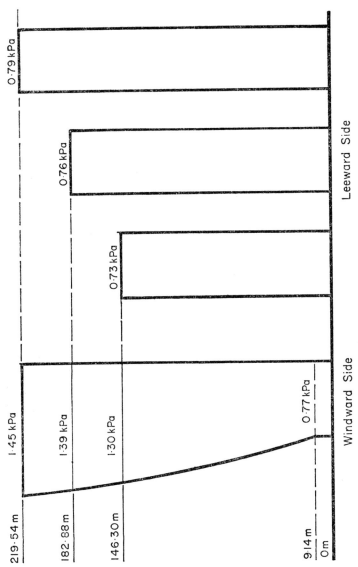

Fig. 11.38. Diagram of wind pressures used in calculating the design guides.

In the tables which follow, the buildings which can be analysed use the notation shown in Fig. 11.37 where

B = the centre to centre distance of exterior columns = $11b$
$\beta = b/h$
b = the centre to centre spacing of columns
h = storey height; set at 3·66 m (12 ft)
H = total height of the building
t_1 = width of column
$\alpha = 1200t$
t_2 = depth of beam
$r = 100t_2/h$
t = thickness of beam and column, set at 305 mm (1 ft).

The values for these parameters in the tables are

β = 0·8, 1·0, 1·2
H/h = 40, 50, 60
α = 20, 33, 45
r = 20, 30, 40

but not all the combinations have been listed.

The tables are based on the wind load as shown in Fig. 11.38 and are designated as Table B/No. of storeys/r–α. For example, Table B 1·0/60/30–33 represents a framed-tube of 60 × 3·660 = 220 m (720 ft) height, having a bay width b = 1·0 h = 3·660 m (12 ft), and therefore a total width of B = 116 = 40·250 m (132 ft). The depth of the spandrel beams is t_2 = 30h/100 = 1·100 m (3·6 ft), and the width of the column is t_1 = 33B/1200 = 1·110 m (3·63 ft). All four walls are uniform throughout the height of the building.

(Table follows on next page)

TABLE BO.8/40/20-20

FLOOR	CO	SUM10	C1	SUM1	C2	SUM2	C3	SUM3	C4	SUM4	C5	SUM5	C6	SUM6
34	35	169	-57	-191	-62	-209	-66	-244	-75	-275	-80	-302	-75	-315
26	88	836	-133	-1010	-146	-1112	-160	-1228	-173	-1326	-177	-1392	-177	-1415
18	142	1873	-204	-2402	-235	-2705	-258	-2950	-271	-3168	-280	-3288	-280	-3328
10	191	3341	-284	-4392	-324	-5015	-351	-5477	-364	-5784	-369	-5962	-373	-6020
2	235	5153	-436	-7217	-422	-8098	-422	-8659	-427	-9029	-427	-9238	-427	-9304

TABLE BO.8/40/20-33

FLOOR	CO	SUM10	C1	SUM1	C2	SUM2	C3	SUM3	C4	SUM4	C5	SUM5	C6	SUM6
34	40	218	-62	-231	-66	-235	-71	-253	-75	-275	-80	-293	-80	-302
26	97	858	-142	-1099	-155	-1197	-169	-1294	-182	-1375	-186	-1423	-186	-1441
18	155	2002	-218	-2576	-244	-2870	-266	-3123	-284	-3310	-293	-3426	-298	-3462
10	209	3582	-289	-4636	-333	-5250	-364	-5727	-382	-6060	-396	-6256	-396	-6218
2	240	5473	-418	-7422	-436	-8401	-444	-9060	-449	-9496	-453	-9745	-453	-9825

TABLE BO.8/40/30-20

FLOOR	CO	SUM10	C1	SUM1	C2	SUM2	C3	SUM3	C4	SUM4	C5	SUM5	C6	SUM6
34	35	169	-62	-213	-62	-222	-71	-249	-75	-275	-80	-293	-75	-302
26	93	832	-137	-1067	-151	-1170	-169	-1272	-177	-1352	-182	-1410	-186	-1428
18	151	1957	-213	-2523	-240	-2816	-262	-3066	-280	-3257	-289	-3373	-289	-3408
10	204	3519	-289	-4556	-329	-5157	-360	-5624	-373	-5949	-382	-6140	-387	-6203
2	244	5420	-436	-7369	-431	-8299	-431	-8895	-436	-9296	-436	-9522	-436	-9598

TABLE BO.8/40/30-33

FLOOR	CO	SUM10	C1	SUM1	C2	SUM2	C3	SUM3	C4	SUM4	C5	SUM5	C6	SUM6
34	35	164	-66	-235	-66	-244	-75	-262	-75	-280	-80	-293	-80	-298
26	97	849	-146	-1134	-160	-1241	-177	-1334	-186	-1406	-191	-1450	-191	-1464
18	164	2051	-226	-2665	-249	-2959	-275	-3203	-289	-3381	-302	-3488	-302	-3528
10	222	3733	-298	-4792	-338	-5384	-373	-5856	-391	-6139	-404	-6390	-409	-6456
2	253	5749	-418	-7578	-444	-8570	-458	-9260	-462	-9723	-467	-9994	-467	-10083

FLOOR	CO	SUMO	C1	SUM1	C2	SUM2	C3	SUM3	C4	SUM4	C5	SUM5	C6	SUM6
TABLE BO.8/50/30-20														
42	66	413	-80	-360	-84	-155	-88	-409	-93	-440	-97	-462	-97	-471
34	124	1170	-155	-1343	-169	-1459	-186	-1575	-195	-1668	-200	-1726	-204	-1748
26	182	2954	-226	-2914	-253	-3221	-275	-3488	-293	-3689	-302	-3809	-307	-3853
18	240	4530	-298	-5055	-333	-5651	-369	-6140	-391	-6496	-404	-6710	-409	-6786
10	284	6715	-373	-7769	-422	-8770	-467	-9549	-489	-10088	-498	-10381	-502	-10510
2	320	9220	-542	-11311	-538	-12722	-538	-13670	-542	-14306	-542	-14676	-542	-14800
TABLE BO.8/50/30-33														
42	66	436	-84	-396	-88	-413	-97	-444	-102	-467	-102	-485	-106	-489
34	133	1375	-164	-1437	-182	-1570	-195	-1686	-209	-1775	-213	-1828	-218	-1846
26	200	2856	-249	-3128	-271	-3457	-298	-3729	-311	-3929	-324	-4049	-324	-4093
18	262	4854	-324	-5446	-360	-6069	-396	-6568	-418	-6928	-431	-7146	-436	-7222
10	315	7297	-400	-8361	-444	-9380	-493	-10190	-520	-10764	-538	-11107	-542	-11222
2	333	9963	-529	-11952	-565	-13487	-578	-14582	-587	-15325	-591	-15761	-591	-15908
TABLE BO.8/50/40-20														
42	62	422	-80	-373	-84	-396	-93	-427	-97	-453	-102	-471	-102	-476
34	124	1317	-160	-1370	-169	-1499	-186	-1615	-195	-1704	-204	-1757	-204	-1775
26	186	2718	-235	-2972	-253	-3292	-284	-3559	-298	-3755	-307	-3875	-311	-3915
18	249	4610	-311	-5175	-342	-5780	-378	-6265	-400	-6617	-413	-6835	-418	-6901
10	298	6933	-382	-7965	-427	-8962	-476	-9745	-502	-10297	-516	-10631	-520	-10737
2	329	9531	-533	-11498	-551	-12967	-556	-13977	-560	-14662	-560	-15063	-565	-15192
TABLE BO.8/50/40-33														
42	66	422	-88	-400	-93	-431	-102	-458	-106	-485	-106	-498	-106	-502
34	133	1379	-169	-1468	-182	-1615	-204	-1739	-213	-1828	-218	-1886	-222	-1904
26	204	2905	-258	-3208	-275	-3555	-307	-3840	-320	-4045	-333	-4165	-333	-4205
18	275	4983	-347	-5606	-369	-6243	-404	-6750	-427	-7115	-440	-7338	-444	-7409
10	329	7547	-413	-8615	-453	-9638	-507	-10453	-533	-11035	-551	-11383	-556	-11498
2	347	10328	-525	-12237	-574	-13803	-596	-14938	-605	-15726	-614	-16184	-614	-16331

TABLE B1.0/40/20-20

FLOOR	CO	SUM0	C1	SUM1	C2	SUM2	C3	SUM3	C4	SUM4	C5	SUM5	C6	SUM6
34	35	173	-57	-177	-62	-200	-66	-244	-75	-289	-80	-320	-80	-329
26	88	809	-133	-992	-151	-1112	-164	-1250	-173	-1361	-182	-1432	-182	-1459
18	142	1864	-204	-2398	-240	-2736	-262	-3021	-275	-3230	-280	-3355	-284	-3395
10	186	3301	-289	-4414	-333	-5077	-355	-5549	-364	-5856	-369	-6034	-373	-6092
2	231	5077	-436	-7293	-422	-8183	-427	-8753	-427	-9113	-427	-9313	-427	-9380

TABLE B1.0/40/20-33

FLOOR	CO	SUM0	C1	SUM1	C2	SUM2	C3	SUM3	C4	SUM4	C5	SUM5	C6	SUM6
34	40	191	-62	-218	-66	-226	-71	-258	-75	-289	-80	-311	-84	-320
26	97	872	-142	-1085	-160	-1188	-173	-1303	-182	-1401	-191	-1468	-191	-1490
18	151	1993	-213	-2558	-249	-2879	-271	-3155	-289	-3359	-298	-3488	-298	-3528
10	200	849	-293	-4632	-338	-5291	-369	-5789	-382	-6127	-391	-6323	-396	-6385
2	235	5348	-422	-7480	-436	-8481	-440	-9135	-444	-9554	-449	-9789	-449	-9865

TABLE B1.0/40/30-20

FLOOR	CO	SUM0	C1	SUM1	C2	SUM2	C3	SUM3	C4	SUM4	C5	SUM5	C6	SUM6
34	35	173	-62	-209	-66	-222	-71	-253	-75	-284	-80	-307	-80	-315
26	97	849	-142	-1072	-155	-1179	-169	-1290	-182	-1388	-186	-1450	-191	-1472
18	151	1975	-213	-2536	-244	-2847	-266	-3114	-284	-3315	-293	-3439	-293	-3479
10	204	3519	-293	-4596	-333	-5233	-364	-5713	-378	-6038	-387	-6225	-387	-6287
2	244	5406	-444	-7484	-436	-8410	-436	-9006	-440	-9402	-440	-9625	-440	-9696

TABLE B1.0/40/30-33

FLOOR	CO	SUM0	C1	SUM1	C2	SUM2	C3	SUM3	C4	SUM4	C5	SUM5	C6	SUM6
34	40	177	-66	-240	-71	-249	-75	-271	-80	-289	-80	-307	-84	-311
26	102	885	-146	-1156	-164	-1259	-177	-1357	-186	-1432	-195	-1486	-195	-1504
18	164	2091	-226	-2701	-253	-3003	-280	-3257	-293	-3448	-307	-3564	-307	-3604
10	218	3751	-302	-4837	-342	-5464	-378	-5954	-396	-6301	-409	-6505	-413	-6572
2	249	5727	-431	-7694	-449	-8708	-458	-9398	-462	-9856	-467	-10119	-467	-10208

TABLE B1.0/50/30-20

FLOOR	CO	SUMO	C1	SUM1	C2	SUM2	C3	SUM3	C4	SUM4	C5	SUM5	C6	SUM6
42	71	471	-80	-373	-84	-387	-93	-427	-97	-462	-102	-489	-102	-498
34	129	1392	-160	-1383	-173	-1504	-191	-1628	-200	-1731	-209	-1802	-209	-1824
26	186	2776	-231	-2990	-258	-3310	-284	-3595	-302	-3813	-311	-3951	-315	-3996
18	240	4605	-307	-5175	-347	-5807	-382	-6323	-400	-6701	-413	-6928	-418	-7004
10	284	6817	-382	-7952	-440	-9020	-480	-9825	-498	-10377	-507	-10697	-511	-10804
2	324	9336	-560	-11632	-547	-13069	-547	-14030	-551	-14671	-551	-15040	-556	-15161

TABLE B1.0/50/30-33

FLOOR	CO	SUMO	C1	SUM1	C2	SUM2	C3	SUM3	C4	SUM4	C5	SUM5	C6	SUM6
42	71	485	-88	-418	-93	-431	-102	-462	-106	-489	-111	-507	-111	-516
34	137	1472	-173	-1508	-186	-1637	-204	-1757	-218	-1851	-222	-1909	-226	-1931
26	204	2990	-253	-3252	-280	-3591	-307	-3875	-324	-4085	-333	-4218	-338	-4263
18	266	5015	-329	-5624	-369	-6278	-409	-6804	-431	-7191	-444	-7422	-453	-7502
10	311	7444	-404	-8592	-462	-9683	-507	-10537	-533	-11138	-551	-11494	-556	-11610
2	333	10097	-551	-12313	-578	-13910	-587	-15027	-596	-15779	-600	-16215	-600	-16358

TABLE B1.0/50/40-20

FLOOR	CO	SUMO	C1	SUM1	C2	SUM2	C3	SUM3	C4	SUM4	C5	SUM5	C6	SUM6
42	71	462	-84	-387	-88	-404	-97	-440	-102	-471	-106	-493	-106	-502
34	133	1410	-164	-1437	-177	-1561	-195	-1682	-209	-1779	-213	-1842	-218	-1864
26	195	2861	-240	-3101	-266	-3430	-293	-3711	-311	-3920	-320	-4053	-324	-4098
18	253	4788	-315	-5375	-355	-6007	-391	-6523	-413	-6897	-427	-7128	-431	-7204
10	302	7124	-391	-8241	-444	-9296	-493	-10119	-516	-10693	-525	-11027	-529	-11142
2	338	9758	-565	-11943	-565	-13443	-565	-14453	-569	-15138	-569	-15534	-574	-15668

TABLE B1.0/50/40-33

FLOOR	CO	SUMO	C1	SUM1	C2	SUM2	C3	SUM3	C4	SUM4	C5	SUM5	C6	SUM6
42	71	462	-88	-422	-97	-444	-102	-476	-111	-525	-111	-520	-111	-525
34	142	1468	-177	-1539	-191	-1682	-209	-1811	-222	-1904	-226	-1962	-231	-1980
26	209	3034	-262	-3328	-289	-3684	-315	-3978	-333	-4191	-342	-4320	-347	-4360
18	275	5153	-342	-5776	-378	-6434	-418	-6968	-440	-7351	-453	-7582	-458	-7658
10	329	7698	-418	-8828	-467	-9910	-516	-10764	-547	-11383	-565	-11734	-569	-11854
2	347	10470	-551	-12584	-587	-14182	-600	-15339	-609	-16126	-614	-16589	-618	-16736

FLOOR	CO	SUM0	C1	SUM1	C2	SUM2	C3	SUM3	C4	SUM4	C5	SUM5	C6	SUM6
TABLE B1.0/60/30-20														
50	80	631	-97	-542	-102	-565	-111	-609	-115	-654	-120	-680	-120	-694
42	137	1628	-169	-1642	-186	-1779	-200	-1913	-213	-2024	-218	-2095	-222	-2122
34	195	3083	-240	-3310	-262	-3644	-289	-3933	-307	-4156	-315	-4298	-320	-4343
26	249	4988	-311	-5540	-347	-6163	-382	-6679	-404	-7062	-418	-7297	-422	-7378
18	302	7329	-382	-8343	-431	-9358	-476	-10177	-502	-10764	-520	-11071	-525	-11236
10	333	10003	-462	-11734	-525	-13265	-574	-14440	-596	-15245	-609	-15712	-614	-15868
2	378	13011	-654	-16077	-640	-18062	-640	-19415	-645	-20327	-649	-20857	-649	-21026
TABLE B1.0/60/30-33														
50	84	667	-106	-614	-115	-645	-124	-685	-129	-720	-133	-747	-133	-756
42	151	1766	-186	-1842	-204	-2002	-222	-2140	-235	-2251	-240	-2318	-244	-2345
34	218	3408	-271	-3715	-298	-4089	-324	-4405	-342	-4636	-355	-4779	-355	-4828
26	284	5584	-351	-6234	-391	-6924	-427	-7480	-449	-7885	-467	-8130	-471	-8214
18	347	8259	-427	-9376	-480	-10475	-525	-11351	-556	-11988	-574	-12370	-592	-12500
10	373	11285	-498	-13100	-565	-14742	-627	-16028	-658	-16936	-680	-17475	-685	-17653
2	400	14538	-663	-17621	-694	-19882	-707	-21484	-716	-22579	-720	-23211	-725	-23420
TABLE B1.0/60/40-33														
50	84	649	-111	-627	-120	-671	-129	-720	-133	-756	-137	-783	-137	-787
42	155	1779	-195	-1895	-213	-2078	-231	-2233	-244	-2354	-253	-2420	-253	-2443
34	226	3479	-230	-3835	-307	-4245	-338	-4579	-355	-4823	-364	-4970	-369	-5015
26	298	5749	-369	-6448	-400	-7173	-440	-7751	-462	-8170	-480	-8446	-485	-8503
18	364	8557	-449	-9723	-493	-10849	-542	-11747	-574	-12397	-591	-12807	-596	-12909
10	396	11765	-516	-13585	-578	-15241	-640	-16509	-703	-17484	-703	-18040	-707	-18213
2	422	15192	-667	-18164	-711	-20478	-729	-22156	-743	-23309	-747	-26206	-747	-24417
TABLE B1.2/50/30-20														
42	71	498	-84	-373	-88	-391	-97	-440	-102	-485	-106	-520	-106	-529
34	129	1441	-160	-1410	-177	-1535	-195	-1673	-204	-1793	-213	-1873	-218	-1900
26	186	2843	-235	-3043	-266	-3386	-293	-3693	-311	-3929	-320	-4080	-324	-4129
18	240	4676	-311	-5273	-355	-5945	-391	-6496	-413	-6893	-422	-7128	-427	-7208
10	284	6888	-391	-8121	-453	-9251	-489	-10083	-507	-10639	-516	-10955	-516	-10849
2	320	9402	-569	-11912	-556	-13385	-556	-14364	-560	-15009	-565	-15374	-565	-15490

TABLE B1.2/50/30—33

FLOOR	CO	SUM0	C1	SUM1	C2	SUM2	C3	SUM3	C4	SUM4	C5	SUM5	C6	SUM6
42	80	529	-93	-431	-97	-444	-106	-476	-111	-511	-115	-533	-115	-542
34	142	1557	-177	-1561	-195	-1690	-213	-1815	-222	-1922	-231	-1989	-231	-2011
26	204	3097	-258	-3346	-289	-3697	-315	-4000	-333	-4227	-347	-4374	-351	-4423
18	262	5117	-333	-5753	-378	-6443	-418	-7004	-444	-7418	-458	-7667	-462	-7747
10	307	7520	-413	-8766	-476	-9936	-520	-10826	-547	-11449	-560	-11814	-560	-11934
2	329	10141	-565	-12606	-587	-14266	-596	-15401	-600	-16153	-605	-16585	-605	-16727

TABLE B1.2/50/40—20

FLOOR	CO	SUM0	C1	SUM1	C2	SUM2	C3	SUM3	C4	SUM4	C5	SUM5	C6	SUM6
42	75	498	-83	-400	-93	-418	-97	-458	-106	-493	-111	-520	-111	-529
34	137	1477	-169	-1477	-186	-1606	-204	-1739	-213	-1846	-222	-1917	-222	-1940
26	200	2963	-249	-3195	-275	-3537	-302	-3835	-320	-4062	-333	-4205	-338	-4254
18	258	4917	-324	-5522	-369	-6194	-404	-6737	-427	-7137	-440	-7378	-444	-7458
10	302	7266	-404	-8463	-462	-9589	-507	-10444	-525	-11031	-538	-11374	-542	-11485
2	338	9923	-582	-12308	-574	-13843	-574	-14871	-578	-15561	-582	-15953	-582	-16086

TABLE B1.2/50/40—33

FLOOR	CO	SUM0	C1	SUM1	C2	SUM2	C3	SUM3	C4	SUM4	C5	SUM5	C6	SUM6
42	75	493	-93	-431	-97	-449	-106	-480	-111	-507	-115	-529	-115	-533
34	142	1521	-177	-1570	-195	-1708	-213	-1828	-222	-1926	-231	-1989	-235	-2006
26	213	3101	-262	-3381	-289	-3737	-320	-4031	-338	-4249	-347	-4383	-351	-4427
18	275	5202	-342	-5838	-382	-6514	-422	-7057	-444	-7453	-462	-7694	-467	-7774
10	324	7716	-418	-8895	-476	-10016	-520	-10898	-551	-11516	-565	-11885	-574	-12010
2	342	10453	-565	-12704	-591	-14355	-605	-15512	-614	-16291	-614	-16745	-618	-16892

TABLE B1.2/60/30—20

FLOOR	CO	SUM0	C1	SUM1	C2	SUM2	C3	SUM3	C4	SUM4	C5	SUM5	C6	SUM6
50	84	694	-102	-569	-106	-591	-115	-645	-120	-698	-124	-734	-129	-747
42	142	1739	-173	-1722	-191	-1860	-209	-2011	-222	-2135	-226	-2220	-231	-2247
34	200	3248	-249	-3462	-275	-3809	-302	-4125	-320	-4374	-333	-4530	-333	-4583
26	258	5210	-320	-5776	-364	-6439	-400	-6999	-422	-7413	-436	-7671	-440	-7756
18	307	7596	-396	-8673	-453	-9767	-498	-10644	-525	-11271	-538	-11645	-542	-11770
10	351	10337	-480	-12197	-551	-13857	-596	-15081	-618	-15913	-627	-16398	-631	-16553
2	382	13358	-676	-16740	-658	-18014	-663	-20216	-667	-21155	-671	-21693	-671	-21867

TABLE B1.2/60/30-33

FLOOR	CO	SUM0	C1	SUM1	C2	SUM2	C3	SUM3	C4	SUM4	C5	SUM5	C6	SUM6
50	97	752	-115	-663	-124	-685	-129	-729	-137	-769	-142	-800	-142	-809
42	160	1931	-200	-1966	-218	-2122	-235	-2273	-249	-2394	-258	-2469	-258	-2496
34	226	3648	-280	-3938	-311	-4325	-342	-4659	-360	-4912	-373	-5068	-378	-5121
26	293	5887	-360	-6554	-404	-7280	-444	-7876	-471	-8317	-489	-8584	-493	-8677
18	351	8597	-440	-9789	-498	-10969	-547	-11917	-578	-12597	-600	-13011	-605	-13149
10	391	11667	-516	-13630	-596	-15414	-649	-16776	-680	-17728	-698	-18289	-707	-18476
2	400	14898	-685	-18351	-711	-20736	-725	-22405	-734	-23522	-738	-24167	-738	-24381

TABLE B1.2/60/40-20

FLOOR	CO	SUM0	C1	SUM1	C2	SUM2	C3	SUM3	C4	SUM4	C5	SUM5	C6	SUM6
50	83	694	-106	-600	-111	-631	-120	-680	-129	-725	-133	-756	-133	-769
42	151	1793	-186	-1820	-204	-1971	-222	-2122	-235	-2242	-240	-2322	-244	-2345
34	213	3404	-266	-3666	-293	-4040	-320	-4360	-338	-4605	-351	-4757	-355	-4810
26	275	5522	-342	-6136	-382	-6826	-422	-7395	-444	-7814	-458	-8072	-462	-8161
18	333	8098	-418	-9211	-471	-10328	-520	-11227	-551	-11872	-569	-12259	-574	-12388
10	378	11049	-498	-12896	-569	-14582	-622	-15864	-649	-16749	-663	-17265	-667	-17435
2	409	14271	-698	-17555	-689	-19735	-689	-21226	-694	-22241	-698	-22824	-698	-23015

TABLE B1.2/60/40-33

FLOOR	CO	SUM0	C1	SUM1	C2	SUM2	C3	SUM3	C4	SUM4	C5	SUM5	C6	SUM6
50	93	703	-115	-649	-124	-685	-133	-729	-137	-769	-142	-796	-142	-805
42	160	1877	-200	-1962	-222	-2135	-240	-2287	-253	-2402	-258	-2478	-262	-2505
34	235	3622	-289	-3956	-315	-4360	-347	-4699	-364	-4943	-373	-5095	-378	-5148
26	302	5931	-373	-6626	-409	-7355	-449	-7947	-476	-8374	-489	-8637	-493	-8726
18	364	8753	-449	-9941	-502	-11098	-551	-12023	-587	-12691	-605	-13096	-609	-13234
10	409	11970	-525	-13848	-596	-15579	-658	-16927	-694	-17880	-711	-18449	-720	-18641
2	422	15352	-689	-18547	-720	-20923	-738	-22619	-747	-23776	-752	-24448	-756	-24670

TABLE B1.2/60/40-20

FLOOR	CO	SUM0	C1	SUM1	C2	SUM2	C3	SUM3	C4	SUM4	C5	SUM5	C6	SUM6
50	80	622	-97	-560	-106	-587	-115	-631	-120	-671	-124	-698	-124	-707
42	142	1655	-177	-1708	-191	-1855	-209	-1993	-218	-2104	-226	-2171	-226	-2198
34	204	3181	-253	-3453	-275	-3809	-302	-4107	-320	-4329	-329	-4467	-333	-4516
26	266	5206	-329	-5802	-360	-6448	-400	-6973	-422	-7360	-436	-7600	-440	-7680
18	324	7707	-404	-8748	-449	-9785	-498	-10617	-525	-11218	-542	-11605	-547	-11707
10	351	10564	-480	-12317	-538	-13839	-596	-17270	-622	-15895	-640	-16393	-645	-16562
2	400	13737	-667	-16705	-667	-18792	-667	-20229	-671	-21208	-676	-21773	-676	-21969

A compact way of presenting the necessary information is to list the variation of the shear force at the centre of each bay as a function of the height of the building; from this all the other structural actions may be calculated.

C_j-values. Figure 11.39 shows one storey of the frame parallel to the load in which the shear forces C_0 to C_6 act mid-way between the columns. The values C_0 to C_6 are listed for every 8th floor in the tables.

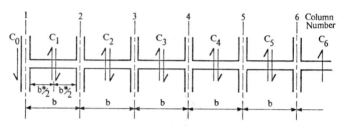

Fig. 11.39.   The shear forces (C_j) in the centre of bays of frame parallel to wind load.

Column axial forces: for example the axial force P_1, in column 1 (i.e. the corner column) just below the 14th floor is given by

$$N_{1,14} = \sum_{k=14}^{n} (C_{1,k} - C_{0,k})$$

where n = number of storeys.

Generally, the axial force N_j, in column j just below the mth floor is given by

$$N_{j,m} = \sum_{k=m}^{n} (C_{j,k} - C_{j-1,k})$$

To simplify these calculations, the tables also contain for each coefficient C_j the value of the sum of all C_j-values from the top storey of the building to the floor under consideration; this value is designated SUMj.

Bending moments in beams: these moments, at the face of a column, are obtained by multiplying the shear force, C_j by half the clear span, $b^*/2$ of the beam (Fig. 11.39).

Bending moments in columns (between spans j and $j + 1$): these moments, at the face of a beam can be obtained with a reasonable degree of accuracy from the relationship

$$M = \frac{(C_j + C_{j+1})b(h - t_2)}{4h}$$

This, of course, will be the moment in the column both above and below the beam.

Example 11.4. A tube building is square in plan, 50 storeys high, with identical floor to floor heights of 3·660 m (12 ft), all perimeter frames are identical and each has 11 bays of 3·660 m (12 ft) width. All columns have a cross-section of 111·0 cm × 30·5 cm (3·63 ft × 1·0 ft) and the cross-section of all beams are 110·0 cm × 30·5 cm (3·6 ft × 1·0 ft). The magnitude and variation of the wind loading is shown in Fig. 11.38. Determine the column axial forces and the moments in the columns and beams at floor 2.

We need first to determine which table to use. The parameters for this building are $b = 3·660$ m (12 ft); $h = 3·660$ m (12 ft); $t_1 = 111·0$ cm (3·63 ft), $t_2 = 110·0$ cm (3·60 ft),

$$\therefore \qquad \beta = 1·0, \quad r = 30, \quad \alpha = 33,$$

no. of storeys = 50
So, use Table B 1·0/50/30–33.
Axial forces in columns are calculated using the SUMj values. The computations are carried out in a tabular form (the -ve sign in the table indicates -ve shear).

Column number	Calculation	Axial force in column below 2nd floor, kN (kips)
1	SUM1 − SUM0 = 12 313 − 10 097 =	2 214 (498)
2	SUM2 − SUM1 = 13 910 − 12 313 =	1 597 (359)
3	SUM3 − SUM2 = 15 027 − 13 910 =	1 117 (251)
4	SUM4 − SUM3 = 15 779 − 15 027 =	752 (169)
5	SUM5 − SUM4 = 16 215 − 15 779 =	436 (98)
6	SUM6 − SUM5 = 16 358 − 16 215 =	143 (32)

Bending moments in beams at the face of the column are calculated using the C_j values and the lever arm of half the clear span

$$b^* = 3.660 - 1.110$$

$$= 2.550 \text{ m } (8.37 \text{ ft})$$

$$\frac{b^*}{2} = 1.275 \text{ m } (4.18 \text{ ft})$$

The following tables gives the moments in the beams at the interior faces of the first six columns

Column line number	Computation	Moment kN m (kip ft)
1	$C1 \times b^*/2 = 551 \times 1.275 =$	703 (520)
2	$C2 \times b^*/2 = 578 \times 1.275 =$	737 (545)
3	$C3 \times b^*/2 = 587 \times 1.275 =$	748 (555)
4	$C4 \times b^*/2 = 596 \times 1.275 =$	760 (560)
5	$C5 \times b^*/2 = 600 \times 1.275 =$	765 (565)
6	$C6 \times b^*/2 = 600 \times 1.275 =$	765 (565)

Bending moments in columns at the face of the beams are calculated using the C_j values and the relationship given earlier. Carrying out the computations in a tabular manner we get

Column number	$b(h - t_2)/4h$	C_j	C_{j+1}	Moment in column kN m (kip ft)
1	0.640	—	551	353 (260)
2	0.640	551	578	723 (535)
3	0.640	578	587	746 (550)
4	0.640	587	596	757 (560)
5	0.640	596	600	765 (565)
6	0.640	600	600	768 (567)

11.9. BEHAVIOUR OF STAGGERED-WALL OR TRUSS STRUCTURES

Behaviour Under Wind Loads

A detailed study of the behaviour of this structural form has been made by the PCA [11.35, 11.36]. To understand the behaviour under wind loads, it is essential to consider the combined action of adjacent transverse frames. Assuming, as we have before, that the floor slabs act as infinitely stiff horizontal diaphragms, all points on any one floor slab will have the same horizontal deflection. Considering each frame separately, it would at first appear that each frame would undergo a stiff beam-flexible column deformation (Fig. 11.40a). However, when adjacent frames are considered, the

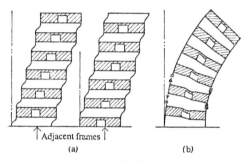

Adjacent frames

(a)   (b)

Fig. 11.40.
(a) Deflected shapes of separate adjacent frames of a staggered-wall structure under wind load.
(b) Deflected shape of combined frames under wind load.

horizontal deformations would not be compatible, so that the deflected shape is much closer to that of an ordinary framed structure with the columns in single curvature (Fig. 11.40b); behaviour similar to that of a shear wall with openings.

Since this structure acts predominantly as a vertical cantilever under lateral loads, the columns are subjected to axial loading.

Methods of Analysis

These structures can easily be analysed as frames with suitable shear stiffness included in the requisite floors. If a shear element does not exist in the computer program, a diagonal which produces the same shear stiffness can be used. The frames are then lumped together as in any other framed building.

Additionally, specialised computer programs for this type of structure are available although any computer program which can handle frames with diagonals lumped to produce the building stiffness will suffice.

Structural Idealisation

The same concepts apply here as those for frames and interacting frames and shear walls aggregated to produce a complete building.

11.10. BEHAVIOUR OF PANELISED CONSTRUCTION

Behaviour Under Wind Loads

Providing the joints develop sufficient strength panelised construction can be treated as thin-walled diaphragm systems with a high degree of rigidity. They may also be conceived of as a series of parallel frames composed of coupled shear walls. Under the action of wind loads these structures behave as coupled shear walls, hence, their deformation is similar to that of a vertical cantilever.

Methods of Analysis

An *approximate method* of analysis is to treat each vertical panel separately and disregard the interaction between panels. The method outlined in Section 10.1 for structural masonry can then be applied. Once the structure is more than 10–15 storeys high this approach is inadequate and a better method is required.

One approach is to treat the entire building as a thin-walled tube with the floors acting as rigid diaphragms. Another is to solve the equations for equilibrium and compatibility of all walls in one plane with the beams connecting them [11.37]. The structure can, of course, be modelled by a frame analysis program such as the one discussed in Section 11.4 provided it can model shear panels either as discrete elements or through the use of diagonals.

Structural Idealisation

The same concepts apply here as those for frames and interacting shear walls aggregated to produce a complete building.

Design Guide

Levy and Varga [11.38] have produced design guides for various configurations of panelised construction. All the configurations can be described by the following geometric information (Fig. 11.41). Because doors are usually provided in the corridor and windows in the facade, the effective width of the corridor wall and facade (when load-bearing) is taken as $0.4S$ or $0.8S$. $t_c = t_f = t_t = t$ in the charts, and where values have been given above these remain fixed.

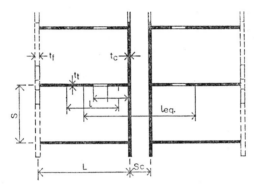

Fig. 11.41. Plan of typical panelised construction showing notation used in design guides.

Key: t_c = thickness of corridor wall; t_f = thickness of facade; t_t = thickness of transverse wall; t_s = thickness of slab = 140 mm ($5\frac{1}{2}$ in); L = length of transverse wall; s = distance between transverse walls; s_c = width of corridor = 0.910 m (3 ft); s_d = width of door = 0.910 m (3 ft); s_{cd} = distance between corridor and door = 2.130 m (7 ft); h = floor to floor height = 2.590 m (8.5 ft); d_1 = depth of lintel = 0.420 m (1.38 ft).

In the design charts the following design conditions have been used:

(i) *Design Loads.* The dead loads are slab 3.3 kPa (69 lb/ft²), facades 3.8 kPa (80 lb/ft²); and corridor and transverse walls according to thickness. The live loads are 1.9 kPa (40 lb/ft²) reduced to 1.2 kPa (25 lb/ft²), an average based on a 25-storey building. Wind load is 1.2 kPa (25 lb/ft²).

(ii) *Design Criteria.* The walls are designed in accordance with the CEB recommendations [11.39], where f'_c = 34 470 kPa (5000 lb/in²). In determining the allowable stresses an eccentricity of

152 mm (0·6 in) was assumed. In checking a typical bay acted upon by wind forces, these criteria must be met:

1. The maximum allowable deflection at the tip is limited to $H/1000$ where H is the height of the building. This requirement is imposed to limit cracking in the walls and lies between current practice, which is 1:500 and the CEB recommendation of 1:2000 based on limit-state of cracking.
2. No tension permitted at the heel of the wall.
3. The compression stress, due to combined wind and gravity loads, cannot exceed 1·33 times the allowable stress.

Figures 11.42a to e contain design charts which give the maximum height of building possible under the above criteria. For the cases when compressive stress limits the height, the graphs are shown as solid lines; when horizontal deflection limits the height, then broken lines are used. For the cases presented tension was not critical.

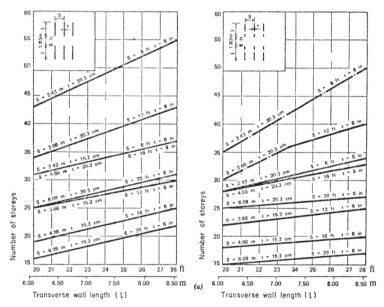

Fig. 11.42a. Design guides for panelised construction—maximum height of building possible versus length of transverse wall, wall spacing and wall thickness. Transverse walls only (after Levy and Varga [11.38]).

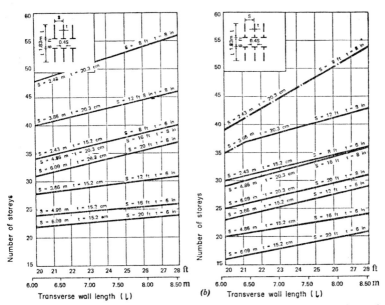

Fig. 11.42b. Design guides for panelised construction—maximum height of building possible versus length of transverse wall, wall spacing and wall thickness. Transverse wall with short corridor wall (0·4*S*) (after Levy and Varga [11.38]).

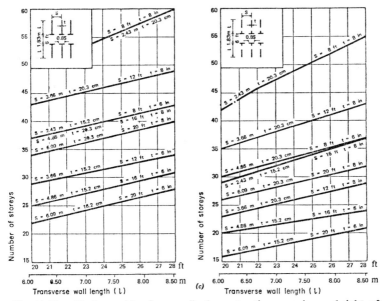

Fig. 11.42c. Design guides for panelised construction—maximum height of building possible versus length of transverse wall, wall spacing and wall thickness. Transverse wall with long corridor wall (0·8*S*) (after Levy and Varga [11.38]).

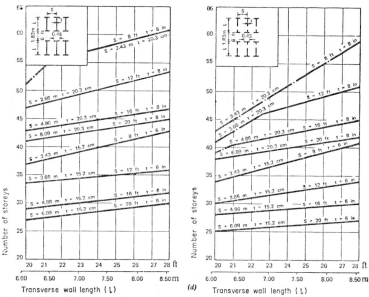

Fig. 11.42d. Design guides for panelised construction—maximum height of building possible versus length of transverse wall, wall spacing and wall thickness. Transverse wall with short corridor and facade walls (0·4S) (after Levy and Varga [11.38]).

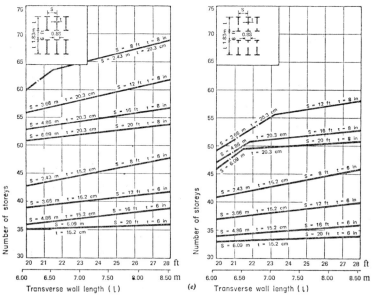

Fig. 11.42e. Design guides for panelised construction—maximum height of building possible versus length of transverse wall, wall spacing and wall thickness. Transverse wall with long corridor and facade walls (0·8S) (after Levy and Varga [11.38]).

Example 11.5. As part of the preliminary design of a multi-storey apartment building, a typical layout has been designed and is shown schematically in Fig. 11.43. The spacing of the walls is 3·660 m (12 ft), the length of the transverse walls is 7·930 m (26 ft) and their thickness is 152 mm (6 in). If the building is to be 40 storeys high determine whether the corridor walls and the facade walls need to be made structural, and if so what effective length of wall is required so that the preliminary design may proceed.

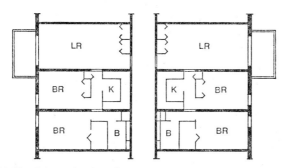

Fig. 11.43.   Schematic plan of preliminary layout used in Example 11.5.

Let us begin by assuming that half the transverse walls have door openings and the other half do not, so we will need to interpolate between the results for these two. One way to solve this problem is to follow the lines on the charts labelled $S = 3\cdot660$ m (12 ft) and $t = 52$ mm (6 in) and see whether they satisfy the requirements when the number of storeys and the transverse wall length is as we have them above.

After examining all the charts we can see that only in Fig. 11.42e do we seem to be able to satisfy our requirements. For our preliminary design, a solid transverse wall of only 7·020 m (23 ft) is required whilst a transverse wall with doors needs to be 8·550 m (28 ft) long. We can assume that if we use a mix of both types of walls we would need a transverse wall of about 7·780 m (25·5 ft) in length. Therefore, we can see that our design requires that both the corridor and facade walls be made structural, at least to the extent that their effective lengths are 0·8 times the spacing between the walls.

11.11. Behaviour of Suspended Structures

Behaviour Under Wind Loads

When considering the behaviour of suspended structures under the action of wind loads we must distinguish between those in which the suspenders are attached to the ground and those that are not. Structures in which the suspenders are not attached to the ground behave as vertical cantilevers, particularly when the joint between the floors and the core is not a rigid one.

On the other hand, structures in which the suspenders are attached to the ground behave in a more complex fashion. Their deflected shapes tend to be closer in appearance to that for interacting frames and shear walls because of the axial stiffness of the suspenders. In addition, the deflection is a non-linear function of the load and the prestress (if any) of the suspender. An increase in prestress up to the value which will not produce any compression in the leeward suspenders reduces the lateral deflection. Beyond this value there is only a marginal decrease.

Attaching the suspenders to the foundations produces significant reductions in lateral deflections as does prestressing the suspenders although this increases the axial load on the core.

Methods of Analysis

Structures which do not have attached suspenders can be simply analysed by treating the entire structure as statically determinate. Another approach is to use a frame analysis program in which the axial stiffnesses of the suspenders on the leeward face are set to zero.

Structures with attached suspenders generally require an iterative approach. The principle of virtual displacements (see Chapter 6) can be applied and the equilibrium equations solved based on compatibility requirements. An alternative method is to use influence coefficients [11.40]. In analysing this structure, attention must be paid to the stresses and deformations arising from incremental loadings during erection.

Structural Idealisation

In both cases the structure may be idealised as a core with one or more cantilever beams and suspenders. It may be assumed that the floors do not contribute to the stiffness.

Chapter 12

Physical Models in Structural Design

In this chapter we briefly examine the use of physical models in structural design as an alternative to the techniques so far discussed. Criteria for their use are derived and then planning of such tests is described. The chapter concludes with an examination of the model study of a 64-storey concrete building.

12.1. THE PLACE OF STRUCTURAL MODELS

The use of structural models in research is well accepted and such a technique is widely utilised in the laboratory. The use of models in design problems is much less well accepted. It would appear that the increasing sophistication of our mathematical models coupled with the availability of computer techniques to manipulate these models would preclude the use of physical studies; however, this has not been so. The reasons for the continued use of physical models may be traced through an examination of the three areas where they have found the most application [12.1].

At the feasibility study stage of a novel design physical models are often used because such models require considerably less assumptions to be made about the behaviour of the structure to be modelled than do mathematical models. It is well known that the use of a linear theory on a non-linear structure will predict that the behaviour of that structure is linear. Often for novel designs no computer based method of analysis exists for analysing such a structure. In addition the realism provided by a physical model can be used to communicate ideas about the structure to both the technical and non-technical personnel associated with the project in a way that reams of computer output could never do. Since the degree of accuracy required from feasibility study models is low, the cost of constructing them is low.

At the other end of the design problem, physical models have been used extensively for the analysis of a detailed region of the structure for stress concentrations and other details. With the development of the finite element method of analysis and the increasing number of elements available physical studies in this area are becoming less competitive, although they are being used to verify results. Which brings us to the third area, that of providing confirmatory evidence for other forms of analysis:

The best way to gain confidence in a computer solution is by comparison with results obtained from laboratory models or full-scale tests of the structure [12.2];

since full-scale testing is both too costly and too time-consuming we usually resort to physical models. In this category we might also include aeroelastic modelling of structures in wind [12.3].

At the conclusion of a report on the feasibility structural model analysis of a 230 m (700 ft) high tower of unusual design [12.4], the authors state that the decision to use a physical model can be directly traced to a number of factors:

(i) no existing computer program could analyse the structure without a number of assumptions of unknown validity being made;

(ii) since the basis of the structure was three-dimensional action, any semi-automated method of calculation using energy principles would have been unacceptably lengthy;

(iii) the time and cost associated with the manufacture and testing of a physical model were assessed to be satisfactory in terms of the expected returns;

(iv) the realism provided by the model and the ability to observe the whole of the model during testing was considered advantageous;

(v) the model could be used not only to obtain quantitative information but could also be used to communicate qualitative ideas about the behaviour of the structure to others, particularly the client and the architect.

The criteria for the selection of this form of analysis are the same as for any method of analysis among possible alternatives, with the added intangible value of realism and qualitative evaluation not readily available in any other method. This aspect of structural models can be very important in itself. The use of model analysis assumes the availability of trained technical staff and suitable equipment; the former are considerably more important than the latter.

12.2. THE BASIS OF MODEL STUDIES

Model analysis as a separate subject has been extensively examined in another volume in this series [12.5] to which the reader is referred for details. The basis of model studies is the concept of similarity and the ability to relate results derived from a model to the equivalent result for the structure being modelled, because the relationships are not necessarily linear even with linear scaling of sizes. Dimensional theory provides the necessary tools for these conversions and the interested reader may examine this subject further in Chapter 3 of Reference [12.5].

Planning structural model tests is essential because structural models are generally expensive since their construction and testing takes much time and care. Any mistake in either the construction or testing may seriously impair the applicability of the results. Most mistakes occur through insufficient planning of the test and often a vital reading is omitted. Decisions regarding the planning of model tests can be grouped under eight headings:

(i) *Purpose and extent*
 The purpose of the investigation must first be defined. What information is sought? Must the whole field be covered or will point-to-point analysis suffice? Is it an elastic or ultimate load study?

(ii) *Materials*
 The choice of the model material is governed by the nature of the test.

(iii) *Dimensions and Scale*
 The approximate size of the model must be decided at the beginning of the investigation; once this has been determined the

scale follows. A large model not only takes up more space, but also needs more material, more labour, a larger supporting frame and greater loads. However, less skill and care in the manufacture of a large model produces the same degree of accuracy, also it produces larger deflections. Often the exact scale is a function of commercially available thicknesses and diameters.

(iv) *Measurements Required*
These determine to a large extent the instrumentation, depending on whether measurements are to be short-term or long-term, static or dynamic, point or field. It is desirable to make a prior assessment of the order of the magnitude of the measurements to be made.

(v) *Instrumentation*
This depends on the measurements required, the environment of the test, the accuracy, the length of test. Availability of equipment, technical assistance and workshop facilities are often over-riding factors. Though models may be tested over a period of months, a set of readings is usually completed in one day so that long term stability of the measuring equipment is rarely important.

(vi) *Loading*
The type of loads and their method of application needs to be considered. It must be realised that the model will be loaded and unloaded a number of times.

(vii) *Data Analysis*
There is little value in obtaining a large number of readings if time is not available to reduce and analyse them. If statistical analysis is contemplated, it is preferable to establish confidence limits so that the test can be planned accordingly.

(viii) *Cost and Time Estimation*
In assessing the cost and time required to perform a model test the principal factors to be considered are:

(a) the cost and time of constructing the model to the required scale and in the appropriate material;

(b) the cost and time of obtaining the measurements necessary to give the desired information reliably;

(c) the cost and time of processing and interpreting the experimental data;

(d) the cost and time for producing the report.

Stage (a) is likely to take longer than the other three stages combined.

12.3. A CASE STUDY

As part of a downtown project in Sydney, Australia, it is proposed to erect a concrete building with 64 levels of almost 250 m (800 ft) in height. In buildings of this height, lateral sway under wind load is one of the primary design considerations. Much of modern structural engineering is directed towards the production of economic solutions to this problem (see Chapter 11); recent studies have indicated the efficacy of axial stiffness away from the neutral axis of the building. The designers of this building had produced a novel design which made use of this concept (Fig. 12.1).

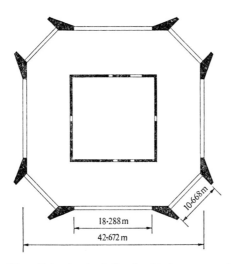

Fig. 12.1.   Plan of structural solution for 64-storey concrete building.

Purpose and Extent

A physical model test [12.6] was called for to provide confirmatory evidence of the feasibility of the concept and to validate a simplified computer model which modelled the entire building as a series of parallel two-dimensional frames. The computer model could have been validated by a full three-dimensional theoretical analysis; however, this was considered to be a rare opportunity to use an alternative validation method for a computer model which was not only going to be used extensively on this project, but also as a standard analysis package for other projects. Additionally the test was unusual in another way. The prototype sizes had not been frozen, as is the case when a finalised design is being modelled, and since this was a feasibility model this gave the model designer more freedom in selecting model scales to utilise commercially available material and where necessary adjust the prototype sizes to match the model.

It was decided to break the building into four segments; maintaining uniform sizes for core and columns for all floors in each segment. The four segments were:

low rise—levels 1–18, low medium rise—levels 19–35, high medium rise—levels 36–51, high rise—levels 52–64.

Materials

The model material chosen was Perspex (polymethyl methacrylate) because of its availability in sheet form, its ability to be easily machined and because of its weldability and glueability.

Dimensions and Scale

It is always difficult to choose dimensions; in this case it was decided to make the model about 2·5 m high because at this height it was possible to reach its uppermost reaches with the aid of a ladder but without the need for scaffolding (except during construction). The precise scale was determined by the available thicknesses for use in the walls of the core. On this basis the length scale became 1:95. Table 12.1 shows the properties of both the prototype and model. Figure 12.2 shows a typical cross-section.

Table 12.1

Property	Prototype	Model
Height (m)	233 (762 ft)	2·44 (8·02 ft)
Beam depth (mm)	1 890 (74·5 in)	20 (0·785 in)
width (mm)	950 (37·6 in)	10 (0·396 in)
Core wall thickness (mm)		
low rise	760 (30·0 in)	8 (0·316 in)
low medium rise	570 (22·5 in)	6 (0·237 in)
high medium rise	475 (18·7 in)	5 (0·197 in)
high rise	380 (15·0 in)	4 (0·158 in)
Elastic modulus (GPa)	21·5 (3 120 × 10³ lb/in²)	$3 \times 10^{-3} \pm 5\%$

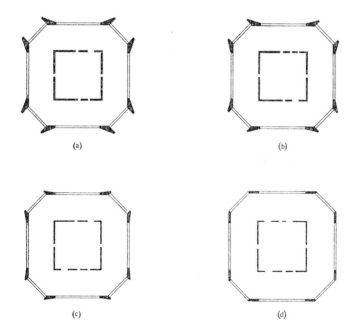

Fig. 12.2.   Details of structural design.
(a) Low rise.
(b) Low medium rise.
(c) High medium rise.
(d) High rise.

Measurements Required

There were two types of measurements required—deflections and strains; from these it is possible to calculate the amount of the lateral load taken by the core and by the external frames, and check for statics.

Instrumentation

Deflections were measured by Baty dial gauges. Electric resistance strain gauges (4 mm gauge length) were applied at 80 points on the core, columns and beams. Strains were automatically read via a data-logger.

Fig. 12.3. Photograph of structural model.

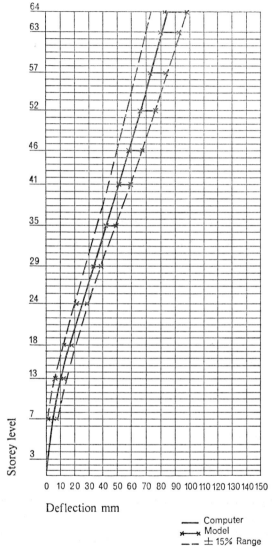

Fig. 12.4.   Comparison of deflection results for both physical and computer
model.

Loading

As only lateral loads were considered important, dead loads were applied at 12 points via a whiffle-tree loading-system.

Data Analysis

Since the results had a very high degree of repeatability no statistical reduction was required; the model results were converted to prototype results through the scale ratios determined from dimensional theory.

Cost and Time Estimation

Because of the urgency of the situation the design, manufacture, construction and instrumentation of this model was completed in nine weeks. Testing took a further week. The labour involved was 4 man-weeks of engineer's time and 20 man-weeks of technician's time.

Figure 12.3 shows a photograph of the model. The deflection and moment results can be seen in Fig. 12.4 and Table 12.2. In models of

Table 12.2

Static resisting moment at Level 6 (kN m)	Results derived from:	
	Model	Computer
Due to outer columns	800 000	735 000
	(590 000 kip ft)	(540 000 kip ft)
Due to inner columns	negligible	negligible
Due to core	440 000	450 000
	(325 000 kip ft)	(330 000 kip ft)
Sum at this level	1 245 000	1 180 000
	(915 000 kip ft)	(870 000 kip ft)

this kind the results produced are reliable only within ±15%. The correlation of the model results with those produced by the two-dimensional computer model increase the degree of confidence in the use of that model. The total static loading moment at this level is 1 190 000 kN m; the moments in the columns themselves are negligible.

Chapter 13

Optimum Design Concepts*

In this chapter we briefly introduce the concepts associated with optimum design and distinguish them from classical or iterative design procedures. It is shown that differential calculus can be used to provide optimal solutions to a certain class of problems. Operations research and in particular mathematical programming are introduced through simple examples. We show that we must distinguish between problems which can be formulated with linear relationships between variables and those that cannot. The chapter concludes with a mention of search methods.

13.1. INTRODUCTION

In Section 7.6 we described how the computer could be used to design building frames; the methods of Chapters 9, 10 and 11 are basically of the same type as that of Section 7.6 in that they are *iterative* in nature. That is, they start with a preliminary design and check that design against the constraints of the behaviour of the design and modify the design if it fails to satisfy those constraints and then repeats the cycle until the constraints are satisfied. Constraints on the behaviour of a structural design would include the three requirements of strength, stiffness and stability. However, there is no guarantee that the final design, *i.e.* the one which satisfies the constraints, will be the best or *optimum* solution, for we have no criteria by which to test solutions for optimality.

If we are going to produce optimum designs we must have a systematic approach. The basis for this approach is given to us by *operations research*. Operations research has been defined as [13.1]:

The application of scientific methods, techniques and tools to problems involving systems so as to provide optimum solutions to the problems.

* This chapter may be skipped at first reading as it contains advanced material.

The application of operations research to design problems involves a number of basic steps:

1. Definition of the system;
2. Delineation of the system variables;
3. Determination, accurately and quantitatively, of the interactions of the system variables;
4. Formulation of a measure of system effectiveness expressible in terms of the system variables;
5. Selection of those values of system variables yielding optimum effectiveness.

The system definition in terms of the design of building frames is normally quite well-defined in that the bulk size of building and its internal functional planning go a long way to deciding the geometry of the structure and hence the boundaries of the structure to be investigated. The design engineer decides the system variables by deciding the choice of structure. This will indicate whether, for example, column spacing is a variable or not. In general, member dimensions are always variables. The interactions between variables are provided by structural theory, which provides a method of *simulating* the behaviour of the system. The measure of system effectiveness is often formulated as minimum weight of structure or minimum total cost of structure, although this may not always be adequate.

In iterative design all the above steps excluding steps 4 and 5 are included in the design process. However, it is step 5 which distinguishes optimum design from other design techniques. The methods by which we locate the optimum solution can be grouped into a number of categories and we shall examine three of these:

1. *differential calculus*, which might be termed a classical optimisation method;
2. *mathematical programming*, of which we shall have more to say later on;
3. *search methods*, which are often used when the above two techniques are not applicable.

13.2. OPTIMUM DESIGN BY DIFFERENTIAL CALCULUS

Differential calculus has been used for a number of centuries to obtain the optimum value of a system defined by a continuous function. In its simplest form we have a function (F) expressible in terms of the variables (x)

$$F = F(x)$$

If the first derivative of this function is zero then the function has a maximum or minimum; if at that value the second derivative is positive, then the function has a minimum value at that point; if the second derivative is negative at that value then the function has a maximum value at that point. In general we are interested in minimisation problems.

Example 13.1. A roof is to be spanned, it is assumed that a series of columns producing equal spans supporting simple rectangular beams to be used with brick end-walls, Fig. 13.1. Determine the optimal span such that the cost of the column/beam system is minimum.

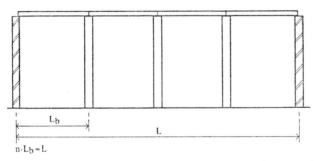

Fig. 13.1. Column/beam system spanning between end walls for Example 13.1.

Let us follow the five steps we outlined earlier:

1. The system is explicitly defined in terms of the above problem statement.
2. There is only one variable in this case; it is the span of a beam L_b.
3. As we have defined the problem in terms of a single variable this step does not apply.

4. It is here, in the formulation of a measure of system effectiveness that we need to decide what level of accuracy we wish to work with. Let us assume that the end walls will not change with a change in beam span. Let us further assume that the weight (per unit length) (w_b) of the beam is directly proportional to its span, i.e.

$$w_b = k_1 L_b$$

where k_1 is the proportional constant.

If c_b is the cost per unit weight of the beam, the total cost of the beams (C_b) is given by

$$C_b = c_b w_b L = c_b k_1 L_b L$$

Further, let the cost of one column be c_c.

Then the total cost of the column/beam system is given by C_t

$$C_t = (n - 1)c_c + c_b k_1 L_b L$$

where n is the number of spans and equals L/L_b, therefore

$$C_t = \left(\frac{L}{L_b} - 1 \right) c_c + c_b k_1 L_b L$$

The objective can now be expressed as

minimise C_t

5. Determine the optimum value of L_b by differential calculus:

$$\frac{dC_t}{dL_b} = -\frac{L}{L_b^2} c_c + c_b k_1 L = 0$$

Therefore

$$L_b = \left(\frac{c_c}{c_b k_1} \right)^{\frac{1}{2}}$$

We need to check the second derivative to ensure that this is a minimum.

$$\frac{d^2 C_t}{dL_b^2} = \frac{2L}{L_b^3 c_c}$$

which is positive.

Therefore, the minimum cost structure is reached when the beam span is equal to

$$\left(\frac{c_c}{c_b k_1}\right)^{\frac{1}{4}}$$

It is interesting to note that we can re-write this expression to make c_c the subject, *i.e.*

$$c_c = c_b k_1 L_b{}^2$$

$$= c_b w_b L_b$$

This implies that the optimum is reached when the cost of one column equals the cost of one beam span.

Let us go back to step 4 and re-examine our assumption that the weight of the beam is directly proportional to the span. We know that the weight of a beam is proportional to its area. For a beam with a rectangular cross-section in which the breadth is arbitrarily set to 0·25 depth, the area (A) may be expressed as

$$A = 0 \cdot 25 d^2$$

where d is the depth of the section.

Now, for a simply supported beam supporting a uniform load (w) the maximum moment (M_m) is given by

$$M_m = \frac{w L_b{}^2}{8}$$

If the allowable stress in bending is F_b, then by simple bending theory

$$F_b = \frac{M}{Z}$$

where Z is the section modulus, which for our rectangular section becomes $0 \cdot 042 d^3$, hence

$$F_b = \frac{3 w L_b{}^2}{d^3}$$

i.e.

$$d = \left(\frac{3 w L_b{}^2}{F_b}\right)^{0 \cdot 33}$$

Therefore, the weight of the section is given by

$$w_b = k_2 L_b{}^{1\cdot33}$$

where k_2 is the constant of proportionality. We can now write the cost of the beams is given by

$$C_b = c_b w_b L = c_b k_2 L_b{}^{1\cdot33} L$$

and the total cost, given by

$$C_t = \left(\frac{L}{L_b} - 1\right) c_c + c_b k_2 L_b{}^{1\cdot33} L$$

The optimum value of this objective function can be determined as before,

$$\frac{dC_t}{dL_b} = -\frac{L}{L_b{}^2} c_c + 1\cdot33 c_b k_2 L_b{}^{0\cdot33} L = 0$$

Therefore,

$$L_b = \left(\frac{c_c}{1\cdot33 c_b k_2}\right)^{1/2\cdot33}$$

Checking the second derivative we get

$$\frac{d^2 C_t}{dL_b{}^2} = \frac{2L}{L_b{}^3} c_c + 0\cdot445 c_b k_2 L_b{}^{-0\cdot67} L > 0$$

which is positive.

Therefore, the minimum cost structure is reached when the beam span is equal to $(c_c/1\cdot33 c_b k_2)^{1/2\cdot33}$. We can rewrite the expression for the beam span at the minimum solution as

$$c_c = 1\cdot33 c_b k_2 L_b{}^{2\cdot33}$$

$$= 1\cdot33 c_b w_b L_b$$

which gives us the relationship between the cost of the column and the beam span at the optimum value.

The models we have developed vary in their degree of accuracy in simulating the real cost behaviour of this structural system. Each produces a different result. We could increase the accuracy of the modelling further by making the cost of a column a function of the span. For example if we made it a linear function of the beam span with a proportional constant k_3 (this is equivalent to assuming that there are only axial forces and no buckling), then the optimum span is given by

$$L_b = \left(\frac{k_3}{1 \cdot 33 c_b k_2}\right)^{1/1 \cdot 33}$$

Example 13.2. A load is to be carried by a two bar truss at a specified location from the supports (Fig. 13.2). Determine the optimum shape (*i.e.* 2θ) to minimise the total material in the truss [13.2].

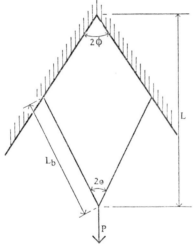

Fig. 13.2.   Two-bar truss whose shape is to be optimised in Example 13.2.

1. The problem is well defined by the above statement.
2. The only variable needed in this case is the angle 2θ, Fig. 13.2, as this is sufficient to define completely the shape of the truss here.
3. In this case we can relate the member area to the member force (F)

$$F = A \cdot f$$

where f is the allowable stress (a constant).
Also, considering equilibrium

$$P = 2 \cos \theta F$$

and

$$L = \frac{\sin(\phi + \theta)}{\sin \phi} L_b$$

4. The total material (M) is simply the volume of the two bars,

$$\therefore \qquad M = 2AL_b$$

where A is the area of one bar and L_b is the length of one bar. Thus, the objective can be expressed as

minimise M

Using the above equations we can reformulate the objective as

$$\text{minimise } M = \frac{PL}{f} \left[\frac{\sin \phi}{\cos \theta \sin (\phi + \theta)} \right]$$

5. Using differential calculus we can optimise this objective in terms of θ

$$\frac{dM}{d\theta} = 0$$

which yields

$$\tan(\theta + \phi) = \frac{1}{\tan \theta} = \cot \theta$$

i.e.

$$\theta + \phi = 90 - \theta$$

$\therefore$ at the optimum

$$\theta = \frac{90 - \phi}{2}$$

An important aspect of optimum design is the *post-optimal analysis* or *sensitivity analysis* in which we wish to see the effect on the optimal solution of perturbations of the variables. It is important to know how sensitive the optimal solution is to these variations.

Example 13.3. Perform a sensitivity analysis on the structure in Example 13.2. Take $\phi = 45°$.
From the result of Example 13.2 we have

$$M_{opt} = \frac{PL}{f} \left[\frac{\sin \phi}{\cos \theta_{opt} \sin (\phi + \theta_{opt})} \right]$$

If we let $PL/f = k$, a constant, we evaluate M_{opt} at $\theta_{opt} = 22.5°$ for this problem, $i.e.$

$$M_{opt} = 0.828k$$

If we let $\theta = 27.5°$, $i.e.$ $\theta = \theta_{opt} + 5°$ then

$$M_+ = 0.837k$$

If we let $\theta = 17.5°$, $i.e.$ $\theta = \theta_{opt} - 5°$
then

$$M_- = 0.837k$$

We can see that the optimum solution is relatively insensitive (about 1% change) to perturbations in the optimum angle value. Sometimes the data are not accurately known and a sensitivity analysis is carried out by varying the data. In this example if $\phi = 45° \pm 5°$ then the value of M_{opt} varies from $0.868k$ to $0.779k$, $i.e.$ a variation of less than 6% from the optimum arrived at previously.

The methods of differential calculus are finding applications in the optimum design of building frames [13.3–7].

13.3. OPTIMUM DESIGN BY MATHEMATICAL PROGRAMMING

One of the most powerful sets of tools of operations research for finding optimum solutions may be grouped under the heading of *mathematical programming*.* These are new mathematical techniques which have only been developed in the last 25 years. Let us look at some simple examples of mathematical programming in order to appreciate its significance.

Example 13.4.† Determine a minimum weight solution for the frame shown in Fig. 13.3a. Assume that both columns are to have the same section [13.8].

---

* The term can be somewhat confusing—it bears no relation whatever to computer programming.

† Chapter 9 is required reading for this example.

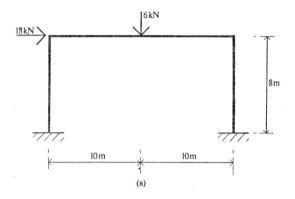

(a)

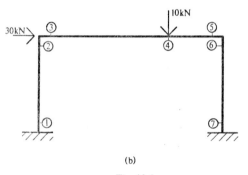

(b)

Fig. 13.3.
(a) Rectangular frame used in Example 13.4.
(b) Points at which plastic hinges are likely to occur labelled 1 to 7.

1. The problem statement defines the system adequately.
2. The system variables will be the section size for the beam and the section size for the columns.
3. The interactions between these variables can be provided by the method of analysis. Let us choose plastic analysis with a load factor of 1·67, Fig. 13.3b shows the frame with the collapse loads shown as well as the points at which hinges are likely to occur numbered 1 to 7. If we let the required moment capacity of the beam be M_b and that of the column be M_c we can use the virtual

displacement method to examine the potential mechanisms of the frame and, hence, develop the interactions. There are four significant mechanisms; these are shown in Fig. 13.4a to d.

To show how to determine these interactions let us look at the mechanism of Fig. 13.4a, the external work is given by

$$W_e = 30 \times 8 \cdot \theta = 240\theta$$

and the internal work by

$$W_i = -4 \cdot M_c \cdot \theta$$

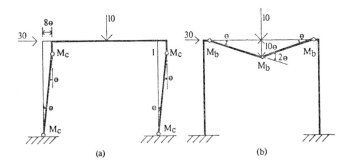

(a)   (b)

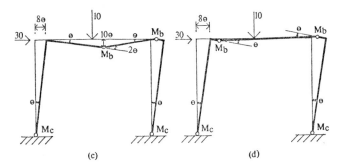

(c)   (d)

Fig. 13.4.   The four significant mechanisms of the frame in Fig. 13.3.
(a) Column mechanism.
(b) Beam mechanism.
(c) and (d) Combined column and beam mechanisms.

From

$$W_e + W_i = 0$$

we get, for equilibrium

$$M_c = 60 \text{ kN m}$$

Now we have to choose a section which has a moment capacity at least equal to that so that collapse will not occur, we may rewrite the expression for M_c as

$$M_c \geq 60 \text{ kN m} \qquad \text{(a)}$$

which represents a constraint on the behaviour of the variable M_c. In a similar manner we can write inequality constraints for the other mechanisms as

$$M_b \geq 25 \text{ kN m} \qquad \text{(b)}$$

$$2M_b + M_c \geq 170 \text{ kN m} \qquad \text{(c)}$$

$$M_b + M_c \geq 120 \text{ kN m} \qquad \text{(d)}$$

4. The objective is to minimise the weight of the frame. Before we formulate this expression, it can be shown [13.8], that the plastic section modulus of beam sections varies almost linearly with their weights. Since plastic moment capacity is directly related to plastic section modulus, we can show a direct relationship between section weight (W) and plastic moment capacity (M_p), i.e.

$$W = kM_p$$

where k is a constant. The expression for frame weight which is the objective function

$$\text{OF} = 20W_b + 2 \times 8W_c$$

can be written as

$$\text{OF} = k(20M_b + 16M_c) \qquad \text{(e)}$$

5. We can select the optimum values if we examine the *solution area* shown in Fig. 13.5a; this solution area can be reduced to the *feasible solution area* by applying the constraints of eqns (a) to (d). If we use shading on one side of a line to indicate that no values can occur on that side we can draw up these four constraints as

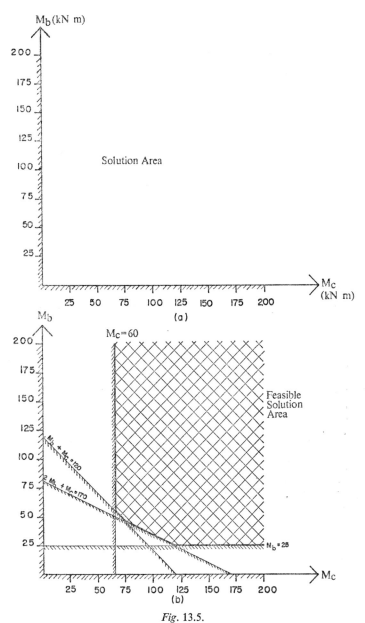

Fig. 13.5.
(a) The solution area of Example 13.4.
(b) The generation of the feasible solution area by the addition of the constraints to the solution area.

shown in Fig. 13.5b with the feasible solution area shown hatched. This area is arrived at by applying each of the constraints in turn. For example the constraint (a) will limit any feasible solution to the right of the line $M_c = 60$, whilst the constraint (b) will limit any feasible solution to be above the line $M_b = 25$, and so on.

In this case we can obtain the optimum value by inspection, by noting that in eqn (e) as the value of OF increases so that line represented by that equation moves to the right, therefore, we move that line as far to the left as we can whilst still letting it pass through the feasible solution area. At the farthest point we have reached the optimum (Fig. 13.6) and the optimal solution is given by

$$M_b = 50 \text{ kN m}$$

$$M_c = 70 \text{ kN m}$$

Thus, the total minimised weight of the frame is given by

$$k(20 \times 50 + 16 \times 70)$$

The approach used here falls into a subset of mathematical programming called *linear programming* because both the objective function and the constraints are expressed in linear terms of the variables.

We can write the linear programming formulation of this class of problem as

$$\text{minimise OF} = \sum a_j x_j$$

subject to

$$\sum_i \sum c_{ij} x_j \leq b_i$$

and

$$x_j \geq 0$$

where x_j are the variables, a_j the coefficients of the variables in the objective function, c_{ij} the coefficients of the variables in the constraints and b_i the constants in the contraint equations.

Obviously, the graphical method we used in the above example cannot be used when there are many variables, however, because of the nature of the feasible solution area there are well defined methods

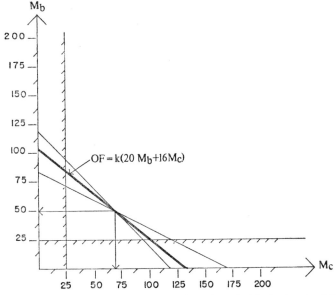

Fig. 13.6. The optimum design for Example 13.4 reached by letting the OF line move as close as possible to the origin whilst still passing through the feasible solution area.

of obtaining the optimum solution of linear programs containing many variables [13.4, 13.5, 13.9–11].

The application of linear programming to optimum frame design based on plastic analysis has been extensively explored [13.12–17]. For large frames the number of collapse mechanisms increases to the point where even a computer solution becomes impractical. In tall building frames a stiff column and flexible beam type of design is often used and this limits the formation of plastic hinges initially to the beams. Work in this area [13.18] has shown that with such simplifying assumptions it is possible to formulate the design of multi-storey frames as a relatively small linear programming problem.

Unfortunately, optimum design of elastic structures does not normally produce linear objectives and linear constraints. Let us look at a simple optimum elastic design problem.

Example 13.5. Design a minimum weight section for the cantilever shown in Fig. 13.7.

1. Note that the cross-section is triangular and is to be made from steel.
2. The only variables are the section depth (d) and the section width (b).
3. Let us develop the interactions by examining the elastic behaviour of the cantilever. Let the allowable stress in bending tension (F_{bt}) be 165 MPa, the allowable stress in bending compression (F_{bc}) be 130 MPa, the average allowable stress in shear (F_s) be 100 MPa and the elastic modulus (E) be 200 GPa. Adopt a deflection to span ratio of 1:360. We shall draw the constraints onto a suitable solution area, as we did for Example 13.4.

Fig. 13.7. Cantilever used in Example 13.5 as an example of non-linear programming.

Physical constraints—obviously b and d must take positive non-zero values, *i.e.*

$$b > 0$$

$$d > 0 \qquad \text{(a)}$$

These are shown in Fig. 13.8a.

Bending stress compression constraint—the maximum moment $M = 150$ kN m.

Now we know that the stresses due to this moment must be less than, or equal to, F_{bc}, *i.e.*

$$\frac{M}{Z_b} \le F_{bc}$$

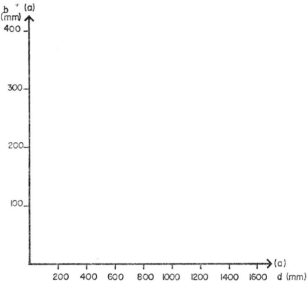

Fig. 13.8a.   The generation of the feasible solution area by the addition of the
constraints. The effect of including the physical constraints.

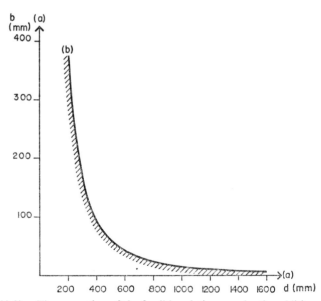

Fig. 13.8b.   The generation of the feasible solution area by the addition of the
constraints. The effect of including the bending-stress compression constraint.

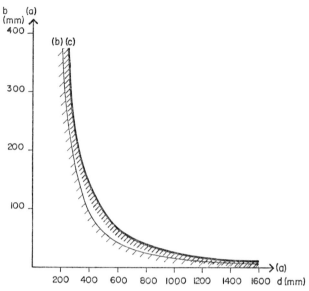

Fig. 13.8c. The generation of the feasible solution area by the addition of the constraints. The effect of including the bending-stress tension constraint.

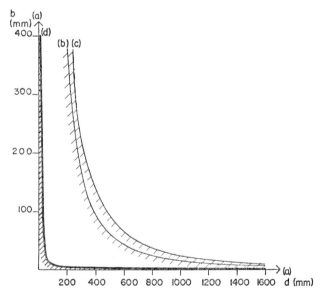

Fig. 13.8d. The generation of the feasible solution area by the addition of the constraints. The effect of including the shear-stress constraint.

The section modulus of the bottom for this section is given by

$$Z_b = \frac{bd^2}{12}$$

substituting the values into the inequality above we get (with b and d in mm)

$$bd^2 \geq 15 \times 10^6 \tag{b}$$

This curve is shown in Fig. 13.8b.

Bending stress tension constraint—the section modulus for the top is given by $Z_t = bd^2/24$, similarly

$$\frac{M}{Z_t} \leq F_{bt}$$

$$\therefore \qquad bd^2 \geq 22 \cdot 8 \times 10^6 \tag{c}$$

This curve is shown in Fig. 13.8c.

Shear stress constraint—we know that

$$\frac{Q}{A} \leq F_s$$

where Q is the maximum shear and A is the section area

$$Q = 50 \text{ kN}$$

and

$$A = \frac{bd}{2}$$

Substituting the values into the inequality above, we get

$$\therefore \qquad bd \geq 1 \times 10^3 \tag{d}$$

This curve is shown in Fig. 13.8d.

Deflection constraint—the deflection (Δ) of a cantilever is given by

$$\Delta = \frac{PL^3}{3EI}$$

but

$$\frac{\Delta}{L} \leq \frac{1}{360}$$

hence

$$\frac{1}{360} \geq \frac{PL^2}{3EI}$$

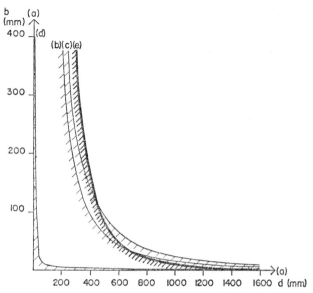

Fig. 13.8e. The generation of the feasible solution area by the addition of the constraints. The effect of including the deflection constraint.

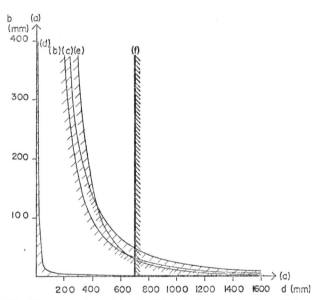

Fig. 13.8f. The generation of the feasible solution area by the addition of the constraints. The effect of including an architectural constraint.

Substituting for P, L, E and I, we get

$$bd^3 \geq 9740 \times 10^6 \qquad \text{(e)}$$

This curve is shown in Fig. 13.8e.

Architectural constraint—let us suppose that there is a limit on the maximum depth of the beam of 700 mm, *i.e.*

$$d \leq 700 \qquad \text{(f)}$$

This line is shown in Fig. 13.8f.
This defines for us the hatched feasible solution area shown in Fig. 13.9.

4. The objective is to minimise the weight, W

$$W = p \cdot A \cdot L$$

where p is the material density, *i.e.*

$$W = kA$$

Therefore, by minimising the cross-sectional area we will be minimising the weight

$$\therefore \qquad \text{OF} = \text{minimise } \frac{bd}{2}$$

5. We can determine the optimum solution by inspection in the same basic manner we did for Example 13.4 by noting that as the value of OF decreases it moves closer to the origin. By trial and error we can determine the value of OF to be 16 250 occurring at $d = 700$ mm and $b = 46.5$ mm as shown in Fig. 13.9.

There is more information on Fig. 13.8e than simply the delineation of the feasible solution area. For example, we can see that we will always satisfy the shear-stress requirement if we satisfy the bending-stress requirements. However, as d increases so these two requirements converge such that for very large values of d (greater than 2800 mm) the shear-stress requirement becomes active and not the bending stresses. Also, we can see that it is the bending stress in tension not the bending stress in compression which is significant for this beam and that there are three constraints which form the

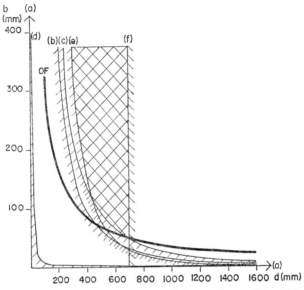

Fig. 13.9. The optimum solution of the cantilever of Fig. 13.7.

boundaries of the feasible solution area. Hence, we can see that depending on the value of a feasible depth, bending-stress tension, deflection or the depth constraint controls the design. In our problem both bending-stress tension and the depth restriction control the design, these are called the *active* constraints.

It is possible to carry out a sensitivity analysis by varying the constraint requirements. For example we could examine the effect on the optimum of, say, a $\pm 10\%$ change in the depth restriction:

d_{opt} (mm)	b_{opt} (mm)	OF ($\times k$) (mm^2)
700	46·5	16 250
630	60·0	18 800
770	36·5	14 400

The above example can be classed as a *nonlinear programming* problem because the constraints and the objective function are not

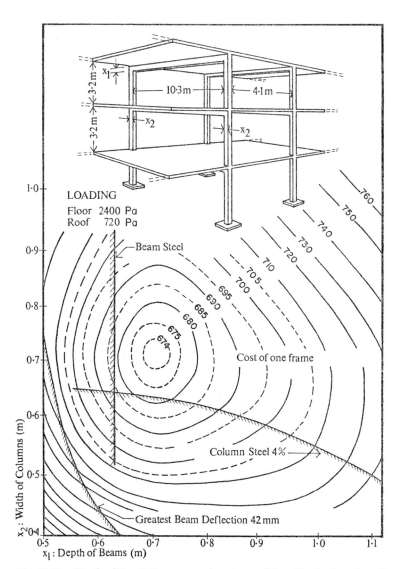

Fig. 13.10. The feasible solution area and contours of the objective function of frame cost for a concrete building frame (after [13.29]).

expressible in linear terms of the variables. There is no simple method for arriving at the optimum solution of non-linear programming problems. A number of approaches are available and they are discussed elsewhere [13.6, 13.8, 13.19–22].

There are techniques associated with other branches of mathematical programming which are beginning to find application in the design of framed structures. Of particular interest is the area known as *discrete optimisation* which is primarily concerned with the situation when the variables are not continuous, as occurs when selecting steel sections from a manufacturer's catalogue [13.23, 13.24]. Another burgeoning technique is that called *dynamic programming* [13.25–27] in which decisions are made sequentially. Dynamic programming can handle both non-linear functions as well as discrete variables, however, it is not computationally efficient when the problem contains more than a small number of variables [13.28].

The basis of all mathematical programming techniques is that of defining a solution area, applying constraints to it to produce a feasible solution area in which the optimum solution lies. Not all optimum solutions lie on the constraint boundaries [13.29, 13.30] as shown in Fig. 13.10 and Fig. 13.11 which show the feasible solution area and contours for different values of the objective function for a concrete building frame and for a concrete continuous-slab integral with tee-beams and columns respectively. It is in situations like this that search methods are used.

13.4. OPTIMUM DESIGN BY SEARCH METHODS

Various search methods have been applied to optimising problems whose solutions have proved intractable by other methods, this applies in particular to non-linear programming problems. It is not proposed to explore these methods here but rather to make mention of them, a notion of what method they employ to reach a solution can be gleaned from their titles. They include such methods as the *random walk* [13.31], various *interpolation* methods [13.5, 13.6], *conjugate directions* and *gradient* methods [13.32–37] and *direct search* methods [13.38, 13.39]. The application of these techniques is only now beginning to produce results [13.29, 13.30, 13.40, 13.41].

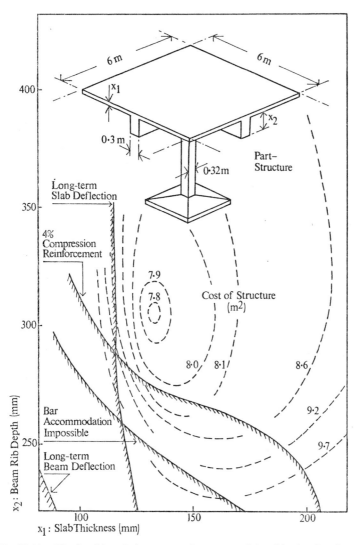

Fig. **13.11.** The feasible solution area and contours of the objective function of cost of structure per square metre for a concrete continuous-slab integral with tee-beams and columns (after [13.30]).

Bibliography and References

General

The literature on this subject is so vast, that any general list of references necessarily reflects the authors' likes and prejudices. However, the general reader may find the following selective list of text-books helpful for general reading. Other books are mentioned in the Chapter References.

History of Structural Design

B 1. TIMOSHENKO, S. (1953). *History of the Strength of Materials*, McGraw-Hill, New York, 452 pp.
B 2. COWAN, H. J. (1966). *An Historical Outline of Architectural Science*, Elsevier, Amsterdam, 175 pp.

Structural Morphology

B 3. TORROJA, E. (1958). *Philosophy of Structures*, University of California Press, Berkeley, 366 pp.
B 4. SIEGEL, C. (1962). *Structure and Form in Modern Architecture*, Crosby Lockwood, London, 308 pp.

Classical Elastic Theory of Structures

B 5. PIPPARD, A. J. S. and BAKER, J. F. (1945). *The Analysis of Engineering Structures*, Edward Arnold, London, 627 pp.
B 6. NORRIS, C. H. and WILBUR, J. B. (1960). *Elementary Structural Analysis*, McGraw-Hill, New York, 651 pp.

Matrix Methods of Structural Analysis

B 7. LIVESLEY, R. K. (1964). *Matrix Methods of Structural Analysis*, Pergamon, Oxford, 265 pp.
B 8. GERE, J. M. and WEAVER, W. (1965). *Analysis of Framed Structures*, Van Nostrand, Princeton, 474 pp.

466

Design of Steel Structures

B 9.   BRESLER, B. and LIN, T. Y. (1960). *Design of Steel Structures,* John Wiley, New York, 710 pp.
B10.   BRITISH STEEL PRODUCERS CONFERENCE (1966). *Steel Designers' Manual,* Crosby Lockwood, London, 1086 pp.
B11.   BEEDLE, L. S. (1958). *Plastic Design of Steel Frames,* John Wiley, New York, 406 pp.

Design of Concrete Structures

B12.   FERGUSON, P. M. (1973). *Reinforced Concrete Fundamentals, with Emphasis on Ultimate Strength,* John Wiley, New York, 750 pp.
B13.   LIN, T. Y. (1963). *Design of Prestressed Concrete Structures,* John Wiley, New York, 614 pp.

Structural Pathology

B14.   McKAIG, T. H. (1962). *Building Failures—Case Studies in Design and Construction,* McGraw-Hill, New York, 261 pp.
B15.   FELD, J. (1965). *Lessons from Failure of Concrete Structures,* Iowa State University Press, Ames, 179 pp.

Chapter 1

1.1.   COLLINS, P. (1965). *Changing Ideas in Modern Architecture,* Faber and Faber, London, 309 pp.
1.2.   SIEGEL, C. (1962). *Structure and Form in Modern Architecture,* Crosby and Lockwood, London, 308 pp.
1.3.   LARSON, L. (1964). *Lighting and its Design,* Whitney Library of Design, New York, 228 pp.
1.4.   *The Co-ordination of Dimensions for Building,* Royal Institute of British Architects, London, 1965, 87 pp.
1.5.   *Dimensional Co-ordination for Building,* Ministry of Public Works, London, 1969, 84 pp.
1.6a. STIGTER, J. (1968). 'Two 50-storey buildings in Australia exemplify the unique use of lightweight concrete,' Proceedings International Congress on Lightweight Concrete (London, 27–29 May 1968), Section C.
1.6b. STIGTER, J. (1966). 'Australia Square, Sydney,' *Constructional Review,* **39** (Sept.), 10.
1.7.   MILLER, H. (1959). 'Chicago's 39-storey reinforced-concrete Executive House,' *J. Am. Concrete Inst.,* **31** (Sept.), 215–22.
1.8.   LIE, T. T. (1972). *Fire and Buildings,* Applied Science Publishers, London, 276 pp.
1.9.   BABICKI, B. (1971). 'Cables support office building,' *Civil Engineering (New York),* **41** (Oct.), 64.
1.10. 'State Office block,' *Architecture in Australia,* **57** (Feb. 1968), 75.

1.11. McKaig, T. H. (1962). *Building Failures*, McGraw-Hill, New York, 119 pp.

1.12. Cassie, W. D. (1968). *Fundamental Foundations*, Applied Science Publishers, London, 226 pp.

1.13. Khan, F. R. and Sbarounis, J. A. (1964). 'Interaction of shear walls and frames,' *J. Struct. Div. Proc. Am. Soc. Civ. Engrs.*, 90, No. ST3 (June), 285.

1.14. Khan, F. R. (1970). 'Recent structural systems in steel for high-rise buildings', *Steel Construction* (Sydney), 4 (March), 2.

1.15. Hall, A. S. (1969). *An Introduction to the Mechanics of Solids*, John Wiley, Sydney, p. 116.

1.16. Lawrence, A. B. (1970). *Architectural Acoustics*, Applied Science Publishers, London, 219 pp.

1.17. Mies van der Rohe, L. (1923). 'Working theses, 1923,' in *Programmes and Manifestoes of 20th Century Architecture*, U. Conrads (ed.), Lund Humphries, London, 1970, p. 74.

1.18. Wilson, J. G. (1955). *Concrete Facing Slabs*, Cement and Concrete Association, London, 23 pp.

1.19. Brown, W. P. (1969). 'Industrialized precast concrete load bearing construction in high-rise flats in Melbourne.' Paper presented at the Biannual Conference of the Concrete Institute of Australia, Brisbane, September 1969.

1.20. Cowan, H. J. and Aynsley, R. M. (1971). Symposium on the environmental aspects of the design of tall buildings, Sydney, 1971. *Architectural Science Review*, 14 (Sept. and Dec.), 65–73 and 89–105, and *ibid.*, (1972), 15 (March), 1–20.

Chapter 2

2.1. *Loading*, Chapter V, British Standard Code of Practice CP3, British Standards Institution, London, 1967.

2.2. *Minimum Design Loads in Buildings and Other Structures*, American National Standard A 58l1, American National Standards Institute, New York, 1971.

2.3. *SAA Loading Code—Dead and Live Loads*, Australian Standard CA 34, Part 1, Standards Association of Australia, Sydney, 1969.

2.4. Johnson, S. M. (1972). 'Dead, live and construction loads,' *Conference on the Planning and Design of Tall Buildings Vol. 5*, Bethlehem (Penn.), pp. 37–55.

2.5. White, C. M. (1931). 'Survey of design live loads in offices,' *First Report of the Steel Structures Research Committee*, Building Research Station, Garston (Herts.), (*out of print*, quoted by [2.11]).

2.6. *Minimum Live Loads Allowable for Use in Design of Buildings*, Report of the Department of Commerce Building Code Committee, Washington, 1924 (*out of print*, quoted by [2.9]).

2.7. Mitchell, G. R. (1968). 'Floor loadings: surveys and analysis,' *Build International*, 1, 36–7.

2.8. Mitchell, G. R. and Woodgate, R. W. (1971). 'Floor loadings in office buildings—the results of a survey,' *Building Research Station Current Paper* 3/71, Department of the Environment, London, 32 pp.

2.9. DUNHAM, J. W., BREKKE, G. N. and THOMPSON, G. N. (1952). 'Live loads on floors in buildings,' *National Bureau of Standards, Building Materials and Structures Report* 133, Superintendent of Documents, Washington, 27 pp.

2.10. BRYSON, J. O. and GROSS, D. (1967). 'Techniques for the survey and evaluation of live floor loads and fire loads in modern office buildings,' *National Bureau of Standards, Building Science Series Paper* 16, U.S. Department of Commerce, Washington, 30 pp.

2.11. MITCHELL, G. R. (1969). 'Loadings on buildings—a review paper,' *Building Research Station Current Paper* 50/69, Ministry of Public Buildings and Works, London, 9 pp.

2.12. MITCHELL, G. R. and WOODGATE, R. W. (1971). 'Floor loading in retail premises—the results of a survey,' *Building Research Station Current Paper* 25/71, Department of the Environment, London, 37 pp.

2.13. JOHNSON, A. I. (1953). 'Strength, safety and economical dimensions of structures,' *Institutionen för Byggnadsstatik, Meddelanden Nr.* 13. Kungl. Tekniska Högskolan, Stockholm, pp. 109–113.

2.14. SCHRIEVER, W. R. and OSTVANOV, V. A. (1967). 'Snow loads—preparation of standards for snow loads on roofs in various countries, with particular reference to the U.S.S.R. and Canada,' in *On Methods of Load Calculation*, C.I.B. Report No. 9, International Council for Building Research Studies and Documentation, Rotterdam, pp. 13–33.

2.15. McCREA, J. D. (1952). 'Wind action on structures,' *Bibliography No.* 5, Division of Building Research, Ottawa, 6 pp. (*This is a comprehensive bibliography of early work, going back, to* 1759.)

2.16. STEVENS, L. K., JOUBERT, P. N. and ROBERTSON, B. D. (1953). 'Wind forces on tall buildings,' *Symposium on the Design of High Buildings*, Hong Kong University Press, pp. 277–95.

2.17. NATIONAL PHYSICAL LABORATORY (1965). *Proceedings Symposium on Wind Effects on Buildings and Structures*, Vol. 1, H.M. Stationery Office, London, 430 pp.

2.18. NATIONAL RESEARCH COUNCIL OF CANADA and UNIVERSITY OF WESTERN ONTARIO (1968). *Wind Effects on Buildings and Structures*, University of Toronto Press, Toronto, 2 volumes, 772 and 461 pp.

2.19. *The Modern Design of Wind-Sensitive Structures*, Construction Industry Research and Information Association, London, 1971, 139 pp.

2.20. *Wind Loads on Structures* (Conference held at the California Institute of Technology), National Science Foundation, Washington, 1971, 137 pp.

2.21. *Wind Loads on Structures* (USA–Japan Research Seminar held at the University of Hawaii), National Science Foundation, Washington, 1971, 374 pp.

2.22. *Wind Effects in High-Rise Buildings*, Northwestern University, Evanston (Ill.), 1970, 224 pp.

2.23. LIGHTHILL, M. J. and SILVERLEAF, A. (Eds.) (1971). A discussion on architectural aerodynamics. *Phil. Trans. Roy. Soc. London*, **269A**, 323–554.

2.24. *Cyclone 'Althea', Part* 1: *Buildings*, James Cook University of North Queensland, Townsville, 1972.

2.25. *Proceedings of the Third International Conference on Wind Effects on Buildings and Structures*, Saikon, Tokyo, 1972, 1267 pp.

2.26. VAN KOTEN, H. 'Wind measurements on high buildings in the Netherlands,' in [2.18], Vol. I, pp. 685–704.

2.27. *SAA Loading Code—Wind Loads*, Australian Standard CA 34, Part 2, Standards Association of Australia, Sydney, 1972.
2.28. RICALDONI, J. and LUMER, G. (1958). 'Nota sobre el efecto de torsion en edificios elevados', *Publicaciones des Instituto de Estatica No.* 16. Facultad de Ingeneria y Agrimensura, Montivideo, 22 pp.
2.29. DAVENPORT, A. G. (1967). 'Gust loading factors,' *J. Struct. Div., Am. Soc. Civil Engrs.*, 93, No. ST3 (June), 11–34.
2.30. KOBAYASHI, S. (1972). 'Vibrational behaviour of tall buildings in strong wind and environmental wind conditions,' *KICT Report No.* 5. Kajima Institute of Construction Technology, Tokyo. (*The research institute of a large construction company, whose address is: Tobutakyu 2 Chome, Chofushi, Tokyo.*)
2.31. MENZIES, J. B. (1971). 'Wind damage to buildings in the United Kingdom 1962–1969,' *Building Research Station Current Paper* 35/71, Department of the Environment, London, 9 pp.
2.32. HOUSNER, G. W. (1972). 'Earthquake ground motion,' *Conference on Planning and Design of Tall Buildings*, Vol. 6, Bethlehem (Penn.), pp. 9–26.
2.33. HANSON, R. D. and DEGENKOLB, H. J. (1969). *The Venezuela Earthquake July* 29, 1967, American Iron and Steel Institute, New York, 176 pp.
2.34. *The Santa Rosa, California, Earthquakes of October* 1, 1968, Environmental Sciences Services Administration, U.S. Department of Commerce, Washington, 1969.
2.35. *The San Fernando, California, Earthquake of February* 9, 1971, National Oceanic and Atmospheric Administration, and Earthquake Engineering Research Institute, U.S. Department of Commerce, Washington, 1972.
2.36. ROGERS, G. L. (1959). *An Introduction to the Dynamics of Framed Structures*, John Wiley, New York, 355 pp.
2.37. NEWMARK, J. M. and ROSENBLUETH, E. (1971). *Earthquake Engineering*. Prentice-Hall, Englewood Cliffs (N.J.).
2.38. ARCHITECTURAL INSTITUTE OF JAPAN (1970). *Design Essentials in Earthquake Resistant Buildings*. Elsevier, Amsterdam, 295 pp.
2.39. GRIFFITHS, H., PUGSLEY, Sir A. and SAUNDERS, Sir O. (1968). *Report of the Enquiry into the collapse of Flats at Ronan Point, Canning Town*, H.M. Stationery Office, London.
2.40. RASBASH, D. J. and ROGOWSKI, Z. W. (1961). 'Relief of explosions in duct systems,' *Proceedings Symposium on Chemical Process Hazards with Special Reference to Plant Design*, Institution of Chemical Engineers, London, pp. 58–68.
2.41. BAKER, J. F., WILLIAMS, E. L. and LAX, D. (1948). 'The design of framed buildings against high explosive bombs,' *The Civil Engineer at War*, Vol. 3, Institution of Civil Engineers, London, pp. 80–112.
2.42. 'The design of structures to resist nuclear weapon effects,' *Manual of Engineering Practice No.* 42, American Society of Civil Engineers, New York, 1961, 150 pp. *Supplement*, 163, 11 pp.
2.43. *International Conference on the Fire-Safety of High-Rise Buildings, Warrenton Va., April*, 1971, General Services Administration, U.S. Government Printing Office, Washington, 1971.
2.44. *Proceedings Reconvened International Conference on Fire-safety in High-Rise Buildings, Washington, Oct.* 1971, General Services Administration, Washington, 1972.

2.45. COWAN, H. J. (1966). *An Historical Outline of Architectural Science*, Elsevier, Amsterdam, 175 pp.
2.46. PUGSLEY, Sir A. (1966). *The Safety of Structures*, Arnold, London, 156 pp.
2.47. INSTITUTION OF STRUCTURAL ENGINEERS (1955). 'Report on structural safety,' *Structural Engineer*, **34** (May), 141–9.
2.48. COWAN, H. J. and SMITH, P. R. (1968). *Design of Reinforced Concrete*. Second Edition, Angus and Robertson, Sydney, p. 60.
2.49. JULIAN, O. G. (1957). 'Synopsis of the first progress report of the Committee on Factors of Safety,' Separate No. 1316, *Proc. Am. Soc. Civil Engrs.*, **83** (July), 22 pp.
2.50. *International Recommendations for the Design and Construction of Concrete Structures*, Published on behalf of *Comité Européen du Béton—Fédération Internationale de la Précontrainte* by the Cement and Concrete Association, London, 1970, 80 pp.
2.51. *Building Code Requirement for Reinforced Concrete* (ACI 318–71), American Concrete Institute, Detroit, 1971, 78 pp.
2.52. *Commentary on Building Codes Requirements for Reinforced Concrete*, American Concrete Institute, Detroit, 1971, 96 pp.
2.53. FREUDENTHAL, A. M. (Ed.) (1972). *International Conference on Structural Safety and Reliability*. Pergamon Press, Oxford, 358 pp.
2.54. BIRKELAND, P. W. and WESTHOFF, L. J. (1971). 'Dimensional tolerances in a tall building,' *Proc. Am. Concrete Inst.*, **68** (Aug.), 600–7.
2.55. SHAH, H. C. (1969). *Statistical Evaluation of Load Factors in Structural Design*, Preprint for a Solid Mechanics Seminar, University of Waterloo, Waterloo (Ont., Canada), 25 pp.
2.56. *Structural Safety and Probabilistic Methods*, Conference on Planning and Design of Tall Buildings Vol. 10, Bethlehem (Penn.), 1972, 105 pp.
2.57. *Load Factor (Limit States) Design for Tall Steel Buildings*, Conference on Planning and Design of Tall Buildings Vol. 19, Bethlehem (Penn.), 1972, 60 pp.
2.58. *Limit States Design for Tall Concrete Buildings*, Conference on Planning and Design of Tall Buildings Vol. 26, Bethlehem (Penn.), 1972, 95 pp.
2.59. 'Structural safety—a literature review,' *J. Struct. Div. Proc. Am. Soc. Civil Engrs.*, **98**, No. ST4 (April), 1972, 845–84.

Chapter 3

3.1. VAN VLACK, L. H. (1964). *Elements of Materials Science*, Addison-Wesley, Reading (Mass.), pp. 44–5.
3.2. RICHART, F. E., BRANDTZAEG, A. and BROWN, R. L. (1928). 'A study of the failure of concrete under combined compressive stresses,' *Engineering Experiment Station Bulletin No. 185*, University of Illinois, Urbana, 104 pp.
3.3. BRAGG, W. L. and NYE, J. F. (1947). 'A dynamical model of a crystal structure,' *Proc. Roy. Soc. (London)*, **A190**, 474–81.
3.4. BROOKS, H. (1957). 'Applications of solid-state science in engineering—an introductory survey,' in *The Science of Engineering Materials*, J. E. Goldman (Ed.), Wiley, New York, Chapter 1, pp. 1–21.
3.5. ROSENTHAL, D. (1964). *Introduction to Properties of Materials*, D. Van Nostrand, Princeton, pp. 84–8.

3.6. FRANKEL, J. P. (1957). *Principles of the Properties of Materials*, McGraw-Hill, New York, pp. 155–79.
3.7. GRIFFITH, A. A. (1920). 'The phenomena of rupture and flow in solids,' *Phil. Trans. Roy. Soc. (London)*, **A221**, 163–98.
3.8. ALI, I. and KESLER, C. E. (1965). 'Rheology of concrete—a review of research,' *Engineering Experiment Station Bulletin No. 476*. University of Illinois, Urbana, 101 pp.
3.9. COWAN, H. J. (1952). 'Inelastic deformation of reinforced concrete,' *Engineering*, **174**, 276–8.
3.10. COTTRELL, A. H. and KELLY, A. (1966). 'The design of strong materials,' *Endeavour*, **25**, 27–32.

Chapter 4

4.1. COWAN, H. J. (1971). *Architectural Structures*, American Elsevier Publishing Company, New York, Chapter 5, pp. 127–80.
4.2. AXELRAD, D. R. (1959). *Strength of Materials for Engineers*, Pitman, Melbourne, pp. 282–91.

Chapter 5

5.1. *Building Code Requirement for Reinforced Concrete (ACI 318–71)*, American Concrete Institute, Detroit, 1971, 78 pp.
Commentary on Building Code Requirements for Reinforced Concrete, American Concrete Institute, Detroit, 1971, 96 pp.
5.2. (a) *The Structural Use of Reinforced Concrete in Buildings, CP 114: Part 2: 1969, Metric Units*, British Standards Institution, London, 1969, 94 pp.
(b) *The Structural Use of Concrete, CP110: Part 1: 1972*, British Standards Institution, London, 1972, 154 pp.
5.3. *SAA Concrete Structures Code AS 1480*, Standards Association of Australia, Sydney, 1974, 102 pp. (*This is in metric units and gives ultimate strength design rules ahead of those for elastic design.*)
5.4. BULL, F. G. and SVED, G. (1964). *Moment Distribution in Theory and Practice*, Pergamon Press, Oxford, 294 pp.
5.5. GLANVILLE, W. H. and THOMAS, F. G. (1939). *Moment Redistribution in Reinforced Concrete*, Building Research Technical Paper No. 22, H.M. Stationery Office, London, 51 pp.

Chapter 6

6.1. HOFF, N. J. (1956). *The Analysis of Structures*, John Wiley, New York, pp. 1–120.
6.2. SHAW, F. S. (1973). *Virtual Displacements and Analysis of Structures*, Prentice-Hall, Englewood Cliffs (N.J.).
6.3. LIN, T. Y. (1963). *Design of Prestressed Concrete Structures*, John Wiley, New York, pp. 252–61.

BIBLIOGRAPHY AND REFERENCES 473

Chapter 7

7.1. MEEK, J. L. (1971). *Matrix Structural Analysis*, McGraw-Hill, New York, 628 pp.
7.2. SPILLERS, W. R. (1972). *Automated Structural Analysis*, Pergamon, New York, 169 pp.
7.3. ROGERS, D. F. (1971). *A Computer Study of the Moment Distribution Method for the Analysis of Structures Consisting of Rectangular Frames and Shear Walls Subjected to Wind Loading*. M.Bdg.Sc. Thesis, Department of Architectural Science, University of Sydney.
7.4. FENVES, S. J. (1967). *Computer Methods in Civil Engineering*, Prentice-Hall, Englewood Cliffs (N.J.), 242 pp.
7.5. GERE, J. M. and WEAVER, W. (1966). *Matrix Algebra for Engineers*, Van Nostrand, Princeton (N.J.), 168 pp.
7.6. ROARK, R. J. (1965). *Formulas for Stress and Strain*, McGraw-Hill, New York, 432 pp.
7.7. WEAVER, W. (1967). *Computer Programs for Structural Analysis*, Van Nostrand, Princeton (N.J.), pp. 81–2.
7.8. ACI Committee 118 (1971). 'Survey of procedures for acceptance of electronic computer calculations by building officials,' *J. Am. Concrete Inst.*, **68**, No. 1 (Feb.), 1–8.
7.9. ANON (1967). *Recommended Procedures for Acceptance of Electronic Computer Calculations by Building Officials*, Structural Engineers Association of Southern California.
7.10. GERO, J. S. (1969). 'Computer-aided design of framed structures,' *Arch. Science Rev.*, **12**, No. 1 (March), 8–11.
7.11. ANON (1968). *ICES STRUDL—II: Engineers User's Manual, Vol. 1 Frame Analysis*, M.I.T., Department of Civil Engineering, Report R68-91.
7.12. ANON (1970). *ICES STRUDL—II: Engineers User's Manual, Vol. 3 Reinforced Concrete Structures*, M.I.T., Department of Civil Engineering, Report R70-35.
7.13. KWOK, H. L. (1969). *A Computer System for the Analysis of Reinforced Concrete Buildings*. Ph.D. Thesis, M.I.T., Department of Civil Engineering.
7.14. BIGGS, J. M., PAHL, P. J. and WENKE, H. N. (1971). 'Integrated system for RC building design,' *Proc. Am. Soc. Civil Engrs.*, **97**, No. ST1 (Jan.), 13–31.
7.15. HARIG, R. F. and McDERMOTT, D. J. (1971). 'Structural and foundation computer based design,' *Proc. Am. Soc. Civil Engrs.*, **97**, No. ST1 (Jan.), 315–28.
7.16. MILLER, C. L. (1963). 'Man–machine communications in civil engineering,' *Proc. Am. Soc. Civil Engrs.*, **89**, No. ST4 (Aug.), 5–31.
7.17. DOUTY, R. and SHORE, S. (1971). 'Technique for interactive computer graphics in design,' *Proc. Am. Soc. Civil Engrs.*, **97**, No. ST1 (Jan.), 273–88.
7.18. BATES, W. F. and COX, W. M. (1969). 'Structural analysis by computer graphics,' *Proc. Am. Soc. Civil Engrs.*, **95**, No. ST11 (Nov.), 2433–48.

Chapter 8

8.1. PIPPARD, A. J. S. and BAKER, J. F. (1943). 'Structs and laterally loaded columns and ties,' *The Analysis of Engineering Structures*, Second Edition, Edward Arnold, London, Chapter 7, pp. 124–67.

8.2. TIMOSHENKO, S. P. and GERE, J. M. (1961). *Theory of Elastic Stability*, Second Edition, McGraw-Hill, New York, 541 pp.

8.3. ROARK, R. J. (1943). 'Elastic stability,' *Formulas for Stress and Strain*, Second Edition, McGraw-Hill, New York, Chapter 14, pp. 291-308.

8.4. 'Design of structures,' *Structural Aluminium*, Aluminium Union Ltd., London, Chapter 4, pp. 22-61.

8.5. WINTER, G. (1958). 'Local buckling of thin elements,' *Commentary on the 1956 Edition of the Light Gauge Cold-Formed Steel Design Manual*, American Iron and Steel Institute, New York, Chapter 3, pp. 5-22.

8.6. COX, H. L. (1965). *The Design of Structures for Least Weight*, Pergamon, Oxford, 134 pp.

8.7. GODDEN, W. G. (1954). 'The lateral buckling of tied arches,' *Proc. Inst. Civil Engrs.*, **3**, 496-514.

8.8. GOLLER, R. R. (1965). 'The legacy of 'Galloping Gertie' 25 years after,' *Civil Engineering (New York)*, **35**, No. 10 (October), 50-3.

8.9. WOOD, R. H. (1958). 'The stability of tall buildings,' *Proc. Inst. Civil Engrs.*, **7**, 69-102.

8.10. GOLDBERG, J. E. (1960). 'On the lateral buckling of multi-storey building frames with shear bracing,' *Final Report of the Sixth Congress, International Association for Bridge and Structural Engineering*, Stockholm, pp. 232-40.

8.11. HORNE, M. R. and MERCHANT, W. *The Stability of Frames*, Pergamon, Oxford, 179 pp.

8.12. McMINN, S. J. (1966). *Matrices for Structural Analysis*, Second Edition, Spon, London, pp. 181-203.

8.13. MERCHANT, W. (1955). 'Critical loads of tall building frames,' *The Structural Engineer*, **33** (March), 84-9.

8.14. SMITH, R. B. and MERCHANT, W. (1956). 'Critical loads of tall building frames,' *The Structural Engineer*, **34** (Aug.), 282-94.

8.15. SWITZKY, H. and WANG, P. C. (1969). 'Design and analysis of frames for stability,' *Proc. Am. Soc. Civil Engrs.*, **95**, No. ST4 (April), 695-713.

8.16. BLEICH, F. (1952). *Buckling Strength of Metal Structures*, McGraw-Hill, New York, 508 pp.

8.17. GREGORY, M. (1967). *Elastic Instability*, Spon, London, 354 pp.

8.18. JAMES, B. W. (1935). *Principal Effects of Axial Loads on Moment Distribution Analysis of Rigid Structures*, National Advisory Committee for Aeronautics, T.N. 534.

8.19. LIVESLEY, R. K. and CHANDLER, D. B. (1956). *Stability Functions for Structural Frameworks*, Manchester University Press, Manchester, 33 pp.

8.20. SOKOLNIKOFF, I. S. and SOKOLNIKOFF, E. S. (1941). *Higher Mathematics for Engineers and Physicists*, McGraw-Hill, New York, pp. 163-7.

8.21. WILDE, D. J. and BEIGHTLER, C. S. (1967). *Foundations of Optimization*, Prentice-Hall, Englewood Cliffs (N.J.), 38-40.

8.22. NAKAMURA, Y. (1966). *Optimum Design of Framed Structures Using Linear Programming*, M.I.T. Research Report R66-4, Jan.

8.23. CHU, K. H. and PABACIUS, A. (1964). 'Elastic and inelastic buckling of portal frames,' *Proc. Am. Soc. Civil Engrs*, **90**, No. EM5 (Oct.), 221-49.

8.24. BOWLES, R. E. and MERCHANT, W. (1958). 'Critical loads of tall building frames,' *The Structural Engineer*, **36** (June), 187-90.

8.25. LU, L. W. (1963). 'Stability of Frames under Primary Bending Moment,' *Proc. Am. Soc. Civil Engrs*, **89**, No. ST3 (June), 35-62.

Chapter 9

9.1. NEAL, B. G. (1963). *The Plastic Methods of Structural Analysis*, Chapman and Hall, London, 358 pp.
9.2. MASSONNET, C. E. and SAVE, M. A. (1965). *Plastic Analysis and Design*, Vol. 1, Blaisdell, New York, 379 pp.
9.3. HODGE, P. G. (1959). *Plastic Analysis of Structures*, McGraw-Hill, New York, 364 pp.
9.4. BAKER, J. F., HORNE, M. R. and HEYMAN, J. (1956). *The Steel Skeleton*, Vol. 2, Cambridge University Press, 408 pp.
9.5. *Plastic Design of Multi-Storey Frames*, Fritz Engineering Laboratory, Lehigh University, Penn. 1965.
9.6. GALAMBOS, T. V. and LAY, M. G. (1965). 'Studies of the ductility of steel structures,' *Proc. Am. Soc. Civil Engrs*, **91**, No. ST4, 125–51.
9.7. HORNE, M. R. (1954). 'A moment distribution method for the analysis and design of structures by the plastic theory,' *Proc. Inst. Civil Engrs*, **3**, Part III, 51–98.
9.8. AMERICAN INSTITUTE OF STEEL CONSTRUCTION (1959). *Plastic Design in Steel*, 94 pp.
9.9. HORNE, M. R. (1958). 'The full plastic moment of sections subjected to shear force and axial loads,' *British Welding J.*, **5**, 170–8.
9.10. CHU, K. H. and PABACIUS, A. (1964). 'Elastic and inelastic buckling of portal frames,' *Proc. Am. Soc. Civil Engrs*, **90**, No. EM5, 221–49.
9.11. MOSES, F. (1964). 'Inelastic frame buckling,' *Proc. Am. Soc. Civil Engrs*, **90**, No. ST6, 105–21.
9.12. HAAISER, G. and THURLIMANN, B. (1958). 'On inelastic buckling in steel,' *Proc. Am. Soc. Civil Engrs*, **84**, No. EM2, 1581–1 to 1581–48.
9.13. LOW, M. W. (1958). 'Some model tests on multi-storey rigid steel frames,' *Proc. Inst. Civil Engrs*, **13**, 287–98.
9.14. HAAISER, G. (1957). 'Plate buckling in the strain-hardening range,' *Proc. Am. Soc. Civil Engrs*, **83**, No. EM2, 1–47.
9.15. LAY, M. G. (1965). 'Flange local buckling in wide-flange shapes,' *Proc. Am. Soc. Civil Engrs*, **91**, No. ST6, 25–43.
9.16. DE VRIES, K. (1947). 'Strength of beams as determined by lateral buckling,' *Trans. Am. Soc. Civil Engrs*, **112**, 1245–320.
9.17. SALVADORI, M. G. (1950). 'Lateral buckling of eccentrically loaded I-section columns,' *Trans. Am. Soc. Civil Engrs*, **121**, 1163–71.
9.18. TOPRAC, A. A., JOHNSTON, B. G. and BEEDLE, L. S. (1951/2). 'Connections for welded continuous portal frames,' *Welding J.*, **30**, Nos, 7, 8, 11, 3485–555, 3975–4045, 5765–835.
9.19. HENDRY, A. W. (1950). 'An investigation of the strength of welded portal frame connections,' *The Structural Engineer*, **28**, No. 11, 265–80.
9.20. OLANDER, H. C. (1954). 'Stresses in the corners of rigid frames,' *Trans. Am. Soc. Civil Engrs*, **119**, 797–809.
9.21. 'Commentary on plastic design in steel,' Progress Report No. 6. *Proc. Am. Soc. Civil Engrs*, **86**, No. EM2 (1960), 107–40.

Chapter 10

10.1. JOHNSON, F. B. (ed.), (1969). *Designing, Engineering and Constructing with Masonry Products*, Gulf Publishing, Houston, Texas, 483 pp.

10.2. HAZELTINE, B. A. (1969). 'Some load-bearing brick buildings in England,' in Reference [10.1], pp. 406-15.

10.3. *Structural Recommendation for Loadbearing Walls*, British Standard Code of Practice CP 111, British Standards Institution, London, 1964.

10.4. *Wall Masonry, Design and Execution*, German Standard DIN 1053, 1962.

10.5. *Standard for Calculation and Execution of Manufactured and Natural Bricks*, Swiss Technical Standard 113, Swiss Engineers and Architects Society, 1965.

10.6. *Detailed Structural Analysis of Loadbearing Masonry*, National Building Code of Canada, Subsection 4.4.9, National Research Council, 1965.

10.7. *Recommended Building Code Requirements for Engineered Brick Masonry*, Structural Clay Products Institute, SCPI, Washington, D.C., 1966.

10.8. *SAA Brickwork Code*, Australian Standard CA47, Standards Association of Australia, Sydney, 1969.

10.9. *Computer Design of Engineered Brick Masonry—Wind Analysis Program*, Structural Clay Products Institute, Technical Note 37A, SCPI, Washington, D.C., April 1971.

10.10. *Computer Design of Engineered Brick Masonry—Torsion Analysis Program*, Structural Clay Products Institute, Technical Note 37C, SCPI, Washington, D.C., July 1971.

10.11. *Computer Design of Engineered Brick Masonry—Bearing Wall Program*, Structural Clay Products Institute, Technical Note 37B, SCPI, Washington, D.C., June 1971.

10.12. SAHLIN, S. (1971). *Structural Masonry*, Prentice-Hall, Englewood Cliffs, N.J., 290 pp.

10.13. *Reinforced Brick Masonry*, National Brick Manufacturers Research Foundation (U.K.), Bulletin No. 5, February 1932.

10.14. THOMAS, K. (1969). 'Current post-tensioned and prestressed brickwork and ceramics in Great Britain,' Chapter 34 in Reference [10.1], pp. 285-301.

10.15. WASS, R. J. and TURNER, D. J. (1969). 'A prestressed clay masonry floor,' Chapter 24 in Reference 10.1, pp. 200-9.

10.16. GERO, J. S. (1969). 'A prestressed masonry–reinforced concrete space structure,' Chapter 25 in Reference [10.1], pp. 210-5.

10.17. ALBERTI, LEONE BATTISTA (Trans. by J. Leoni) (1955). *Ten Books on Architecture*, Alec Tiranti, London, 256 pp. (*This is a facsimile of the first English Edition of 1755. The first printed edition was published in Latin in Florence in 1485.*)

10.18. *Fire Tests on Building Material and Structures*, B.S. 476, Part I. British Standards Institution, London, 1953, pp. 13-14. (*Similar information is given in most national fire-test standards.*)

10.19. HIMMELWRIGHT, A. L. A. (1905). *The San Francisco Earthquake and Fire.* Roebling Construction Company, New York, 270 pp.

10.20. MARSH, C. F. (1904). *Reinforced Concrete*, A Constable, London, 545 pp.

10.21. *Reinforced Concrete Design Handbook*, American Concrete Institute, Detroit, 1965, 271 pp.

10.22. LIN, T. Y. (1963). *Design of Prestressed Concrete Structures*, Second Edition, John Wiley, New York, 614 pp.

10.23. ABELES, P. W. (1964, 1966). *Introduction to Prestressed Concrete*, Concrete Publications, London, 2 volumes, 742 pp.

10.24. COWAN, H. J. and SMITH, P. R. (1966). *Design of Prestressed Concrete in accordance with the SAA Code*, Angus and Robertson, Sydney, 212 pp.
10.25. SIESS, C. P. (1952). 'Review of research on ultimate strength of reinforced concrete members,' *J. Am. Concrete Inst.*, **23**, 833–59.
10.26. HABERSTOCK, H. K. (1951). *Die n-freien Berechnungsweisen des einfach bewehrten rechteckigen Stahlbetonbalkens*, Deutscher Ausschuss für Stahlbeton Heft 103, Berlin, 160 pp.
10.27. HOGNESTAD, E. (1951). *A Study of Combined Bending and Axial Load in Reinforced Concrete Members*, University of Illinois Engineering Experiment Station Bulletin No. 399, 128 pp.
10.28. 'Report of the A.S.C.E.-A.C.I. joint committee on ultimate strength design,' *Proc. Am. Soc. of Civil Engrs*, **81**, Paper No. 809 (1955), 68 pp.
10.29. FERGUSON, P. M. (1965). *Reinforced Concrete Fundamentals*, Second Edition, Wiley, New York, 718 pp.
10.30. JOHNSON, R. P. (1967). *Structural Concrete*, McGraw-Hill, London, 271 pp.
10.31. COWAN, H. J. and SMITH, P. R. (1968). *The Design of Reinforced Concrete in accordance with the SAA Code*, Second Edition, Angus and Robertson, Sydney, 545 pp.
10.32. FENLON, H. F. (1960). *Reinforced Concrete Column Tables—Ultimate Strength Design*, F. W. Dodge, New York, 462 pp.
10.33. GLANVILLE, W. H. and THOMAS, F. G. (1939). *Moment Redistribution in Reinforced Concrete*, Building Research Technical Paper No. 22, H.M. Stationery Office, London, 51 pp.
10.34. BAKER, A. L. L. (1963). 'Ultimate load design of reinforced concrete frames—a recapitulation and appraisal,' *Publ. International Association for Bridge and Structural Engineering*, **23**, 33–50.
10.35. AOYAMA, H. (1965). 'Moment–curvature characteristics of reinforced concrete members subjected to axial load and reversal of bending,' *Flexural Mechanics of Reinforced Concrete*, American Society of Civil Engineers, New York, pp. 183–212.
10.36. JAEGER, L. G. (1964). *Elementary Theory of Elastic Plates*, Pergamon Press, Oxford, 107 pp.
10.37. WOOD, R. H. (1961). *Plastic and Elastic Design of Slabs and Plates*, Thames and Hudson, London, 343 pp.
10.38. JOHANSEN, K. W. (1962). *Yield Line Theory*, Cement and Concrete Association, London, 181 pp.
10.39. JONES, L. L. and WOOD, R. H. (1967). *Yield Line Analysis of Slabs*, Thames and Hudson, London, 405 pp.
10.40. D.S.I.R. BUILDING RESEARCH (1961). *Principles of Modern Building*, H.M. Stationery Office, London, Vol. II, p. 31, Fig. 2.5.
10.41. WESTERGAARD, H. M. and SLATER, W. A. (1921). 'Moments and stresses in slabs,' *Proc. Am. Concrete Inst.*, **17**, 415–538.
10.42. BLAKEY, F. A. (1965). 'Towards an Australian structural form—the flat plate,' *Architecture in Australia*, **54**, 115–7.
10.43. FRANCIS, A. J., BROWN, W. P. and ARONI, S. (1957). 'Full-scale tests of precast multi-storey flat construction,' *Symposium on Full-Scale Tests on House Structures*, Special Publication No. 210, American Society for Testing Materials, Philadelphia, pp. 50–60.
10.44. WHITE, R. B. (1965). *Prefabrication—A History of its Development in Great Britain*, National Building Studies, Special Report No. 36, H.M. Stationery Office, London, 354 pp.

10.45. SEBASTYEN, G. (1965). *Large Panel Building*, Publishing House of the Hungarian Academy of Sciences, Budapest, 401 pp.
10.46. DRZDOV, P. F. (1963). 'The design of buildings with box units,' *Beton i Zhelezobeton*, **8**, No. 2, 89–92. (Translated as *Library Communication No. 1198*, Building Research Station, Garson 1963, 6 pp.)

Chapter 11

11.1. ACI Committee 442 (1971). Response of buildings to lateral forces, *J. Am. Concrete Inst.*, **68**, No. 2 (Feb.), 81–106.
11.2. ANON (1940). 'Wind bracing in steel buildings,' *Trans. Am. Soc. Civil Engrs*, **105**, 1713–37.
11.3. ACI Committee 435 (1968). 'Allowable deflections,' *J. Am. Concrete Inst.*, **65**, No. 6 (June), 433–44.
11.4. ROBERTSON, L. (1967). 'On tall buildings,' in *Tall Buildings*, A. Coull and E. Stafford-Smith (eds.), Pergamon, Oxford, pp. 591–607.
11.5. STEFFANS, R. J. *Some Aspects of Structural Vibrations*, B.R.S. (U.K.), Eng. Series, Current Paper No. 37.
11.6. FINTEL, M. and KHAN, F. R. (1965). 'Effects of column exposure in tall buildings—temperature variations and their effects,' *J. Am. Concrete Inst.*, **62**, No. 12 (Dec.), 1533–56.
11.7. FINTEL, M. and KHAN, F. R. (1966). 'Effects of column exposure in tall buildings—analysis for length changes in exposed columns,' *J. Am. Concrete Inst.*, **63**, No. 8 (Aug.), 835–42.
11.8. Anon (1972). 'Radisson Hotel South, Minneapolis, Minnesota,' *Acier-Stahl-Steel*, Feb. 1972, pp. 82–6.
11.9. GERO, J. S. (1969). 'A prestressed masonry–reinforced concrete space structure,' in *Design, Engineering and Construction with Masonry Products*, B. Johnson (ed.), Gulf Publishing, Houston, pp. 210–15.
11.10. SEBASTYEN, G. (1965). *Large Panel Buildings*, Akademiai Kiado (Publishing House of the Hungarian Academy of Science), Budapest, 401 pp.
11.11. KONCZ, T. (1968). *Manual of Precast Concrete Construction*, Vol. 1, Bauverlag, Wiesbaden, 304 pp.
11.12. JENNINGS, A. (1968). 'Frame analysis including change of geometry,' *Proc. Am. Soc. Civil Engrs*, **94**, No. ST3 (March), 627–44.
11.13. NORRIS, C. H. and WILBUR, J. B. (1969). *Elementary Structural Analysis*, McGraw-Hill, New York, 303–15.
11.14. FRISCHMANN, W. W., PRABHU, S. S. and TOPPLER, J. F. (1963). 'Multi-storey frames and interconnected shear walls subjected to lateral loads,' *Concrete and Constructional Engineering*, **43**, No. 6 (June), 227–34.
11.15. KHAN, F. R. and SBAROUNIS, J. A. (1964). 'Interaction of shear walls and frames,' *Proc. Am. Soc. Civil Engrs*, **90**, No. ST3 (June), 285–335.
11.16. MEEK, J. L. (1971). *Matrix Structural Analysis*, McGraw-Hill, New York, 628 pp.
11.17. WEAVER, W. (1967). *Computer Programs for Structural Analysis*. Van Nostrand, Princeton, N.J., 300 pp.
11.18. CLOUGH, R. W., WILSON, E. L. and KING, I. P. (1963). 'Large capacity multistorey frame analysis programs,' *Proc. Am. Soc. Civil Engrs*, **89**, No. ST4 (Aug.), 179–204.

11.19. CLOUGH, R. W., KING, I. P. and WILSON, E. L. (1964). 'Structural analysis of multistorey buildings,' *Proc. Am. Soc. Civil Engrs*, **90**, No. ST3 (June), 16–34.
11.20. WEAVER, W. and NELSON, M. F. (1966). 'Three dimensional analysis of tier buildings,' *Proc. Am. Soc. Civil Engrs*, **92**, No. ST6 (Dec.), 385–404.
11.21. ACI Committee 318 (1963). *Building Code Requirements for Reinforced Concrete (ACI 318-63)*, American Concrete Institute, Detroit, 144 pp.
11.22. COULL, A. and SMITH, B. S. (1967). 'Analysis of shear walls: a review of previous research,' in *Tall Buildings*, Pergamon, London, pp. 139–55.
11.23. ROSMAN, R. (1964). 'Approximate analysis of shear walls subjected to lateral loads,' *J. Am. Concrete Inst.*, **61**, No. 6 (June), 717–32.
11.24. ROSMAN, R. (1964). 'An approximate method of analysis of walls of multistorey buildings,' *Civil Engineering and Public Works Review*, **59**, 67–9.
11.25. ZIENKIEWICZ, O. C. (1967). *The Finite Element Method*, McGraw-Hill, London, 272 pp.
11.26. COLACO, J. P. (1971). 'Preliminary design of high rise buildings with shear walls,' *J. Am. Concrete Inst.*, **68**, No. 1 (Jan.), 26–31.
11.27. PARME, A. L. (1967). 'Design of combined frames and shear walls,' in *Tall Buildings*, Pergamon, London, pp. 291–320.
11.28. GOULD, P. L. (1965). 'Interaction of shear wall–frame systems in multistorey buildings,' *J. Am. Concrete Inst.*, **62**, No. 1 (Jan.), 45–70.
11.29. ROSENBLUETH, E. and HOLTZ, I. (1960). 'Elastic analysis of shear walls in tall buildings,' *J. Am. Concrete Inst.*, **56**, No. 12 (June), 1209–22.
11.30. CARDAN, B. (1961). 'Concrete shear walls combined with rigid frames in multistorey buildings subjected to lateral loads,' *J. Am. Concrete Inst.*, **58**, No. 3 (Sept.), 299–316.
11.31. GRUNDY, P. and WATHEN, G. R. (1972). 'Frame–shear wall interaction,' *Civil Eng. Trans. Inst. Eng. Australia*, CE14, No. 1 (April), 102–9.
11.32. MAZZEO, L. A. and DE FRIES, A. (1972). 'Perimetral tube for 37-storey steel buildings,' *Proc. Am. Soc. Civil Engrs*, **98**, No. ST6 (June), 1291–307.
11.33. COULL, A. and SUBEDI, N. K. (1971). 'Framed-tube structures for high-rise buildings,' *Proc. Am. Soc. Civil Engrs*, **97**, No. ST8 (August), 2097–105.
11.34. SCHWAIGHOFER, J. and AST, P. (1972). *Tables for the Analysis of Framed-Tube Buildings*, Publication 72-01, Dept. Civil Engineering, University of Toronto.
11.35. FINTEL, M. (1968). 'Staggered transverse wall beams for multistorey concrete buildings,' *J. Am. Concrete Inst.*, **65**, No. 5 (May), 366–78.
11.36. FINTEL, M., BARNARD, P. R. and DERECHO, A. T. (1968). *Staggered Transverse Wall Beams for Multistorey Concrete Buildings—A Detailed Study*, PCA, Skokie, XS6735.
11.37. COULL, A. and CHOUDHURY, J. R. (1967). 'Stresses and deflections in coupled shear walls,' *J. Am. Concrete Inst.*, **64**, No. 2 (Feb.), 65–72.
11.38. LEVY, M. P. and VARGA, I. S. (1972). 'High rise panel structures,' *Proc. Am. Soc. Civil Engrs*, No. ST5 (May), 975–87.
11.39. *International Recommendations for the Design and Construction of Large-Panel Structures*, Translation No. 137, Cement and Concrete Association, London, 1967.
11.40. SKORUPA, A. (1971). 'Statics of buildings with suspended floors,' *Int. Civil Eng. (Israel)*, **2**, No. 3 (Sept.), 110–23.

Chapter 12

12.1. GERO, J. S., *et al.* (1968). 'Economic potential of physical model analysis in engineering,' *Build International*, **1**, No. 3 (Dec.), 16–21.

12.2. BECK, C. F. (1972). 'Responsibilities of computer-aided design,' *Civil Engineering*, **42**, No. 6 (June), 60.

12.3. VICKERY, B. J. (1972). 'On the aeroelastic modelling of structures in wind,' *Structural Models Conference*, Cement and Concrete Association, Sydney, pp. Vickery 1–9.

12.4. GERO, J. S., ROSENMAN, M. and ALEXANDER, P. (1970). *Feasibility Structural Model Analysis of a 700 ft High Tourist and Telecommunications Tower*, Models Lab. Report MR3, Dept. Architectural Science, University of Sydney.

12.5. COWAN, H. J., GERO, J. S., DING, G. D. and MUNCEY, R. W. (1968). *Models in Architecture*, Applied Science, London, 228 pp.

12.6. GERO, J. S. (1973). *Structural Model Test of the M.L.C. Centre Tower Building*, Models Lab. Report MR10, Dept. Architectural Science, University of Sydney.

Chapter 13

13.1. CHURCHMAN, C. W., ACKOFF, R. L. and ARNOFF, E. L. (1957). *Introduction to Operations Research*, John Wiley, New York, 645 pp.

13.2. SPUNT, L. (1971). *Optimum Structural Design*, Prentice-Hall, Englewood Cliffs, N.J., 168 pp.

13.3. HANCOCK, H. (1960). *Theory of Maxima and Minima*, Dover, New York.

13.4. PIERRE, D. A. (1969). *Optimization Theory With Applications*, John Wiley, New York, 612 pp.

13.5. WILDE, D. J. and BEIGHTLER, C. S. (1967). *Foundations of Optimization*, Prentice-Hall, Englewood Cliffs, N.J., 480 pp.

13.6. FOX, R. L. (1971). *Optimization Methods for Engineering Design*, Addison-Wesley, Reading, Mass., 270 pp.

13.7. GRUNDY, P. (1971). 'Optimum beam layout for large areas,' *Proc. Am. Soc. Civil Engrs*, **97**, No. ST8 (Aug.), 2085–96.

13.8. GERO, J. S. (1969). 'The application of operations research to engineering design—a review,' *Architectural Science Review*, **12**, No. 3 (Sept.), 67–77.

13.9. FRAZER, J. R. (1968). *Applied Linear Programming*, Prentice-Hall, Englewood Cliffs, N.J., 174 pp.

13.10. WAGNER, H. M. (1969). *Principles of Operations Research*, Prentice-Hall, Englewood Cliffs, N.J., 1062 pp.

13.11. AU, T. and STELSON, T. E. (1969). *Introduction to Systems Engineering*, Addison-Wesley, Reading, Mass., 374 pp.

13.12. BIGELOW, R. H. and GAYLORD, E. H. (1967). 'Design of steel frames for minimum weight,' *Proc. Am. Soc. Civil Engrs*, **93**, No. ST6 (Dec.), 109–31.

13.13. FOULKES, J. (1953). 'Minimum weight design and the theory of plastic collapse,' *Quart. Appl. Math.*, **10**, No. 4 (Jan.), 347–58.

13.14. CHARNES, A. and GREENBERG, H. J. (1951). *Plastic Collapse and Linear Programming*, Abstracts No. 56, American Math. Soc.

13.15. NAKAMURA, Y. (1966). *Optimum Design of Framed Structures Using Linear Programming*, Research Report, R66-4, M.I.T. Dept. Civil Eng.

13.16. GRIERSON, D. E. and GLADWELL, G. M. (1971). 'Collapse load analysis using linear programming,' *Proc. Am. Soc. Civil Engrs*, **97**, No. ST5 (May), 1561–73.

13.17. KUZMANOVIC, B. O. and WILLEMS, N. (1972). 'Optimum plastic design of steel frames,' *Proc. Am. Soc. Civil Engrs*, **98**, No. ST8 (Aug.), 1697–723.

13.18. KARAGOZIAN, J. (1963). *An Engineering Approach to Plastic Design of Tall Steel Buildings*, M.S. Thesis, U.C.L.A.

13.19. REINSCHMIDT, K. F., CORNELL, C. A. and BROTCHIE, J. F. (1966). 'Iterative design and structural optimization,' *Proc. Am. Soc. Civil Engrs*, **92**, No. ST2 (Dec.), 281–318.

13.20. ROMSTAD, K. M. and WANG, C. K. (1968). 'Optimum design of framed structures,' *Proc. Am. Soc. Civil Engrs*, **94**, No. ST12, (Dec.), 2817–45.

13.21. REINSCHMIDT, K. F. and RUSSELL, A. D. (1970). *Linear Methods in Structural Optimization*, Research Report R70-41, M.I.T., Dept. Civil Eng.

13.22. ZANGWILL, W. I. (1969). *Non-linear Programming*, Prentice Hall, Englewood Cliffs, N.J., 356 pp.

13.23. REINSCHMIDT, K. F. (1971). 'Discrete structural optimization,' *Proc. Am. Soc. Civil Engrs*, **97**, No. ST1 (Jan.), 133–56.

13.24. TOAKLEY, A. R. (1968). 'Optimum design using available sections,' *Proc. Am. Soc. Civil Engrs*, **94**, No. ST5 (May), 1219–41.

13.25. BELLMAN, R. E. and DREYFUS, S. E. (1962). *Applied Dynamic Programming* Princeton, University Press, Princeton, N.J., 363 pp.

13.26. PALMER, A. C. (1968). 'Optimum structural design by dynamic programming,' *Proc. Am. Soc. Civil Engrs*, **94**, No. ST8 (Aug.), 1887–906.

13.27. PORTER GOFF, R. F. (1969). 'Dynamic programming and the shape of a bridge truss,' *Computer Aided Design*, I.E.E., London, pp. 296–305.

13.28. GERO, J. S. (1973). *The Application of Sequential Decision Making in Optimization Problems in Architecture*, Computer Report CR23, Sydney University, Dept. Arch. Science.

13.29. BOND, D. (1973). 'The optimum design of concrete structures,' *International Symposium on Optimization in Civil Engineering*, Liverpool Univ. 1973 (Preprint, 27 pp.)

13.30. SKELTON, R. (1972). *Analytical Methods for the Optimum Design of Reinforced Concrete Beam and Slab Structures*, Ph.D. Thesis, Queen's Univ. Belfast.

13.31. BROOKS, S. H. (1958). 'A discussion of random methods for seeking maxima,' *Operations Res.*, **6** No. 2, 244–51.

13.32. POWELL, M. J. (1962). 'An iterative method for finding stationary values of a function of several variables,' *Computer J.*, **5** No. 2, 147–51.

13.33. POWELL, M. J. (1964). 'An efficient method for finding the minimum of a function of several variables without calculating derivatives,' *Computer J.*, **7** No. 4, 303–7.

13.34. FLETCHER, R. (1965). 'Function minimization without evaluating derivatives—a review,' *Computer J.*, **8** No. 1, 33–41.

13.35. DANIEL, J. W. (1967). 'The conjugate gradient method for linear and nonlinear operator equations,' *SIAM J. Numerical Analysis*, **4** No. 1, 10–26.

13.36. FORSYTHE, G. and MOTZKIN, T. S. (1951). 'Acceleration of the optimum gradient method,' *Bull. Am. Math. Soc.*, **57**, 304–5.

13.37. FLETCHER, R. and POWELL, M. J. (1963). 'A rapidly convergent descent method for minimization,' *Computer J.*, **6** No. 2, 163–8.

13.38. LUND, S. (1969). *Experiences with Direct Search Methods for Nonlinear Structural Optimization*, Nord-DATA-69, Stockholm, June 1969.

13.39. HOOKE, R. and JEEVES, T. A. (1961). ' "Direct Search" Solution of Numerical and Statistical Problem,' *J. Assn. Comp. Machinery (ACM)*, **8** No. 2, 212–29.

13.40. LAMONT, J. H. (1972). *Techniques for the Analysis and Optimum Design of Reinforced Concrete Column Slab Structures*, Ph.D. Thesis, Queen's Univ. Belfast.

13.41. GALLAGHER, R. H. and ZIENKIEWICZ, D. C. (1973). *Optimum Structural Design—Theory and Practice*, John Wiley, London, 358 pp.

Appendix: Metric Conversion

Length
1 yard (yd)	$= 0.914$ m
1 foot (ft)	$= 0.3048$ m
1 inch (in)	$= 25.40$ millimetres (mm)

Area
1 yd^2	$= 0.836$ m^2
1 ft^2	$= 0.092$ m^2
	$= 92\,900$ mm^2
1 in^2	$= 645.2$ mm^2

Second moment of area
1 ft^4	$= 86.3$ dm^4
1 in^4	$= 41.62$ cm^4
	$= 416\,231$ mm^4

Mass
1 long ton (2240 lb)	$= 1016$ kilograms (kg)
	$= 1.016$ tonnes
1 short ton (2000 lb)	$= 0.907$ tonnes
1 pound (lb)	$= 0.4536$ kg
1 ounce	$= 28.35$ g

Mass per unit area
1 lb/ft^2 (psf)	$= 4.882$ kg/m^2
1 lb/m^2 (psi)	$= 703$ kg/m^2

Force
1 lbf	$= 0.4536$ kgf
	$= 4.448$ newtons (N)

Moment of force
  1 lbf ft $= 1\cdot356$ N m
  1 lbf in $= 0\cdot1130$ N m

Pressure and stress
  1 lbf/ft^2 (psf) $= 47\cdot88$ N/m^2
                         $= 47\cdot88$ Pa
  1 lbf/in^2 (psi) $= 69\cdot0$ millibar (mb)
                         $= 6900$ N/m^2
                         $= 0\cdot0703$ kgf/cm^2
  1 inch of mercury $= 33\cdot86$ mb
                         $= 3386$ N/m^2

Temperature
  °F (Fahrenheit) $= 1\cdot8$°C $+ 32$ (Celsius or
                            Centigrade)
  °R (Rankine) $= 1\cdot8$°K (Kelvin)
                         $=$ °F $+ 459\cdot67$

2. Metric to Imperial Units

Length
  1 m $= 1\cdot094$ yd
  1 cm $= 0\cdot3937$ in
  1 mm $= 0\cdot039\ 37$ in
  (*Note* 1 μm (micrometre or
        micron) $= 10^{-6}$ m
      1 nm (nanometre or
        millimicron) $= 10^{-9}$ m
      1 Å (Ångström) $= 10^{-10}$ m)

Area
  1 m^2 $= 1\cdot196$ yd^2
  1 mm^2 $= 0\cdot001\ 55$ in^2

Mass

1 tonne	$= 0.984$ long tons (2240 lb)
	$= 1.102$ short tons (2000 lb)
1 kg	$= 2.205$ lb
1 g	$= 0.035\ 27$ oz

Mass per unit area

1 kg/m^2	$= 0.2048$ lb/ft^2 (psf)
1 kg/mm^2	$= 0.1422$ lb/m^2 (psi)

Force

1 N	$= 0.2248$ lbf
1 kgf	$= 2.205$ lbf
(*Note* 1 kgf	$= 981$ N
1 dyne	$= 10^{-5}$ N)

Moment of force

1 N m	$= 0.738$ lbf ft
1 kgf m	$= 7.233$ lbf ft

Pressure and stress

1 kN/m^2	$= 20.89$ lb/ft^2 (psf)
	$= 0.1450$ lb/in^2 (psi)
	$= 0.2953$ inches of mercury
(*Note* 1 millibar	$= 100$ N/m^2
1 kgf/cm^2	$= 98.1$ kN/m^2
1 mm of mercury	$= 1$ torr
	$= 133.3$ N/m^3
1 atmosphere	$= 101.3$ kN/m^2)

Temperature

°C	$= (°F - 32)/1.8$
°K	$= °R/1.8$

Index